Collaborative Power Grab

Collaborative Power Grab

A Step-by-Step Guide for Every Leader on
How to Invite, Attract, and Cultivate Collaborative Power

Robert M. Donaldson

Title: Collaborative Power Grab
Cover Layout: TBD
Interior Layout: Pickawoowoo Publishing group
Edited: Amy Scott (amy@nomadeditorial.com) with help from Kersten Jaeger
Index: Paul Sutliff
Printing & Distribution: Ingram (USA, UK, AUS, EUR)
"The Lost Art Of Collaboration" is trademarked by Robert Donaldson Reg. No. 4,985,392

Robert M Donaldson
ISBN: 979-8-9864436-0-7 (paperback)
ISBN: 979-8-9864436-1-4 (ebook)

First Printing, 2022

To Mom and Dad

My lifetime of successes
were launched by these folks
stalwart in their quest to "Carry On"
who forever had my back
no matter the magnitude of my failures

I miss them so...

About Bob's Book

From the first words to the last, Bob's energy and knowledge jump off the page. There is no denying his genuine aspirations to improve our individual and collective world through the teaching of his vast experience. A short time after I began reading Collaborative Power Grab, I started applying these tools and I felt a positive shift in my outlook, and in the way others perceived me. Bob is teaching us that we can move mountains, but first we must cultivate and align the boulders. The lessons abound within the covers of this book, laid like stone steps at our feet. A step-by-step guide to obtaining that which you desire. Grab some notecards and highlighters, because nearly every page of the book you are about to read holds some gem of wisdom that can help take you to that next level. I am truly thankful to Bob for sharing his toolbelt, and helping me move forward feeling empowered.

Todd Phillips, Reception Supervisor
Pacific Veterinary Emergency and Specialty Hospital

An incredibly valuable read for people at all levels of any organization. Unlike most books about leadership or influence, this book is filled with big-picture context and is loaded with specific, actionable guidance that anyone can learn and implement. When I met Bob, I noticed that the organization he worked for ran very smoothly, and his projects had cohesive teams and were completed on-time and within budget. After reading this book, I am beginning to see why. The steps for inviting and attracting collaborative power are things everyone should be doing on a daily basis. Bob has crystalized these into a specific recipe for anyone who wants to become a truly inspiring leader.

John Schwarz, Founder
JHS Consulting

Bob has encapsulated decades of collaboration and leadership experience into single recipe for success. It's easy to follow and implement in order to see immediate results.

This is a must read for leaders and front line supervisors that want to take advantage of Bob's experience and get a head start to creating collaborative power within your team. This recipe for success can also be used to empower and enrich your personal relationships as well.

E. J. Shalaby, General Manager (Ret.)
West Contra Costa County Sanitation

Being in a leadership position I always seek ways to develop my leadership skills and, in turn, enhance my team's performance. Bob has a knack for providing clear step-by-step guidelines to make accessible the most complex of topics. This book is no exception. The world needs more collaborative power, in our individual spheres of influence and in the larger context of human experience. Bob has provided a proven method by which to gain such collaborative power. If you want to expand your own and/or your group's effectiveness, satisfaction, and leadership skills, this is the book for you.

Teresa Herrera, P.E., General Manager
Silicon Valley Clean Water

An essential learning tool and guidance document for all leaders - no matter what stage of their career they may be in. Bob interlaces organizational psychology and behavior, judgement, and high-level cognitive decision-making, and distills it into well-thought, practical and proven processes yielding high-functioning teams, positive work environments and successful outcomes. I've read this more than once, and each time I learn something new. Definitely an annual read!

John A. Mahoney, President
Professional Land Services Inc.

Collaboration on any activity is one of the most difficult forms of human interaction. Much like an automobile is a form of transportation requiring integration of multiple parts to achieve the desired outcome of moving occupants to a desired location. Collaboration represents the same type of integration of people with their skills and experience, along with their respective organizational entities to achieve a desired outcome. Collaboration requires more than cooperation by causing commitment to various actions by the individuals involved. It is an art form on how 2 or more people and entities strive to achieve certain results beyond their self-interest. Each situation is different depending on the scope and people involved. *Bob Donaldson is a master artist* in realizing the importance of collaborative activities during his career *and now he presents, in readable form, many of the lessons* and ideas on how *to achieve collaborative results* for the common objectives of any activity. Recommended reading for anyone engaged in working on multitask activities leading to desired outcomes.

Bob Whitley, Founder (Ret.)
Whitley, Burchett and Associates

Bob Donaldson's book is straight forward, detailed, and contains a wealth of knowledge. I followed many of the concepts described in this book during my 30-year career in the United States Navy. The concepts are simple, but the details are important. Practicing ideas like checking your ego at the door, bring a pad and pen, eliminate fear, and ask for ways to improve, will help anyone looking to move up in their organization. I highly recommend this book if you are looking to improve your ability to collaborate, and to improve your leadership and development skills.

David Peters
CMDCM, USN, (Ret)

I have worked with Bob for well over 20 years, each time as part of the team that reports to him in pursuit of successfully completing a project mission. *There are so many notable passages in this book there are too many to start listing. Bob has a rare level of wisdom coupled with zero arrogance that you just don't find every day.* This incredible wisdom and humble nature makes being part of his team a privilege. His book captures all these attributes which can now provide any leader the instructions necessary for their successful collaborative power grab, if they merely follow the instructions provided.

Todd Beecher, P.E., Founder
Beecher Engineering, Inc.

I offer that this book is not only the cure for a dysfunctional workplace but a complete manual for the rescue and survival of humanity. If one seeks to change the world, I recommend one start with reading this book. If comprehended correctly, the world between one's shoulders will transform and be equipped to change the world around them. Together with others blessed with the knowledge, wisdom, and the experience of implementing these lessons, become enabled to collaborate with all involved to grab the necessary and positive power to change the workplace, the human condition and hence the world.

Everything needed for those who seek the truth of how the human brain functions, the ability to lead with mutually beneficial results and leave a trail of prosperity, competence, communication, and innovation in values of the highest order, lie within the pages of this book. Mastering the formula set forth in this book will not only produce the best leaders and groups humanly possible but guarantees excellence in all that follow in these ancient teachings. The mostly long forgotten but essential teachings are now verified, enhanced, and explained in detail by this book using science, research, practice, intelligence, and the lifelong experience of the author.

John William Selig
Professional Contractors

About Bob

Bob is able to condense the best from decades of study and his own experience with transforming an organization and individuals, and deliver it in concentrated immediately usable packages. During Bob's presentations I found my head moving up and down in agreement and mentally holding on while experiencing a tour de force of tried and true concepts and rules for the road of becoming a super employee and an effective human being.

Ray Busch, Facility Manager (Ret.)
City of Hayward, California

Bob Donaldson gets it. He identifies the ailment of a fledgling organization that is slowed by a culture of mediocrity and timidity, and then lays out the cure. His no-nonsense leadership and organizational philosophy provide practical steps to help groups and teams of all sizes obliterate their status quo and establish a foundation for the team to thrive by inducing outstanding individual performance. As individuals are truly empowered to perform within the dynamic team environment, be prepared for revolutionary results!

Hugh Logan, Operation Specialist
Logan services Inc.

I have known and worked with Bob Donaldson for nearly thirty years. Our professional relationship has seen us tackle a variety of technically challenging construction projects that involved both physical and environmental risk for all parties involved. Bob has always displayed a cool head and a level of professionalism in his approach to these difficult challenges. Bob has the ability to quickly recognize the strengths individuals bring to the table on a particular subject. Given his communication skills, he quickly guides the team to identifying the issues and then works with the various team members in finding the best solution. He displays an upbeat attitude and a focus on solving the problem without alienating team members. Working with Bob has always been a pleasure and an inspiration.

Ken Lindberg, Owner
Power Engineering Contractors

Wetland restoration at Bair Island of the Don Edwards National Wildlife Refuge is becoming a reality through the assistance of Bob Donaldson. His collaborative approach helped us find ways to make this complex project work for both wildlife and people. When we ran into problems with a contractor Bob used his skills of dealing with difficult people to help us solve our problems. We couldn't have done it without his help.

Mendel Stewart
Chief of Budget, Performance and Workforce
United States Fish and Wildlife Service

Collaborative Strategies' Bob Donaldson is a tough and fair-minded person with years of experience in negotiating and representing the public good. California Wildlife Foundation has witnessed first-hand his ability to take a complex issue with multiple party interests and bring projects to successful completion, on time and on budget. He is skillful and determined in meeting his contract obligations. We do not hesitate in recommending him to others based upon his past performance.

Janet Cobb, Executive Officer
California Wildlife Foundation

I have known and worked with Robert Donaldson for nearly 30 years. Bob is a progressive policy thinker while maintaining personnel accountability within the workforce. In the mid-1980s we shared employment at an organization that was recovering from a labor strike. Employees were at odds; personal property was being vandalized and communication between work teams was inconsistent at best. Morale was low, and organizational efficiency was extremely poor. Bob believes a strong workforce begins with employee empowerment. He initiated programs that increased employees' viability to their current (and as it turns out also to future) employers. In the face of internal resistance he maintained his beliefs and persevered with these changes. These programs eventually provided increased educational opportunities and coupled with defined lines of communication within the organization became the cornerstones of greater efficiency and employee empowerment. Within five years, this group became the model that the industry held as an example. Individual and organizational awards began flowing in. The organization became a well-oiled machine that translated into highly motivated and efficient work teams that either met or exceeded all objectives of its mission statement.

Karl Royer O&M Manager
East Bay Dischargers Authority (Ret.)

I have known Bob for over 12 years. Bob is an extremely trustworthy and ethical person. He has demonstrated a very steady and even character. He follows through on all projects in a timely manner and is very dependable. He has demonstrated the ability to work under a high pressure, fast paced environment while maintaining a good sense of humor. He is very comfortable and experienced talking with the board, making presentations and answering questions. I strongly believe that his work experience and character provides for the confidence you need in order to utilize Bob on any project.

Jeff Ira, City Councilman
Redwood City, California

Bob's capabilities and capacity to distill complex and challenging issues into systematic approaches to solutions is near genius. Over the 25 years I have known Bob professionally, he has consistently achieved measurable improvements in staff development and productivity, team-focused direction, and success where success is hard to derive.

Teresa Herrera PE, Manager
Silicon Valley Clean Water

I have been working with Bob Donaldson on complex infrastructure projects for nearly 20 years. When you work with Bob on a challenging, full-of-potential-pitfalls kind of project, you are in for one of the most rewarding professional achievements of your life. He is a master at leading mission-oriented teams who respect, challenge, and support each other in working towards a common goal. For Bob, collaboration is not just a bunch of people sitting around a table making nice. Collaboration is work – hard work – real work. And the stakes for the outcome of the process are often very high. It is in this kind of environment that Bob thrives and excels.

Valerie Young
Environmental Planning

I have closely witnessed the work and accomplishments of Robert Donaldson for more than 25 years in the various capacities he has held. Bob was able to facilitate the best solutions to a myriad of problems including technical, personnel, organizational, regulatory, functional, operational and administrative issues that he was continually confronted with. I have always been impressed by how honestly and respectfully he treated each participant and conducted his activities in a manner that allowed everyone to express themselves and yet lead the discussion candidly and productively. Bob's talents are many and I heartily and unequivocally recommend his engagement in any assignment that fits these talents.

Joseph Covello, P.E., Board Chairman (Ret.)
The Covello Group

I've worked with Bob for more than 25 years on a wide array of efforts/projects ranging from public health emergencies to multi-year planning efforts. Inevitably, the successful completion of these projects required the collaboration of parties with vastly different agendas and definitions of success. Bob has displayed an unusual ability to assess the needs of the parties involved and craft a strategy for cooperation that will benefit everyone. He has a large toolbox of strategies on how to get a team working together. He does his homework and comes with a plan that works. I don't recall ever second-guessing his methods or the outcome.

Mike Joyce, Principal
Kennedy/Jenks Consultants

I had the honor and pleasure of working both for and with Bob Donaldson for 20 years. Bob brought qualities such as clarity, focus, objectivity and equitable treatment of those working for and with him on the teams he led. I learned a great deal from him about how to manage and lead. I was consistently impressed with his ability to navigate the complexities of multi-disciplinary projects involving lots of people with a wide variety of expertise while keeping the overall project on time and within budget parameters. As a Minister and spiritual leader, I have come to appreciate Bob's more subtle qualities as well. Developing collaborative strategies requires "keeping one's head while all about are losing theirs." For many years I witnessed Bob's remarkable ability to do just that.

Reverend C. Michael Woodstock

I have worked with Bob Donaldson and under his guidance for 20 years. No one is better at creating a collaborative environment than Bob. What I have learned from him is that as you navigate through the rest of your life, be open to collaboration. He has taught many of us that other people's ideas are often better than our own and that when we find a group of people who challenge and inspire us, spend a lot of time with them and it will change your life.

Duane Sandul
Public Outreach Specialist

I highly recommend "A Lifetime of Empowerment for the First Line Supervisor" training course to anyone wanting to improve his or her performance, professionally or personally. There was not one example that I have not experienced in twenty years and Bob gives you the tools to make great leaps in being successful if you choose to apply them.

David Delzer, Ops Supervisor
City of Palo Alto

I have had the pleasure of working with Bob Donaldson for more than 20 years on numerous issues and projects. During that time I developed an appreciation for Bob's ability to successfully deliver on every project and honor every commitment. Bob uses a disciplined, thoughtful process for breaking down highly complex issues into more easily understood parts. He also has a talent for seeing a problem from the perspective of those on the other side of the table and is able to build trust and work effectively with people at every level of an organization. I came to enjoy working with Bob because I knew that at the end of the day any project or problem we were working on would be handled with integrity, professionalism and a sense of humor.

Mark Larson, Director of Airports (Ret.)
San Mateo County

As someone who has worked with Bob on numerous projects for over 20 years, I got to know him on a professional and personal basis. Many of these projects were large and complex from both a technical and organizational point of view. Bob needed to manage many parties ranging from engineering firms, consultants, and contractors as well as several departments within the utility he served. Through keen insight Bob was able to sort out challenging issues and help bring positive results that helped fulfill the operational mission of his utility while being fair to all parties involved. He is a man of outstanding character and integrity.

Dewitt Smith, M.S.E.E., P.E.

Bob Donaldson combines many unique qualities into one powerful personality. He fosters strong team interactions by establishing clear lines of communication and a common understanding of chain of command. He keeps projects moving by focusing on the project objective, and identifying and removing impediments to progress. Bob builds teams of people with the necessary skills required for the assignment and he shares the credit with his collaborators. He provides an emotionally safe environment and encourages honest conversations. Bob mentors and coaches everyone he works with by sharing generously his good advice, which he has in abundance.

Roanne Ross, P.E., Senior Engineer (Ret.)
West Yost Associates

Table of Contents

Figures

Figure development compliments of Nathaniel Prophet for Collaborative Strategies Consulting Inc.

Introduction

It's easy to follow and implement in order to see immediate results. This is a must-read for leaders and front-line supervisors that want to take advantage of Bob's experience and get a head start to creating collaborative power within your team. This recipe for success can also be used to empower and enrich your personal relationships as well.

—E. J. Shalaby

FIRST THINGS FIRST: YOU CAN ALWAYS JUMP RIGHT TO CHAPTER 1 AND 2 IF YOU WANT

Regardless of where you start this book you can always jump to chapters 1 and 2 right away and start moving forward on using the *Starting Now* actions immediately. While knowing why this all works is certainly something you want to catch up on, you do not have to read the entire book before you start. If you do choose to start right away then Chapters 5 and 6 would be the chapters you would want to read *as you are using* Chapters 1 and 2. I know this sounds a little crazy however this book is a training manual and an implementation manual *all at the same time*.

ON-LINE COURSE – *THE JOURNEY OF HEROES*

Joseph Campbell was more than a famous author, he spent a lifetime comparing mythologies, cultures and religions and he is most famous for finding a common thread between all these modalities that he called: The Hero's Journey. While prolific in his writings and in his lectures, the one book that is perhaps his most important work is the book entitled *The Hero with a Thousand faces*.

What Campbell had found are ***common themes*** between mythologies, cultures and religions that support the same story that all humans experience as they grow, as they mature and as they may or may not become their own hero to the challenges, trials and tribulations that life has to offer. As we examine the pathways and pathology of the leaders journey, there's a similar motif in leadership development that parallels Campbell's work. I should also note that Campbell's work often spoke in terms of men. However, as a single Dad of three daughters I can tell you, we all, woman or man, go through a Hero's Journey as we face the challenges of life. In this book I'm speaking to everyone. While he has been criticized by some folklorists, his work simply makes sense to me as related to the human experience and is more than good enough for our purposes of helping leaders to be heroes.

The most essential part of the Collabortive Power Grab is the ***Starting Now*** actions. This is the backbone of the promise I made to you in the subtitle, making this a practical step-by-step manual that will lead to your leadership success.

In order to help you become successful I am also offering these same ***Starting Now*** actions in an online course found at The Lost art of Collaboration™ :

Go to: **TheLostArtOfCollaboration.com** and see the on-line course entitled "The Journey of Heroes."

This is not another long drawn out online course that will bore you to tears. The course allows you to earn badges and by earning badges enter into drawings that will offer free one-on-one coaching sessions with me and cash prizes. Sounds different doesn't it? Listen, this is all about encouraging your progress by adding some fun to the process ***while also teaching you some of the most successful, practical and effective <u>Starting Now</u> actions <u>a leader could ever learn</u>***.

As part of the membership you're able to join my weekly seminar where I answer questions that people have submitted in advance. I will also be regularly blog answers to any questions submitted by email or by phone and text messages.

- <u>**What is most important to me for you to know**</u>:
  I'm not just selling a book and I'm not just selling an online course.
  I'm here to create a community that will focus on the **Collaborative Power Grab** and **The Journey of the Heroes**.

I'm here to support you and have your back as you face the challenges in front of you.

A NOTE ABOUT THE FIGURES AND DOWNLOADS
All the figures in this book as well as selected portions of chapter 5 and 6 are used as guides in the on-line course. Once you've joined all of these guides can be down loaded.

The Landscape Survey (found in Chapter 4) is free to download. Go to:

TheLostArtofCollaboration.com and follow the menu to the **free stuff**.

Hope to see you there!

THE RESULTS YOU CAN EXPECT

Immediately using the *Starting Now* actions in Chapter 2 and in the sequence as laid out in chapter 1, these are the trends you will be setting in place that will mature overtime:

- Examples of negative human behaviors drop
- Fear-caused behaviors drop
- Quality and quantity of communication increases
- Mission statement moves to center stage
- Respect and dignity become preferred behaviors
- Professional relationships dominate
- Clear and achievable performance expectations abound
- Leadership provides a support role without giving up power
- Problem-solving becomes a team sport
- Productivity and smart work rules over mediocrity
- Group members become involved in creating outcomes
- Inappropriate, toxic behaviors are trounced
- Group members accept more responsibility over time
- Ability to deal with adversity increases
- Ideas for improvement is a constant conversation
- Team members become very good at what they do
- Leaders grow to very high levels of effectiveness
- Group members have confidence to make decisions and know when to include their supervisor
- Continuous improvement strategy becomes an organic function
- The need for direct supervision continuously dries up
- Leaders learn to check their ego at the door

After Chapters 1 and 2 are implemented you can read the rest of the book. Once Chapters 3 through 7 are fully implemented along with the expertise and knowledge base you have gained, these are the results you will gain over time as the group matures:

- Identifying a list of behaviors **to stop using** if you want more group collaboration
- Implementing a list of behaviors **to start using** if you want more group collaboration
- Smartly addressing and eliminating the causes of fear generation in the work environment
- Reducing complexity of the policies, procedures, and how-to of day-to-day operations
- Training every group member to expert levels in collaboration and technical competency
- Reducing expensive direct supervision time by providing more autonomy
- Creating clearly understood objectives that are directly supported by that person's training
- Ensuring smooth productivity by removing roadblocks, adjusting workloads, and setting reasonable deadlines with clear expectations as part of every delegated task
- Having leaders conscientiously train, mentor, and guide the success behaviors of their direct reports
- Having leaders actively solicit and assertively implement improvement proposals from non-leader group members
- Having leaders who train others in the use of a systematic problem-solving process in order to neutralize deeply embedded cognitive biases, fallacious reasoning, and emotional blocks
- Having leaders who privately hold individuals accountable to collaborative behaviors and publicly advance ambitious but achievable objectives
- Having leaders who assist in performance recovery when inevitable errors come to pass
- Having leaders recognize the exceptional performance events of their direct reports so this same performance is encouraged to be repeated in the workplace by them and others

ABOUT POWER

Whether it's the power of the sun that supports all life on Earth, the flow of electrons through a wire, the contest of political will playing out in the debate hall or on the battlefield, or the power that money brings, *we all have an intrinsic relationship with power whether we like it or not.*

The word "power" also has some very negative connotations, so let me address that issue first.

Some of these negative connotations come from experiences where we might not like the power that our opponent possesses. We might feel powerless at times, which can be exacerbated by not knowing how to gain more power as we feel vulnerable and helpless against those who might exercise power against us.

Some of this comes from systemic problems that work to overpower us.

Systemic issues can lead to negative impacts as a result of a car collision, an inoperable tumor, a fall from a ladder, an accidental poisoning, you name it. Yes, the *system errors* that lead to these problems need to be addressed, but I want you to remember that a lot of times being faced with the overwhelming circumstances in front of us *can start to feel personal when it's not.*

I also want to acknowledge that there are systemic biases in our world based on many factors, including economic status, race, sexual orientation, ethnicity and religion. These challenges require a response and *we should all take community action that can contribute to correcting these system biases.*

That being said, in this book I'm here to empower you in your more immediate circumstances as a leader-manager (please see Appendix 7) in your organization and *to assist you in taking charge of the things you have direct influence over.* I'm focused on building your collaborative power -play.

Taking positive actions at the personal level will empower you, the supervisors you follow, and the direct reports who follow you.

Sure, diabolical corruption and greed might disempower us, we may encounter enemies along life's path, or a broken system may bankrupt us, but *there is no invisible force that wakes up every morning and says,* "I'm going to find some way to overpower [place your name here] today."

Just because something feels personal doesn't mean it is. More importantly, if it's not personal but more systemic, *there's a better way to fight it than to fight it as if it were personal.*

Personal power plays and systemic power plays require *two entirely different strategies*, and if you take systemic issues personally you are just *wasting huge amounts of energy you could be using to instead move forward to establish your own personal collaborative power base.*

Whether you agree with me or not on that last point, please take this piece of advice: *stop wasting time concentrating on forces that are beyond your influence.* Instead, I now invite you to concentrate on how you can empower yourself *in spite of* the forces lording over you.

Despite evidence to the contrary, there are ways to use power for good, to help others as well as ourselves. And it's hard to be helpful to the people in your world *if you as well feel helpless in your world*, so let's change that.

I grew up witnessing the world's penchant for leap frogging past calmer-heads-prevailing solutions and instead jumping towards passive or active violence *as a first step option,* and it took me a little blood, sweat, and tears to come to the conclusion that my intrinsic power was indeed *intact.* I found it early in life, thankfully, with mentors at my side. Later in life, in the face of needless death of friends, destruction, and sometimes personal danger, I then figured out how to actually *implement my power from an empowered position.*

My learning process for how to best wield power came with its own set of errors. I have woven the results of those lessons into this book so you can learn from them without repeating them. Please take special note that any mentor not willing to admit to failure is not someone you want to learn from. The greatest gift a mentor can give you besides their depth and breadth of experience is the permission to fail. ***Failure hurts at the time, but not taking risks in order to avoid it means you never improve.***

What I often see occurring with people is they do not appropriately, critically, and selectively determine which encounters they will enter into and which ones they won't, when given the option one way or the other.

When you engage power, you want to pick and choose your battles. My advice: ***you only want to pick the battles that are worth fighting.***

Now there are a lot of other considerations that you should take into account when deciding whether to enter into battle as it relates to a power play such as: can I prevail in this challenge?

Right now, I'm just narrowly addressing what I think are the questions everybody should be asking themselves before they take the next step at doing almost anything:

Is this a worthy challenge? Is this a worthy opponent? Is this a decision that's worthy of my time, that's worthy of my effort, that's worthy of my life's purpose?

If you decide that it's not worthwhile and you nonetheless pursue the next steps against your best judgment, you're just wasting a good life.

Life is filled with challenges. Life is filled with opponents. Life is filled with life-changing decisions.

But again, ask yourself: Are those ***worthy*** challenges? Are those ***worthy*** opponents? Are those ***worthy*** decisions?

Once you have decided to engage, you will need ***power*** to create the desired outcome.

With worthy ***challenges,*** you will need power to manage them.

With worthy ***opponents,*** you will need power to effectively respond to them.

With worthy ***decisions,*** you will need power to contemplate your best next steps.

When we feel powerless, ***challenges*** are robotically met with brute force. Often to our own detriment.

When we feel powerless, ***opponents*** are instinctively met with sharp weapons (metaphorically) - often to our own detriment.

When we feel powerless, important life-changing *decisions* become catastrophic cortisol-pumping dilemmas, *deceptively* presenting *only* a limited list of horrific outcomes as our *apparently narrow list of options* from which to select. *False-choicest-maximus.*

Again, this is often to our own detriment.

These types of tragic powerless responses are a life-sucking psychic wasteland, needlessly ineffective and often damaging to the forward movement of the very same goals we are hoping to achieve in life.

However, when we feel *empowered*, we innately sense that:

> *Challenges are potential opportunities.*
> *Opponents are potential allies.*
> *Decisions are potential collaborative win-win outcomes.*
> *Opportunities, allies, and collaborative win-win outcomes* create enormous amounts of power *that you can use*!

I'm not Pollyanna-ish when it comes to power, and I don't want to be accused of skipping over uncomfortable realities lest I be accused of avoiding the obvious. So let me be clear: *unquestionably, in more extreme circumstances*, some challenges do indeed require brute force, some opponents do require a sharp object, and some decisions do require the heavyweight reluctant acceptance of a life-changing decision. I've seen it all.

However, using any of these responses *as a first step in situations that don't warrant it* is 100 percent ineffective at moving your power base forward. It's always about figuring out the best first step, and power *misunderstood* denies you the truth-telling sight necessary to first see, second measure, and third *effectively respond to the world around you regardless of what your world is presenting you.*

Power *misunderstood* never gives you the information needed for making that best first step *that is in your best self-interest.*

This last statement has been true since the beginning of time.

Give me a chance to convince you to stay focused on things you can change. Further, *let me convince you there are many more things you can change than perhaps you previously thought.*

There's plenty you can do *and you are far more powerful than you realize.* That's not a pep talk. As a leader in a group you already think you have power, *but you have so much more power than you realize,* and how to utilize that power is *exactly* what we're going to be talking about in this book.

If you were empowered by mentors growing up, if you're empowered today by a good friend or a wise elder or a work supervisor, if you are empowering your direct reports, friends, or children with knowledge, skills, and ability that will help support them in a joyful life, what say you? Let's do this! Let me add to your palette of options.

However, if you were not so fortunate in the past and are currently not so fortunate as to have these people in your life, we are going to be talking about how you can invite mentoring into your work life and how you can learn to effectively mentor those you lead **all at the same time.** If that sounds like what you want, this book is definitely for you.

I'm encouraging you to look at power in a different way than you might have experienced it in your life. Different than what you have perhaps come to know power to be — the systematically indifferent societal bulldozer that unilaterally adjusts your position in life.

Power is ever present in nature — just think of the incredible power unleashed by hurricanes, earthquakes, and volcanoes. This includes the more subtle examples as well, such as the wind blowing through the branches of a tree or the water wandering through a creek. It's no mistake that we've been using the wind and water to power our machines for thousands of years. It's important for me to point this out because **power as a natural force is a concept I need you to agree with.**

I'm here to convince you there is an **abundance** of this tool.

It doesn't have a limited supply, and just because I have somehow gained more power **doesn't mean I've somehow also magically limited the size of the world's power pie** from which you too can eat. **It's ever abundant.**

Unfortunately, power is often framed as a zero-sum game, but that is sorely inaccurate at best. **At its worst,** that zero-sum game is purposely practiced with deceptive intent. **It is a power play in itself.** Every zero-sum power play is either trying to convince you that your opponent has more power than you do or that you have less power than they have, or more likely a combination of both. The zero-sum power game is bullshit, a false choice proposition that is robbing — that's right — **your intrinsic power.**

As a leader in a group there are many actions you can take that will empower you in the eyes of the other members of the group. That's the type of collaborative power we are now going to concentrate on. The bottom line here: **collaborative power is abundant, it is available to you for the taking, so take it.**

Fire can save your life on a cold night or it can burn you to death. The water necessary to quench your thirst and keep you alive for a handful of days? The **same exact amount,** well placed, can also drown you. Many things that can take your life can save your life as well, and **power is no exception.**

Power is nature's currency.

Currency that can either pay for good or pay for evil.

So let us now turn our attention to how we use that currency to pay for good.

What you will find in this book is as a series of **Starting Now** actions that when employed as a *phased step-by-step process* will allow you to empower the people above you and the people below you from your particular leadership position. Whether you're a division chief, department head, middle manager, or first line supervisor, **all of it applies.**

Why is that?

Because humans are humans wherever you go.

Certainly, we all have differences. But my philosophical arguments (I'll save those for another book) and, *more importantly, my experience and modern brain science* tell me that our *sameness* is so intrinsic to our true common nature that by now focusing on the sameness of the human brain the differences indeed melt away, glowing ever more dim with each **Starting Now** action employed.

So much so that our differences rightfully appear to be unimportant misaligned pettiness. In our world where *pettiness abounds* it often partners with *normalized mediocre performance* (a concept you will be learning about in this book).

Unimportant misaligned activities and normalized mediocre performance issues can inappropriately and deceptively take center stage in a workplace and result in a massive distraction that will sideline your climb to power just as it has for many leaders for many years.

So where do you think true power resides? With the sameness of the human brains in your group or with unimportant misaligned pettiness?

Yes, those were test questions. I hope you passed.

These **Starting Now** actions are specifically designed to empower the people above you and to empower the people below you, and those deeds *will cause a return of power from them to you.*

That's exactly how it happens.

What you're about to read also provides you a diagnostic tool to examine, excavate, and calculate the current lack of collaboration and other problems your organization is facing. You can't fix it if you don't know what's broken.

Throughout this book you'll notice I'm offering a phased step-by-step process so you can implement these actions effectively, as well as outlining the basis for why this approach is so incredibly effective in Chapter 3: Using Superior Knowledge in All Areas of Required Expertise. I truly stand on the shoulders of giants who have come before me as they stand on those that came before them. It just so happens I agree with those giants, and as I compare their experiences with my experiences *there is an unquestionable resonance*. I'm not alone here as I promote what you might encounter as new ways of looking at old problems.

If you disagree with anything you read in Chapter 3, I recommend that you suspend judgment for now. I say this because for some of us, our inner critic has no problem shaming us and pushing us back to the same old *ineffective powerless approaches* that this new information calls into question.

Also, don't automatically assume that your current leadership approach — accepted on face value, perhaps from other leaders or, even worse, because "we've always done it that way"— will be compatible with what I'm recommending here. There are a lot of things modern-day leaders do *that should've been stopped long ago*.

To that end, Chapter 3 also covers, in exact detail, why powerless leaders remain that way. I would recommend every leader take special note of these descriptions so these types of leadership deficiencies can be avoided. Essentially this section describes the list of *Stop Now* actions. If you see yourself in these descriptions: stop now. If you see other leaders in your group in these descriptions, you might want to pass them a copy of the book. I know that recommendation sounds self-serving, but most of us know the incredible sensitivity necessary when calling into question the actions of fellow leaders in our group in an attempt to reduce their poor *Stop Now* behaviors.

While this book could be much longer because I have a lot more to say on the subject, what's between the two covers of this book will certainly deliver on its promise if implemented in the way I recommend. Speaking of implementation, attempts to implement phases and steps out of sequence will negatively impact your process, so hear me now.

I don't think I'm so exceptional that I somehow possess such a magical touch that what I am about to teach won't work for you as well. In fact, I know it will because I have taught many.

This entire system has been field tested over the last 45 years of my life—that's right, 45 years. Some of what you'll find here goes all the way back to lessons gleaned from hours of public debate with my high school and college political science, history, and sociology teachers. I have a rather assertive quality to my personality and my quest has always been to become an ever more effective human starting at an early age, as witnessed by others. Some lessons were hard learned, but they were learned. What you're getting in this book is how you can use what I learned *to your benefit*.

Changing your approach to power isn't easy and will likely *require you doing something different than what you're doing today*. It may even require you to do some things that *make you feel uncomfortable*.

If you can *develop a relationship* with feeling uncomfortable and can *get used to doing something different* in the pursuit of building your collaborative power base, then you're up for some radical change.

I'm here to support you as you build your own Collaborative Power Grab in a way *you likely didn't ever think possible*.

Okay?

Let's go.

ABOUT INVITING, ATTRACTING, CULTIVATING

When I use the term Collaborative Power Grab, it's up for interpretation as to what I mean and some of those interpretations could be highly suspect of my motives. As inferred earlier, thanks to some of the power grabs that we have experienced in human history, I would opine their concern is not without merit.

When you read the term "power grab" in this book, know that I'm referring to a Collaborative Power Grab and this is what I mean to say:

Leaders who want to build a high-performing group with the intention of achieving mission success by motivating and empowering the members of the group, who then respond with enthusiastically contributing to that high performance, *can only pursue this process of building a highly collaborative group if that leader has enough collaborative power*.

Said another way: The leader who wants to build a high-performing group with the intention of achieving mission success and doesn't have the power to do so *will never be successful*!

In this introduction we'll look at some examples of what happens when leaders are powerless and why they are powerless, and likewise examples of what an organization looks like where the leaders have successfully invited, attracted, and cultivated collaborative power.

This book is a practical toolbox that gives you **step-by-step** *instructions on how to best* **gain collaborative power** *by:*

1. Learning how to implement your Collaborative Power Grab strategy (Chapter 1)
2. Using superior knowledge in all areas of required expertise (Chapter 3)

3. Understanding *exactly* what's going wrong in your organization (Chapter 4)
4. ***Inviting Collaborative Power*** from the Top Down (Chapter 5)
5. ***Attracting Collaborative Power*** from the Bottom Up (Chapter 6)
6. ***Cultivating Collaborative Power*** by Implementing Collaborative Group Behaviors (Chapter 7)

Let's take these one at a time:

1 – Learning how to implement your Collaborative Power Grab strategy: Without a successful implementation strategy concerning anything you do in your life, what you're hoping to achieve is just a nice thought. You need to figure out how you're going to deliver the desired outcome. How you move forward with a Collaborative Power Grab requires certain specific steps that if not done correctly will cause you to be slowed or stopped in your attempt to improve your group performance and promote mission success. ***Without following specific steps in Chapter 1, you will actually disempower yourself instead of empowering yourself.***

The other issue concerning implementation is this: my reputation is very vulnerable to your success. Or said another way, if you read this book and ***don't implement it as I'm describing***, you're going to be walking around saying, "Yeah, I read that guy's book and it doesn't work." Skipping steps hurts both of us. I know this stuff works because I've already done it and I've taught it to others successfully who have then went on to successfully apply these same concepts in their leadership positions. I'm placing all my bets on your success and the only way that happens is if you implement it as described, so don't let me down.

2 - Using superior knowledge in all areas of required expertise: I'm giving you some significant reading in Chapter 3. This part does move away from the step-by-step process, but I cannot emphasize enough how important it is for you to know exactly what the big picture is, which includes what is ***really*** happening behind the scenes that is responsible for human motivation.

We now know at a scientific level the highly detailed descriptions of how the high-performing group either successfully arrives to achieve mission success or how people and groups can ultimately nose-dive into catastrophic failure. This includes what you're about to read below concerning normalized mediocre performance. I have spent a lifetime accumulating and using successfully and unsuccessfully everything I have poured into this book to do and not do.

This allows you to focus on success and also allows you to avoid the pitfalls that lead to failure.

Many of the descriptions I'm using to describe a group in deteriorated conditions are from my personal experience. I'm now at nearly five decades of trying to figure out how to build better performance by empowering the people in the group and this is what I have to say: by gaining ***superior knowledge*** your level of expertise will surpass perhaps 90% of the people in leadership positions on the planet today. An outlandish statement? Perhaps, but I'd like to hear your thoughts about it after reading this book.

3 - Understanding *exactly* what's going wrong in your organization: In Chapter 4 I will supply you with a Landscape Survey that you can answer as you observe your group and the people working in the group. The result of this initial series of questions will pinpoint the problems you're experiencing that need to be addressed if you want to move forward with creating a collaborative group. The survey also becomes an ongoing assessment tool allowing you to track progress (or not) and focus in on the problem areas while not wasting time on what you might perceive to be problems but determine from completing the survey are in fact areas where the group is already strong. *It also happens to be an exquisite checklist for every leader that might already be in a high-performing group that nonetheless wants to improve their group.*

4 - Inviting Collaborative Power from the Top Down: Inviting power from the top down is exactly that. The power source is your supervisor and the entire senior leader-managers above them (did you read Appendix 7?) . And while some power grabs attempt to take that power unilaterally from the senior staff, *that is exactly what we are <u>not</u> talking about here.*

When you start to understand, integrate, and respond to their challenges and respond with superior strategies and tactics necessary to meet those challenges, most leaders who are looking for high performance will leap at the opportunity to share power with you. From their perspective you will be a breath of fresh air. You'll be somebody who works for them that now presents to them a unique experience compared to their past experience.

At first they might be just pleasantly surprised, but then they'll start to understand what it really means to be supported by a direct report that knows exactly what the f*** they're doing coupled with being intent on helping their supervisor achieve mission success. Not every supervisor is going to respond that way, however, because some people in leadership positions shouldn't be there, and one of the reasons they shouldn't be there is if they become insecure based on your superior knowledge. We will go over that in the implementation section.

As you invite collaborative power, what your supervisors will learn is the more power they share with you *the more powerful they become as well*, as you increase the qualitative performance level of your work unit which then directly impacts *their* performance in an extremely positive way. When I say "qualitative" what that means is that the work group of *your direct reports will now align their performance outputs with the needs of your supervisor* and senior leader-managers. So: *you empower your supervisor first, then she empowers you.* That's the secret.

5 - Attracting Collaborative Power from the Bottom Up: When you can convince people that by following you and having you as their leader they've made a good decision, it radically expands your power base.

I know some of that sentence doesn't make sense because leaders typically pick followers and followers don't pick leaders. The most powerful people in the world only get that way by convincing a bunch of people to follow them. When you start to look at it from that perspective everything starts to change, *in your favor.* As leader-managers we all know we have to work through other people; we can't do it all on our own or else we would, right? So let me use a metaphor to explain my point, an undeniable reality that describes exactly what you're about to do.

As a leader you have a choice:

> Don't empower the people that work for you and they're like bumper cars at the county fair bouncing around chaotically, working hard, and having the best of intentions but being highly ineffective, with one jolt after another keeping the group away from mission success.

> Or, empower your people and they become more like a bunch of Formula One race cars with fast, exquisite, and precise movements, all in pursuit of a singular vision of mission success, of winning the race.

How you empower them is what we will be covering in this book.

Let me ask you this: if your work unit creates extraordinary levels of performance *based on the fact that you empowered them in ways they've never been empowered before*, what's that going to do for your reputation as a leader? That's correct, you will have Attracted Collaborative Power from the Bottom Up from a group of people that are so highly trained that their performance, their professionalism, and their ability to collaborate will be at such extraordinary levels that their dedication to mission success will carry you along and empower you as their leader. When you empower your direct reports they reward you by handing power back by creating extraordinary levels of high performance. It's just like with inviting collaborative power:

You empower them first, then they empower you.

See a trend starting to form here?

<u>*6 - Cultivating Collaborative Power by Implementing Collaborative Group Behaviors:*</u> Humanity's problems are solvable by integrating information we already know works *but that remains unused*. The issues of empowering groups to higher levels of performance is no exception. What you're going to learn about cultivating collaborative power is to start to use a very sophisticated human behavior dos and don'ts list. You'll see this one-two reference used regularly as you read through the book. What this means is that there is a long list of human behaviors that naturally excite the human brain to create an environment of collaboration. What is also true is that there is a long list of human behaviors

that naturally demotivate the human brain to create an environment of collaboration. So there you have it:

> *Don't list:* a list of behaviors that people are using that we want them to stop using now in order to create a more collaborative, high-performing work group.

> *Do list:* a list of behaviors that people are not using right now that they need to start using if we want a more collaborative, high-performing work group.

In Chapter 7: Cultivating Collaborative Power, I'll give you the initial dos and don'ts list that will get you rolling, and I'll also help you figure out how to add your own dos and don'ts with the method that I've used for years. I will also be rolling out a series of books in the future that will have more and more dos and don'ts separated into the Big 8 categories of group performance, but know I'm not holding back on you. What you have in this book will certainly help successfully launch your Collaborative Power Grab.

Once you have successfully invited and attracted collaborative power then cultivating collaborative power will not come as a shock to the group and will be welcomed by most of the people in the group. Quite frankly this step will be met with some resistance by some people and we'll talk about that too. *The order of implementation is important and cultivating collaborative power is always the last step towards completing the Collaborative Power Grab.*

Moving forward, what takes power away from leaders who want to improve the performance of their groups in order to achieve mission success? It is a deadly hidden menace that covers the globe. Does that sound a little too dramatic? In future sections we will talk about *normalized mediocre performance*. For now, let me introduce myself.

ABOUT ME

Looking back on over 45 years of work experience, I see that I was making Collaborative Power Grabs because of the circumstances I found myself in. I just didn't realize it at the time. But before you accuse me of being power hungry, let me explain.

I wasn't born knowing how to do this like the birds that know how to build their first nest with no training and no experience whatsoever. I had a significant number of failures along the way. Trying stuff that didn't work, understanding why it didn't work, and learning to avoid those actions.

And likewise, every time I found something that worked that either Invited Collaborative Power from the Top or Attracted Collaborative Power from the Bottom, I just kept reusing those techniques only to find they never go out of date. The results of that process are what you're finding in between the two covers of this book.

I know different generations think differently. But my experience is that there's no expiration date on actions that empower the people above you and empower the people below you. And in my observation it's going to remain that way unless the human brain changes its operating systems. And I think we can both agree that's not going happen anytime soon (and probably never).

Again let me emphasize: it's a **Collaborative** Power Grab. A power grab without a compass point has been the downfall of many individuals simply because **absolute power corrupts absolutely.**

If the purpose of your power grab is solidly founded upon improving the lives of the people around you, it's been my experience that mission accomplishment will always follow. As well, if you're grabbing power to help increase your ability to gain shelter, water, food, or safety for you and your family, that is also perfectly understandable and is a natural human thing to do as part of the evolutionary prerogative.

However, if your primary reason for grabbing power is for mission success **at the expense of all else** you will definitely have some significant short-term gains but it is a proposition that has diminishing returns over time. Additionally, if the primary reason for grabbing power is just so you could have more of it then I don't think you're helping your group or planet to progress.

If you're the type of human that always wants more control but not the responsibilities that come along with it then I would lump you into the same group. Regardless of my opinion on the matter, in my experience people who want to grab power just so they have more of it never seem to be able to satisfy that need. It seems to be a bottomless pit that regardless of how much power they shovel into it it's never enough. In this sense, and for this reason, I think people who want more power just for the sake of having more of it demonstrate a severe character defect at best and potentially a very significant psychological problem at worst. Read: **Without Conscience** by Robert Hare and **Snakes in Suits** by Paul Babiak and Robert Hare.

WHAT I LEARNED

The complete story of my work history is beyond the scope of this book and there are enough stories that it's probably its own book. However, suffice it to say I've worked in many different jobs where the working conditions and accepted practices were as such that we were subjected to very dangerous conditions. Unfortunately, those dangerous situations were also coupled with inadequate industry standards and ineffective company policies, all of which were being implemented by somewhat incompetent leaders and managers.

A terrible mix, indeed.

On the one hand, you're doing a job that can kill you and, on the other hand, your chances of survival are lessened because the groupthink knowledge base not only doesn't protect you but actually places you in harm's way based on the concept of "*We've always done it that way, so again, what's the problem you're having here?*"

While at the same time the people that are telling you what to do don't know what they are doing when it comes to leading people or managing organizations. After all, they're just doing the same thing the same way as *we always have*. And having a conversation with them concerning the concepts that *you don't know what you don't know* and *the things that you don't know are definitely things that can hurt you* is met with a silent blank stare (true story).

Or when you find a condition or a practice that is inherently unsafe and you bring it to the attention of your supervisor and he responds, "It's not really unsafe, we're just asking you to do the job as safely as possible." All it took was a quick 10-minute meeting with my supervisor's supervisor's supervisor (that's right—three levels up in the leadership hierarchy) in a newly founded safety committee meeting, and the deadly practice I was objecting to, which had been in place for over 20 years, was changed forever and for the better.

- The combination of inadequate industry standards and ineffective company policies, all of which were being implemented by somewhat incompetent leaders and managers, typically gets people *injured*, sometimes *maimed*, and sometimes *killed*. And in the case of some of my coworkers and nearly me a couple times, *all three* of those outcomes was *exactly what was happening.*

INVITING COLLABORATIVE POWER FROM THE TOP DOWN WAS BORN

This is when I started developing these techniques and didn't even realize I was doing it. Listen—I didn't have the flexibility to just quit my job and go someplace else. I had rent to pay, food to put on the table, and eventually kids to raise, and good-paying jobs don't grow on trees. I had to figure out another way.

As it turns out, when I was bringing these issues up to my supervisor and the various leaders above me, there was always somebody listening to what I was saying. In every single job I've ever had in my entire life there was always somebody in the leadership stack listening when I brought stuff up, even though it wasn't always obvious at the time.

And when I brought things up and started to hear the problems that my supervisors were confronted with, *I started working on their problem with what they were hearing from me.* I know that sounds a little confusing so let me explain.

What was happening with some of these *listening leaders* is they were simply involving me in their own challenges. They weren't denying what I was saying was a true fact; they were simply saying that what I was bringing up created a challenge for them that they had to work on before they could figure out what to do next.

The moment I learned what their challenges were I started focusing on their challenges 100 percent. In doing so I never experienced a situation where I could not contribute to an outcome that helped to support my supervisor, which resulted in a positive outcome for me and my coworkers!

The only way I could remedy these situations was to *invite collaborative power from the top down*.

What happened next was fascinating. I had my direct supervisor and his supervisor and sometimes even his supervisor's supervisor starting to contact me about the other challenges they were having *that had nothing to do with my original concern*. I became part of the problem-solving team for all my bosses above me, and as I empowered them with this level of support they handed the power back to me as well.

This happened at every job I've *ever* had.

And that's how Inviting Collaborative Power from the Top Down was born!

ATTRACTING COLLABORATIVE POWER FROM THE BOTTOM UP WAS BORN
A few years later I moved up in a different organization.

Unfortunately and unknowingly, I then found myself faced with a cataclysmic workplace culture that was so deteriorated there were about three different groups vying for power, walking around hating each other's guts, keying each other's cars, putting nails up against people's tires, stealing personal property from each other's lockers, and routinely using drugs and alcohol on company time. People showed up with whiskey on their breath, and some of them would routinely kick the trashcan after they were assigned a task or were heard slamming doors as they left the building. It was *the Wild West*.

However, what I did find over time, buried in that chaotic, fear-generating mess called a workplace, was a group of people that later formed the core of my future success.

But it couldn't happen until I helped to empower them. I did that by using my authority to create programs that would train them to become experts, after which I was able to then turn around and rely on them as the experts they now were. So not only did I empower them with information, knowledge, process, and know-how, I then empowered them with the decision making that came along with it. Once somebody is trained to an expert level and given the power of decision making, *everything changes*.

They returned the favor by empowering me. In this sense, as I noted earlier, I didn't necessarily select them as *my* followers but by empowering them first, *they selected me as their leader*.

I was standing on the shoulders of giants, the very same giants that I helped create.

They carried my collaborative power agenda forward with their extraordinary performance, focusing on mission success like a laser beam. I will forever be in their debt.

The only way I could remedy such a deteriorated work environment was to *attract collaborative power from the bottom up.*

And that's how Attracting Collaborative Power from the Bottom Up was born!

CULTIVATING COLLABORATIVE POWER WAS BORN

After that phase, I advanced in the organization and that's when I started *Cultivating Collaborative Power* by starting the development of what I now call Collaborative Group Behaviors. I trained on those behaviors frequently and rigorously, after which I converted them into *performance expectations placed directly on the personnel performance evaluations.*

Turnover initially went up as those who desired to play out their personal agendas (I'm being kind in my description of their activities here) slowly found themselves in an environment that didn't allow for destructive behavior.

Over a short period of time this group became an industry leader, receiving numerous individual awards from various professional organizations, with many of those people going on to give professional presentations on the exceptional performance of the programs we had developed in our organization. There was also regionwide recognition for our group achievements. Many of the people that worked for me went on to advance in their careers as senior leader-managers in other organizations.

I'm here to tell you, these practices — Inviting Collaborative Power from the Top Down, Attracting Collaborative Power from the Bottom Up, and Cultivating Collaborative Power by using Collaborative Group Behaviors — *work.*

The primary reason they work is because they empower people up and down the hierarchy, providing them with an extraordinarily satisfying work experience that has, as its result, mission success for the group. There is no better combination than that.

- You empower everyone, up and down the hierarchy, by supporting them with assertive loyalty, insightful care, and dynamic competence, *and they will respond by handing back more power than you can imagine.*

The entire book is captured in this sentence you just read.

All the *Starting Now* step-by-step actions I am about to give you, when consistently applied over time, communicate that same authentic message. The result is you change people's lives for the better.

When you change people's lives for the better, of course they want to keep you around, ***and they do that by handing you power.***

WHEN A LEADER GAINS ENOUGH COLLABORATIVE POWER

When a leader is able to ***Invite*** enough collaborative power from above and ***Attract*** enough collaborative power from below and then start influencing the culture by ***Cultivating*** Collaborative Power from the larger workplace landscape (in that order), things start to change.

When a group of leaders in the same group follow the same Collaborative Power Grab, the following is an exact description of what will happen once a collection of collaborative leaders gain collaborative power:

- **Mission:** The significant amount of reliable, mission-centered, independent decision-making climbs to very high levels as management program responsibilities cascade downward, significantly reducing the need for supervision at every level in the group. All work is now appropriately prioritized. As new work arrives both the new work and previous work are reprioritized based on the needs of the mission, never again to be doing the second most important thing first and therefore never again doing the fifth most important thing first.

- **Culture:** There are some immediate benefits when those who demonstrate destructive behavior, such as bully behaviors, are effectively addressed: lowering fear in the workplace and promoting a psychologically safe environment for the human brain to remain in the prefrontal cortex. Sounds kind of scientific because it is. Take special note with what you are about to read concerning the operating rules of the human brain and how our behaviors are governed by obvious and hidden fears. As you will learn it makes all the difference; the impact of this benefit will grow and grow as group members *mature* with the ***Starting Now*** step-by-step collaborative group behaviors.

- **Effective Interpersonal Relationships:** As the collaborative group behaviors that are embedded within the ***Starting Now*** step-by-step instructions become integrated into the group, people problems will start to dry up, again significantly lowering the need for direct supervision and decreasing the huge amount of time that interpersonal problems consume.

- **High-Quality Communication:** When people learn how to talk and write to each other because we are now "talking about how we talk," misunderstandings and the damage they do are reduced. The other big reason problems drop in this area is because Cultivating Collaborative Power using the Collaborative Group Behaviors defines when a person should initiate communication. Once people are using the ***Starting Now*** step-by-step collaborative group behaviors, their jobs and the expectations placed upon them become very clear, causing confusion to drop radically. When confusion goes down, so does the need for direct supervision, and time is no longer needed to fix communication problems.

- **Technical Competency:** The more highly trained the group members become, the more they become very technically competent in their respective positions; that competency, combined with ***Starting Now*** step-by-step collaborative group behaviors as time goes on, means each person will now make better decisions and error rates will drop significantly, again further reducing the need for direct supervision. People are now trained in their weakest skill set first and are constantly retrained to levels that allow for them to produce ***expert-level outcomes and decisions.*** And from there the next weakest skill set is improved and so on and so forth. The group is able to reduce the amount of risk, reduce the number of unexpected consequences, reduce the number of problems, now for the lowest amount of resource expended. How does that not sound good to every single leader reading these words right now?

- **Productivity:** Is now important. It might have always been important to you as a leader, but not necessarily to the group at large. That's all changing now as people get recognition for their achievements and workflow directives are now a fine-tuned machine that uses time limits for activities. As a planning mindset takes root, productivity goes up, time for more training and delegated tasks opens up, and the need for direct supervision drops again for yet another reason, allowing all leader-managers, including first-line supervisors, to now inherit additional mission-promoting management tasks from the level above them. Bam!

- **Problem-Solving:** Problems stop showing up on your desk and the ones that do become smaller and smaller in magnitude because you now have a ton of expert problem solvers working for you. Once every group member starts to incrementally get better at recognizing and solving problems using the Recognizing Problems SOP (Appendix 1) and the Eight Step Problem-Solving Process SOP (Appendix 2), the average problem half-life drops. As people get better at solving problems, again, the time available for more delegated tasks opens up and the need for direct supervision drops again for yet another reason, allowing everyone in the group—including leadership—to have a more interesting and rewarding work life. One other observation you will have: there is a long list of unsolved problems in your group right now *that you don't know about. As with every group, these hidden unknown problems are doing damage and they are sucking up time like a magnet.* Not only that, they are creating secondary problems. ***These problems are like a big parent hurricane creating all the children tornadoes around it.*** Once problem-solving becomes a team sport, things really change for the better and opportunities to save time start showing up from the least expected places.

- **Continuous Improvement:** Most requests for ideas for improvement positively impact productivity. As people start to learn how to ferret out the good ideas from the not-so-good ideas *before* they submit the idea using the idea evaluation process provided, it saves management time. Once leaders become much more empowered, much more willing to take appropriate risks, and much more motivated to stretch themselves, their people, and their resources in the pursuit of extraordinary levels of improvement, *continuous improvement starts to become an organic process within the culture.*

That's right: when implemented consistently and passionately over time, *continuous improvement eventually becomes an organic function of the group.* When continuous improvement begins to operate organically within the group you have created a situation where *the larger strategic objectives of the organization become a daily practice by your front line people.* Take a moment and think about the power that resides within these last two or three sentences.

When everybody becomes an expert as a result of extraordinary levels of training, ideas for improvement begin to flow like an unstoppable river. Ideas for improvement no longer clutter the desks of upper management and the group no longer suffers from having critical performance-increasing good ideas getting stalled in a manager's overflowing inbox. (That was me at one point.)

- **Recognition:** People now get recognition for their achievements and positive performance is now no longer being taken for granted. Remember: those who are recognized for their demonstration of desirable technical and collaborative behaviors *will repeat that same desirable behavior in the future.* Recognition by the leader of those worthy acts is like using a collaborative glue patching back together the human emotional need to be part of something larger than ourselves. This results in creating an *esprit de corps* that generates *extremely loyal and dedicated high performers.* Once you have a group of those people your *highly collaborative workforce will also become a juggernaut of organic continuous improvement.* For every behavior you want repeated, effectively and officially recognize it and *it will be repeated forevermore by them and others.*

- **Recovery:** Substandard behavior is clearly defined. No one is a victim any longer; performance, one way or another, is now a *choice.* Negative performance events are met with recovery behaviors (provided with each collaborative group behavior). One of the more hidden reasons group productivity is hurt and the mission is compromised is the accumulation of error. People err and will continue to err in part because they don't know how to recover from their errors. It's not something we learned growing up necessarily. Not having a strategic approach to error mitigation is a huge, missed opportunity for many groups. Teach a person how to recover from error and the gift is returned to the group as extraordinary levels of high performance. Look for similar errors being made in seemingly unconnected events and trace them back to their common source with the intent of eliminating *systemic error generation by turning them into teachable moments for the next version of the training program.* By changing the training program to include teachable moments as a preventative measure against future instances of the same error, group performance again climbs systematically. And when people do err, keep the feedback session private and safe, deliver the feedback unemotionally, focus on improvement, and be specific so the individual *receives usable information for improvement*. As noted earlier take this information and modify the training program to prevent the error from being repeated by others in the future. *This same basic method has created the best fighter pilots in the world.* More on that later.

In summary, when leaders have collaborative power the following changes will occur in the group:

- Examples of negative human behaviors drop
- Fear-caused behaviors drop
- Quality and quantity of communication increases
- Mission statement moves to center stage
- Respect and dignity become preferred behaviors
- Professional relationships dominate
- Clear and achievable performance expectations abound
- Leadership provides a support role without giving up power
- Problem-solving becomes a team sport
- Productivity and smart work rules over mediocrity
- Group members become involved in creating outcomes
- Inappropriate, toxic behaviors are trounced
- Group members accept more responsibility over time
- Ability to deal with adversity increases
- Ideas for improvement is a constant conversation
- Team members become very good at what they do
- Leaders grow to very high levels of effectiveness
- Group members have confidence to make decisions and know when to include their supervisor
- Continuous improvement strategy becomes an organic function
- The need for direct supervision continuously dries up
- Leaders learn to check their ego at the door

IT'S REALLY JUST ABOUT YOU

None of this happens without the leader first gaining *collaborative power*.

The first thing any leader needs to do is to Invite the power from above. There are very specific and effective ways to do that and I'm going to be outlining them, step-by-step.

At about the same time you can start Attracting Power from the Bottom Up by influencing the behaviors of the people that follow you in such a favorable and effective way that you will build loyalty to the mission based on your dedication to them. And again, I'm going to be outlining exactly what to do, step by step.

After the people above you hand over collaborative power to you based on their experience of your effectiveness, and after the people below you hand over collaborative power to you based on their experience of your support for them, you can start to influence the larger landscape and promote the building of an enhanced culture by bringing in a very sophisticated human dos and don'ts list called collaborative group behaviors. I have provided a very solid first list of collaborative group behaviors for your use and will again give you a step-by-step process of how to use them.

At this point you can start creating your own collaborative group behaviors; it's a very simple process if you have gained enough power.

What are the behaviors that are being demonstrated in the group right now that need to stop in order for you to create a collaborative group?

What are the behaviors that are not being demonstrated in the group right now that need to start in order to create a collaborative group?

By answering these two questions you can start to create new performance expectations for everyone in the group, leader and non-leader alike, that will vault overall group performance in ways you have not thought possible.

And again, I'm going to take you through this process step-by-step.

Simply said: all you have to do is use it.

Simply said but not *simply done*, right?

And in my experience the biggest obstacle you are going to need to deal with is *you*.

The only way this works is if you participate and demonstrate these behaviors on a regular basis in a reliable fashion.

I have trained others in what I'm about to give you, so I know it works, I know it can be learned, and I can confirm my experience was not unique.

If you're not ready to use the information that's in this book, I would invite you to return it for a refund.

I don't want you to read this book and start telling people this will never work because you *didn't have it in you* to actually use the information provided. I'm sorry if that sounds aggressive but I'm tired of the endless excuses articulated by disempowered leaders who don't use information and then diss the same information simply because they didn't have the ability to change their leadership behavior, didn't have the *intestinal fortitude* to take the risks necessary to move their group towards extraordinary levels of performance and do the hard work to gain the power necessary to create an enhanced high-performance workplace culture.

This book might ask you to demonstrate certain behaviors you're not comfortable demonstrating. And in my experience if people are not comfortable demonstrating a particular behavior it makes changing from their current less-effective behavior extremely difficult. From what I've seen, the primary motivating factor that causes a person to change habit patterns is *desire*. This desire is typically sourced from one or both of the following situations: either the current situation is so painful that a person becomes highly motivated to move away from that painful situation, or a new potential situation is incredibly attractive compared to their current circumstances.

- The key to changing is to *simply start*. When people don't start a new habit pattern there can be many reasons why they don't take the first step. *The first step is the biggest step*, so when you *simply start* by taking the very first step the rest of the change that you are participating in becomes more sequential, more matter of fact, and less decisional.

Are you up for this challenge?

Are you up for changing your behaviors to gain the power necessary to become a highly effective high-performing leader?

Gaining collaborative power from above you (Invite), below you (Attract), and around you (Cultivate) is a simple step-by-step process, but it is likely to mean *you need to change some of your current approaches to leadership.*

A lot of people talk about doing but don't *walk* about doing. If you're not willing to take the risks necessary to gain collaborative power by inviting it, attracting it, and cultivating it, your desire to become a highly effective leader will never become a reality.

All right?

Let's move forward.

Next step: read Chapter 1: Implementation Plan. Even if you want to read the entire book before you implement any of the steps (which I recommend, by the way), *please read about the implementation plan next.*

Chapter 1

Implementation Plan

Bob's energy and knowledge jump off the page. A short time after I began reading
Collaborative Power Grab, I started applying these tools and I felt a positive shift in my outlook,
and in the way others perceived me.

—TODD PHILLIPS

The Five (or Six) Factors You Need to Know About
    Number One
    Number Two
    Number Three
    Number Four
    Number Five
    Number Six
Logbook and Record Keeping
Implementation Steps
    Phase 1
    Phase 2
    Phase 3
    Phase 4 (Optional)

If you have not read the introduction, please go back and read that now and then come right back to this chapter. Thank you!

THE FIVE FACTORS YOU NEED TO KNOW ABOUT

This implementation chapter is Chapter 1 for a reason. You can read the rest of this book in whatever order you want, but before you dive in here are five factors for implementing your Collaborative Power Grab that you need to know about right now!

NUMBER ONE

How well you implement what's in this book is entirely dependent on your ability to start new habits and your ability to implement a skill set that might not be familiar to you.

This can be difficult for many people so be aware of it and watch yourself here. If you're feeling resistance or if you have a voice in your head saying, "don't do this," you need to address the resistance if you're going to excel by pushing through *as leaders are expected to*, and you need to talk back to that voice with a different message that says: "Hey voice, get on board because we are going all in."

If you're not willing to do those two things you might want to consider a different career as an alternative to leadership.

NUMBER TWO

I have promised you a *Starting Now* step-by-step process, so that's what I'm going to give you in Chapter 2: Action-Only Phasing Plan. Following the instructions in that chapter allows you to jump in directly with using the new *Starting Now* actions.

However, what's important for you to know is that in order to completely understand at an in-depth level everything I'm giving you, you must familiarize yourself with the content in the rest of this book as well. If you want to jump in and start using the Action-Only Phasing Plan now go right ahead, but please parallel those actions with the reading assignments found in Chapters 5, 6, and 7.

There is a giant boatload of additional information in this book that goes beyond the *step-by-step Starting Now* actions and can cause your performance as a leader to skyrocket. Reading *Chapter 3: Using Superior Knowledge in All Areas of Required Expertise* will give you a level of expertise few leaders possess.

NUMBER THREE

Do not use your own implementation plan that strays from the recommendations in this implementation plan. This is because this sequence of steps helps you to *avoid the mistakes that I have made in the past*. Implementing this plan out of sequence can hurt you and slow you down in terms of excelling your collaborative power base as a leader.

The two exceptions here are:

A. It's perfectly acceptable to go ahead and read the entire book before you come back to the implementation plan and start to implement. There's nothing wrong with that approach, and in fact there's a lot right with that approach. And…

B. If you're already a successful leader operating a successful group, then by all means you can cherry pick information out of this book and use some of the items that you might be seeing for the first time. And follow the sequence even if you are cherry picking.

NUMBER FOUR

This plan is broken down into phases, and every step within a phase can be implemented all at the same time. That being said, when it comes to Inviting and Attracting Collaborative Power, you want to follow the sequence of the phases, *making sure you have completed and stayed in each phase for an extended period of time before moving to the next phase.*

NUMBER FIVE

This effort is going to require you to take notes regularly. I recommend a pen and a yellow pad because you're not going to be able to bring your laptop or phone to every venue that will require some record keeping. Plus, using a laptop or a phone to take notes during a meeting can make people nervous. Everybody uses to a pen and a yellow pad. *If you don't take notes, you are not going to succeed.*

NUMBER SIX

I know this is going to sound self-serving but if it will makes sense to you later and you might want to take me up on this deal: If you like what you're reading here and you think it'll be effective at increasing the performance of your group towards mission success, I would recommend you get copies of this book for each of the leaders in your follower group. If you're serious about implementing what you find here, I think you'll come to realize that the easiest thing for you to do is to use this book as a training manual and start setting up meetings for some open conversation about skyrocketing group performance. *There's no better way to do that than turning every leader into an expert on this subject matter.*

LOGBOOK AND RECORD KEEPING

As I mentioned above, you have to take notes in order to succeed in your Collaborative Power Grab. Be prepared to *take notes at all times in the following scenarios:*

- When performing the Landscape Survey
- When writing down your recipe for success describing how you're going to exceed each one of your performance expectations
- When meeting with your direct reports
- When recording problems that you were unable to solve right away
- When recording ideas for improvement that come from your direct reports
- When keeping an active list of each person's weakest skill set that they need to be trained on next
- When recording exceptional performance that needs to be recognized
- When participating in performance improvement meetings
- When recording and tracking the various deadlines you've incorporated into the directives you have assigned to your direct reports
- When meeting with your supervisor for any reason
- When recording the priorities to be followed, the problems to be solved, and the goals established by your supervisor

- When recording performance feedback that needs to be incorporated into your recipe for success
- When meeting with the senior leadership-management team for any reason
- When receiving information that's going to be critical for you to remember

When thinking about this list I couldn't resist sharing something I read in Jeffery Pfeffer's book *Power: Why Some People Have It and Others Don't.* In a section on self-knowledge, Pfeffer shares the story of Joe Beneducci, who became CEO of the Fireman's Fund at 39 years old. Beneducci told Pfeffer he reached such a high level at such a young age not because of his educational background but because of a simple habit he'd developed: after every significant meeting or interaction he would make notes about what he had done well and what happened, what people had said and done, and the outcome of the meeting, so he could make future interactions more effective.

A similar story came from Dr. Modesto Maidique, a Cuban American who served as president of Florida International University for 23 years. When Pfeffer asked Maidique what leadership habits he thought made him effective, his response was immediate: making notes about decisions, meetings, and other interactions and reflecting on what he had done well or poorly so he could improve his skills.

Pfeffer goes on to say, "There is no learning and personal development without reflection." According to Andy Hargadon, a business school professor at University of California, Davis, many people who think they have 20 years of experience really don't — they just have one year of experience repeated 20 times. Structured reflection takes time. It also requires the discipline to concentrate, make notes, and think about what you're doing. *It is very useful for building a path to power.*

Back to my thoughts. Just like the people profiled in Pfeffer's book, I recognize the importance of taking time to make notes and reflect. You can't reflect unless you can also reference what's happened in the past. The best way to do that is to *write it down*. While I consider myself a voracious reader by anybody's standards, I sometimes think I've written more than I've read. And I can see that looking back on last year's strategic plan or last week's senior management meeting or yesterday's notes when developing a new program *was critical to my future success*.

Bottom line: *write it down.*

IMPLEMENTATION STEPS

As noted, everything in each phase can be implemented all at the same time. Where there are steps it's best to follow those steps in order within the phase. The important issues here are:

A. You need to activate and have fully implemented everything within a phase before going to the next phase.

B. Once you go to the next phase you want to continue to use and activate everything in the previous phase. In other words, you're not *replacing* **Starting Now** action items when going from one phase to the other; instead you're *adding* to your list of **Starting Now** action items.

PHASE 1
Implement and use all *Starting Now* actions with supporting information as follows:

1.1 Get ready to take notes.

1.2 Perform an initial Landscape Survey (in Chapter 4) This can be a quick first pass (you can download a free copy of this from TheLostArtOfCollaboration.com).

1.3 Read and become an expert on Operating Rules of the Human Brain and Quadrant 2 Behaviors (in Chapter 3) with special attention to fear reduction and the hidden sources of fear.

1.4 Read: Bumps in the Road (in Chapter 3).

- **You can refer to and use the *Starting Now* actions in Chapter 2 they are the same Chapter 5 and 6. I broke they out in chapter 2 so you had a quick guide. I recommended reading Chapter 5 and 6 as you are implementing Chapter 2**

PHASE 1 – START USING THESE *Starting Now* actions NOW:

1.5 See Chapter 2 (read Chapter 5): Inviting Collaborative Power from the Top Down, then implement:

Step 1: Know and Exceed Your Performance Expectations
Step 2: Basic Rules That Apply to Most Situations
Step 3: Determine Which Quadrant Your Current Boss Falls Into (you will need to read this section in Chapter 5)

1.6 See Chapter 2 (read Chapter 6): Attracting Collaborative Power from the Bottom Up, then implement:

Step 1: Emulate the Behaviors You Want from Others
Step 2: Support Timely Decision Making and Problem-Solving
Step 3: Build to Expert Levels of Technical and Collaborative Competency
Step 4: Continually Make Observations of Examples of Good Performance

Before Step 2 – get used to performing these **Starting Now** actions on a daily basis. Nothing wrong with taking a couple weeks before going to Step 2.

PHASE 2
Implement and use all *Starting Now* actions with supporting information as follows:

2.1 Get ready to take notes.

PHASE 2 – START USING THESE *Starting Now* actions NOW:

2.2 See Chapter 2 (read Chapter 5): Inviting Collaborative Power from the Top Down, implement:

Step 4: Develop a Mentoring Relationship with Your Boss

2.3 See Chapter 2 (read Chapter 6):Attracting Collaborative Power from the Bottom Up, implement:

Step 5: Keep the Group Focused on the Mission, Values, Directives, and Their Performance Expectations at All Times
Step 6: Teach and Promote All Productivity Behaviors
Step 7: Encourage the Group to Innovate New Ideas for Mission Success

Before Step 3 – get used to performing these *Starting Now* actions on a daily basis. Nothing wrong with taking a couple weeks before going to Step 3.

PHASE 3
Implement and use all *Starting Now* actions with supporting information as follows:

3.1 Get ready to take notes.

PHASE 3 – START USING THESE *Starting Now* actions NOW:

3.2 See Chapter 2 (read Chapter 5): Inviting Collaborative Power from the Top Down, implement:

Step 5: Start Initiating Your Support Role Activities

3.3 See Chapter 2 (read Chapter 6): Attracting Collaborative Power from the Bottom Up, implement:

Step 8: Help Your People Recover from Low Performance or Errors with Training Sessions Focused on Improving Performance
Step 9: Protect and Promote the Culture
Step 10: After Full Implementation, Implement, Implement, Implement all the above at Every Chance

PHASE 4 (OPTIONAL)
<u>**Implement as follows:**</u>

<u>4.1 Read Chapter 7: Cultivating Collaborative Power in its entirety.</u>

<u>4.2 Do a Power Check</u> and make sure you have enough power to implement this before moving forward. If you don't think you have enough power **then don't do it** and leave this for the senior leaders.

<u>4.3 Don't hesitate to cherry pick!</u> Read Chapter 7 thoroughly and cherry pick any ideas that you think you want to start implementing now because it will help you with Attracting Collaborative Power or help solve a problem.

AGAIN, One Last note: If you want to start right now you can. The *Starting Now* actions in Chapter 2 of Inviting and Attracting are highly supportive of the direct supervisor and those above you and highly supportive of the people that follow you.

These actions do not create a threat to either your supervisor or your followers.

Chapter 2

Action-Only Phasing Plan

*Bob has a knack for providing clear step-by-step guidelines to make accessible
the most complex of topics. This book is no exception.*

—TERESA HERRERA

Phase 1
    Inviting
    Attracting
Phase 1
    Implementation figures 1 through 7
Phase 2
    Inviting
    Attracting
Phase 2
    Implementation figures 8 through 11
Phase 3
    Inviting
    Attracting
Phase 3
    Implementation figures 12 through 15
Phase 4 (Optional)
    Cultivating

This **action-only phasing plan** includes the **Starting Now** action items for Inviting Collaborative Power from the Top Down (Chapter 5) and Attracting Collaborative Power from the Bottom Up (Chapter 6), but with all the supporting information **removed** so you can easily find the actions to take in each phase. It doesn't mean the other information in Chapters 5 and 6 isn't important, however, because it is.

This section is merely being provided for ease of reference.

Before we dive into the action items, let me start out with a quick note on the phases and steps. You'll see in Chapters 5 and 6 that Inviting Collaborative Power from the Top Down and Attracting Collaborative Power from the Bottom Up are divided into three phases each.

While Inviting and Attracting are two entirely different action groups and are presented in separate chapters, you want to implement both the Inviting and Attracting steps of a phase simultaneously.

In other words, implement Steps 1–3 for Phase 1 of Inviting along with Steps 1–4 in Phase 1 of Attracting for an extended period of time as explained in Chapter 1: Implementation Plan. Then, move on and implement the Inviting and Attracting steps in Phase 2 and so on.

PHASE 1 - INVITING AND ATTRACTING

INVITING

Step 1: Know and Exceed Your Performance Expectations

- Build a plan for how you are going to exceed all your performance expectations.
  - ° **Starting now:** Take your logbook and write down in two or three sentences *exactly* how you're going to exceed each and every performance expectation. This is your *recipe for success*. As new expectations might be placed on you, stop and create a plan that describes in two or three sentences how you're going to exceed that performance expectation. *Take an active and thoughtful approach to planning out how you're going to exceed your performance expectations.*
  - ° **Starting now:** Take note of any performance expectation you don't completely understand and use that as part of your conversation with your supervisor. Always: If you need input on filling out your *recipe for success* go ask your mentor—yes that's also your boss. See Step 2.
  - ° **Starting now:** Start acting on your plan. Start implementing your *recipe for success* and make adjustments to the plan *when you find opportunities to improve* your approach. You want to start to integrate a *continuous improvement strategy* into how you're going to exceed your performance expectations. Your question: what do I need to learn next in order to improve my performance? Once you answer that question: *implement.*
- Note: Building a recipe for success requires some work up front. However, the mere fact that you are methodically assessing each performance expectation and adding the actions you are going to pursue *is extremely powerful*. For any performance expectation that requires a more complex approach just break down your recipe for success into easily understood steps. Any complex concept or practice can be broken down into sequential steps and *I can honestly say every time I did this it was time well spent investing in my successful future.*

Step 2: Basic Rules That Apply to Most Situations

- One of the best ways to make your boss a success is to complement their weaknesses.
  - ° **Starting now:** Examine the quadrant advice given below and follow it.
  - ° **Starting now:** If it looks like one of your boss's weaknesses is about to blindside them: *immediately meet with them privately and bring it to their attention.* If they insist on disagreeing with you let the issue go. If the issue becomes a reality, then the second time you bring something up they will probably be listening a little more closely and will be less likely to disagree with you. However, if the issue does not become a reality, they may still realize that you brought it to their attention because you care about their success. If for some reason they do not come to that same conclusion you are free to remind them that the way you see your job, in part, as their direct report is for you to protect them and in doing so protect mission success.
- Take extreme care in how or if you disagree with any of your supervisors : *it needs to be done in private.* Anytime you're in a situation where it appears that you're having to disagree with your supervisor in public, *just don't do it.*
  - ° **Starting now:** If you're going to be in a meeting with your boss and you know that your boss's boss will be there, *first have a pre-meeting meeting with your direct supervisor and ask them how they want things to go.* Then do as they say. *From this point forward treat your boss with dignity and respect whether that be in private or public meetings.* Note: there is a lot going on in the leadership stack above you that you may never know about. And this means you don't want to assume that you know the whole situation. If you do make this assumption it could lead to serious mistakes that could mortally wound your relationship with your boss. This is why it's always important to take your boss's behavior as an example of the dynamics in larger meetings that have higher level management around the table.
- Don't complain about your boss to your followers.
  - ° **Starting now:** When you receive information from your boss that you know your followers are going to have problems with, you need to soften the blow. Yes, certainly acknowledging any faults in the information, but at the same time acknowledge that the boss has their eye on a larger field than what we are participating in and it's our job to get the job done. *Do not under any circumstances participate in a whine session with your direct reports about your boss or their directives.* The more you can draw parallels between yourself and your supervisor and the group's mission statement in the eyes of your followers, the more you become an extension of your leadership team and therefore an extension of their power as well. *The only specific exceptions to this rule are found within the quadrant information below.*
- Something going wrong?
  - ° **Starting now:** Get to your supervisor ASAP and let them know what's going on. The sooner you do it the better off you are. Some supervisors may criticize you for not solving the problem when they think you should have, but the alternative of you knowing about a problem and not contacting them sooner is orders of magnitude worse for you and your supervisor.

Note: as noted previously, train yourself on Appendices 1 and 2 and know the material like the back of your hand. When you become an expert problem solver the whole world will want you around.

- Take responsibility for poor outcomes.
  - **<u>Starting now:</u>** If you or your crew is responsible for poor outcome, the sooner you bring that to the attention of your supervisor the better. It doesn't mean you won't get a dose of medicine that maybe will leave a very bad taste in your mouth, but over time this falls under the category of perception management. By demonstrating that you hold yourself responsible, ***they learn that you are somebody they can trust.*** This is big. The moment your supervisor *is convinced that you are legitimately trustworthy, your power expands massively.*
- Don't bypass your boss.
- **<u>Starting now:</u>** Always follow the chain of command and do not bypass your boss on the way up. Nor let your boss bypass you on the way down to your direct reports. There is no other situation that is more ripe for misunderstanding and misdirected perceptions along with misdirected anger than the chain of command getting bypassed or the chain of command going unused. The messaging can get confusing and people won't really know what to do next or they will think they know based on poor-quality information. When bypassing has occurred, and nothing goes wrong it gives people the impression that bypassing the chain of command is not only not wrong, but it can be very effective and useful. However, whenever a breakdown in the chain of command causes problems it's usually a very messy situation with a lot of finger-pointing to go around. Essentially with a healthy chain of command in use it will make sure that the right decisions are being made at the right authority level with the right people being held responsible. Note: the only exception to this rule is if for some reason your immediate supervisor is directing you to perform activities that are clearly illegal, unsafe, against company polices or are diametrically opposed to the directives issued by senior management. If that happens you have to have a, probably uncomfortable, conversation with your direct supervisor before you go over their head. In any situation like this, which we can all agree is a difficult situation, you need to talk to your direct supervisor first before you do anything else. ***Welcome to leadership.*** The only exception to this rule is if you suspect the end result of your conversation could be violence. In that rare situation going directly to your boss's boss before a conversation with your supervisor is entirely appropriate. Study, follow and enforce Appendices 3 and 4 and follow chapter 7 high-quality communication collaborative behaviors in order to promote a high-quality communication system.

<u>Step 3: Determine Which Quadrant Your Current Boss Falls Into (See Quadrant Ratings in Chapter 5)</u>

  - **<u>Starting now:</u>** Carefully and slowly examine the quadrant descriptions of the various bosses in the section on Quadrant Behaviors. This guide is just that: a guide. Everybody has fingerprints, but it's those same fingerprints that make us very different. The quadrant thinking of your boss is no different. There is no doubt that your boss is going to land predominantly in one of these quadrants, just as you do. By combining your understanding of your quadrant and your boss's, you can bring a very intelligent level of support to your boss. Step 3 is imperative before you make any future moves into Phase 2.

Starting now: This guide is provided so not only do you understand what quadrant your boss is in but what quadrant you are in. If you haven't already figured out which quadrant you are in, do so now by referring to the Quadrant Thinking section in Chapter 3 and the quadrant information provided below. The advice that's given to you in this section when comparing your quadrant to your boss's quadrant *needs to be an essential component of your plan moving forward if you want to succeed.* Note: there are many benefits to understanding Quadrant Thinking, however one of the primary purposes of understanding your and your boss's quadrant is to *protect Mission success against your combined inherent weaknesses.* Your boss could be very strong in an area where you are weak, and that's *complementary strength.* You could be very strong in an area where your boss is weak, and that is also *complementary strength.* However, when discovering areas where you're both weak you can empower the both of you by *acquiring the resources and knowledge necessary to resolve your combined weakness.*

ATTRACTING

Step 1: Emulate the Behaviors You Want from Others

Starting Now

- Here are the three actions you need to start taking immediately:
  1. **Starting now:** Consistently demonstrate a positive work ethic *by reliably and consistently demonstrating all the following Steps 2 through 10 in Attracting Collaborative Power.*
  2. **Starting now:** Consistently demonstrate your dedication to integrity and professionalism *by treating all your followers with the dignity and respect that every one of us deserves.*
  3. **Starting now:** Build predictability in your relationships *by explaining your decision-making philosophy.* As noted, by building in predictability your direct reports will start to *design their decision making based on your philosophies*!

Step 2: Support Timely Decision Making and Problem-Solving

Starting Now

Here are the four actions you need to start taking immediately:

1. **Starting now:** Hold training sessions on how to recognize problems and train your group to *always communicate to you about any problems*, including roadblocks they encounter during their

workday. Each day: remind them to tell you about *anything getting in the way of them doing a good job today*.

2. **Starting now:** Train your direct reports on the first step of the problem-solving process, which is to communicate problems to you *immediately*.
   Note: when a problem occurs, the statement I hear from leaders most often is: *"If they had just told me about the problem earlier a lot of damage could have been avoided!"*

3. **Starting now:** Hold training sessions on *how to use the step-by-step problem-solving process and require its use*. Use Appendix 2 for training your direct reports on the step-by-step problem-solving process. Make sure to also go over the list of cognitive biases supplied in Appendix 1. It's a real eye-opener if people are learning about cognitive biases for the first time.

4. **Starting now:** Promote that every group member have an open-minded approach that (a) encourages people to *allow new facts to change their minds* and (b) *ensures* that finding the right answer is more important than *being right*. It's *not about being right*, it's about *learning right* so we can *do right*, therefore they need to leave their ego at the door.

Step 3: Build to Expert Levels of Technical and Collaborative Competency

Starting Now

Here are the three actions you need to start taking immediately:

1. **Starting now:** Provide training for each individual's weakest skill set first. And then the next weakest skill set, working your way up from the weakest to the strongest skill set. Ask them what they think they need training on and make sure they know why you're asking. *This should be a routine training process within the entire group.*

2. **Starting now:** Provide training that advances the trainee to an expert level for whatever task they are being trained on. *Once they are an expert, start relying on them as an expert.* Start encouraging them to make independent decisions so you can relieve yourself of the burden of direct supervision. Note: training your people to be experts might seem like overkill, especially in a world that has normalized mediocre performance. However, I'm of the opinion most of the planet is under-trained. And if you look deeply into the problems of many organizations the biggest issue is almost always *incompetency*. When people are trained to expert levels, both the tangible and intangible advantages are significant towards achieving mission success. Tangibles are results such as less direct supervision, better decision making, and fewer problems. Intangibles include increased job satisfaction from increased job control, higher self-esteem, and significant fear reduction.

3. **Starting now:** Provide *quarterly refresher training on the performance expectations* everyone is expected to meet. This would include making sure that Q1 and Q3 individuals receive more collaboration training and that Q4 and Q3 individuals receive more technical training. This

also includes moving Q4s to jobs that better fit their skills if it looks like training is not resolving their technical incompetencies. ***The moment the Q4 is moved to a job where they are very technically competent, they instantly become a Q2.***

Step 4: Continually Make Observations of Examples of Good Performance

Starting Now

Did someone:

- go beyond the call of duty?
- become the best at a routine duty?
- do an exceptional job responding to an emergency?
- do an exceptional job responding to a customer complaint?
- take on additional responsibilities?
- volunteer?
- solve a problem?
- help during a stressful situation?
- come up with a great idea for improvement?
- come up with a great idea for increasing productivity?
- Here are the three actions you need to start taking immediately:
  1. **Starting now:** If somebody qualifies for recognition go up and tell them that you're aware of what they did and personally thank them.
  2. **Starting now:** The next thing you're going to do is write a short one-on-one email to your supervisor noting the individual and the exceptional performance. Then copy that email and send it to the person who you are recognizing. This is a very powerful way of recognizing somebody, when they know that you're passing this information on to your boss. Do not underestimate how empowering this is.
  3. **Starting now:** As you train more people to become Q2s their performance will start to increase and you need to be ready and willing to recognize them ***as quickly as possible.*** Your goal is to send one of these emails ***about once every two months for each person on your crew.*** And you want to make sure that all of these events are collected and placed in their semi-annual or annual evaluation so people understand that what they do in the field ***directly impacts their performance evaluation scores.***

The following figures are not as comprehensive as the *Starting Now* instructions above but instead have been developed as quick guides to help keep you focused on what's important. These quick guides are also included as downloads from the online course.

PHASE 1

IMPLEMENTATION FIGURES 1 THROUGH 7

Inviting Steps 1, 2, 3

Attracting Steps 1, 2, 3 ,4

>INVITING< COLLABORATIVE POWER FROM THE TOP DOWN

PHASE 1: STEP 1: *Know & Exceed Your Performance Expectations*

HOW TO **EXCEED** ALL OF YOUR PERFORMANCE EXPECTATIONS (P.E.s)

Preparation:
- Purchase a spiral **notebook**
- Locate your **company P.E.s**

A–Starting Now: Recipe for Success
- *Copy down your P.E.s into **your logbook.***
- *For each P.E., write down **two or three sentences** describing exactly how you're going to exceed each and every performance expectation.*

B–Starting Now:
Clarify Unclear P.E.s
- *Note the P.E.s you **don't fully understand** as you go.*
- *Take "unclear" P.E.s **to your Boss**/mentor for discussion.*

C–Starting Now:
Take Action on the Plan
- ***Take action** on the "Recipe" you created in Step A.*
- ***Make adjustments** to your Recipe for Success as you find opportunities to improve it.*

D–Starting Now:
Continuous Improvement
- ***Ask daily:** What do I need to learn next in order to improve my performance?*
- *Once you answer that question: **implement.***

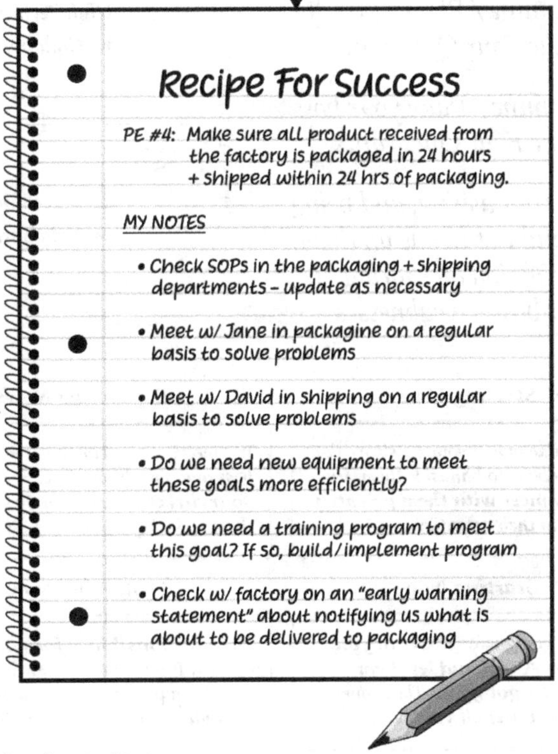

Recipe For Success

PE #4: Make sure all product received from the factory is packaged in 24 hours + shipped within 24 hrs of packaging.

MY NOTES

- Check SOPs in the packaging + shipping departments – update as necessary
- Meet w/ Jane in packaging on a regular basis to solve problems
- Meet w/ David in shipping on a regular basis to solve problems
- Do we need new equipment to meet these goals more efficiently?
- Do we need a training program to meet this goal? If so, build/implement program
- Check w/ factory on an "early warning statement" about notifying us what is about to be delivered to packaging

Fig. #1 & #24

15

>INVITING< COLLABORATIVE POWER FROM THE TOP DOWN

PHASE 1: STEP 2: *Basic Rules That Apply To Most Situations*

Fig. #2 & #25

MAKE YOUR BOSS **A SUCCESS** - COMPLEMENT THEIR WEAKNESSES BY SUPPORTING THEM WITH SKILLS THEY DON'T HAVE

Warning: When supporting your boss with a *strength of yours* to compensate for a *weakness of theirs,* it can appear to them *as if* you are trying to **one up** them.

Basics... {
- AVOID OVERTLY DISAGREEING WITH YOUR BOSS
- FIND WAYS TO SUPPORT THEM W/O ASKING PERMISSION

A–Starting Now:
Use the Four Quadrants

- *Examine / Place yourself in the Four Quadrants*

- *Examine / Place your boss in the Four Quadrants*

- *Without asking, and being careful not to one up them, take action on shoring up your boss's weaknesses*

FOUR QUADRANTS

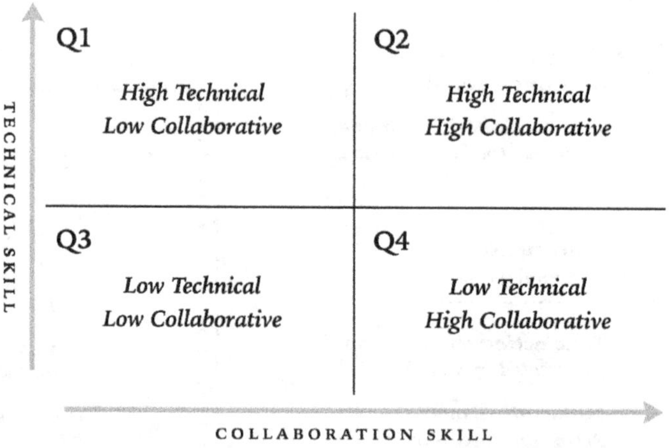

Q1 High Technical Low Collaborative	**Q2** High Technical High Collaborative
Q3 Low Technical Low Collaborative	**Q4** Low Technical High Collaborative

TECHNICAL SKILL

COLLABORATION SKILL

B–Starting Now:

If it looks like one of your boss's weaknesses are about to blindside them, immediately meet with them privately & bring it to their attention.

C–Starting Now:

If a meeting is taking place with your boss and your boss's boss, meet with your direct supervisor first and ask them how they want the meeting to go.

D–Starting Now:

When you receive information from your boss that you know your followers are going to have problems with, you need to soften the blow.

E–Starting Now:

Something going wrong? Get to your supervisor ASAP and let them know what's going on. The sooner you do it the better off you are.

F–Starting Now:

Take responsibility for poor outcomes. If you or your crew is responsible for a poor outcome, the sooner you tell that to your supervisor the better.

G–Starting Now:

Always follow the chain of command and do not bypass your boss on the way up. UNLESS—you are asked to do something illegal or unsafe.

>INVITING< COLLABORATIVE POWER FROM THE TOP DOWN

PHASE 1: STEP 3: *Detect What Quadrant Your Current Boss Falls Into*

Fig. #3 & #26

UNDERSTANDING YOU AND YOUR BOSS'S QUADRANT PROTECTS MISSION SUCCESS AGAINST YOUR COMBINED INHERENT WEAKNESSES.

FOUR QUADRANTS

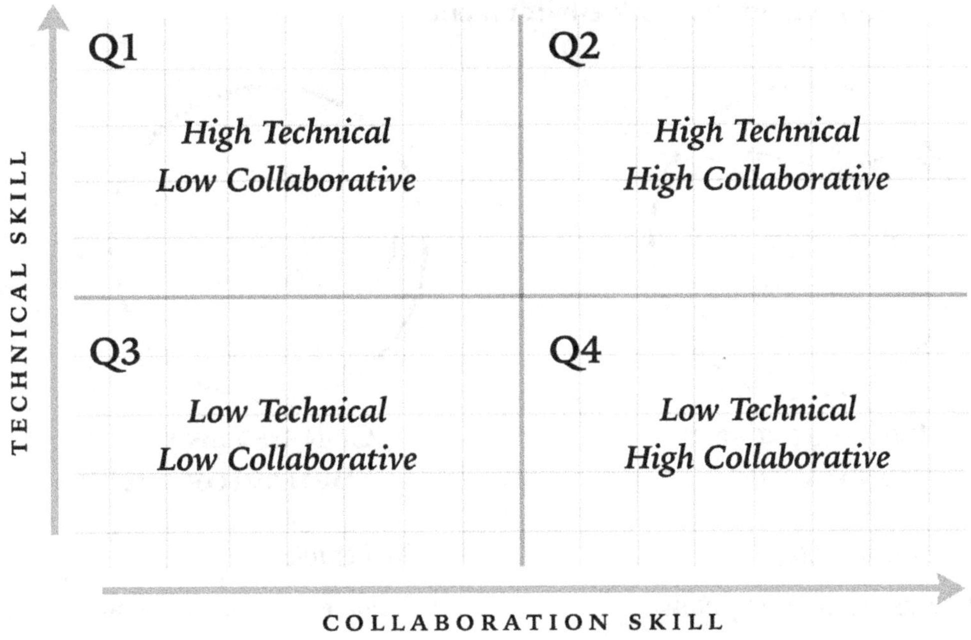

Q1 High Technical Low Collaborative	**Q2** High Technical High Collaborative
Q3 Low Technical Low Collaborative	**Q4** Low Technical High Collaborative

TECHNICAL SKILL (vertical axis)

COLLABORATION SKILL (horizontal axis)

Start Now Actions	*More Info*
A–Starting Now: *Read the Quadrant Descriptions*	• *Go to chapter 5 and study the quadrant descriptions.*
B–Starting Now: *Place Your Boss In the Quadrants*	• *Using the material you've read, place your boss in the appropriate quadrant.*
C–Starting Now: *Place Yourself In the Quadrants*	• *Using the material you've read, place yourself in the appropriate quadrant.*
D–Starting Now: *Protect Mission Success From You & Your Boss's Combined Weaknesses.*	• *Find where you and your boss are weak.*
E–Starting Now: *Where You're Both Weak: Secure Outside Help.*	• *Protect your weaknesses as necessary and recruit outside help if needed.*

PHASE 1: STEP 1: *Emulate the Behaviors You Want From Others*

Don't underestimate the power this has on the people who follow you. ***By reducing inconsistent and unpredictable behaviors**** and instead increasing the consistent and predictable use of a positive work ethic, dignity, and respect, the supervisor significantly reduces fear in the work environment.

Inconsistent Behavior

- *Unpredictable / no pattern*
- *No set example to follow*
- *Generates fear*
- *Destroys productivity*

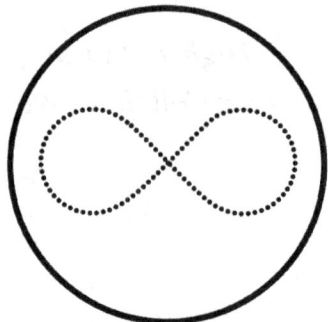

Consistent Behavior

- *Predictable*
- *Reliable example to follow*
- *Generates safety*
- *Maximizes productivity*

As **COLLECTIVE FEAR** GOES DOWN, GROUP **PERFORMANCE** GOES UP

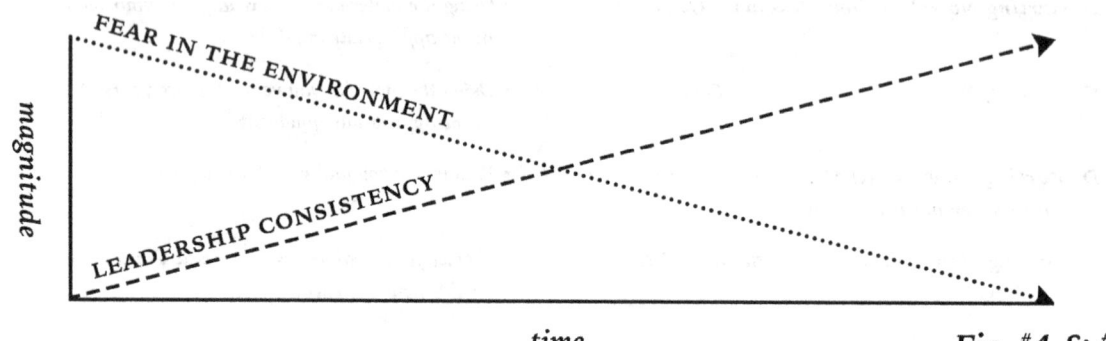

Fig. #4 & #33

>ATTRACTING< Collaborative Power from the Bottom Up

PHASE 1: STEP 2: *Support Timely Decision Making & Problem Solving*

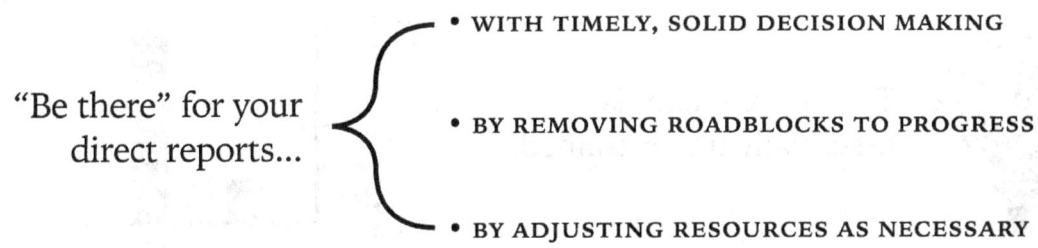

"Be there" for your direct reports...

- WITH TIMELY, SOLID DECISION MAKING
- BY REMOVING ROADBLOCKS TO PROGRESS
- BY ADJUSTING RESOURCES AS NECESSARY

When field personnel are waiting an inordinate amount of time on a management decision, *the group is falling behind on meeting its deadline.*

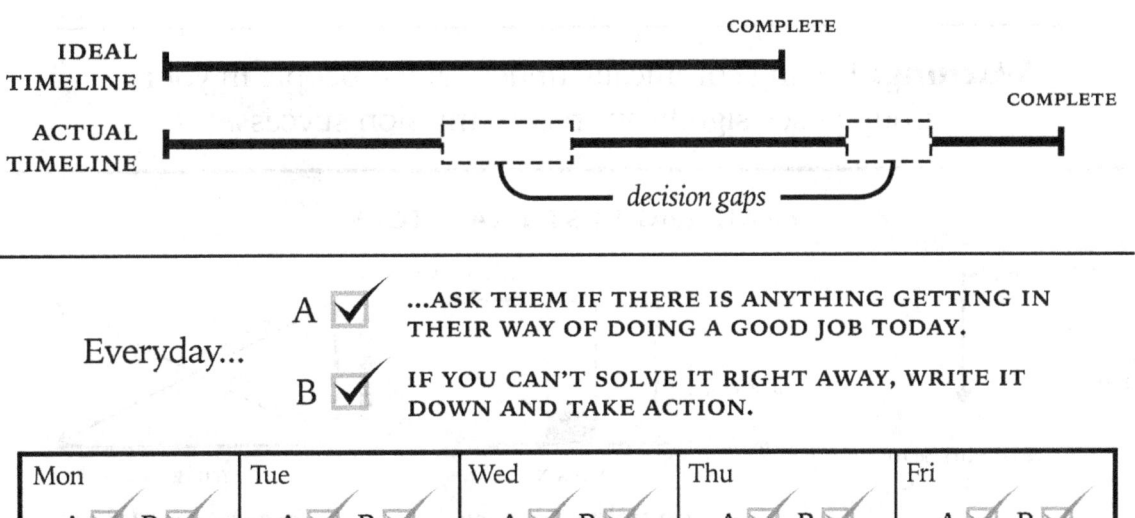

Everyday...

A ✓ ...ASK THEM IF THERE IS ANYTHING GETTING IN THEIR WAY OF DOING A GOOD JOB TODAY.

B ✓ IF YOU CAN'T SOLVE IT RIGHT AWAY, WRITE IT DOWN AND TAKE ACTION.

Mon	Tue	Wed	Thu	Fri
A ✓ B ✓	A ✓ B ✓	A ✓ B ✓	A ✓ B ✓	A ✓ B ✓

Starting Now, train your group on...

> how to recognize problems

> telling you any time a roadblock appears

> communicating problems to you immediately

> using the step-by-step problem solving process

> taking an open-minded approach that:
- allows new facts to change their mind
- prioritizes the right answer over being right
- prioritizes leaving their ego at the door

Fig. #5 & #34

>**ATTRACTING**< Collaborative Power from the Bottom Up

PHASE 1: STEP 3: *Build to Expert Levels*
of Technical & Collaborative Competency

The <u>entire planet</u> is
essentially under-trained.

Fig. #6 & #35

WELL-
TRAINED

UNDER-
TRAINED

UN-
TRAINED

*avg.
person* *avg.
expert*

Most error
& destruction
in the world...

...*is a result of...*

...incompetence
rather than
maliciousness.

Warning: Having chronically undertrained people in your
group poses significant risk to mission success.

TRAINING BEST PRACTICES

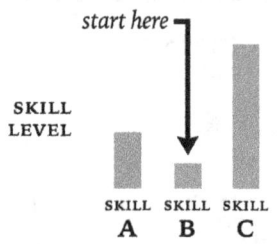

start here

SKILL
LEVEL

SKILL SKILL SKILL
A **B** **C**

*Train to the weakest
skillset first.*

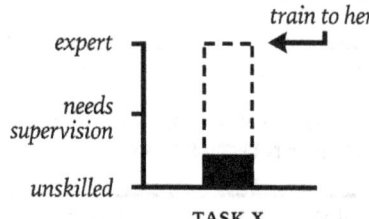

expert

*needs
supervision*

unskilled

train to here

TASK X

*Your training programs
should build trainees into
experts for each task.*

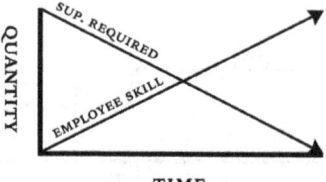

QUANTITY

SUP. REQUIRED

EMPLOYEE SKILL

TIME

*Once you've created an
expert, your supervision
requirements will drop.*

Train Q1s & Q3s in **collaboration**. Train Q3s & Q4s in **technical skills**.

Starting Now:

A—Provide training for each individual's weakest skillset first.

B—Provide training advances the trainee to an expert level in the task
they are being trained.

C—Provide everyone with quarterly refresher training on their
performance expectations.

PHASE 1: STEP 4: *Continually Make Observations of Examples of Good Performance*

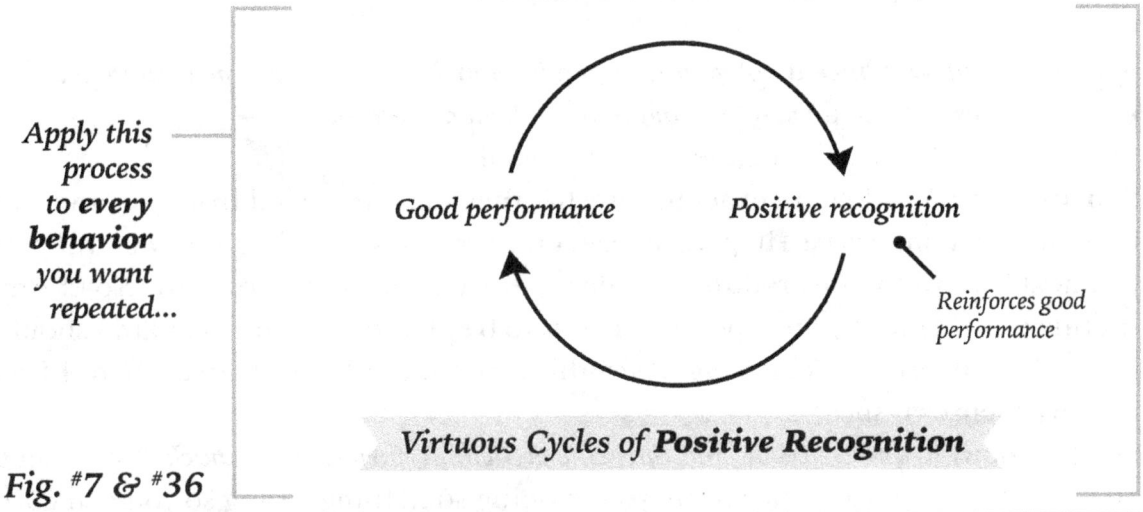

*Apply this process to **every** behavior you want repeated...*

*Virtuous Cycles of **Positive Recognition***

Fig. #7 & #36

Behaviors that are recognized with positive feedback are *always* repeated.

DID SOMEONE...

☐ *...go beyond the call of duty?*

☐ *...become the best at a routine duty?*

☐ *...respond exceptionally to an emergency?*

☐ *...respond exceptionally to a customer complaint?*

☐ *...take on additional responsibilities?*

☐ *...volunteer?*

☐ *...solve a problem?*

☐ *...help during a stressful situation?*

☐ *...come up with a great idea for an improvement?*

☐ *...come up with a great idea for increasing productivity?*

...THEN LET THEM KNOW WITH POSITIVE RECOGNITION.

Starting Now:

A—If somebody qualifies for recognition, go up and tell them you're aware of what they did and personally thank them.

B—Next you're going to write a short one-on-one email to your supervisor noting the individual and the exceptional performance.

C—Then copy that email and send it to the person you are recognizing. This is a very powerful way of recognizing somebody.

D—As you train more people to become Q2s, their performace rises and you need to be ready to recognize them as quickly as possible.

PHASE 2 - INVITING AND ATTRACTING

INVITING

Step 4: Develop a Mentoring Relationship with Your Boss

- *Always, always, always have a notepad and pen in your hand when you meet with your supervisor. Take a lot of notes, refer to them often, and update them as necessary.*
- You are asking: What are their expectations of you?
  - **Starting now:** Ask them in exact terms what they want and need from you and then follow those instructions with a 110 percent execution response. Finding out what they want from you next is a continuous routine conversation from this point forward. Note: Any type of routine meeting with your supervisor needs to be placed on your calendar. I shouldn't have to say that but after *writing things down* this is the second largest area where I find people hurting their own success.
  - **Starting now:** *Request, accept, and integrate critical performance feedback.* Ask them to please give you direction when they think you're doing something wrong so you can correct your performance immediately. Just know that once they start doing this it might not feel very good, but it's the exact thing you need to know. Every time they give you critical feedback on your performance *and you make an adjustment they will be very impressed with you*, as well they should. Professionals making adjustments in their performance quickly and effectively is always impressive. One of the reasons it's so impressive is because this is a very difficult thing for many people to do. *You, however, are going to become an expert at it.*
  - **Starting now:** When setting the goals for your performance objectives try to ensure that you have a clear and realistic approach to achieving those objectives. Ask your supervisor for any *practical advice* that they can offer so you have a better chance of achieving those objectives.
  - **Starting now:** Make sure every directive you receive has a clear objective, an achievable deadline, and the resources available to complete the directive as assigned. Talk things out with your supervisor until those three requirements are met with each assignment they give you. By approaching every directive this way, it increases your chances of success, which increases your supervisor's chances for success. Lastly, if you find during implementation of your assignments that for whatever reason you're not going to be able to meet the deadline, *the earlier you inform your supervisor the better.* Prior to you presenting this information think through the options of what could be offered to help move the objective forward in spite of the new roadblock just encountered, *but don't take too long doing this.*
  - **Starting now:** Have and demonstrate a strong work ethic. Certainly having a strong worth ethic will benefit your entire life, however the key word there is *demonstrate*. It's not enough to be good at what you do; if your boss doesn't know it, then their perception

of you is incomplete. As I'm sure you've heard before perception is reality. It's up to you to make sure their perception of you matches the reality. *You are an authentic support to the leadership structure above you. There's nothing wrong with you making sure they know that.*

    ○ **Starting now:** Have periodic meetings with your supervisor from this point forward. Keep your communication level with them extremely high. Again, any routine meeting with your supervisor needs to be placed on your calendar.

        ■ However, *don't get in the way of their already crowded calendar.*

        ■ You want to keep them informed of *all the information you're in possession of that can help them do their job.*

ATTRACTING

Step 5: Keep the Group Focused on the Mission, Values, Directives, and Their Performance Expectations at All Times

Starting Now

- Here are the three actions you need to start taking immediately:
    1. **Starting now:** Meet periodically (say, once a quarter) with your entire follower group with handouts of the mission, values, and other senior leadership materials and directives. Go over the materials and specifically promote that *every group member brings value to support the overall mission and in this sense everyone should be considered important regardless of rank or standing.* Open up the conversation and get people talking. During meetings, promote the ethos that *"if it's important to you then it's important to me"* and specifically speak to the need for breaking down barriers between departments. We all succeed or we all fail together, including the people in other departments. As noted earlier, initially start out with one-on-one meetings to lay the groundwork. Once your one-on-one meetings have developed a basic understanding you can switch over to group meetings.
    2. **Starting now:** Meet often with your immediate direct reports. Give them sufficient face time so they are able to talk about the directives they have received from you and *focus on giving them the right priority for the day and reprioritizing their work as necessary.* Encourage them to contact you anytime concerning any challenges they might be having. *Of all the meetings you hold as a leader, these should be considered the most important.*
    3. **Starting now:** Meet occasionally with your larger follower group, separate from the mission and values meetings, and give training presentations on their performance expectations and answer any questions they might have. I'll talk about this in the building experts step as well.

Step 6: Teach and Promote All Productivity Behaviors

Starting Now

Here are the four actions you need to start taking immediately:

1. **Starting now:** *Identify a time period within which each and every task needs to be completed.* If the people who work for you are not used to this it gets a little tricky when you first introduce this concept. But it's an essential move, because if you don't have specified time limits for all tasks, *there's no way to predict or track productivity.* And if you can't predict and track productivity, I don't care what your mission statement says, it can't be achieved. *If you are not tracking productivity, you have normalized mediocre performance.* Be willing to take the time and explain this to everybody that works for you. The reason this is tricky is because if the members of your group have not been given deadlines and timelines in the past then they are essentially used to being *independent contractors* so with that change there might be resistance at first, however everyone will get used to it at some point.
   - One of the best ways to approach this is *by collaborating with your direct reports.* Using a timeline that THEY recommend is the key to removing resistance because they have a sense of control. Be flexible – the timelines can be adjusted if they aren't quite right. If they aren't sure what the timeframe should be, *help them come to the right answer.* Over time, people will get better and better at this. Lastly, be sure to encourage them to communicate to you any problems that come up *before the deadline.* This way, you have time to work out a solution and hopefully still make the deadline.
   - When giving directives always include these eight important components:
     1. **A clear and achievable objective**
     2. **A time frame/deadline**
     3. **The number of people assigned to the job**
     4. **The name of the responsible party for completing the directive**
     5. **The reason the assignment needs to be completed**
     6. **The request for any ideas that can get the assignment completed in less time or for less money**
     7. **The request that they contact you before the deadline if it appears the deadline cannot be met**
     8. **Encourage questions and discussion and give advice as requested**
2. **Starting now:** Teach your direct reports that it's about working smarter by constantly reviewing how work is being completed. ASK them to tell you about procedures currently in use *that can be changed or eliminated to reduce the effort, time, or cost of completing tasks.*
3. **Starting now:** Reduce complexity at every opportunity. *Complexity is the arch enemy of higher productivity.* Having everyone on your team constantly looking for ways to reduce complexity is

highly effective. If you find somebody who is especially good at it *then make them the person in charge of reducing complexity*.

4. **Starting now:** While always making yourself available for advice, solving problems, or removing roadblocks, also encourage your new experts to make independent decisions. *As your experts improve the quality of their decision making, give them more responsibilities over time.* Give them positive feedback each and every time they make good independent decisions (see Step 9).

Step 7: Encourage the Group to Innovate New Ideas for Mission Success

Starting Now

- Here are the three actions you need to start taking immediately:
  1. **Starting now:** At your various meetings start promoting this process. Let people know that if they have an idea that they think can improve productivity, you want to hear about it. *Along with improvements to productivity be sure to mention that the improvement of working conditions will not only make our lives better but it will make our lives smarter.*
     - *Improving working conditions also means that safety issues should be communicated and addressed, with unsafe conditions being mitigated effectively, so everybody goes home to their families at the end of their workday.*
     - Ideas that improve productivity and improve working conditions at the same time get special focus. Encourage people to submit ideas and come to you and talk about what they're thinking. When they start talking you start writing down their ideas start working on implementation for high-benefit, low-cost, low-risk ideas (see Appendix 5).
  2. **Starting now:** Provide training on the standard operating procedure that helps people understand and define what a good idea actually is (see Appendix 5). *This should be a routine training process within the entire group.*
  3. **Starting now:** Keep your logbook handy. You should have a running list of all the ideas you have implemented, all the ideas that have been submitted, and all the ideas that you are actively working on implementing now.

The following figures are not as comprehensive as the *Starting Now* instructions above but instead have been developed as quick guides to help keep you focused on what's important. These quick guides are also included as downloads from the online course.

PHASE 2

IMPLEMENTATION FIGURES 8 THROUGH 11

Inviting Step 4

Attracting Steps 5, 6, 7

>**INVITING**< COLLABORATIVE POWER FROM THE TOP DOWN

PHASE 2: STEP 4: *Develop A Mentoring Relationship With Your Boss*

Preparation:
Always-always-**always** have a note-pad & pen in your hand when you meet with your supervisor. Take a lot of notes, refer to them often, & update your notes as necessary.

YOU ARE ASKING: WHAT ARE THEIR EXPECTATIONS OF YOU?

A–Starting Now:
Ask supervisor what they want & need, then execute on their wants & needs with a 110% response.

B–Starting Now:
Request / accept / integrate feedback from your boss.

C–Starting Now:
Use a clear & realistic approach to meeting performance objectives.

D–Starting Now:
Get practical advice from supervisors on staying clear & realistic while pursuing your performance objectives.

E–Starting Now:
Make sure every directive you receive has
 - a clear objective
 - an achievable deadline,
 - the resources available to complete
  the directive as assigned.

F–Starting Now:
*Have and demonstrate a strong work ethic. No doubt having a strong work ethic will benefit your entire life, however the key word there is **demonstrate**.*

G–Starting Now:
Starting now: Have periodic meetings with your supervisor from this point forward. keep them informed of all information you possess that can help them do their job.

Fig. #8 & #27

PHASE 2: STEP 5: *Focus Your Group on The Mission, Values, Directives, & Performance Expectations*

CREATE A GROUP DIALOGUE USING THE FOLLOWING TOOLS:

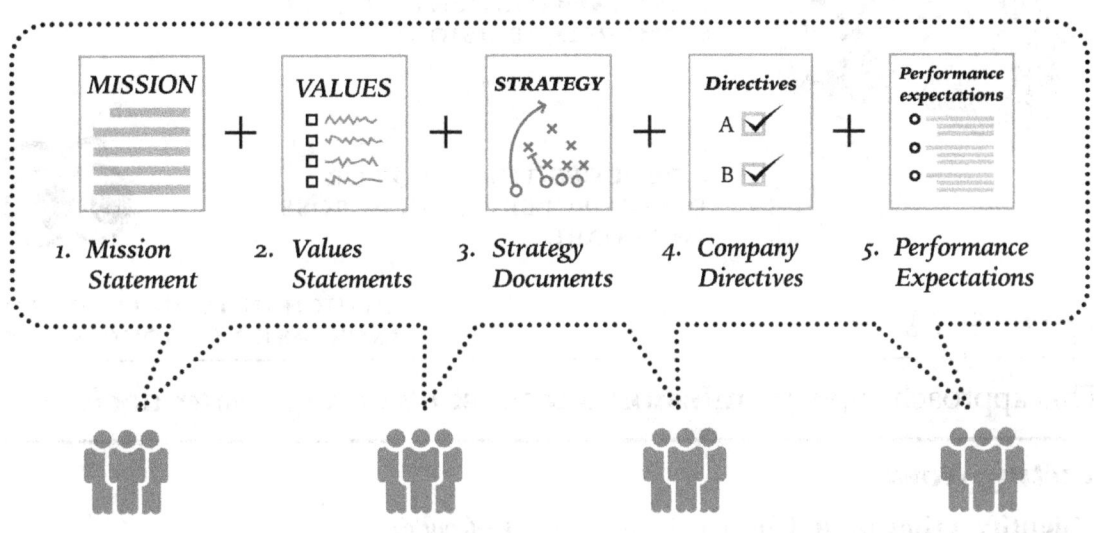

1. Mission Statement   2. Values Statements   3. Strategy Documents   4. Company Directives   5. Performance Expectations

This dialogue will range from...
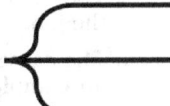
- WHERE THE GROUP IS HEADING...
- & WHAT THE GROUP HOPES TO ACHIEVE...
- TO HIGHLY DETAILED MEETINGS DISCUSSING PERFORMANCE EXPECTATIONS.

Keep the group focused on mission, values, directives, and performance expectations *at all times.*

Starting Now: *Fig.* #9 & #37

A—Meet periodically with your entire follower group with handouts of the mission, values, and other materials.

- Go over the materials
- Promote the message that every individual brings value
- Promote that: "if it's important to you, it's important to me."
- Lay the groundwork with 1-on-1 meetings.
- When your 1-on-1s have built understanding, meet as a group.

B—Meet often with your immediate direct reports.

- Give them sufficient facetime so they are able to talk about the directives you've given them and help them prioritize those directives.
- Consider these your most important meetings.

C—Meet occasionally with your larger follower group and give training presentations on their performance expectations. Also provide Q & As.

PHASE 2: STEP 6: *Teach & Promote*
All Productivity Behaviors

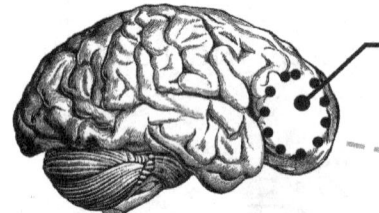

TRAINING DIRECT REPORTS TO MAKE **INDEPENDENT MISSION-CENTERED** DECISIONS...

...**REDUCES** THE NEED FOR DIRECT SUPERVISION ACROSS THE BOARD...

Fig. #10 & #38

...WHICH IN TURN LEADS TO **INCREASED PRODUCTIVITY.**

This approach supports **mission success.** *It's working smarter,* **not** *harder.*

Starting Now:

A—Identify a time period for completing each task.

- If you don't have specified time limits for all tasks, there's **no way** to predict or track productivity.

- If you can't predict and track productivity, *it can't be acheived.*

- *Collaborate with your direct reports:*

  "We need to make sure we are comp--leting work in a reasonable amount of time, how much time would you recommend that this task require?"

  Then use their timeframe.

- If they don't know what the time--frame should be, *keep negotiating* and help them come up with an answer that works for them.

- Let them know that if something comes up that was unexpected, they should communicate with you before the deadline.

B—When giving directives, always include these 8 components.

1. A clear & achievable objective.
2. A timeframe/ deadline.

B—(cont'd)

3. The number of people assigned to the job.

4. The name of the person responsible for completing the directive.

5. The reason the assignment needs to be completed

6. A request for any ideas that can get the assignment completed with--in less time or for less money

7. A request that they contact you if they think the deadline can't be met.

8. Encourage discussion and give advice as requested.

C—Teach your direct reports to work smarter **by constantly improving** how work is being completed.

D—Reduce complexity at every opportunity.

E—While **always** making yourself available for advice, solving problems, or using your authority to remove roadblocks, also **encourage your new experts** to make more **independent decisions.**

>**ATTRACTING**< Collaborative Power from the Bottom Up

PHASE 2: STEP 7: *Encourage the Group to Innovate New Ideas for Mission Success*

Innovating means changing **HOW** you are doing something.

The people **actually doing the work** will come up with the best ideas for innovation.

Fig. #11 & #39

 When they start talking, you *start listening*. After listening, implement the ones that will *lower effort, save time,* and *save money* with the lowest risk.

 **At all times** you should have a running list of ideas that your people have collected and are working to implement.

Implementing 10, 30, or even 50 large, medium, and small time & money-saving ideas over a one year period creates epic outcomes. Don't underestimate the *POWER* of continuous improvement!

Starting Now:

A—At your various meetings start promoting this process. Let people know that if they have an idea that they think can improve productivity, **you want to hear about it.**

B—Provide training on the standard operating procedure that helps people **understand** and **define** what a good idea actually is (see Appendix 5). This should be a routine training process within the entire group.

C—Keep your logbook handy. You should have a **running list** of all the ideas you have **implemented,** all the ideas that have been **submitted,** and all the ideas that you are **actively working on** implementing now.

PHASE 3 - INVITING AND ATTRACTING

INVITING

Step 5: Start Initiating Your Support Role Activities

…by supporting your boss. Find out from them, ***during the course of your conversations with them*** or by asking them directly, if you think they would be comfortable discussing these issues with you at some point in the future once you've had the chance to establish a good relationship:

- What are their goals for the group?
  - ° **Starting now:** Make them your goals as well.
- What are their most important priorities?
  - ° **Starting now:** Those are your most important priorities as well.
- What are the problems they are facing?
  - ° **Starting now:** Those are the same problems you're going to start working on the solutions to in addition to your normally assigned work.

Note: The power of these three actions cannot be overstated. In fact, if I was going to distill the idea of inviting collaborative power to just three actions it would be these. They are pivotal both to the success of your boss and to you. At some point your boss will realize your success is linked and this realization has the tendency to morph your relationship into a partnership.

Important Side Note:

- It would also be good to know what performance expectations are being placed on your supervisor by their higher-ups. However, this is a bit tricky as your boss probably won't feel comfortable discussing these items with you. Extreme caution needs to be exercised here. If they ever think that you're wanting to find out their performance expectations so you can determine whether you think they're meeting those expectations, it's a ***game stopper*** in building the mentoring relationship you need to build. If you can't safely find out what expectations are being placed on your boss by their boss, it's best to leave it; it is not necessary to find out.
  - ° **Starting now:** If you are able to find out, then use their performance expectations to guide your future decisions so can support your boss where they need you the most.

ATTRACTING

Step 8: Help Your People Recover from Low Performance or Errors with Training Sessions Focused on Improving Performance

Starting Now

Here are the five actions you need to start taking immediately:

1. **Starting now:** If someone has made an error or is suffering from substandard performance, pause and plan ahead exactly what you want to say to the individual before you meet. You should be making notes that you will use in your meeting with them and *your advice to them for making improvements should be very, very specific.*

2. **Starting now:** Meet with them one-on-one and make sure the *first* thing you tell them is that you're meeting with them *to help them improve their performance.* The *second* thing you want to tell them is that you understand they might be feeling uncomfortable, and that you understand why that might be. *Keep the meeting psychologically safe* and reduce fear by reassuring them over and over again, as many times as necessary, that the reason for the meeting is to improve their performance. *Be specific*—the more specific you are the better chance they have at recovering. *Schedule a follow-up meeting* so you can give feedback on their improvement. *This second meeting is very important—don't skip it.* Always keep the meeting as a private one-on-one meeting and the contents of the meeting should always be confidential.

3. **Starting now:** If it's the *second time correcting the same problem*, place some additional pressure by mentioning this fact. If a person persists in substandard performance after repeated retraining sessions, consult your supervisor for next steps.

4. **Starting now:** Bullying behavior, acts of intimidation, or other hostile behaviors need immediate action on the part of the leader. Regardless of how busy you might be destructive behavior needs to be dealt with at the moment it's discovered. Also, the solution needs to have staying power which means if continued training does not bring about the desired outcome your immediate supervisor needs to be involved. More detail is provided below in Step 9.

5. **Starting now:** Do not over-supervise or micromanage your veterans. It's inefficient and ineffective, not to mention demoralizing and demeaning. That being said, do not under-supervise your newcomers. They can become anxious when they're not quite sure what to do. Your steady guidance is critical to their success. Note: I have seen many situations where supervisors do not adjust their level of supervision according to the experience of their individual team members. This becomes just another way of normalizing mediocre performance. When you successfully train people to expert levels, the best thing you can do is get out of their way.

Step 9: Protect and Promote the Culture

Starting Now

Here are the four actions you need to start taking immediately:

1. **Starting now:** *Don't allow inappropriate comments and behaviors in public forums.* This includes, but is not limited to, angry outbursts, inappropriate humor, any type of harassment, and bullying behavior.

Have a private meeting with these folks and let them know it's not okay to pursue this type of behavior. If it seemed to them that this behavior was acceptable in the past, let them know you are trying to build a better workplace and that you need their help to do that. If the behavior persists, escalate your response by bringing this to your supervisor's attention and seek their guidance on next steps.

2. **Starting now:** Protecting the culture from destructive behaviors is critical because it protects your high performers. As I mentioned above in Step 8, no matter how busy you might be, destructive behavior needs to be dealt with at the moment it's discovered. If you are unable to create the outcome you need from repeated retraining, you need to involve your immediate supervisor. Uncorrectable destructive behavior needs to be removed from the group culture one way or the other.

3. **Starting now:** *Promote that getting along with your fellow employees is now part of their job.* Stress to your direct reports that from now on their ability to develop professional collaborative relationships is as important as their technical competency.

4. **Starting now:** Teach all your followers that when they feel angry that they are not to attack. Instead, they are to step back, reassess, and *go talk with their supervisor about finding solutions*.

Step 10: After Full Implementation, Implement, Implement, Implement All the above at Every Chance

Starting Now

Starting now: Implement the steps in *Chapters 2 and 3 in order to fully integrate Attracting Power from the Bottom Up.*

PHASE 4 (OPTIONAL)

CULTIVATING

Before moving forward with Cultivating Collaborative Power, read Chapter 7 in its entirety; you have a judgment to make.

Do a Power Check: Your position in the leadership hierarchy and the amount of power that position gives you, along with the amount of power you have acquired by Inviting and Attracting Collaborative Power, will be the determining factors in whether you use this option at all. If you're not sure you have enough power to implement this section, don't do it and leave it for the senior leaders.

Cherry Pick: That being said, you don't have to implement all of the collaborative group behaviors that are listed in Chapter 7. You can pick and choose and implement the ones you think are most necessary to solve problems and encourage Q2 thinking.

The following figures are not as comprehensive as the *Starting Now* instructions above but instead have been developed as quick guides to help keep you focused on what's important. These quick guides area lso included as downloads from the online course.

PHASE 3

IMPLEMENTATION - FIGURES 12 THROUGH 15

Inviting Step 5 / Attracting Steps 8,9,10,

>INVITING< COLLABORATIVE POWER FROM THE TOP DOWN

PHASE 3: STEP 5: *Start Initiating Your Support Role Activities By Supporting Your Boss*

THROUGH THE COURSE OF **CONVERSATIONS** WITH YOUR BOSS, OR BY ASKING THEM **DIRECTLY** (IF YOU THINK THEY'D BE COMFORTABLE WITH THAT), FIND OUT ABOUT THEIR PRIORITIES IN THE FOLLOWING **3 CATEGORIES.**

> **1. *What are your boss's goals for the group?***
> *Starting now,* make their goals into your goals.

> **2. *What are your boss's most important priorities?***
> *Starting now,* those are your most important priorities as well.

> **3. *What are the problems your boss is facing?***
> *Starting now,* support your boss by taking owner-
> -ship of those problems where it makes sense.

NOTE: THE POWER OF THESE THREE ACTIONS **CANNOT BE OVERSTATED.** IN FACT, IF I WAS GOING TO DISTILL THE IDEA OF INVITING COLLABORATIVE POWER TO JUST THREE ACTIONS, **IT WOULD BE THESE.** THEY ARE PIVOTAL, BOTH TO THE SUCCESS OF YOUR BOSS AND TO YOU.

Fig. #12 & #28

>**ATTRACTING**< Collaborative Power from the Bottom Up

PHASE 3: STEP 8: *Help Your People Recover from Errors with Training Focused on Improving Performance*

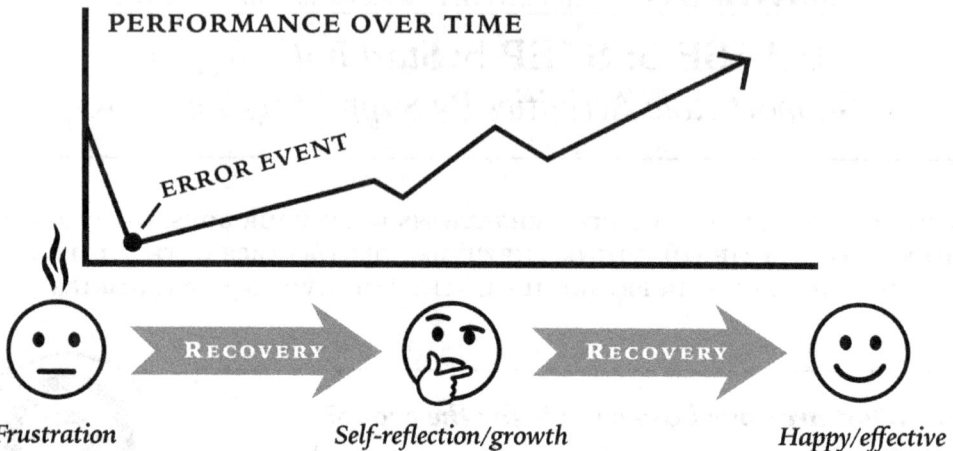

Help them improve their performance by helping them recover after making an error or *any instance* of less-than-standard performance.

When you *help people improve their performance* and *recover from an error* the chances of them repeating the mistake is much lower than if you were to reassign a new person to the job who *hasn't* committed the same error. Think about that.

Starting Now:

A—If someone made an error, pause & plan exactly what you will tell them be--fore you meet. *How you suggest they improve should be very specific.*

B—Meet with them one-on-one. The first thing you say: this meeting is to help you improve. If they feel uncomfortable, reassure them of the meeting's purpose.

"THIS IS TO HELP YOU IMPROVE."

Fig. #13 & #40

C—If it's the second time correcting the same problem, place some additional pressure by mentioning this fact.

D—Bullying behavior, acts of intmidation, or other hostile behaviors need im--mediate action on the part of the leader.

E—Do not over-supervise or micromanage your veterans. It's ineffient and in--effective, not to mention demoralizing and demeaning.

That being said, do not under-supervise your newcomers.

>ATTRACTING< COLLABORATIVE POWER FROM THE BOTTOM UP

PHASE 3: STEP 9: *Protect and Promote the culture*

USE YOUR LEADERSHIP POWERS TO PROTECT YOUR PEOPLE.

High performance & high performers **need a psychologically safe work environment** for all the human brain reasons we've already covered.

A protected and promoted culture is *not a nice to have.* This is **a required intrinsic foundation** to a high-performing human enterprise.

Weird, chaotic, and inappropriate behaviors in the culture definitely **generate fear**, pushing everybody out of their prefrontal cortex.

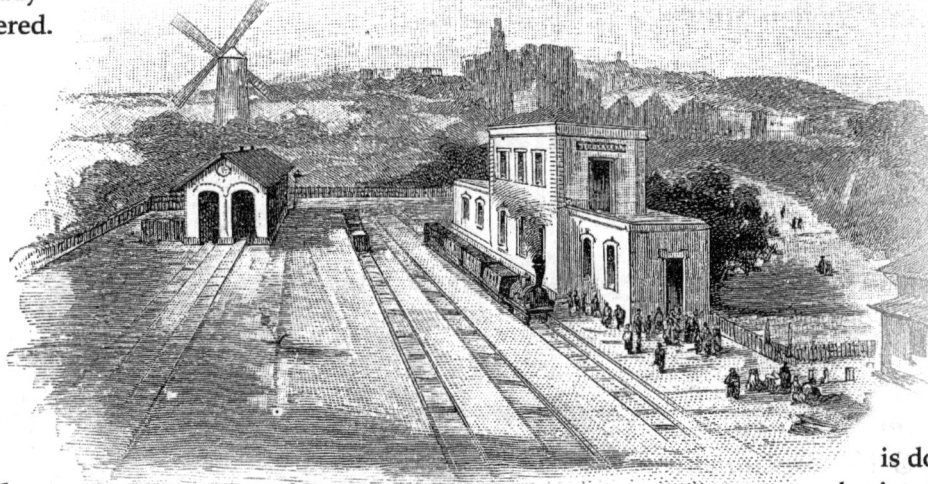

Without a protected and promoted culture your best performers **will leave** for greener pastures.

Keep people **in their prefrontal cortex** by evoking *logical, rational, & ethical thinking* which turns into *logical, rational, & ethical behavior.*

Protecting the culture is done through having people **stop** behaviors that they shouldn't be using and *promoting the culture* by having people **start** to do things they're not doing now.

Starting Now: Fig. #14 & #41

A—*Don't allow inappropriate comments & behaviors in public forums.* This in--cludes, but is not limited to, angry outbursts, inappropriate humor, any type of harassment, & bullying behavior.

B—No matter how busy you might be, *destructive behavior needs to be dealt with at the moment it's discovered.*

C—Promote that getting along with your fellow employees is *now part of their job.*

D—Teach all your followers that *when angry that they are not to attack.* Have them step back, assess, & discuss solutions with their supervisor.

PHASE 3: STEP 10: *After Implementing Steps 1-9, Implement, Implement, Implement*

Fig. #15 & #42

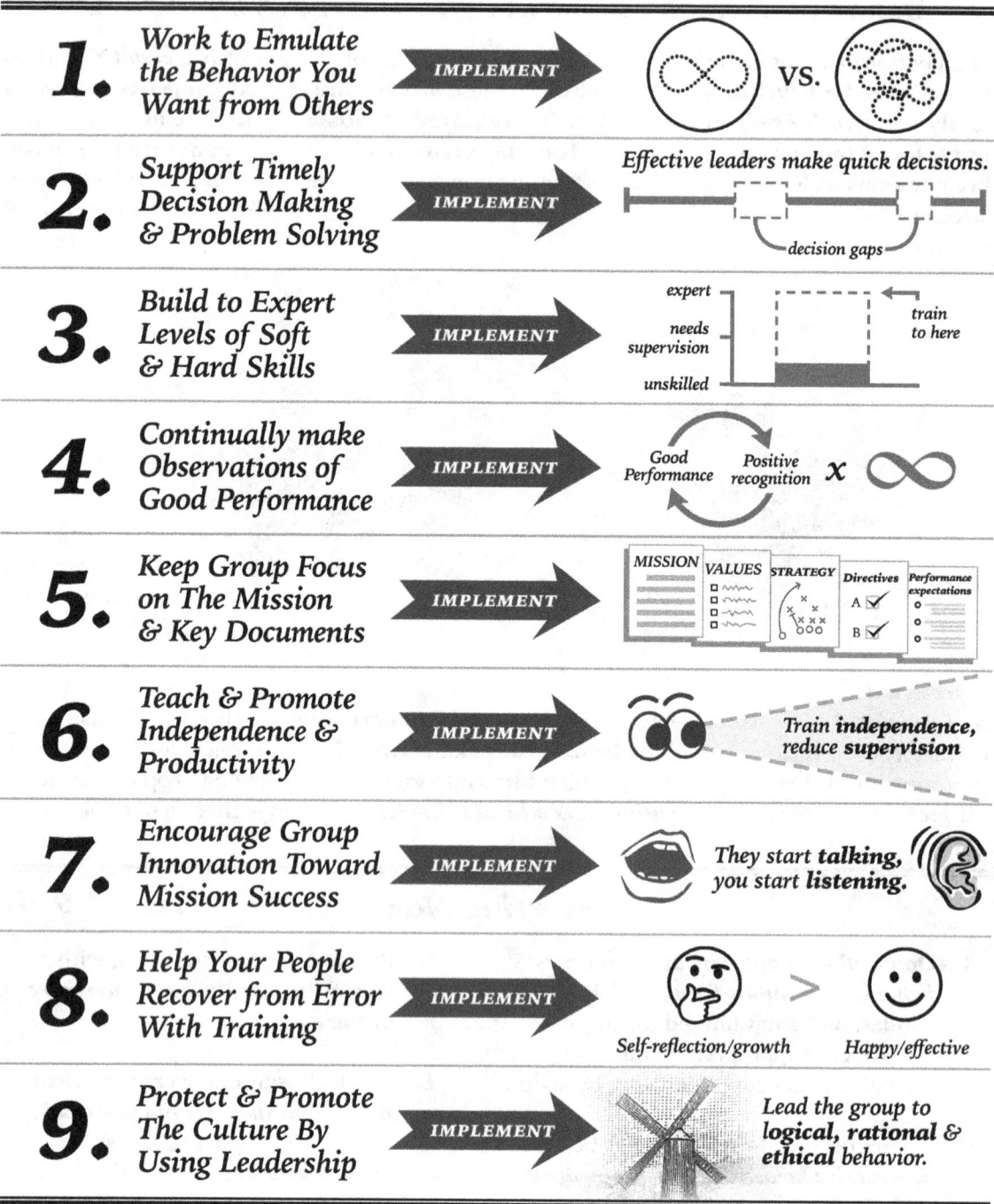

1. *Work to Emulate the Behavior You Want from Others* — IMPLEMENT — ∞ VS.

2. *Support Timely Decision Making & Problem Solving* — IMPLEMENT — *Effective leaders make quick decisions.* —decision gaps—

3. *Build to Expert Levels of Soft & Hard Skills* — IMPLEMENT — expert / needs supervision / unskilled / train to here

4. *Continually make Observations of Good Performance* — IMPLEMENT — Good Performance / Positive recognition *x* ∞

5. *Keep Group Focus on The Mission & Key Documents* — IMPLEMENT — MISSION VALUES STRATEGY Directives Performance expectations

6. *Teach & Promote Independence & Productivity* — IMPLEMENT — Train **independence**, reduce **supervision**

7. *Encourage Group Innovation Toward Mission Success* — IMPLEMENT — They start **talking**, you start **listening**.

8. *Help Your People Recover from Error With Training* — IMPLEMENT — Self-reflection/growth > Happy/effective

9. *Protect & Promote The Culture By Using Leadership* — IMPLEMENT — Lead the group to **logical, rational & ethical** behavior.

Chapter 3

Using Superior Knowledge in All Areas of Required Expertise

I offer that this book is not only the cure for a dysfunctional workplace but a complete manual for the rescue and survival of humanity.

—JOHN WILLIAM SELIG

The Big Picture
    What's Happening Today and Why It's Important to Know
    Why Collaborative Power Works Based on Our Collective Collaborative Roots
    Why Intentional Human System Designs Are Important for Group Success
    Implementing Enhanced Cultures/Need Proof?
    Modifying the Environment to Create Collaborative Relationships
    Recovery
    Recognition
    A New Future
    Once Cultivating Collaborative Power Is Implemented
    Bumps in the Road
Operating Rules of the Human Brain and Quadrant 2 Behaviors
    Our Human Brain
    Quadrant Thinking
    If You Are Already a Q2 Leader
Normalized Mediocre Performance
    Not Bad People
    Normalized vs. Enhanced
    Leader in Title Only
    Eight Categories of Mediocre Performance
Why Powerless Leaders Don't Have Power
    Types of Disempowered Leaders
    They Can't Invite Collaborative Power from the Top Down

THE BIG PICTURE

When leaders gain collaborative power, it's an outcome that was created by intention. I use the term "collaborative power" with intention; I didn't just say "power." As noted previously, power without an embodied compass point that combines individual needs with community needs is dangerous and may or may not work to the benefit of all the people in the group.

The primary objective of collaborative power is to create a high-performing group that has its focus on two primary functions. One is empowering performance for mission success and two is empowering the people to create high performance through job enrichment and satisfaction for the group's members.

Those two objectives are complementary functions. I'm sure you can see that without me having to point out to you why those two objectives would support each other.

Said another way, when you empower leaders and non-leaders alike with collaborative power you're essentially laying the groundwork for an extremely high-producing, highly effective group that's going to be able to prioritize mission success.

The next term you need to be familiar with is "enhanced culture."

An **enhanced culture** is a consciously sculpted social experience that uses the primal operating rules of the human brain to reduce fear, elicit our sense of meaning, and feed our desire to be part of something larger than ourselves in order to promote the mission success of the groups we participate in.

Understanding these two realms—the individual human brain and human group cultures—and then finding a way of melding them to leverage human capital has been a deep pursuit for thousands of years. Whether it be waging war, growing food, building pyramids, or running a mom-and-pop furniture store down the street, *how humans feel, think, decide, and act continues to be the most important four-step sequence in determining the success or failure of any group enterprise.*

This treatise is as intricate as the humans we hope to support and motivate with the clear intent to promote mission success by creating an enhanced culture. The information is presented here to help you follow the trail to a better understanding of enhanced culture and its significant advantages by way of promoting *co-prioritizing* individual human needs and group mission success.

WHAT'S HAPPENING TODAY AND WHY IT'S IMPORTANT TO KNOW

- *There are millions of groups struggling with inadequate performance despite the fact that research, many studies, and living illustrations of enhanced cultures have given us the tools to use the examples to follow to mitigate deteriorated conditions.*

While *Fortune* magazine seems to abound with high-performing groups, they are not many compared to the millions upon millions of groups worldwide that continue to rely on wasteful, outdated, ineffective, and significantly inefficient methodologies to do their work. Normalized mediocre performance, marginal mission execution, and antiquated and nonsensical working conditions led by people who may well be hardworking and well-intended but are nonetheless ineffective in their leader-manager role all result in less-than-optimal outputs for the consumer.

I will talk more about normalized mediocre performance in a later section of this chapter. It is a mostly hidden-cancer-type environment that eviscerates group success worldwide. But let me touch upon it briefly here.

You might hear some economists say that ineffective and inefficient groups, like an organism existing outside its niche, *will eventually die off.* Anecdotal examples of inefficient companies being systematically eliminated can be found where market conditions couple very narrow profit margins *with* severe competition. But taken in light of our larger human society with hundreds of millions of groups, the general statement is *pure fiction.* As long as a group is minimally effective it can and will survive in spite of its own dysfunction. The bottom line is this: most groups are surviving not because they are performing optimally but because they just barely meet the minimum requirements to stay alive.

While many behavioral models developed over the last 50 years have advanced to become reliable methods for predicting, supporting, and motivating high-performing humans, there remains a serious lack of mainstream application of what we have learned.

In other words, we have solutions to a lot of the problems that ail society yet they aren't put to use.

Why is this?

First of all: Groups that have normalized mediocre performance ***don't see the need to improve.***

From a larger context, we experience a consistent inability to problem solve *even though we know how to systematically solve problems.*

We suffer by not implementing the protective measures necessary to mitigate the significant negative impacts of fear upon brain function and decision making.

Our inability to sufficiently memorialize information continues to hamper our ability to replicate past successes. Yes, even when we find success we can stumble hard *by not being able to **repeat it**.* Because we don't like using anything new even if it's good. An obvious opportunity left vulnerable to the group's momentum to instead simply do today what they did yesterday or do again today what they did *10 years ago.*

Continuous improvement strategies trying to emerge in a group are fatally injured by "if it's not broken don't fix it" or "it's good enough" or "don't rock the boat," which are the rallying cries for the status quo. *It is broken, it's not good enough,* and yes, ***it needs rocking.***

We suffer under the chronic inability to freely empathize and collaborate with our fellow humans. The circumstances of our modern age muscle against the advantage we would all gain by uniting to address common problems. Yet the emphasis on what makes us different keeps some of us from helping to bail water as the lifeboat fills. This is despite our genetic expression and long history that demonstrates our ability to do rather well in collaborating with our fellow humans given the environment that excites this natural tendency.

Our world grows more complex with each passing day. The existence of people and groups that can't keep up in their understanding of how the world works, aside from knowing how to leverage the information if they had it, does not result in a neutral outcome.

Buckminster Fuller asserted through the Knowledge Doubling Curve that knowledge was doubling every century up to around the early 1900s. By the end of WWII it was doubling every 25 years. Moore's Law is still in play even though its prediction that the computational power of our computers is doubling every 18 months is debated. Nanotechnology is doubling every two years, genetic technology every 18 months. As of 2012, human knowledge was generally doubling *every 13 months.* In an article on the Industry Tap website, David Schilling notes that not only is human knowledge, on average, doubling every 13 months, but IBM is predicting we are quickly on our way, with the help of the Internet, to the doubling of knowledge *every 12 hours.*

The more our educational and training support for our neighborhoods falls behind, the inability to keep pace widens the margin between the available useful information and those that *need it but don't receive it.*

This ever-widening margin results in our communities becoming spawning grounds for ignorance.

Untested theory becomes fact, which results in all unverified information being treated equally, which results in a blizzard of commingled data of facts and fiction. We're lost in snowy white-out conditions of information so we do the best we can and, simply stated, it's just not good enough knowing the growing challenges we face.

Likewise because the issue is so huge it also means that the opportunity for improvement is just as large. We already have information that would benefit us all and actually solve most of our problems, so let's start using it. That's exactly what I am attempting to do here; join me.

Takeaway: We have learned enough about human behavior in the last 50 years and about science—from brain function to economics—over the last 20 years that has confirmed essentially everything we need to know in order to build high-performing human groups, *and we are not applying what we have learned.*

WHY COLLABORATIVE POWER WORKS BASED ON OUR COLLECTIVE COLLABORATIVE ROOTS

- *Humans are mentally and emotionally built to collaborate depending on the environment they experience.*

The exact scientific underpinnings of how collaboration evolved go beyond the central scope of this book. But suffice it to say we now have reliable data that demonstrates thousands of centuries of collective activities including large-scale animal hunting along with sharing food with non-kin members of relatively small tribes that resulted in the tremendous success of intra-collaborative tribes—so much so that it allowed the collaborative tribes to outcompete tribes that were using alternative methods.

By the way, I'm talking about *your* ancestors, who are the reason you are here today. The current population of humans was preceded by an estimated 100 billion people, which means many family lines died off before modern times—but not yours, obviously. There are reasons for that.

This time-tested process a thousand centuries long allowed for a handful of positive precise impacts, one of which is a co-evolutionary physical modification called gene expression that cemented our reaction to the collaborative environments we encounter by *responding with like-minded reciprocal acts of collaboration when met with such an environment.*

Our long-ago collaboration "training" will also cause us to sometimes appear as if we are *uncollaborative.* However, in those cases, more often than not, we are actually demonstrating appropriate hyper-protective reactions as a necessary response to a deteriorated human group environment. The decisions we humans make just so happen to come from the emotional centers of the brain. If it's unknown and potentially generates fear, perceived or real, we often decide to not engage for safety reasons. No engagement means no collaboration.

The demonstration of anger-behaviors typically has its basis in fear—fear of a new initiative deemed harmful or fear of *a loss* and every fear in between. We could talk forever about whether those reactions are justified, but that's not my point. My point is to draw attention to *how the human brain reacts to threats and fears* and how we use that information to build high-performing groups.

The brain on fear has limited options from which to choose for its best next steps and the options list typically doesn't have the right answer for what would benefit the human at that moment. This statement is news we can use, and you will see it woven into many of the proposals that follow to support creating an enhanced culture in the workplace.

This brings me to a quick piece of advice: *A healthy actor in an unhealthy environment will often first appear as an antagonist.* Yes, not every antagonist is a frustrated healthy actor. But if you can get past your own defensiveness when you have an angry person sitting in your office and can determine they are indeed a healthy actor, *what they are about to tell you about what is going wrong in your group is pure gold. Listen up, then act on what they tell you.*

Create an enhanced *human-centric, fear-reducing* environment and the collaborative side of the human will arrive. Along with loyalty and hardwork-smartwork tendencies, a *bonus feature will be their motivation to simultaneously and passionately demanding cooperation from others.*

It's true: Highly cooperative people will more likely **demand** reciprocal cooperation from others. This is why once highly collaborative people come to dominate a group population *some problems are self-corrected by the group members.* This is a function of what's called **strong reciprocity**. This comes from another primal training program that was able to *bake into the mindset of high cooperators* that even if it costs you to hold non-cooperators accountable, you're going to do it anyway.

Strong reciprocity also creates a culture momentum that will convert those individuals that may have a tendency towards free-riding. Most of that conversion occurs with simply watching their peers become great collaborators and determining that they want to join them.

Think about some of the most collaborative people you know personally. Isn't it true they typically also come with a bit more passion than other people you know? Yep, that's what I'm talking about.

Takeaway: Humans come ready-built to collaborate if experiencing an environment specifically designed to enhance that tendency. Likewise, the lack of collaboration on the part of the human is often motivated by deteriorated environmental conditions. Once you have enough collaborators in the group, some problems are *self-corrected by the group members*. It's been a long time coming, but we now know enough to know *we can reliably go back to our roots*.

WHY INTENTIONAL HUMAN SYSTEM DESIGNS ARE IMPORTANT FOR GROUP SUCCESS

- *The well-designed human system is the best option available for influencing higher individual and group performance.*

Essentially, this system is using the *collaborative default settings* of human behaviors instilled over the last 100,000 years. The superior design of the human system essentially **invites** these collaborative default behaviors.

By defining the design based on *human need*, the outcome of mission success for the group is no longer counter to the individual's goal of needing to feel satiated while simultaneously helping the group achieve mission success.

The superior human design carefully borrows from the fundamental need for humans to be part of something larger than themselves, a desire so deeply planted so many centuries ago that most are completely unaware of its central role in creating a successful human collaborative effort.

In this sense our search for meaning becomes a group basis-of-design requirement. Symmetry between *what I have to do* and *why I am doing it* has such a profound influence on group success it deserves a completely separate treatise. Viktor Frankl wasn't wrong; more about that some other day.

In many respects, we are simply going back to what we did before the emergence of the city-state which then slid into the nation-state which eventually then slid into the Industrial Revolution. With each of these steps the *human **desire** from the **bottom up*** was sequentially sidelined by the *human **demand** from the **top down*** until we could no longer recognize ourselves as **individuals** *contributing*, instead becoming **individuals** *drafted*.

Mass enculturation—while key to group security and success today and in the time of our primal ancestors—if indeed taken too far by imposing a one-sided mission that ignores basic human needs, *replaces the name with a number. **Replaces the soul with a cog.***

Human behavior and how humans respond to any particular environmental conditions are no longer a mystery. Our knowledge of the human brain, our ability to use new economic models such as game theory, and our ability to collect and interpret data from leading industrial psychologists over the last five decades compounded with the more recent findings of biological behaviorists all point towards creating a reliable and repeatable collective understanding where we can now often typically predict *what people will do* and *why they do it* **as influenced by a commonly experienced environment between the individuals within the same group**.

There are wrong ways to lead people and wrong ways to manage a culture, and *nonetheless they persist and are still accepted practices in many if not most groups today*, but your group doesn't have to be one of them.

Successful group cultures become that way because they have created an enhanced culture that is consistent with the operating rules of the human brain. If you start with the human brain you can always get to the bottom-line profits. However, if you focus on seeking bottom-line profits first, skipping over the fundamental operating rules of human capital, you get nowhere fast. You might start out great, but sustainability as a high performer will prove costly as the diminishing returns over time will force the culture-building leaders back to the steps they skipped.

Much of how we respond to the people around us is based on what we are thinking. Much of what we are thinking is based on how we are feeling. Essentially (and this is a proven fact), many decisions are made in the emotional centers of the brain. When leaders properly manage the work environment they influence how people are feeling, which influences how people are thinking—*which then influences the decisions they make and the actions that follow.*

While treating people with dignity and respect certainly has an intrinsic moral imperative, it also happens to produce the best results when trying to accomplish a group task that relies on human capital. The connection between the two, the intrinsic moral imperative and the positive human group outcome, *is not an accident.*

The relationship between ***reducing*** fear or threat and ***increasing*** predictability and fairness, for instance, is just one example of the many ways we can create an enhanced work culture that results in extraordinarily high levels of human performance.

Simply finding behaviors that the group is *demonstrating now **that need to stop*** (in order to advance collaboration) and finding behaviors the group is *not demonstrating now **that need to start*** (in order to advance collaboration) becomes a powerhouse combination resulting in a dramatic swing towards an enhanced work environment.

The initial steps to implement for enhancing the culture are really that concept-simple!

Influence the environment with this sophisticated human *dos and don'ts list* that asserts human collaboration as a priority, and **practically any leader** can inspire and promote the desired mission-centered outcomes *simply based on the proper caretaking of the human psyches under their charge.*

In deteriorated conditions our thinking is affected by the amygdala and our decision-making capacity has a short-term toolbox of fight, flight, or freeze. When we remove threats and fear and add collaboration training and recognition for best skills demonstrated by group members, decision-making advances to the prefrontal cortex, whose toolbox uses logical, rational, and ethical thoughts as the precursors of logical, rational, and ethical actions. Which toolbox results in the best group performance?

I ask the obvious question sarcastically because many groups today have absolutely no idea they are using any type of **human brain toolbox**, much less *the wrong toolbox*! Ugh.

Takeaway: We have become accustomed to *enforcing our way to meeting goals* even though we use some pseudo-organizational-development window dressing that attempts to make the approach more palatable. Instead, enhance the system based on the operating rules of the human brain by building in the new dos and don'ts rules. Then train on the required use of best-practice collaborative behaviors on par with the same importance we currently place on technical competency, *and your group's ability to meet mission success is increased by orders of magnitude.*

IMPLEMENTING ENHANCED CULTURES/NEED PROOF?

- *Enhanced cultures embed strategic objectives into daily practices.*

Pause and think about the power of that statement for just a moment.

Enhanced cultures ensure that relationship-building behaviors are part of the training process and are positively recognized when observed and are privately addressed when lacking. Enhanced cultures teach others how to make quick solid decisions and how to use systematic problem-solving processes. Negative events are dealt with immediately and the group environment is actively protected from rogue amygdala-sourced destructive behavior.

Productive behaviors, along with process innovation, are encouraged by using a relentless continuous improvement strategy supported with a positive recognition process that *excites humans to simply repeat the successful behaviors they have been honored for demonstrating.*

All of these values become *enhanced shared values* through a comprehensive training program supported by an effective set of performance expectations driven forward by the *bold leader.* I say *bold* because protecting a culture so that high-performing, effective humans can flourish might require a few *uncomfortable conversations* with those wanting to instead demonstrate personal agendas and potentially destructive behavior that essentially controls the work environment through a means of active *and passive* intimidation.

My observations over the last 40 years inform me that not every leader is up for this challenge as some of them do not possess the *emotional creds* to pull off these necessary uncomfortable conversations successfully. Yet these same leaders will remain in place, unaware that they are in fact the primary impediment to a higher-performing group. They grow fond of the status quo, as do the boards of directors or commissions who hire and maintain them. *There are many in leadership positions that shouldn't be for this exact reason.*

To counter any past assumptions: *If leaders can only be effective by assertively fulfilling their role, then by definition the vacuum resulting from a neutral leaders' inactivity does damage to the group.*

Takeaway: The human-enhanced culture is a superior design because it's built to encourage something we already know how to do and quite frankly want to do given the right circumstances. Once collaborative behavior becomes an active skill set that is prioritized equally with the current technical skill sets, the results are nothing less than revolutionary. Rules for creating and managing our professional relationships need to be a performance expectation *if the group is to gain the benefits of an enhanced culture.*

- *Enhanced cultures are not pipe dreams; they already exist.*

For their groundbreaking work *Corporate Culture and Performance*, John Kotter and James Heskett did a study that tracked numerous blue-chip companies in several industries <u>over an 11-year period</u>. They measured cultural values, behavioral patterns, and shared attitudes and classified the companies as either having enhanced or non-enhanced cultures.

The results:

Increases over 11 years	Enhanced Cultures	Non-Enhanced Cultures
Net Income	+756%	+1%
Stock Price	+901%	+74%
Workforce	+282%	+36%
Revenue	+682%	+166%

Look at those numbers…

Takeaway: Enhanced cultures lead to greater group success. Hands down.

MODIFYING THE ENVIRONMENT TO CREATE COLLABORATIVE RELATIONSHIPS

Exponential Relationships

- *Part of the challenge is we are simply overwhelmed by a numbers game we don't know enough about and we have a hard time overcoming its impact.*

Because we don't know what we are up against, understanding the problem is a good first step. Let me explain.

Metcalfe's Law gives us that with 5 people in the room there are 10 relationships to manage. With 6 people we *jump to 15 relationships*. See what happened there? Add a sixth person to a five-person group and the 20 percent increase in the number of people leads to the number of relationships jumping by 50 percent.

Adding to the number of people in a linear fashion increases the number of active relationships in the group *exponentially*. Humans, which includes leaders, don't do well with things that grow exponentially. The negative impact on our relationship management prowess promoted by the hidden acceleration of the number of relationships is something very few even know about.

With 10 people we jump to 45 relationships, and *with 15 people—a 50 percent increase—we jump to 190 relationships, or a 300 percent increase in the number of relationships*. With 300 people in a fair-sized organization, we are now at 44,850 relationships. With a 1,000-person organization we are essentially at a half a million possible relationships (499,500 to be exact).

While they're no doubt busy, I don't think anyone leading an organization with a thousand people realizes they are managing half a million relationships.

This is another reason why if we want a collaborative culture we need to have collaborative *relationships*.

If we don't focus on managing the behaviors used in our relationships within the culture, we are *missing a key metric*. If the true definition of developing a culture is based on managing the relationships in the group, it's safe to assume the focus should be on creating rules by which we guide and manage *our relationship behaviors*. By managing those behaviors with training and by installing those behaviors via performance expectations the culture then supports high performance towards mission success.

When people *are assumed* to know how to create and manage professional relationships when in fact many don't, the culture is degraded as a result. Many company policies rightfully restrict negative behaviors of sexual harassment and other culture-breaking behaviors. Yet most have no policies, no training, and no performance expectations that require the demonstration of behaviors *that create and positively manage the professional relationships in the group.* Certainly there is more training on these topics than there used to be, *but how often do you see them transferred into job descriptions and, more importantly, performance expectations?*

Lastly, two key points worth knowing.

One, the only time the number of people is higher than the number of relationships is when it's just you and me in the room. That's right: two people, one relationship. After that, it's three people with three relationships, and even that can start to get tricky. Then four people creating six relationships and so on and so forth.

Two people co-managing a single relationship is the type of relationship we have the best chance of succeeding at. Long successful relationships, whether it be personal between best friends or spouses or a professional relationship such as business partners, are the ones we have shown to be effective at implementing. And even then, how many challenges in the two people–one relationship scenario do each of us know about that ended in failure?

The relationship rules change significantly when we add more and more people and the ***need for relationship rules grows significantly as we add more and more relationships exponentially.***

A fun fact but nonetheless relevant insight to gain a better understanding of the nightly news: According to Metcalfe's Law, with 7.5 billion astronauts on spaceship earth our number of possible relationships now outnumbers the current estimate for the number of grains of sand on our planet.

We are overwhelmed by a hidden set of numbers that is working against us. The sheer volume of relationships tells us it's really about understanding and influencing ***the relationships.***

A superior human system design will influence relationship behaviors on the front end by A) influencing the brain's precursor feelings and thoughts that then promote the behaviors that follow and B) at the same time, define then provide training on the required collaborative behaviors help to adjust the relationships during the active use of those behaviors in the group environment.

Takeaway: Another success factor that will become a *failure factor if ignored* is to *focus on the overwhelming number of relationships in the group if you want an enhanced culture.* The best way to do that is to simply influence the behaviors used in those relationships with a well-designed human system that (a) concentrates on influencing the precursor feelings and thoughts that occur before the demonstrated behavior, then (b) follows up with collaborative behavioral training to influence the demonstrated behavior once it is active in the group in order to promote the formation of professional relationships. And then importantly, use those same collaborative behaviors ***as performance expectations.***

RECOVERY

- ***One of the more hidden reasons group productivity is hurt and the mission is compromised is the accumulation of error.***

People err and will continue to err in part because they don't know how to recover from the errors they've already made, and the group is not effectively addressing the issue from a training standpoint.

Not having a strategic approach to error mitigation is a huge missed opportunity for a group.

Repetition of the same errors hurts us more than we realize.

Also, and perhaps more importantly, systemic error creation can be unknowingly embedded in the methods used and the training provided.

Because an error by an individual first appears to be solely sourced to the originator, the blame game is piled on the person who erred. There are times, however, when upon further examination the error might also be found to be promoted by the system of methods used or by the training. Tracing back a collection of individual errors for the express purpose of finding systemic error is something you find pursued only by the most advanced groups, as you shall see in a moment.

Dealing with individual and systemic error creation is not a skill set that we're born with and therefore it requires training. Making the same error twice, including ***notably the same error by two different people***, not only hurts group productivity and can create risk to mission success, ***it can often be traced back to a single systemic issue that created the duplicate errors.***

As leaders, we can learn how to teach people to recover from the errors they make, so at the very least they're making new errors *and not repeating the same errors.*

A word of caution: We want to develop a healthy relationship to errors because they also come with experimentation and continuous improvement. Out-of-date, risk-averse reactions to error are still employed by many leaders, resulting in squelched efforts for improving. The solution is to teach group members how to differentiate between the two. Like I just noted, this is not a skill set that we were born with.

When recovery behaviors are properly employed to help a group member improve from past errors, the results become extraordinary. *The more experienced they get and the more training they receive, the fewer errors they will make.*

Stop getting mad at people when they make a mistake. ***We cannot punish our way to success.*** People will err on a regular basis; the key is to simply not repeat the same error in the future. ***If you want less error, give them more training!***

Certainly there are those people that find themselves in the wrong job where regardless of the training the issues don't abate; that's not who I am talking about. I would also be cautious here: Sometimes it's the training or even a particular trainer that can't stop error. In some cases, we found improvement by simply *switching the trainer.*

The big problem: When people are continually, and oftentimes collectively, repeating the same errors. In these cases you have a golden opportunity to find a ***systemic connection*** to the errors made by other group members.

Sometimes I found the source of a collective error *embedded within a flaw in the training program.*

We typically used errors made in the field to regularly go back and upgrade our training program. In these cases a training program flaw was not causing the errors, but by changing the training to address typical errors we could save the group from the misery and reduced productivity of the errors by simply stopping them from being repeated in the future. ***We added it to the training program as a teachable moment.***

With every Collaborative Group Behavior that we teach we also teach the leaders how *to help anybody recover from failure.* With every behavior the group is also trained on the recovery behaviors at the point of failing by either *using a behavior they were not supposed to* or *not using a behavior they were supposed to.*

- The feedback session is private and safe.
- The feedback is delivered unemotionally and is focused on improvement.
- The feedback messaging is very specific so the individual can use this information for improvement.
- The information is also used to modify the training program to prevent the error from being repeated by others in the future.

This same basic method has created the best fighter pilots in the world.

Takeaway: Teach a person how to recover from error and the gift is returned to the group as extraordinary levels of high performance. Look for similar errors being made in seemingly unconnected events and trace them back to their common source with the intent of eliminating *systemic error generation.* Look for opportunities to change the training program as a preventative measure against future instances of error by converting it into a teachable moment.

These issues can be hard to remember so Figure #16 is provided as a quick guide to help you focus on what's important.

Fig. #16: The Hidden Costs of Error Accumulation

RECOVERY: *One of the more hidden reasons group productivity is hurt & the mission is compromised is* **the accumulation of error.**

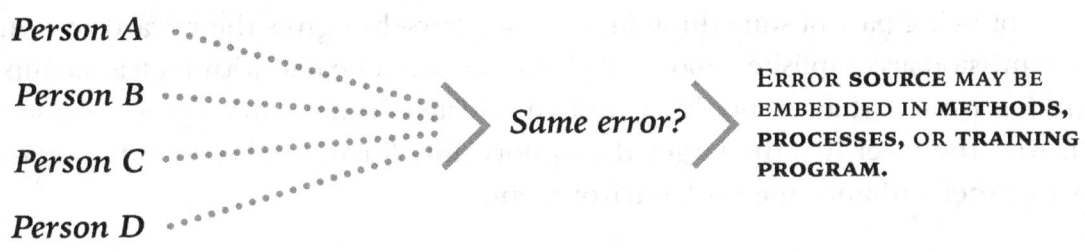

Person A		
Person B	Same error?	ERROR **SOURCE** MAY BE EMBEDDED IN **METHODS**, **PROCESSES**, OR **TRAINING PROGRAM**.
Person C		
Person D		

Repetition of the same error hurts us more than we realize.

Generating the same error twice, especially by two different people is often **a sign of systemic error.**

LIKELY CAUSE	NO. OF ERROR REPETITIONS PER TASK						
individual error	1-2 X						
word-of-mouth training	3≤ X	X	X				
training program	4+ X	X	X	X	X	X	X ...

An individual error can often (but not always) be a mistake on the part of **that person.** Further examination may reveal that the source of the error is found in the *system of methods* used, or *within a training program.* ***Advanced groups will trace a collection of related individual errors to find the source of the error.***

WE WANT TO DEVELOP A **HEALTHY RELATIONSHIP TO ERRORS** BECAUSE THEY ALSO COME WITH EXPERIMENTATION & CONTINUOUS IMPROVEMENT. RISK-AVERSE REACTIONS TO ERROR **DISCOURAGE HEALTHY RISK TAKING.**

When your people are trained to improve on past errors, the results are **extraordinary.**

Stop getting mad at people when they make a mistake. ***We cannot punish our way to success.*** People will err on a regular basis. The key is to simply not repeat the same error in the future. ***If you want less error, give them more training!***

RECOGNITION

- *Those who are recognized for their demonstration of desirable technical and collaborative behaviors will repeat that same desirable behavior in the future.*

Recognition by the leader of those worthy acts is like using a collaborative glue patching back together the human emotional need to be part of something larger than ourselves. This results in creating an esprit de corps that generates *extremely loyal and dedicated high performers.*

The satisfaction of being part of something larger than ourselves gives the reward of ownership and the verve to see mission accomplished above all else and cannot be had without leadership setting the stage. Recognition is rarer than it should be and an effective leader can empower those around her with this gift. And the rarer it is the larger the opportunity for mutual success between leader and follower who, together, enhance the work environment.

Like mercy, recognition is twice blessed, first for the receiver but also for the giver.

Once you have a group of "those people" by creating an enhanced culture, your *highly collaborative workforce will also become a juggernaut of organic continuous improvement.* That's when you start to see the accelerated results that Kotter and Heskett recorded over 11 years.

Takeaway: For every behavior you want repeated, effectively and officially recognize it and *it will be repeated forevermore by them and others.*

A NEW FUTURE

You're going to be taking baby steps into the future. As outlined, the first step is to assess the problems in your group so you have an idea of what's going wrong, which is going to be important as you move forward in your plan to gain collaborative power.

If you know what is wrong then you know what to fix, and when you fix the things that are going wrong that will improve your group not only for your boss or your followers but also for your customers and your CEO.

And once again you need to do it in a specific order.

Inviting Collaborative Power

The first step will be gaining the trust and support and mentorship of your boss to the extent they're able to give those things to you. And essentially we're going to gain that collaborative power from your boss simply by supporting him in ways that his previous direct reports haven't supported him.

You're going to find out what keeps your boss awake at night when it comes to his work responsibilities. You're going to find out what the largest problems are that he's having to confront. You're going to find out exactly what he expects from you, and you're going to fulfill it. Once you know some of the problems that he is dealing with, you and your direct reports are going start working so you can solve those problems and get them out of the way. You're going to stop using any type of narrowmindedness and self-centeredness from this point forward. You are becoming a powerful leader and the best way to start that process is to invite that power from your boss and even your boss's boss and make sure that you are supporting them in ways that they have never been supported before. We will go through that process step by step.

Attracting Collaborative Power

Whether you're a first-line supervisor or a CEO you can Attract Collaborative Power from the Bottom Up. And you're going to do that in a similar way to Inviting Collaborative Power from the Top Down but using very different tools. You're going to support your direct reports in ways they've never been supported before. Whether they realize it or not, you are going to be teaching them skills that they can use not only on the job but wherever they go. You are essentially going to be building more effective humans so they can support you in your group effort but at the same time once they have those skills they'll be more effective as humans in general. And again we will go through the process step by step.

Cultivating Collaborative Power

This is the last section in the Collaborative Power Grab. And it needs to wait until you have fully fleshed out the first two phases because this last step can be the most challenging and its success (or not) is highly dependent on how much power you possess.

Cultivating Collaborative Power is optional. Yes, you have been laying the groundwork for building strong relationships above you (Invite) and below you (Attract). Prior to this you have already been helping people to grow by encouraging them and modeling the very collaborative behaviors that might be missing from your group. You have already been trying to reduce fear by squelching the types of behaviors that stop people from collaborating in your group. Cultivating Collaborative Power will require you to take a more assertive role in stopping destructive behavior. How far your group has already advanced on the collaboration path will help dictate your decision on when and whether to cultivate power.

Success with Cultivating Collaborative Power needs to be built on a strong foundation of Inviting and Attracting Collaborative Power for as long as it takes to set the stage. That being said, this stage of implementation might have to be reserved for those that have enough power to overcome any resistance. Therefore, implementation might have to reside with those who are higher up in the organization.

When making the full conversion to an enhanced culture by Cultivating Collaborative Power, most will thrive in this highly human nurturing collaborative environment when you start implementing collaborative group behaviors as the third step in the power trifecta.

As we support, train, and encourage those that thrive under collaboration, those that don't will move on. As new group members are trained in the use of collaborative group behaviors during your onboarding training process, the available positions will be filled by those who thrive in a highly collaborative *human-centric, mission-successful,* enhanced culture.

Working in an environment that effectively corrects destructive behavior while building human capabilities by teaching skills such as *problem-solving*, the leader is essentially *commingling the two goals of advancing better individual life skills and achieving group mission success.*

Improving the collaborative life skills of the individuals in the group and then receiving the use of those same skill sets for mission success *is one of the most important keys to creating an enhanced work environment.*

Making fundamental changes in how collaboration is valued in the group by redefining how we act and treat each other contributes to abating the sources of hidden fears. Seeking good advice from those who use their hands by now also asking them for what is in their brains for creating improvement not only lowers *hidden fears* but simultaneously supports advancing a continuous improvement strategy.

When fear is present in the human brain not only do people feel bad and are perhaps more reactive and less responsive than we need them to be, but, as noted previously, fear will also place in motion a series of faulty decision-making practices that will generate more problems.

Expecting an unenhanced work group to be well led without first modifying some of the most fundamental aspects of human behavior *is one of the most unfair proposals we can place on the shoulders of good leaders.*

Takeaway: Without first Inviting and Attracting Collaborative Power, Cultivating Collaborative Power needs to wait until the time is right. However, aligning and then implementing a clear set of new collaborative performance expectations within the group's mission and desired culture, *and then requiring their use as performance expectations*, will vault the group forward because as the work environment reduces fear, as the number of problems drop, as the training reduces direct supervision, and as your boss's problem list gets shorter, people are going to be wide open to this next move.

The last point here: You will have been able to influence your part of the organization very favorably by Inviting and Attracting Collaborative Power. But depending on where you are in the leadership stack, you may not have been able to influence other areas.

- If you are a division chief or a department head, or even the CEO or general manager, you're going to have a lot more influence over implementing the cultivation stage than if you are a middle manager or a first line supervisor.

Takeaway: The lower you are on the leadership stack, the less influence you have to institute collaborative group behaviors, which are the basis of Cultivating Collaborative Power. *Therefore, this phase might need to be implemented by those leaders that are higher up in the organization.*

ONCE CULTIVATING COLLABORATIVE POWER IS IMPLEMENTED
The enhanced culture *is protected, promoted, and supported using very specific actions with very specific intentions to create very specific outcomes.*

Using specific behaviors—in this case collaborative group behaviors, with a concerted effort spread over eight specific but overlapping performance categories that I call the Big 8—the leader supports individual competency and expands opportunities for individual significance and likability. The result: the hidden fears of being ignored, humiliated, or rejected are substantially lowered.

By using collaborative group behaviors *as performance expectations*, significant changes will be observed over the entire range of the Big 8 performance categories:

1. Mission
2. Culture
3. Effective Interpersonal Relationships
4. High-Quality Communication
5. Technical Competency
6. Productivity
7. Problem-Solving
8. Continuous Improvement

By using this process, over time the group population will become dominated by those who want to collaborate. Led by those who protect the culture and support and mentor them with recovery and recognition in the Big 8 performance categories, the group becomes resilient to setbacks and eventually becomes a group of stalwart veterans co-owning the mission. Once that starts to happen managers will manage less and leaders can lead more.

Good leaders who are helping their reports to achieve great things in their professional lives *can become heroes*. Good leaders fashion their reputation with their direct reports by first protecting the culture then training, supporting, and mentoring them towards successful outcomes that benefit the individual *and* the group.

This is an essential message for any leader that wants to improve their culture:

> Using this process as described might cause some turnover among those that don't do well in a collaborative group, yet it will create an *enhanced culture* with shared values for those that stay, and eventually all you will be left with is a bunch of highly skilled, collaborative humans…*imagine that.*

What the Cultivating Collaborative Power phase will do:

> Enhanced cultures follow collaboration rules in order to influence Mission, Culture, Effective Interpersonal Relationships, High-Quality Communication, Technical Competency, Productivity, Problem-Solving, and Continuous Improvement. Promoting specific behaviors to start using and preventing specific behaviors to stop using, combined with converting all these activities into performance expectations upon which group members are evaluated, is the key to success.

An enhanced culture can be created by any leader in any group by first inviting an adequate amount of power and by next attracting an adequate amount of power prior to cultivating power. But cultivating power has its basis in the following bullet list. I wanted to offer a simplified version of this list now so you have an idea of what the future brings.

And again this list will be repeated at later points in the book and I will help you with each and every task listed here. DO NOT get overwhelmed by the following list. I'm going to give you a step-by-step process to build your toolbox.

The grand trifecta of *Inviting Collaborative Power, Attracting Collaborative Power*, and *Cultivating Collaborative Power* will have you doing the following:

- Identifying a list of behaviors **to stop using** if you want more group collaboration
- Implementing a list of behaviors **to start using** if you want more group collaboration
- Smartly addressing and eliminating the causes of fear generation in the work environment
- Reducing complexity of the policies, procedures, and how-to of day-to-day operations
- Training every group member to expert levels in collaboration and technical competency
- Reducing expensive direct supervision time by providing more autonomy
- Creating clearly understood objectives that are directly supported by that person's training
- Ensuring smooth productivity by removing roadblocks, adjusting workloads, and setting reasonable deadlines with clear expectations as part of every delegated task
- Having leaders conscientiously train, mentor, and guide the success behaviors of their direct reports

- Having leaders actively solicit and assertively implement improvement proposals from non-leader group members
- Having leaders who train others in the use of a systematic problem-solving process in order to neutralize deeply embedded cognitive biases, fallacious reasoning, and emotional blocks
- Having leaders who privately hold individuals accountable to collaborative behaviors and publicly advance ambitious but achievable objectives
- Having leaders who assist in performance recovery when inevitable errors come to pass
- Having leaders recognize the exceptional performance events of their direct reports so this same performance is encouraged to be repeated in the workplace by them and others

In the final step, the above desired attributes are supported in the form of specific behavior descriptions used in the performance evaluations for every member of the organization.

By turning each *specific behavior description* into a performance expectation for evaluating performance, feedback given during evaluations is more accurate, more relevant, more specific, and therefore more effective at creating improvement.

Not using specific behaviors as benchmarks and instead telling somebody they need to *improve their communication* or *be more cooperative* or *work harder* won't get you very far, but I hear leaders do it all the time.

Takeaway: The power of high performance is always within reach by taking the right steps. These steps—finding out what's going wrong so you know what needs to be fixed, Inviting Collaborative Power from Above you so you're supporting the mission accurately and effectively, Attracting Collaborative Power from Below so your people are supported and well trained and become experts at what they do, and finally implementing Cultivating Collaborative Power—all work if you and your fellow leaders don't stop until the group arrives at its enhanced culture.

These issues can be hard to remember so Figure #17 is provided as a quick guide to help you focus on what's important. .

Fig. #17: Inviting, Attracting, & Cultivating Collaborative Power

The GRAND TRIFECTA of

INVITING
ATTRACTING
& CULTIVATING
Collaborative Power

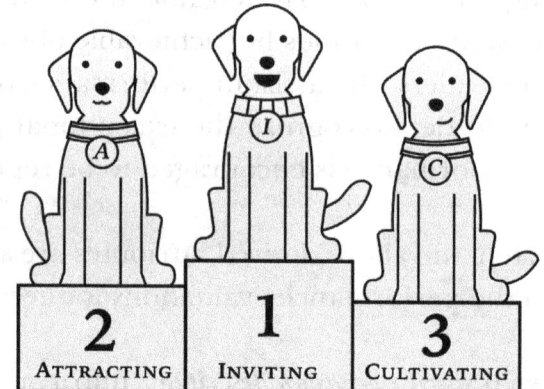

2	1	3
ATTRACTING	INVITING	CULTIVATING

Will have you doing the following:

- Identifying a list of un-collaborative behaviors to **stop using**
- Implementing a list of collaborative behaviors to **start using**
- Locating/removing the sources of **fear generation** in the environment
- **Reducing complexity** at every opportunity
- Training group members to expert levels of **collaboration & technical** competency
- Reducing costly **direct supervision time** by training for autonomy
- Giving **clear objectives** that are supported by training programs
- Fixing **roadblocks**, adjusting **workloads**, & setting **sensible deadlines**
- Having leaders **train & mentor** the success of their direct reports
- Soliciting & implementing **improvement proposals from non-leaders**
- Training your group in a **systematic problem-solving process** to neutralize the impact of **cognitive biases, logical fallacies, & emotional blocks**
- Having leaders privately **hold individuals accountable** to collaborative behaviors & publicly advance ambitious but achievable objectives
- Having leaders **promote recovery when inevitable errors come to pass**
- Encouraging **repetition of exceptional performance by recognizing the exceptional performance** events of their direct reports

Support the above attributes with specific behavior descriptions used in the performance evaluations as performance expectations for every member of the organization.

BUMPS IN THE ROAD

Many people that I have spoken to misunderstand the term "collaboration" as it relates to the human enterprise. They think collaboration is always *just making nice* when in fact *making the hard decisions and doing it the right way* is not always easy.

Collaboration doesn't mean *easy*.

Human collaboration needs to result in mission success or else the human group fails. And in some cases, the human group failing means people get hurt or people go hungry or people become homeless or people die.

Implementing a more collaborative culture can be challenging and at times confusing if leaders have some of the more "make nice" misunderstandings concerning the foundational requirements necessary in order for human collaboration to flourish in group settings. It is for this very reason that the *Starting Now* actions are specifically designed the way they are. That being said, here is a list of resistance actions that might be encountered when converting over to an enhanced workplace environment.

Mission: When it comes to reprioritizing work, some people don't like stopping what they're doing in the middle and then starting a new task that just showed up. That won't always be the case but sometimes it will be. Because some people become annoyed at always having to make sure we're doing the most important thing first, they would see this as something that's not collaborative. Well, they're wrong. If people think that collaboration is allowing people to do the second or fifth most important thing first because nobody wants to annoy them then they're wrong, and their definition or their understanding of what it means to be collaborative as it relates to the mission is simply incorrect.

Culture: When it comes to maintaining a culture that supports high performers by reducing the amount of fear in the work environment, this includes employing the industrial-strength actions necessary to correct destructive behavior, offering counseling, and perhaps even demoting people that are fear generators who are susceptible to angry outbursts and thereby destroying collegiality. And maybe the people that the leader is having to correct have friends that think maybe a leader is going too far. Maybe there are people in the group that think, *"well, they've always been that way, it's not that big of a deal."* There might be people in the group that think a psychologically safe work environment and this whole thing about fear reduction is pampering—after all, we're not a bunch of babies. Collaboration means you clamp down on destructive human behavior.

Effective Interpersonal Relationships: Collaboration means that you develop professional relationships, even with people in the group that you don't like. There might be some people who really don't like collaboration if that's what it's going to mean. Collaboration means getting along with your fellow group members *is now part of your job*. If somebody's not used to doing that and they don't really like doing that then they're not going to like collaboration, are they?

Technical Competency: Collaboration means that you always step up to the plate and make a decision to fulfill the technical competency that you've been trained in. Not everybody likes doing that. A lot of people like to think they have the option to step into their technical role, or not, depending on the situation. However, in a collaborative group it's mandated that you do so. Also, in a collaborative group you're not allowed to operate outside your area of expertise, and a lot of people like to do that. How are they going to feel about being told that they are no longer allowed to operate outside their area of expertise?

Productivity: If people are not used to being given a deadline for their work they don't like it very much when it starts to occur. Sometimes when objectives are developed it's to solve a problem that the person assigned to the task is unaware of. As such, the objectives of the assignment may not make immediate sense to them as they are receiving the assignment. When people are not informed as to why the objective is being put forth, they can be mystified, and mystified people can become resistant. Certainly, the supervisor should be educating their people when assignments are made and sometimes they have to give those explanations quickly on the fly. Either way an explanation as to why they are having to meet an objective carries a lot of positive weight for those carrying out the assignment. I know this seems like an obvious point but I have witnessed quite a few supervisors that really didn't see the need for explaining *why* to the people that were receiving these assignments. This is a necessary step in promoting productivity. Additionally, some individuals don't like being held responsible by name for getting an objective completed, especially if they're not used to doing it. Well, in a collaborative group it's essential that assigned tasks are *by name of the individual that's responsible for meeting the deadline*. Not doing so adds risk to the group activities. So again if people are not used to collaborating in this way they're not going to like it when they're exposed to it for the first time.

Problem-Solving: This requires a higher cognitive function that goes beyond how we typically measure intelligence. Many people automatically think that they are good problem solvers when in fact they're not. How are people going to respond to the problem-solving training and the training on how to best recognize problems if they already think they don't need the training? I only bring this up because I've run into it before. In a highly collaborative group, the training to recognize problems and act on those problems with a systematic problem-solving process is exactly what people *are required to do*.

Continuous Improvement: This comes in two forms. One is to give people feedback so they can excel in their performance, and the other is to collect ideas on improving future operations.

Of these two components it is giving people performance feedback that can be a difficult task for some leaders to perform. It's not a bad thing when you're helping people to achieve outstanding levels of performance, but the sticky part comes in when people are operating at substandard performance and they disagree with your assessment concerning their performance when you give them feedback. Well that's what you need to do if you are in a highly collaborative human group.

So does that sound like collaboration making nice?

OPERATING RULES OF THE HUMAN BRAIN AND QUADRANT 2 BEHAVIORS

The fact is collaborative power is floating all around you regardless of your station in life. It falls from the sky and it fills up our lives like a giant reservoir. Even though I'm employing what seem to be lofty metaphors, what I'm trying to illustrate is that the power of collaboration is not always obviously available yet *its building blocks are always available*. All that's necessary is for the leader to gather those blocks and assemble them correctly and BAM there you have it.

The two intermingled subjects addressed in this section offer the best clue to understanding how those building blocks fit together.

First, we need to know what's going on in our brains, how our brains operate, and how we need to modify our work environment based on the operating rules of our brains.

Second, I want to introduce you to a model that's going to be used throughout the remainder of the book that classifies each of us within a single quadrant out of four available quadrants. This matrix and our individual classifications allow us to have a better understanding of the people we work with and, more importantly, a better understanding of ourselves as to where our strengths and weaknesses lie.

When these two building blocks are commingled it will help you better develop the tools necessary to Invite, Attract, and Cultivate Collaborative Power.

When leaders learn the methods to Invite Collaborative Power, Attract Collaborative Power, and Cultivate Collaborative Power, that's exactly what you'll be doing: *Learning the building blocks in the series of building maneuvers in order to get the power you need to have a positive impact on your group by increasing its performance with a bunch of enthusiastic group members hurtling you towards mission success.*

When the most effective brain-activating methods are not used or not clearly understood to Invite, Attract, and Cultivate Collaborative Power, the human brain does not do well in supporting mission success.

The best way to understand exactly what's going on internally is to stop for a moment and gain clarity on how the human brain works as this is a key component for understanding how to achieve and maximize collaborative power for the leader and the group.

OUR HUMAN BRAIN

Some of what I'm about to explain, if you're hearing it for the first time, you're not going to believe. So let me start and we'll just see how this goes.

You need to know that even though we have the availability to make choices it's far more limited than we ever thought. That even though we are making choices we're making those choices based on sets of embedded scripts that we gained over the past, spanning from last week to the last thousand centuries.

We are influenced so significantly by the subconscious, embedded scripts that our brains employ that the number of choices we make not using embedded scripts is very low. What we have interpreted previously as *free will* might exist in just a small number of the choices we select. If you don't believe me, give me a chance; don't stop reading.

This is not bad news; it's just most people don't want to admit to themselves that so much of their decision making is made by subliminal scripts.

The good news is that being aware of this information means you can use it to your benefit. We have a lot of cognitive biases operating in our brain right now and one of them is called confirmation bias. Whether we like it or not, we have a tendency to collect information to support the decisions we've already made and avoid information that undercuts our decisions. Now that you know about confirmation bias, you can start to be aware of how you look at information.

Looking at new information and new ways of analyzing new information helps you modify your next steps to approach any given situation. This places you in the driver's seat and gives you power like you've never had before.

Starting now, by allowing new facts to change your mind, that's exactly what we're doing. We're putting you in the driver's seat so you can Invite, Attract, and Cultivate Collaborative Power.

Even though you're hearing that free will actually doesn't exist and that many of your choices are coming from places you were not previously aware of, please be reassured that the upside is this is why humans are so successful, more so than any other species that have ever landed on the planet. Quite simply, these same scripts have proven themselves to promote our survival as individuals and as groups.

What we know from extraordinary leaps in brain science over the last quarter century, from game theory on how people respond to economic decision making under various circumstances, and from 50 years of organizational analysis and inquiry is beyond reproach. And I say that because it almost doesn't matter who you talk to; most everyone is coming up with very similar conclusions based on their analysis or their observations and most often both.

A thorough examination of this combined effort is a separate book, so I'm just going to stand on the shoulders of some giants and give you some names and references in the bibliography at the end of this book.

So let me get to the heart of the matter:

Because we know what the scripts are and how these scripts generate outcomes based on the circumstances the brain is experiencing, we can build supremely high-performing human groups based on this knowledge.

This is not a pipe dream. We already have proof, and there are groups that already do this, so lower your doubt shield and keep reading.

We know what these scripts are based on studies of the reactions to the various environments that humans have been exposed to. One of the reasons this field of study is so astounding is that many of the subjective assumptions that were generated by many brilliant multidisciplinary humans over the last 80 years or so are starting to be supported by the undisputed conclusions of science.

We therefore know what type of environment creates what type of reaction, in a general sense, and from there it provides us the opportunity to design environments to create the outcomes we desire from the human brains in our groups.

I know this might sound a little robotic but I can't help that; I'm just going with the science. Propagandists know this extremely well and we have seen this used in very diabolical forms and for very diabolical reasons. This is why people consider this subject matter scary talk. I can't say that I blame them.

However, there's no getting around it: our brains operate with scripts that were generated over thousands of years. This time-tested process starting a thousand centuries ago allowed for a handful of influential precise impacts, *one of which is a co-evolutionary physical modification called gene expression that cemented our multitude of reactions to the multitude of environments.*

There's a lot to go over here so I'm going dive in with a series of bullets:

- The decision-making centers of the brain—where we go to access the scripts on what to do next based on the environment we are experiencing—so happen to also be *the emotional centers of the brain.*
- The brain has multiple decision-making centers and it's too much to go into here so we are just going to focus on two of them, the prefrontal cortex and the amygdala.
- Different parts of the brain developed at different times during human evolution. The amygdala is a part of the brain that developed at the very beginning of human evolution. The prefrontal cortex developed last as part of our brain evolution. And in fact in the modern human the prefrontal cortex doesn't fully develop until about the mid-20s.
- The amygdala has been keeping humans alive for millions of years. This is the part of the brain that receives information coming in from the outside world before the rest of the brain has had a chance to look at it. The amygdala has multiple filters or pieces of information stored,

which it then compares to the incoming information it's receiving from the environment that the human is experiencing *in order to determine if the current environment produces a threat to its survival.* And one of the reasons you're here today is because the amygdala of your ancestors not only determined whether they were in danger, it also gave them a set of limited options with which to respond to that threat.

- The prefrontal cortex is the more advanced thinking portion of the brain and demonstrates the qualities of the human at its best, its most sophisticated, and its most collaborative. When you see a human talking and acting with logic, rational responses, and ethical behavior, you know that's the prefrontal cortex in action. The prefrontal cortex receives the incoming information long after the amygdala has already had a chance to look at it and decides what to do with that information *using a very different set of criteria.*

- Conversely, when you witness a human fighting or running or simply freezing like the proverbial deer in the headlights, you know that they're in their amygdala. As you can see the amygdala and the prefrontal cortex have what I call very different *toolboxes.* And I don't think anybody disagrees with the fact that sometimes freezing and doing nothing, running like hell, or fighting is the most appropriate thing to do based on certain environments that humans might find themselves in. Sometimes the amygdala gets a bad rap but it has gotten us this far, after all.

- If a person happens to be in their prefrontal cortex and something happens that creates fear or *that merely appears to be a threat* the decision-making center of the brain switches from the prefrontal cortex to the amygdala. *And here's where things either go terribly right or terribly wrong.* If it's a true threat, if it's something the person really should fear, then things are going terribly right.

- The big problem is that if the threat (or whatever is generating the fear) is not an authentic threat but the person perceives it to be, the amygdala takes charge when in fact we want the prefrontal cortex to remain in charge. In other words, based on the actual situation that the human is experiencing the best toolbox they could be using is that of the prefrontal cortex not the amygdala, *but the amygdala toolbox is nonetheless now in charge and things start to go terribly wrong.*

  - In complex human situations one of the best things the person can do, even for their own survival, is to remain in the prefrontal cortex so they can use the power of logic, the power of rational thinking, and the power of ethical thinking in order to develop complex solutions to complex challenges that are complementary not only to one's own survival but also the survival of others in their group.

In many situations that humans face that create fear or a sense of threat, *the worst thing we can do is to respond with fight, flight, or freeze.* However, because we already feel fearful and threatened, it's too late to employ the prefrontal cortex toolbox. By the time our prefrontal cortex gets the information we're already too busy *inappropriately fighting* or *inappropriately running* or *inappropriately freezing.*

In other words, in a lot of situations humans finds themselves in *with other humans in workplace settings* they are simply responding with the wrong toolbox for that environment which then makes things sometimes explosively worse.

In our complex system of human relationships we can generate threat and fear, but because this type of threat and fear is qualitatively different than the threat and fear the amygdala was raised on millions of years ago (e.g., a growling saber-tooth tiger in the bushes next to you) oftentimes in group situations the best way to face these more complex human problems is by creating solutions that will emanate from the prefrontal cortex *not the amygdala*. When faced with many of these modern human threats and fears we are using the amygdala toolbox instead of the prefrontal cortex toolbox and this one of the reasons the nightly news looks the way it does.

Here's the bottom line: *this is why it is absolutely essential that when designing any type of human enterprise fear reduction and knowing how to lower perceived threats need to be at the very top of the list.*

The story gets worse; follow me here.

Not only are some of our human situations forcing us from the prefrontal cortex into the amygdala based on obvious factors like humans treating other humans badly or unkindly or with intimidation, there are also less obvious sources of fear. Compliments of Will Schutz we learned:

- Each person wants Inclusion to feel significant. *Without feeling significant their fear is being ignored.*
- Each person wants Control to feel competent. *Without feeling competent their fear is being humiliated.*
- Each person wants Openness to feel likable. *Without feeling likable their fear is being rejected.*

So what is this telling us?

For humans, the possibility of being ignored or the possibility of being humiliated or the possibility of being rejected from their group, any group that they belong to, is a devastating prospect which will then push the human brain from the prefrontal cortex to the amygdala, which then employees a toolbox that makes collaboration and the gathering of collaborative power very difficult.

What's happening in groups where group members don't collaborate or in groups where the expectation to collaborate is not being placed on the group members by their leaders?

What's happening if supervisors are not managing well or not leading well or mismanaging resources and creating their own level of emergencies that have to be dealt with by the front-line people? What about situations where the work is not prioritized well, causing confusion and miscommunication? What about working in a group where any of the following is true, where leaders:

- don't emulate the behaviors they want from others,
- don't protect the culture which means they're not protecting you,
- treat their direct reports like mushrooms by not being transparent with information,
- don't support their people with timely decisions and problem-solving,
- don't give their people the training they need,
- attempt to increase productivity by simply working people harder,
- don't want to hear your opinion about anything,
- don't mentor their direct reports,
- don't help people recover after making an error, or
- don't recognize exceptional performance?

Even with a small handful of these issues plaguing a work environment, what do you think is going to be happening with feelings like *inclusion, control, or openness*?

Or the needed feelings of *significance* or feelings of *competency* or trying to assess whether or not you *are liked*? Don't underrate wanting to be liked.

Whether you know it or not, your human brain is constantly wanting to figure out whether your group future includes a scenario where you are ignored or humiliated or rejected.

So if I know that at a minimum I might be "liked" by my fellow group members, does that play a role in this constant ignore-humiliate-rejection assessment that's going on in my brain?

The answer is unquestionably *yes*.

Do those examples listed above sound like a collaborative workplace or is it a workplace that's going to be generating hidden sources of fear catapulting everybody from the prefrontal cortex into the amygdala?

Do those examples listed above sound like a work environment that has any empathy, any dignity, any respect? Of course not, so what's happening?

That's right: Everybody is sliding towards the *fear of being ignored or the fear of being humiliated or the fear of being rejected*. And they're not completely conscious of it, but as noted their brains are, their amygdalae are.

These issues can be hard to remember so Figure #18 is provided as a quick guide to help you focus on what's important. .

Fig. #18: *Inclusion, Control & Openness*

Warning: Fear conditions in an environment, such as unkind treatment or intimidation, can push us into *amygdala thinking.*

THE **AMYGDALA** GENERATES FIGHT-OR-FLIGHT THINKING FROM **LESS OBVIOUS FEARS:**

<u>NEEDS MET</u>	*OR*	<u>HIDDEN FEARS</u>
Each person needs **Inclusion** to feel significant.		Without feeling significant, their fear is **being ignored.**
Each person needs **Control** to feel competent.		Without feeling competent their fear is **being humiliated.**
Each person needs **Openness** to feel likeable.		Without feeling likable their fear is **being rejected.**

INCLUSION   CONTROL   OPENNESS

IGNORED   HUMILIATED   REJECTED

Source: Will Schutz

LEADERS GENERATE **FIGHT-OR-FLIGHT** THINKING WHEN THEY:

- **don't emulate behaviors they want from others**

- **don't protect the culture & the people.**

- **are not transparent**

- **don't support the mission with timely decisions & problem-solving**

- **don't give their people needed training**

- **force people to work harder without working smarter**

- **don't want to hear your opinion about anything**

- **don't mentor their direct reports**

- **don't help people recover after making an error**

- **don't recognize exceptional performance**

Even with a small handful of these issues plaguing a work environment, everybody is sliding towards the *above fears: being ignored, being humiliated, being rejected.*

HERE IS THE SEQUENCE THAT FORCES THE AMYGDALA TO BE IN CHARGE:

1. A poor work environment is defined as an environment that allows unchecked destructive human behavior to occur, which creates a "negative" *condition.*
2. The negative *condition* experienced by the human provokes an *adverse feeling.*
3. The *adverse feeling* causes the presence of *fear or perceived threat.*
4. Fear causes the brain function into the amygdala section of the brain, ergo giving only three possible options of how to respond: *fight, flight, or freeze.*
5. Fight-flight-freeze behaviors are naturally self-centered because the person feels the need to protect themselves, so by definition it is in opposition to collaborative action as a way of interacting with other humans.
6. Collaboration is not able to occur and as a result the workplace further deteriorates, taking mission success down with it.

(This is happening on a global scale, promoting human misery along the way, but that will be a separate book.)

This sequence might appear to some like I am making some big leaps in logic. I don't think I am. Between the giants whose shoulders I stand on and my life experience of over five decades of witnessing chaos destroy collaboration, every bone in my body is telling you: I really think it's that simple.

HERE IS THE SEQUENCE WHEN THE LEADER HAS BEEN ABLE TO INVITE, ATTRACT, AND CULTIVATE COLLABORATIVE POWER.

1. A positive or enhanced work environment is defined as an environment that specifically classifies behaviors into two categories: those behaviors that should not be demonstrated (but *are* in many group settings) and those behaviors that are not demonstrated (but need to be in order for the group to "grow"). As collaborative power is Invited, Attracted, and Cultivated, destructive behaviors are reduced and collaboration-building behaviors are enhanced.
2. The enhanced workplace environment experienced by the human provokes a *favorable feeling.*
3. The *favorable feeling* reduces the presence of *fear or perceived threat.*
4. Reduced fear causes brain function to shift away from the amygdala and moves it to the prefrontal cortex, so instead of the limited options of how to respond such as ***fight, flight, or freeze,*** now with the prefrontal cortex in charge the options of how to respond include ***rational, logical, and ethical behaviors that produce collaborative outcomes.***
5. Rational, logical, and ethical behaviors are multi-centered, so thereby include the wider scope of the human needs of self *and* others, *promoting* collaboration as a way of interacting with other humans.

6. Collaboration is now not only able to occur, it is promoted, and as a result the wealth-generating benefits of mission success it provides *are now gained*.
7. Wealth-generating benefits gained, on a global scale, promotes human welfare and helps to mitigate human misery.

In closing, it is absolutely essential for you to understand the operating systems of the human brain and how those operating systems are highly influenced by the environment humans finds themselves in. Armed with this knowledge, you as the leader can start to modify the environment to create the outcomes necessary for mission success.

Everything that you are going to learn about quadrant thinking in the next section, and everything you're going to learn about the step-by-step instructions on how to Invite, Attract, and Cultivate Collaborative Power, *is going to help you to create a workplace environment that influences the outcomes created by all the human brains that you can persuade in the group.*

QUADRANT THINKING
So let's talk about how to Invite, Attract, and Cultivate Collaborative Power using the concept of quadrant thinking.

The two measuring criteria that we will use will be our *technical competencies* and *collaborative competencies*. How competent we are in those two criteria will determine our quadrant rating.

We either:

- are highly technically competent but not competent in collaboration
- or vice versa: are highly competent in collaboration but not highly technically competent
- need to improve at both technical and collaboration
- are really good at both technical and collaboration

Which influences:

How well we do our jobs
How well we treat other people
How we supervise and lead the people that follow us
How we treat our boss
How we treat our boss's boss

If you break down each one of our tendencies within one of the four quadrants based on these two basic measuring criteria you can start to generate different quadrants *that are practical tools* we can use to better understand:

1. our supervisors
2. the people that follow us
3. ourselves

Let's take a look at the quadrant matrix.

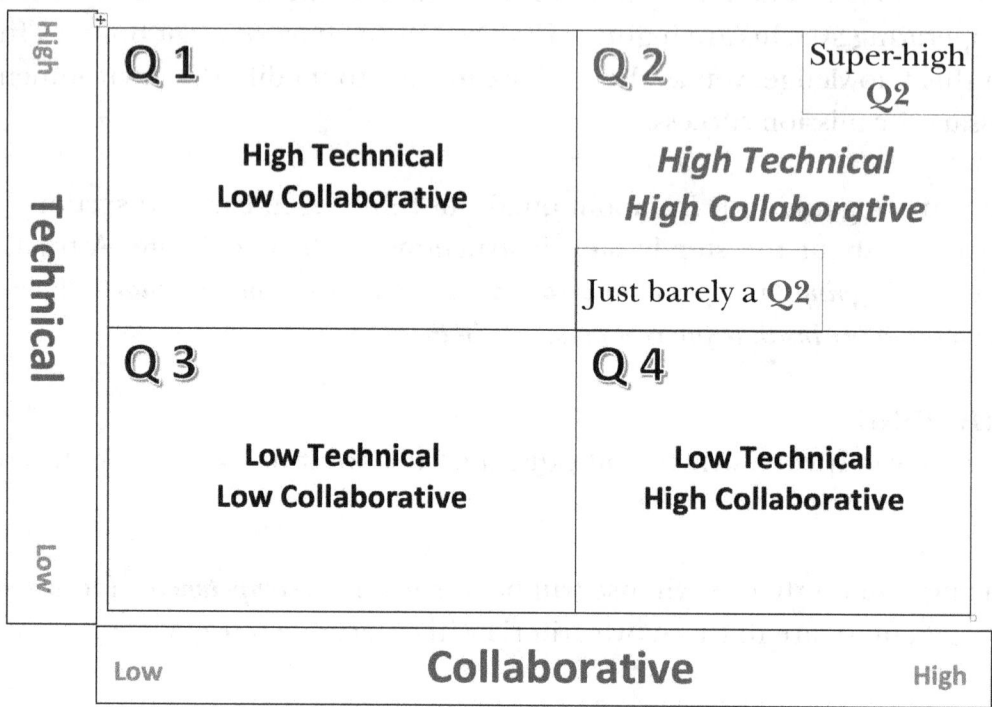

As illustrated in this diagram we can compare technical and collaborative competencies of the four types/quadrants.

Q1s are highly technically competent but not competent in collaboration. These individuals are the backbone of a highly technical system. They do extremely well at the technical aspects of their job and they do extremely well at maximizing productivity and finding ways of reducing effort.

- *If you are supervising a Q1 you want to make sure you give them a lot of collaboration training to move them towards Q2.*

Q4s are highly competent in collaboration but not highly technically competent. These individuals work really well as team members and they do extremely well at thinking outside the box when it comes to collaborating between team members. That being said they need to improve on their technical skill sets if they are to survive as the group moves towards mission success.

- *If you are supervising a Q4 you want to make sure you give them a lot of technical training to move them towards Q2.*

Q3s need to improve at both technical competency and collaborative competency. This can be quite a challenge and typically Q3 individuals are washed out of many groups. As I have experienced Q3s in my career there were quite a few of them that just simply did not get the training and mentoring that could have improved their life and most importantly improved their work life.

- *If you are supervising a Q3 you want to make sure you give them a lot of technical and collaboration training to move them towards Q2.* Moving a Q3 to a Q2 is a heavy lift but you might be pleasantly surprised. If you can get the Q3 to at least a standard level of performance with both dimensions, barely edging them into the Q2 quadrant, *you'll find a dedicated and loyal direct report who will support you because you were willing to invest in them when they needed you the most.*

Q2s are going to respond well to all of this training. They already have a lot of things figured out so a lot of the things in this book that you're going to expose them to make perfect sense to them. Some Q2s in your group might be barely within the quadrant. In other words, they're just slightly above the midpoint technically and slightly above the midpoint collaboratively. The key here is to give them both technical and collaboration training so they can start to reach towards the far top right-hand corner of that quadrant. All that's going to do is cause their performance to skyrocket, *the contents of this book essentially giving them the perfect fuel for their fire.*

- *If you are supervising a Q2 continue to add more training and add more responsibility as fast as they're willing to take it. As opportunities permit put these people in charge of something then be prepared to get the hell out of their way as their performance trajectory continues to explode into the far top right-hand corner of the matrix.*

In looking at the world in general terms, most work groups stress technical training over collaboration training, and as such the performance expectations stress technical competency over collaborative competency and motivate the population in the group to shift towards Q1, which is the predominant type you see in most groups. The truth is if you don't know how to do your job technically your future employment is in question.

So while the Q1 does need some improvement in their collaboration actions they play a vital technical role.

Technical competency is extremely important. However, if people are not also collaboratively competent, sustainable mission success becomes doubtful unless success is being downgraded through the acceptance of normalized mediocre performance.

This results in a very large pool of Q1 individuals and it is from this quadrant that most leaders are selected. One of the most significant problems with groups today is an overabundance of Q1 leaders. And we'll talk about that later in the book.

These are not bad people; they're hardworking, well intentioned, and, yes, perhaps ineffective in their leadership and perhaps management duties based on their less-than-adequate skill in collaboration.

Are there some leaders who then naturally pursue training to improve their Q4 performance and move towards Q2? Yes of course. However, when looking at the millions of groups in the world today, finding leaders who voluntarily train or were mentored by their leader in order to move towards the Q2 quadrant is not as common as we would like.

When a group prioritizes collaboration training—*which is exactly what you're going to be prepared to do after reading this book*—the group explodes with a high population of Q2 individuals.

As the pool of available Q2 group members expands, it is from this enlarged Q2 pool that future leaders are selected. Any group that has a predominant population of Q2 leaders is where you find high performance and a very satisfied population of group members all moving the group to mission success.

Grow Q2 team members first and mission success will always follow closely behind.

Inviting, Attracting, and Cultivating Collaborative Power promote Q2 thinking and Q2 actions keeping everybody, including you, in the prefrontal cortex and appropriately avoiding the amygdala at every opportunity while navigating complex human systems at the same time.

This book is designed to help you become a Q2 follower for your boss and a Q2 leader for your direct reports.

You might already be a Q2 leader, and if you are this book will just simply enhance what you're already good at.

However, if you want to be a Q2 leader and you're not one now, understanding and implementing everything that you're reading in this book will get you there.

Full disclosure: Not everybody agrees on the type of collaboration that you will be trained in with this book. Counter to the opposition that this training might expose you to, I think after you read this book you'll be the best judge as to whether it makes sense to you to become the Q2 I'm talking about. *I'm betting what I'm about to give you in this book is going to make complete sense to you.*

IF YOU ARE ALREADY A Q2 LEADER
If you are already a Q2 leader and you're looking for a guide to help your direct reports to become Q2s as well, this book is an excellent training manual. I know that sounds self-serving but I've already done all the work for you, so why wouldn't you take advantage of it?

NORMALIZED MEDIOCRE PERFORMANCE

NOT BAD PEOPLE

The powerless leader who wants to do well, who wants to build collaboration within their group, who wants to experience a high-performing group, who wants to be able to support the people that follow them and support their boss's agenda but doesn't know how to develop any of these outcomes *lives an extremely frustrated life on a daily basis.*

These are not bad people. They work hard and mean well but unfortunately, to some degree, they are ineffective. They are trapped and need help getting out of the mess they find themselves in that, indeed, *is a mess they didn't create* but sometimes unknowingly propagate, simply because their response to what they've been handed is ineffective, typically due to their being overwhelmed by processes that they have little power to change.

This is exactly what the Collaborative Power Grab can change by empowering the people you work for and also empowering the people that work for you and then receiving back permission from your supervisor to excel and support from your direct reports in the form of high performance.

The area most ripe for improvement as well as the area most ripe for finding fault is the world's inability to support and empower these hopeful *someday-collaborative-leaders* due to a ubiquitous phenomenon I call *normalized mediocre performance.*

Normalized mediocre performance is a fire built, and also unfortunately a fire *fed*, by the very same ineffective leadership that then works against not only their own best interests but those of every leader within the group as well. What I mean by this is that normalized mediocre performance is unknowingly promoted by ineffective leaders, yet at the same time this normalized mediocre performance causes a lot of frustration for the very same leaders.

Here it is:

Normalized mediocre performance *lowers the bar of accomplishment in order to achieve success.*
Without *having to expend significant effort.*
Without *having to hurt anybody's feelings.*

Without *having to rock the boat.*
Without *having to take any risks.*

Without having to call their own concept of leadership into question and lose reputation in front of those who hired them or those who follow them.

The "without" list is near endless in my observations.

There is always an attraction and an excuse to lower the bar of accomplishment in order to achieve success by simply redefining what success is.

Not every group does this 100 percent of the time, but many groups do, to one degree or another, find themselves slightly moving the bar of accomplishment in order to redefine success. If you're finding yourself in an already highly performing group then obviously this is a rare occurrence, but it could be happening with one of your first-line supervisors who mostly operate out of sight.

These issues can be hard to remember so Figure #19 is provided as a quick guide to help you focus on what's important. .

Fig. #19: *Normalized Mediocre Performance*

ARE YOUR LEADERS HIDING BEHIND A CARDBOARD CUTOUT OF MEDIOCRITY & EXCUSES?

Normalized mediocre performance gives every leader a **get out of jail free** card.

It lets leaders off the hook from **hard decisions** & from work that challenges their *comfort zone.* Leaders need to take healthy risks to promote high performance in the group. Mediocre groups avoid healthy risk.

When leaders feel disempowered by mediocrity, they *unknowingly promote the same mediocrity that is driving them crazy.*

If everybody's making out on the deal then why in the world would there ever be an **incentive for change?** When ignoring critical group metrics, one comes to the convenient conclusion that **"we're doing just fine."**

Leader in Title Only

The calling cards of powerless leaders:

- They don't have the **force** necessary to implement a mission.
- They are are unable to protect & promote **a collaborative culture.**
- They are incapable of modeling **effective interpersonal relationships.**
- They are inept at transmitting **high-quality communication.**
- They are **technically incompetent** at what they do.
- They lack the keys to **unlocking the productivity enigma.**
- They are unconscious of the methods for **astute problem-solving.**
- They will never be able to develop a **continuous improvement strategy.**
- They don't realize that **they are suffering from a lack of power.**

WE HAVE TO ADDRESS THE AREAS WHERE WE'RE GETTING HURT, & THAT MEANS ADDRESSING NORMALIZED MEDIOCRE PERFORMANCE.

NORMALIZED VS. ENHANCED

You might remember that in an earlier section of this chapter I referenced a study found in *Corporate Culture and Performance* by John Kotter and James Heskett. You might remember that in that study they were able to prove that an enhanced environment creates high levels of performance that produce very successful outcomes in terms of net income, stock price, workforce expansion, and revenue.

I'm going to bring that chart back up here so we can actually make a different observation.

There seems to be a meme out there that says inefficient and ineffective groups naturally die off because they can't survive and you might remember that I had a severe disagreement with that conclusion.

The study also included non-enhanced cultures. These are the cultures that do pursue normalized mediocre performance *yet they didn't go out of business during the 11-year study.*

They stumble along *unimproved but just good enough to survive.* This constitutes a very large number of groups in the world community.

Increases over 11 years	Enhanced Cultures	Non-Enhanced Cultures
Net Income	+756%	+1%
Stock Price	+901%	+74%
Workforce	+282%	+36%
Revenue	+682%	+166%

With the non-enhanced cultures or what I will also call the normalized mediocre performance group, does an average annual growth rate in revenue of 15 percent keep you in business? Sure it can—you'll notice net income was essentially zero but the stock price still averaged an annual increase of almost 7 percent over the same decade. Lastly they were hiring more people each year on average with an expanding workforce of a little over 3 percent a year. So what's the big problem?

What these numbers show is that normalized mediocre performance can give you the misdirected perception that the group is excelling and growing towards mission success. But if you look at the groups that are enhanced you quickly learn that yes, that was an inaccurate perception. As long as you don't compare the groups suffering from normalized mediocre performance to the groups that have enhanced cultures, it turns out that the normalized mediocre performance groups *look just fine.*

Normalized mediocre performance also does not escape some boards or commissions that hire C-level leaders, perpetually advancing the normalized mediocre performance agenda.

Normalized mediocre performance gives every leader a "get out of jail free" card from having to make hard decisions or expend effort that calls into question their current level of success. It gets leaders off the hook from taking the risks *they're supposed to be taking in order to promote the high performance of the group.*

Regardless, it is nonetheless a very disempowering situation for the leaders in the group. And as the leaders become successively more disempowered it encourages them to continue to promote, unknowingly, the same mediocre performance that's driving them crazy.

With normalized mediocre performance, if everybody's making out on the deal then why in the world would there ever be an incentive to change?

If the budget is stable and overhead costs aren't too high, nobody is getting fired, and complaints are relatively low, then what are the incentives for taking risks that promote the steps for creating a high-performing group? If you're not looking at the metrics that really count as a group, one easily comes to the conclusion that *we're doing just fine.*

As you can see there are a lot of reasons to go along with the normalization of mediocre performance, not just one reason. Ergo the reason this phenomenon is so dominant in our work groups today.

LEADER IN TITLE ONLY

Unaware of the artful best practices necessary to understand, obtain, and wield power, some appear to be leaders based on their title but suffer from one or more disabilities. They either:

- Don't have the force necessary to implement a mission
- Are unable to protect and promote a collaborative culture
- Are incapable of modeling effective interpersonal relationships
- Are inept at transmitting high-quality communication
- Are technically incompetent at what they do
- Lack the keys to unlocking the productivity enigma
- Are unconscious of the methods for astute problem-solving
- Will never be able to develop a continuous improvement strategy
- Don't realize that *a lack of power is the problem that they are suffering from*

These are the calling cards of the powerless leaders.

Listen, there is a significant number of excellent leaders out there doing a great job with their groups.

However, the groups that normalize mediocre performance hurt us more than the incredible help contributed by groups operated by great leaders. Meaning, it's not enough to have a significant number of great groups with great leaders if the world is going to move forward. We have to also address the areas where we're getting hurt. And that means addressing normalized mediocre performance.

This is one of the many reasons I am writing this book. I don't want to just empower disempowered leaders, I want their empowered groups to make this a better planet to live on.

We'll talk more about the Big 8 performance categories in another section of this book, but I'll list them here so I can use them to give you examples of how normalized mediocre performance shows up in groups in very specific terms.

The Big 8 performance categories are:

1. Mission
2. Culture
3. Effective interpersonal relationships
4. High-quality communication
5. Technical competency
6. Productivity
7. Problem-Solving
8. Continuous improvement

MEDIOCRE PERFORMANCE IN THE BIG 8
The following sections demonstrate how *normalized mediocre performance* can play out in a group within each of the Big 8 performance categories listed just above.

Mission
If people in the group are not trained on the mission, goals, and values that need to be demonstrated in the group, I can guarantee you that there is a significant amount of work that's not appropriately prioritized. This means you might have groups of priorities that look good on the surface, but let's dig a little deeper here.

If a hospital emergency room is operated like an auto shop things are not going to go well. With an auto shop it's first come, first served—after all, customers needing their cars repaired would want nothing less. But we all know what happens in an emergency room when the more important case that comes through the door is not placed in front of the less-important cases that have already arrived and are now sitting in the waiting room. One of the most frequent complaints of people sitting in waiting rooms is watching other cases be moved in front of them. Most of those complaints are resolved, however, once people acknowledge the fact that the bullet wounds and chainsaw accidents need to be moved ahead of the broken ankles and ear infections.

I'm not saying that every group has to operate like an emergency room. But what I am saying is that most groups that are *not* mission-centered *operate first come, first served* when they should be instead prioritizing the work and, if necessary, *reprioritizing the work according to the mission not according to this is what we were doing yesterday so we should just do the same thing today.* That, my friends, is no way to run a world.

Takeaway

If people are not well trained on the mission, goals, and values, and all the things that help them make good decisions, I can guarantee you in many areas embedded deeply within the group *the second-most-important thing is being done first.*

And that is the slippery slope. The moment an organization is susceptible to doing the second-most-important thing first I can also guarantee you there are areas in the group where the fifth- or 10th-most-important thing is being done first.

This hidden disaster plagues many groups, unbeknownst to hardworking and well-intentioned leaders working in a culture of normalized mediocre performance.

<u>Culture</u>

If people in the group are not held accountable to avoiding behaviors that destroy collaboration and they are not trained on promoting behaviors that *are* collaborative then you have hidden fears that are causing people to make poor decisions, and I can guarantee things are going wrong without leaders knowing it. I'll talk more about "hidden fears" later. If fear reduction is something that's new to you, you really need to take the time now to learn more about it.

I'm describing many groups here. How many groups do you know specifically have identified behaviors to avoid and behaviors to use to advance collaboration actually listed and embedded within the performance evaluation process (not just company policies, ugh) *as performance expectations* that each employee is *trained on* and *held accountable to* on a regular basis?

Because most groups remain untrained in these most essential collaborative behaviors, the disempowered leader will simply go along with the program and unknowingly promote hidden fears that then result in poor decision making.

But because the situation has been normalized they can't tell that is what is happening. The moment that collaborative skills take the same prominent role in determining a person's success in the group as their technical skills *everything changes for the better.*

Right now many groups are typically led by Q1 leaders. What we really want are Q2 leaders that can make the same hard judgments as well as they are made in the emergency room, not the auto shop.

Takeaway

Suffice it to say, and this will not come as a shock to you, people are typically promoted into leadership positions because of their past technical competency. What this means is the leadership staff is typically not populated based on a person's expertise at creating a highly collaborative high-performing mission-successful group.

Which is exactly why most groups don't have leaders who are **experts** at creating high levels of collaboration or high levels of performance and high levels of mission success based on a collaborative approach. Sure, they know how to do the technical aspects of their job, they might even manage well, but as a collaborative leader to advance super-high performance of mission success: they don't know shit from Shinola.

This is a gaping problem that is not obvious to most groups. They know something is wrong but they can't quite put their finger on it. ***Well I just put my finger on it for them.***

If we want high performance our leaders need to be collaborative experts, and if they were hired into their leadership position ***because they were good at what they did in their previous technical role*** then we've got a problem that needs solving.

Effective Interpersonal Relationships

If people in the group are not trained in how to create professional relationships, and if creating professional relationships is not a performance expectation for every person in the group, I can guarantee you we could make huge progress in building a higher-performing team by simply incorporating this into a group performance metric.

There are huge opportunities for higher productivity here but if we normalize mediocre performance nobody wants to take the risk. Somehow holding people accountable for creating professional relationships, while an essential attribute in a high-performing collaborative group, is nonetheless not seen as a necessary activity in a group that's already accepted normalized mediocre performance.

Instead, in a group that has accepted normalized mediocre performance teaching people how to create professional relationships is seen as a high-risk activity. In a normalized group it becomes hard to imagine people being trained on how to create trust-filled professional relationships by teaching people dignity and respect in how they treat and talk to each other.

Takeaway

How people treat each other is important. I know we all already agree with that statement. But at the same time, if it's so important why don't we have ***performance expectations*** that describe how people should treat each other?

If we want people to develop professional relationships and we don't give them the training on how to do that and we don't give them performance expectations that hold them accountable for using the training then one of the most important things we could possibly do in any human group and in any situation where we want a high-performing group is being completely, 100 percent ignored!

High-Quality Communication

If people in the group are not trained and not given direction defining how communication should occur within the group I can guarantee you things are going wrong, but you can't tell. Let me explain.

You can't prove a negative. ***In other words, we can't prove that we lost an opportunity for higher performance based on the lack of high-quality communication.*** In the passive sense we don't know what opportunity was missed because the improved communication didn't occur ***so it's impossible to measure a missed opportunity***.

And if you're already a very busy leader, and no doubt you are, if you can't measure something then it's not part of the conversation in your group. I'm here to tell you that if we're not now paying attention to high-quality communication then amount of opportunity that could be available to us that's not available to us now ***is jaw-dropping***.

Takeaway

This starts to fall under the category of non-violent non-cooperation or perhaps even passive violence.

No one is intentionally looking the other way, but because we don't even realize there was a lost opportunity from a lack of high-quality communication we have no idea that we have the problem.

If people are not trained and are not held accountable towards using high-quality communication and ***instead are just relied upon to do the right thing based on their life experience***, we have no understanding of the magnitude of this problem.

When you combine reducing fear in the culture with higher expectations for interpersonal relationships and then add high-quality communication then we can start to avoid the nightly news replication process.

Anytime we rely on people to do the right thing based on their life experience instead of our group ***performance expectations and the training necessary to support those expectations*** related to a fear-reducing culture or effective interpersonal relationships and high-quality communication, we are setting ourselves up for dismal failure if we want a high-performing group.

The opportunity for increasing group performance by giving people training and performance expectations necessary for high-quality communication is simply so profound we typically have no idea how significant it is until we actually start changing it. Leaders who just don't acknowledge this issue are simply creating a group of people who are hardworking, well intentioned, and missing out on the hidden opportunities found within better communication as a performance expectation within the group.

Technical Competency

If people in the group are not constantly trained on their weakest skill set first, the group is experiencing an extraordinary amount of risk that could be reduced for the lowest possible cost.

The world is pathetically undertrained. Go watch how people drive, or how people deal with each other during a conflict, or almost any situation that either requires more than one activity within a short time span or an issue that requires multiple sequenced dynamic thinking patterns in order to devise the best outcome for a given situation.

In the group that has normalized mediocre performance they compare their training program to similar agencies or organizations through benchmarking and reassure themselves that they're keeping pace with their competition. And that approach is complete bullshit if we want to improve.

When one group that has normalized mediocre performance compares themselves with another group that has normalized mediocre performance or a group of other groups that have normalized mediocre performance, how are we going to improve?

I know the process can help create improvements if the study includes groups that are experiencing an extraordinarily higher performance than the rest of the groups compared to—in other words, if we find outliers of high performance from the group of groups that have normalized mediocre performance. However, if the outlier doesn't exist *everybody takes solace from at least being competitive within the pack*. That's the problem.

Titanic lifeboats were half full; they had room for hundreds more people. But because the training drills had been not performed as anticipated and as required, the junior officers were not familiar with the new rigging system. During the disaster a junior officer felt that the rigging of the lifeboats would not have supported a full lifeboat. It turns out that that was not true but his best judgment was not based on good training but rather his best estimate at the time. It turns out his judgment was horribly wrong. He was doing the best he could based on what he knew, *but he didn't know any better because of a lack of training*. As a result numerous lifeboats were lowered into the water half full and literally hundreds of lives are lost that could have been saved, all because of a lack of training.

It's important that we don't place the blame on this junior officer. We have a tendency to scapegoat the individual when in fact it would be more appropriate if we place the blame on senior management that decided to not go through with the training as required.

Yet another example where the incompetence of a single individual was actually based in the lack of training. We see this same mistake repeated over and over again.

Takeaway

We want to accelerate training each person on their weakest skill set first and then work our way up from the bottom for every single person in the organization.

The other issue here that goes unseen is that when somebody is technically incompetent we never know when that's going to show up because we haven't done the hard work to find out what they don't know. The reason this is such a cancer in so many organizations is because when the incompetency shows up it is blamed on the individual when in fact the true cause might be instead a slightly dysfunctional training program that looks nice on the outside but is selectively incompetent on the inside. What leader wants to admit that to themselves?

This is a stunning example of how the disempowered leader helps to promote normalized mediocre performance.

Remember this: *the blame for incompetency can be misdirected towards the individual if you have not first confirmed the true source of the issue to be a flaw in the training program.*

What we need to do is not only blame supervisors for the lack of performance of their crew as we typically do but also *start blaming training programs for the lack of performance of their trainees.*

Don't tell me it doesn't make sense. There are too many situations where people who do not adequately pass the minimum criteria for being able to produce optimal outcomes are nonetheless given a passing grade after their training has been completed.

That is the ubiquitous signature of the normalized mediocre performance we see before us on our planet.

If we want to create a better world and at the same time have more people using their training and being able to pass the minimum qualifications of their training program, *then we must increase the quality and increase the quantity of training* and we will move this world forward away from normalize mediocre performance.

Not everybody learns at the same pace, not everybody learns using the same types of tools, not everybody responds to the narrow set of lesson plans we might hold, as trainers, in high esteem. If this is new news to us as trainers, we are definitely part of the problem.

If we want groups to advance away from normalized mediocre performance we need to accept the fact that in order to progress we need to start looking at how we train people, how they learn, and what we can do to improve the training experience in order to increase the number of people passing their minimum qualifications, instead of letting leaders and trainers off the hook and just scapegoating the trainees for all the failures that will undoubtedly show up in the future.

Productivity

Are we measuring productivity?

IF we're not measuring it **THEN** we don't know what it is.

In every single case that I know about when a leader doesn't know what their productivity rates are or they are not including productivity as part of their performance expectations training program, the actual productivity the group is experiencing *is ALWAYS much lower than what it can be and should be if we are wanting a high-performing collaborative group that meets mission success.*

Are there any performance expectations that hold people accountable for productivity levels? If not, that's a risk disempowered leaders will never take because they know that if you start setting deadlines for people when they are used to working without them the pushback from the group can be very uncomfortable for that low-performing leader. In this situation, what's the incentive for them to require people to stick to deadlines?

In a group where there are no deadlines, essentially everybody starts to become independent contractors setting their own deadlines. Does that sound like high performance? Does that sound like mission success?

Takeaway

- When directives are issued:
  - Are they assigned to a specific person that is now held directly responsible for completing the task?
  - Is the objective of the directive specifically and clearly defined for the person receiving the directive?
  - Is the objective achievable based on the time resources available to the person responsible?
  - *Is there a deadline attached to that directive?*
  - *Is there a discussion about the deadline?*
  - Is there a step-by-step process that determines the individual receiving the directive has the training necessary to provide an expert level of response in meeting the directive safely and effectively?

- ° Is the person receiving the directive given the incentive to come up with a better way to do it faster, easier, and less expensively (or any combination thereof), and are they encouraged and given the recognition for developing a better approach?
- ° Is the person told that you'll be available to help with unexpected roadblocks that come up?

Is anyone even asking these questions about a directive before they issue it?

Or is it just a top-down, *do as I say* directive? Or a directive *with no deadline*? If so, egads, we have a giant problem.

In our organizations are there any performance expectations that address the issue of deadlines not being met?

It's important that deadlines are established so as to avoid damage to the group and they should not be established willy-nilly. If deadlines are established to avoid damage to the group that means when deadlines are not met the group is damaged; therefore, there need to be consequences for not meeting deadlines if everything else is in place to support success.

That kind of talk is a little too scary for a lot of groups that participate in normalized mediocre performance and certainly for every disempowered leader.

The fact is if we train our people to expert levels, give them achievable objectives, and make the supervisor available for removing unexpected roadblocks we can then hold people accountable to expected outcomes based on the training that they've been provided.

If we also simultaneously are quick to recognize their brilliant efforts at improving upon the outcome that we've asked for our group productivity will skyrocket:

One directive at a time, one person at a time, one empowered leader at a time.

Problem-Solving
Problem-solving requires a higher cognitive function that's not connected to our typical definitions for intelligence. People that are considered really smart make some of the dumbest decisions I've ever seen.

There is a certain process necessary to recognizing a problem, understanding a problem, examining the problem, and then, yes, ultimately solving the problem. Many problems don't get solved simply because they are not initially seen as a problem at all. The inability to recognize a problem that's starting to occur is probably the most significant impediment to solving problems. It goes without saying (or at least it should) that a problem not recognized is a problem not solved.

The other big fat problem about problems is that nobody uses a specific well-trained, well-disciplined problem-solving process when they're asked to solve problems in the group. Just because a person is able to acquire shelter for themselves, get a driver's license, and carry on a reasonable conversation doesn't mean they're a good problem solver.

Additionally, leaders don't necessarily have an incentive to find more problems and add them to their ever-growing list of problems needing solutions. I'm not accusing leaders of doing this on purpose but you will find in groups with a penchant for normalized mediocre performance that unempowered leadership behaviors are often guided by incentives and disincentives and not necessarily a compass point that is saying "*it might be the hard thing to do but it's also the right thing to do.*"

Certainly it's smart to design a system of incentives for actions you desire in the group and disincentives for actions you want your group members to avoid. But sometimes the achievement of mission success calls for a compass heading that requires you to swim upstream, meeting resistance all the way until the group also starts to acclimate to the new compass heading.

My observation is that if the resistance is too high and leaders find themselves in a place of normalized mediocre performance and they are unknowingly contributing to that same dilemma, *they're not going choose the compass heading required for mission success if it also means they will encounter significant resistance.*

Does that make sense to you? Have you had similar observations?

Additionally, if I am a lower-level under-empowered leader that's not supported by a good training program for my people or inadequate resources coming from above, *why in the world would I add yet another problem to my overflowing basket of unsolved problems?*

Takeaway
A person's life experiences does not necessarily prepare them to be a good problem solver.

Some people have good intuition that works in their favor from time to time when solving problems, but some of the most disgusting solutions to some of the most challenging problems that have ever been invented have come from a person's *gut*. Yeah, go with your gut, that's always the best way, right? Wrong.

We have a seemingly endless list of examples taken from human history that show the incredibly flawed way in which humans think that destroys their ability to solve problems. And the more complex the problem the worse it gets. In other words, the more complex the problem the more elusive an effective solution.

I give you as examples the two space shuttle failures. I know that 20-20 hindsight is harsh. But in my training classes I go through the decision-making processes that were used that ultimately created unsolved problems that caused these multi-billion-dollar disasters and the loss of 14 dear souls. As I step through those scenarios you start to understand just how egregious, how misplaced, and just how horribly wrong people's attempts at problem-solving can go.

Challenger. The O-rings for the solid rocket booster had not been tested below 32° so an engineer with contractor Morton Thiokol recommended that the flight not go forward until the booster rockets warmed up later in the day. Morton Thiokol management initially backed their engineer's recommendation. But NASA management was under a lot of pressure to get *Challenger* in space because of the multiple highly public canceled launches of the *Challenger*'s now-famous teacher-in-space flight. When Morton Thiokol informed NASA management of their decision to not recommend a launch until things warmed up a bit out at the launch pad, some of the NASA flight managers were apoplectic. The phone dialogue between the two management teams was extremely confrontational. While there were also NASA engineers who were highly concerned about the issue, once NASA management found out that it could not be verified that the O-rings wouldn't work below 32° because they had not been tested, and that the primary O-ring had failed before but was always successfully backed up by the secondary O-ring, averting past shuttle launch disasters, NASA management pressured Morton Thiokol management and they relented and gave a **_Go for the_ Challenger _launch_**.

If you reread this last paragraph a couple times you can find a boatload of really poor problem-solving at multiple intersections. Suffice it to say that because NASA management **_had narrowly escaped past disasters more than once their risk aversion started to inappropriately decline at just the right moment_**. This lowered risk aversion came in handy when they needed to respond to the political pressure to launch the teacher into space. This small group of NASA managers was able to convince themselves that the decision to launch was the right decision. The pressure to launch now evoked by the highly public cancellations, one after another, then cemented the wrong decision in their minds as being the right decision. In this sense this is not just a problem with the individuals involved but a problem with the culture in general, which started to become inappropriately less risk averse because past O-ring failures did not create an adverse outcome.

It was only later that we found out that NASA's Associate Administrator for Space Flight and the Launch Director **_were never told_** about the knockdown drag-out fight that had been going on for 24 hours between some of the NASA managers and the Morton Thiokol group (with every engineer on both sides telling their bosses to not launch). As we discovered during the investigation, the communication pipeline to the NASA Associate Administrator for Space Flight and the NASA Launch Director had been plugged **_purposely_** along the way by a few people who thought they were making the right decisions.

Columbia. Upon launch of this space shuttle some of the foam separated from the liquid fuel tank. This had happened before on multiple launches with no harm done so concerns were mostly sidelined. Are we seeing a trend here? If you narrowly escaped disaster multiple times it's now something you don't have to worry about? From the standpoint of some of the NASA engineers, however, there was something different about this particular incident. Not only was it a fairly large piece of foam, it came down just at the right spot where they thought it may have hit the leading edge of the shuttle wing. Before NASA engineers contacted NASA management they sent a request to the Defense Department to see if they could swing their satellite-mounted telescope to inspect the wing in space. When NASA management caught wind of this plan they nixed it. A long series of horrible decisions followed.

Suffice it to say that during meetings the NASA managers in charge inappropriately decided even if there was a hole in the wing there was nothing they could do about it. The *Columbia* crew was not alerted to the concerns of NASA engineers and they reentered the atmosphere thinking everything was fine. As we know they burned up upon reentry because of the hole in the wing caused by the foam separation during the launch.

As it turns out a spacewalk or an inspection of some type, of which they had several options, may have determined whether there was in fact a hole in the leading edge of the wing. If there was a hole discovered in the wing, in hindsight the options for rescue were limited, however, the *Atlantis* shuttle was already being prepped and, according to the *Columbia* Accident Investigation Board (CAIB) report, while mounting a rescue was challenging, *it was feasible* (page 174). Feasible but never given a chance because it was drowned in a culture of lousy decision making and abysmal problem-solving.

And just in case we are thinking that this can't happen to our group, the fact is NASA was and is still considered a high-end, super-effective agency even though it did have its challenges. So if it can happen to them it can happen to our group too if we're not paying attention to the right things.

One last note from the CAIB report:

"Cultural traits and organizational practices detrimental to safety were allowed to develop, including: reliance on past success as a substitute for sound engineering practices (such as testing to understand why systems were not performing in accordance with requirements); organizational barriers ... prevented effective communication of critical safety information *and stifled professional differences of opinion*; lack of integrated management across program elements; and *the evolution of an informal chain of command and decision-making processes that operated outside the organization's rules*."

Unfortunately if you read the 1986 *Challenger* report you find some of the same organizational deficits they found here in 2003. Yep, 17 years later, the culture either had never changed or had reverted back to its myopic view of risk, reassured and lowering their guard over a series of near misses thinking that "we'll be okay" and no longer served by having the sting of the *Challenger* disaster in their recent rearview mirror.

It can be very hard for groups to change even when faced with catastrophic disasters that, looked back upon, could have been avoided.

There is so much going on there it's head spinning, so let's close up this section with clarity:

If we want to advance problem-solving in our group, we need to:

A. teach people the myriad of ways in which problems go unrecognized and how to now recognize them (I will be providing this later in the book), then

B. teach them a systematic problem-solving system (I will also be providing this later in the book), and then

C. hold them accountable for using both A and B as performance expectations (that's something you'll have to do, but I'll be giving some guidance on that as well).

I know this process seems oversimplified and I'm here to tell you A, B, and C are the keys to unlocking the treasure chest full of solutions that you need in order to get problems solved that then leads to the high performance necessary to support mission success.

If you do as I will be coaching later in the book, the problem about problem-solving starts to get solved.

Continuous Improvement
People are naturally inventive and most of the good ideas that are going to improve your group come from the people *that are actually doing the work*.

You need every brain in the game to increase performance, and while it is probably more fashionable to ask people what they think actually putting a program in place that guarantees continuous improvement is typically out of the reach of most groups.

There are two forms of continuous improvement.

One is continuous improvement in execution by giving people the recognition and recovery skills necessary to execute their performance expectations.

Two is teaching people how to pursue smart-think and smart-work techniques to use in developing ideas that allow the group to create high-quality outcomes for less time and less money.

Takeaway
Simply training people and helping them to determine what a good idea is for improvement before they submit it creates a huge advantage for the process of continuous improvement.

I help you do that. Part of the problem is everybody thinks their idea is a good idea so when they get turned down they feel rejected and they stop submitting ideas for improvement. The solution to this problem is to train them in advance about how their idea will be judged so they can determine whether they want to submit it or improve it before they submit it and therefore avoid the feelings of rejection.

The other component of an effective continuous improvement strategy is that the decision to try new things needs to be risked based by the empowered leader. Risked based decision making involves asking several questions concerning benefits as compared to costs and as compared to causing other problems as a result of implementing this improvement idea (See Appendix 5: Submitting Ideas for Improvement SOP)

Along with that review process the empowered leader should be asking one additional question: **what are the risks associated with not implementing the new idea?**

Leaders that are not empowered are risk averse, which means they're not weighing the risks, which means they do not try new things, which means the group does not improve to levels of high performance necessary for mission success. Additionally, by also not asking the question concerning the risks associated with **not implementing an improvement idea** the lost opportunity is never recognized as a lost opportunity. It's a very simple sickness that infects every group I've ever seen **that is systematically risk averse.** Yet another example of the normalized mediocre performance group; unrecognized lost opportunities. In groups that systematically avoid exploring opportunities they then typically never recognize the lost opportunities.

By giving people a process by which they can measure risk, risk taking becomes a solid decision-making process instead of the notorious shoot-in-the-dark approach most people assume it to be.

I have found that most leaders who are risk averse have never been trained on how to assess risk, so they run for safety in an attempt to hermetically seal themselves from risk. And of course this outcome means much less performance from the group than what would normally have been otherwise achieved.

When you have a high population of risk-averse leaders in your leadership group you can actually watch the multiple opportunities that would promote your group towards high-performance mission success **circling the drain just before they disappear forever.**

Forever.

WHY POWERLESS LEADERS DON'T HAVE POWER

The powerless become that way or remain that way based on a myriad of reasons. **The purpose of this section is to outline to you what a disempowered work environment looks like so you can recognize it when you see it.**

I thought long and hard about not including this content in the book. I wanted to focus in on the positive aspects of the types of behaviors you want to pursue in order to Invite, Attract, and Cultivate Collaborative Power in your group as a leader.

At the same time, *if you don't know* what's going wrong with the leadership team, *if you don't know* what is disempowering your fellow leaders, *then you don't know what is going wrong and you don't know what behaviors to avoid.*

What I'm about to describe for you is what the disempowered workplace looks like *when leaders cannot Invite Collaborative Power from the Top Down, when leaders can't Attract Collaborative Power from the Bottom Up, and when they can't Cultivate Collaborative Power from the workplace landscape.*

As you read this section try to remember that we are not talking bad about good people, necessarily. I say "necessarily" because while they might say some rather disturbing things (that I'm about to share), they're saying them out of ignorance. So yes these people can be hardworking and well intentioned but again very ineffective based on their ignorance and incompetence. In order to understand what not to do, it's essential that we talk about some of the highly dysfunctional actions demonstrated by people who hold leadership positions.

Even neutral leaders damage their groups horribly, in a passive sense. Doing nothing or avoiding uncomfortable situations hurt people. When action is necessary in order to protect the people in the work group and that same action is not taken the group is damaged, and so is mission success. Workplace issues like bullies or the lack of safety rules can be the hallmarks of leaders that don't feel comfortable holding people accountable for their behaviors. So in that sense neutral leaders are not necessarily bad people but they do damage by taking a passive approach to their work life because they want to avoid uncomfortable situations.

In my descriptions below I will move from the tendencies of the neutral leader to those who are highly dysfunctional because they either have significant character flaws or they have psychological problems or they are horribly incompetent and perhaps just because they have a very distorted set of assumptions they use to operate their leadership lives.

Starting from the neutral leader all the way to the horribly incompetent leader, as long as they're in charge of other people's work lives they have a significant negative impact on those people that can even spill into their personal lives.

I have personal experience with every disempowered leader I will be describing below.

Psychological Projection-ist

One supervisor was quick to judge and develop a perception about other people. He didn't really spend the time to tease out and learn about others but he nonetheless prided himself on being able to make a quick study of those people around him and those that worked for him. The moment he had gained his perception, that was it, he knew he had the truth about the other person. And in practice he was not even close in his assessments. Regardless of whether it reflected reality, if it was a perception he held of you *as true* then it became a reality to him. However unfair this is, it's simply a fact that some people make snap judgments and that wrongful perception is now wrapped around the neck of a person who works for that supervisor. Unearned fault, misdirected inscription into the something-that's-really-wrong hall of fame. This is essentially the same thing as psychological projection, which is a process whereby people assign certain negative or positive qualities upon another person while having no real proof that the qualities that they are assigning to the other person have any basis in fact whatsoever. And truth be known, most humans do this to one extent or the other.

Know It ALL
Another supervisor had a nasty habit that went something like this: if you disagree with me that means *you are automatically 100 percent completely wrong*. If this person is your boss or a fellow leader or a direct report then that attitude is going to be a problem. And just like all problems that one would need solving. If it's a fellow laterally placed leader that can be a difficult problem to solve; if it's a direct report that is something that can be solved rather easily. However if it's your boss and she wants to persist in that way of thinking the options for solving that problem is a very short list.

There a many types of issues beyond the Psychological Projection-ist and the Know-it-all, I site these examples to make you aware that *every weakness or incompetence a person might have is often carried with them, unchecked, as they advance into leadership*. The process of leaders bringing their incompetencies and character flaws, as part of their leader-manager approach, is ubiquitous for many organizations to deal with. We often are unaware of their weaknesses until it's a bit too late. Therefore, a discussion of the Peter Principle is necessary and timely.

The Peter Principle
Remember I'm not trash talking these people. They just simply have no business being in charge. In other words, this supervisor or middle manager or CEO is incompetent and everybody knows it and everybody's getting hurt by them.

This can happen for a number of reasons. One of the most typical is the Peter Principle based on the concept developed by Laurence Peter. The Peter Principle describes a situation where a person rises in the group hierarchy to the point of their incompetence and stops and oftentimes remains there.

It is a real phenomenon and it makes complete sense in that people are going to continue to be promoted as long as they're doing well. "Doing well" means they are adequately demonstrating the core competencies that the position requires. The moment they advance to a position where they are not demonstrating performance that meets the core competencies, they will stop advancing, and in an organization with normalized mediocre performance a lot of times they won't be fired but just remain at their level of incompetency.

If you are in an organization that does not fire incompetent people or demote incompetent leaders, chances are that right now you have some of the people that Laurence Peter talked about in your group, where they remain doing damage every day they walk through the door.

When I found that I had inadvertently promoted people to their level of incompetence and it was compromising their ability to remain as an employee, instead of firing them I demoted them back to their level of competence.

These types of situations are uncomfortable for everybody but when you give the opportunity for people to shine again by moving them back down to their level of competency it's certainly a better alternative been firing them in most cases. But it takes a while for the hurt to go away and I've ended up with some extraordinary results and that person was able to continue their employment which allow them to support their family.

Specific Examples – Inability to Invite, Attract, or Cultivate Collaborative Power.
Now let me get into the specifics of the areas every leader should be concerned about when managing their Collaborative Power Grab by Inviting, Attracting, or Cultivating Collaborative Power.

I've never met a leader that has actively demonstrated all of the following behaviors. But I have seen every one of these issues demonstrated by different leaders and yes, in some cases several of these issues coming from the same supervisor. However, all it takes is one, two, or three well-placed key issues that I identify in the three separate "can't" lists below and that's enough to do a significant amount of damage to the group and to the people this person leads, manages, and supervises.

What I'm about to explain in this chapter certainly tells us enough to know that they're in the wrong job, and yet here they are.

THEY CAN'T INVITE COLLABORATIVE POWER FROM THE TOP DOWN
The only way you can invite more collaborative power from your supervisor and those more senior in the leadership stack is to convince them to share power you. And the only way you convince them to share power with you is to demonstrate that it is to their advantage to give you some of their power. The most effective way to convince your superiors to give you more power is to invite it based on your demonstrated behaviors employed specifically for that purpose. How you do that is outlined in detail in this book.

It just so happens the more power they share with you based on the actions I'm giving you in this book the more empowered they actually become as well. As leaders share power with other competent leaders, both leaders make out on the deal. As one collaborative leader shares a piece of their power pie their piece of the power pie is not getting smaller. What's happening is both of your pieces are getting larger because when leaders share power the whole pie is getting larger. Excuse the metaphor but it applies. You want more collaborative power so you have the power to positively impact the lives of the people above you and the lives of the people below you and, quite frankly, positively impact your own life too. It should go without saying but I'll say it here: people that have more power usually enjoy more personal freedom and typically enjoy a better income. Everybody is winning here as long as your power grab has a compass point that supports the people in your group and your group's mission statement.

In this section I am going to give you examples of how the powerless leader makes horrible mistakes that convince their supervisor and their senior supervisors to never, ever share power with them. These are things you should not do as a leader if you want to better manage how you are perceived by your supervisor.

Here are some of the mistakes leaders make with their supervisor:

- They don't have a relationship with their boss. Or they might but it's a contentious relationship.
- They don't empathize with their boss's agenda or the problems they're facing.
- In fact, they're not even aware of the problems their boss is facing because they've never thought it was important to ask.
- They just think it's important to issue directives and follow directives. And after that nothing extra is really required of them—after all, they can't do their supervisor's job for them. Why in the world would they be expected to do that?
- They have no idea what challenges are being faced by the larger group, their department, or their division because they haven't bothered to find out. They haven't found out because...? (You supply the answer here.)
- Look, they already have enough problems to solve on their own; why be an idiot and just add to my own list of problems? Really, everybody should just stay in their lane and just do their job.

Here are some examples as to why invitations made by a direct report to gain more collaborative power are not being well received by their supervisor. In this situation, these are issues with the *direct report*, not the supervisor.

They are not collaborative.
Either because they just don't know how—in other words, they're incompetent at being collaborative—or they don't believe that collaboration is important in a human enterprise.

- If the boss notices that, for example, people are not getting along and that their direct report is not dealing with people problems adequately or in a timely fashion, this disempowers the direct report in the supervisor's eyes. If I'm that person's supervisor, why would I hand over power to somebody who is obviously not doing a good job with human collaboration?

They don't see the big picture.

They aren't savvy to the mission or management by objective or the strategic objectives of the larger group or division, department, etc. Nor do they know the pain and agony suffered by their boss or senior management.

- When a direct report is not empathetic to the needs of their boss or the larger organization, it shows. They are just myopically centered on their own world and their boss and senior management know this because the person is mystified when called upon to do something unusual or extra or new. It requires the supervisor to do a lot more heavy lifting to get his point across as to what problems he wants his direct report to be working on. And if a person is not going into their supervisor's office asking: "Hey, boss, do you have anything going on you think I can help you out with?" then these disempowered leaders are missing a massive opportunity to Invite Collaborative Power.

They don't lead effectively.

They inadvertently commingle leadership initiatives and management functions, which are two completely different areas for people who are in leadership-management hierarchies. See Appendix 6 for a comprehensive guide on this subject.

- This is a long list but let me mention just a few here. They don't create a culture that protects success when what they should be doing is eliminating any procedure that moves the group away from mission success. If you're this person's supervisor you'll notice problems popping up that could've been avoided. If they're not focusing on the important stuff as leaders are supposed to, eventually all that unfinished important business is going to land on the boss's desk.

They don't manage well.

Managers that are overworked (and most are, in a group with normalized mediocre performance) can often feel satisfied because they are very busy. Obviously being very busy doesn't necessarily mean you're getting a lot of things done, nor does it mean you're getting the right things done, but this is how very busy managers can see themselves. It's not unusual for a very busy manager to stay that way because they're not training the people underneath them to take on some additional responsibilities so they can move stuff off their desk and then take on some of the problems their boss is suffering from. All of this shows.

- Again another very long list but let me hit on a few important ones. Solid problem-solving is a pretty important aspect of the management function, especially when it comes to technical issues or troubleshooting. If a person is not good at this and there are problems starting to show up on their supervisor's desk that the supervisor thinks the direct report should have been able to solve, that is bad news for the direct report that's trying to invite power from their supervisor. A good manager is also good at communicating complex concepts in usable terms and if their supervisor gets the impression that their direct reports can't do that, again it's not a good look.

They don't manage resources well.

"Resources" might be money or time or both. They're constantly making excuses about needing more money or more time to complete the directives that they've been given. They're not asking at the beginning of the process, which is where they need to get these questions asked and answered. Instead they are informing their supervisor that they need more time or more money moments before the deadline. So now we have two problems, right? Not managing resources and not communicating. It's not unusual that these two things go hand in hand simply because the direct report is incentivized to not communicate knowing that they'll probably get dinged for their lack of resource management because that's what happened the last time they failed to properly manage resources. Makes sense?

- Nothing is going to drive the boss crazier than when the direct report fails to communicate particularly sensitive items and then does so very late in the process. Meanwhile the deadline lapses, hurting the group and now adding insult to injury because the short-notice request means the supervisor has to now add more money or more time to reach the solution that they were asking for originally. If this happens enough the face of that direct report is seared on to the brain of the supervisor and things are not going to go well for the direct report if it keeps happening. Sound like someone you would share power with? Not.

Here is a recap about why the invitation for power is avoided by a person's supervisor:

- They don't prioritize well and don't prioritize the boss's needs.
- They don't stop destructive behavior when it's their job to do so and the results land on the boss's desk.
- They are unable to resolve conflicts between employees when it is their job to do so and the results land on the boss's desk.
- They don't communicate as well as they should be able to and it makes it more difficult for the boss to address issues.
- They complain about their boss to others. (If anybody thinks that won't get back to the boss eventually they are kidding themselves...)
- They are incompetent in some areas of their job. If their incompetence results in additional work for their supervisor they are never going to be able to invite power from their boss.

- Anytime a team lacks the adequate productivity to get the job done regardless of the reason, and it impacts the supervisor, the blame will rightfully fall directly in the lap of the direct report who is the next leadership position below them. This is another reason why the supervisor would never share power.

- A scenario where they're not solving problems, the problems land on the supervisor's desk, and the supervisor holds the opinion (correctly or incorrectly, right?) that this is a problem his direct report should have solved instead, *is a disaster*.

- If there's not a general feeling that regular improvement to the systems, processes, conditions, or work environment is occurring when the expectation is placed upon an individual to do so, that will get noticed by the supervisor and is yet another black eye that reinforces the supervisor's opinion that this direct report is somebody who cannot be trusted to take on more responsibilities.

- Lastly, if meek and risk-averse leader-managers are in management positions, it results in not having continuous improvement activity. The meek leaders always take the safest path, the path that avoids risks, the path that simultaneously avoids opportunity as well.

These issues can be hard to remember so Figure #20 is provided as a quick guide to help you focus on what's important.

Fig. #20: If They Can't Invite Collaborative Power from the Top Down

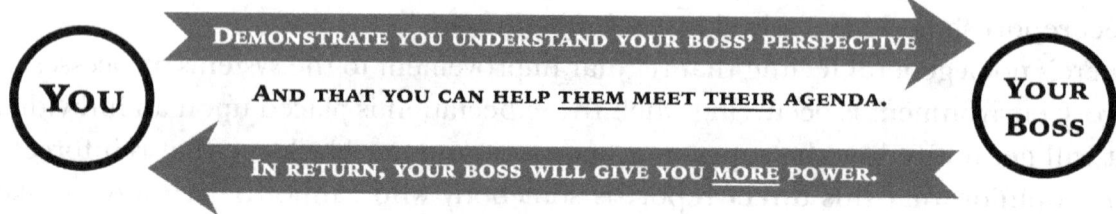

YOU → DEMONSTRATE YOU UNDERSTAND YOUR BOSS' PERSPECTIVE AND THAT YOU CAN HELP <u>THEM</u> MEET <u>THEIR</u> AGENDA. → YOUR BOSS

← IN RETURN, YOUR BOSS WILL GIVE YOU <u>MORE</u> POWER.

The only way you can invite more collaborative power from your supervisor & senior leadership is to **convince them to share power with you.**

You convince them to do this by demonstrating to them that it is **to their advantage** to **share power with you.**

Effective leaders share power with other effective leaders because **both leaders make out on the deal.** As one collaborative leader shares a piece of their power pie, their piece of the power pie actually grows.

Contrary to zero-sum thinking, when leaders share power, the **entire pie** gets larger.

More collaborative power allows you to **positively impact** the lives of the people above you, the lives of the people below you & your own life too. People that have more power also typically enjoy **more freedom** & a **better income.**

Avoid these errors to invite collaborative power from the **Top Down.**

Six Mistakes Leaders Make With Their Supervisors:

1. They have a low quality or contentious relationship with their boss.

2. They don't empathize with their boss's agenda or challenges.

3. They're not aware of the problems their boss is facing because they don't ask.

4. They know it's important to issue directives & follow directives—but don't take accountability for outcomes, mission, or the big picture.

5. They have no idea what challenges are being faced by the larger group, their department, or their division because they don't ask.

6. Look, they already have enough problems to solve on their own; "Why be an idiot and just add to my own list of problems?"

THEY CAN'T ATTRACT COLLABORATIVE POWER FROM THE BOTTOM UP

When you can convince the people that follow you that they've made a good decision by having you as their leader, it expands your power base. You are the leader—there's no doubt about it, you hold all the cards—but when you can support your people in ways they need supporting you are going to empower them to become more effective humans and therefore you will end up empowering them to be more effective employees.

As a result of those types of actions your direct reports become experts at what they do. And when you have a whole bunch of direct reports that are expert problem solvers, that are super-high produc-ers, that are innovators, and a crew that will just simply get the job done because they received expert training, *they empower you*. They give you explosive levels of performance that moves your entire team to something that's exceptional, empowering you along the way to be the exceptional leader. There's probably nothing more empowering to you as a leader than being carried along by an explosively high-performing team that knows how to meet mission success under almost any condition.

That being said if you're doing just the opposite you're going to end up with direct reports that are constantly running in the opposite direction. They're going to avoid you, they're not going to be incentivized to solve any problems, higher production only results from direct supervision, you're not going to get good ideas that support innovation, and getting the job done falls to the wayside as a typi-cal burden of the disempowered leader.

<u>Here are some of the typical thoughts of a disempowered leader when it comes to their direct reports:</u>

- I have a lot to do and I just need to keep people focused on their tasks to get things done. I really want them to just shut up and do their job.
- Building relationships is not part of the job. It's really that simple, right? All this bullshit about culture and psychological safety is just a bunch of coddling. Psychobabble, right? I never needed coddling to get the job done.
- They get the same amount of training I got when I was doing their job. They don't need more training, they just have to suck it up, figure it out on their own, and get it done, just like I did.
- It's not my job to kiss anybody's ass to get work done.
- As far as good ideas go: I'll do the thinking around here, they'll do the doing, thank you very much.
- Every time somebody shows up at my door giving me another problem it just places me fur-ther behind, so it's pretty obvious to me that the person giving me problems is the problem. ("Shooting the messenger" is a fun phrase but it's more typical than anybody wants to admit.) I have seen several examples where people presenting problems to their supervisor and notify-ing them that something was wrong resulted in a passive-aggressive move by the supervisor to

demonize the messenger. Passive-aggressive behavior on the part of humans is rather ubiquitous, though not universal. Someone who has an advanced case of passive-aggressiveness who also so happens to occupy any type of leadership position is going to be the source of massive *subliminal* problems over time.

- The world is a lot simpler than most people think, it's up or down or black or white and it's not this many shades of gray crap, that's just a distraction, that's just over-complicating something that's very simple.
- There's nothing I can do about Fred mouthing off in the lunchroom or yelling at you again. He's been doing that for the last 20 years, that's just the way he is, so do what we've been doing, just ignore him.

Now I've just given you some pretty extreme examples here.

And yes, it's unrealistic that they're all coming from the same person, but I've heard these exact statements come out of various people's mouths, *all of whom were in charge of other people at their workplace*.

It's easy to see how these people would never be able to Attract Collaborative Power from the people that work for them.

Here are some examples as to why supervisors can't Attract Collaborative Power from their direct reports:

They don't emulate the behaviors they want from others.

- When they get stressed out they start blaming the people that work for them for their problems and they act like a three-year-old throwing a temper tantrum. They are inconsistent and unpredictable when giving directives or placing any type of expectations on their direct reports. Based on these behaviors they are very difficult people to work for because you never know how they're going to react. And when it comes to dignity and respect they can't walk the talk.
  - Nobody wants to follow a person like this. Many of us have to one degree or another worked for people like this, but I'm here to tell you they are out there in droves. They create their own hell then bring it along with them wherever they go, exposing you to the same dread. People do not feel safe working for a person like this who moves everybody's thinking pattern from the prefrontal cortex into the amygdala. And as I've already noted when people are in the prefrontal cortex their mental toolbox possesses thoughts and actions that are logical, rational, and ethical. Yet when we're not feeling safe or feel disempowered we as a necessity have to go to the amygdala and our toolbox is essentially fight, flight, or freeze.

They don't protect the culture which means they're not protecting you.

- They ignore destructive behavior. They ignore conflicts between team members. It doesn't seem to matter how uncivilized things become, and as a result it's kind of a scary place to work. They don't hold people accountable for anything, practically speaking. You end up having some people do a lot less work than other people while everybody at that level is paid the same, creating a lot of resentment. This supervisor never seems to notice any of that as looking away from problems seems to be their way of solving them. They don't respond to requests for anything that's going to place them in an uncomfortable position. You would think the bullies would get their attention and that they would do something about it, but they don't, so there's a lot of fear to go around.
  - Nobody wants to work at a place like this and the moment they can move on they will. If there's anything that's going to make sure you cannot hold on to your best talent and your best employees, this type of supervisor is the number one reason.

They treat their direct reports like mushrooms.

- That's right—they keep them in the dark and just feed them shit. When someone feels or knows that you're not being transparent they feel less valued as a person. When supervisors aren't letting their people know what the big picture looks like then people will feel unimportant as a natural response to their environment. They don't feel valued and people that don't feel valued aren't going to give you a very good work product. They'll just do the absolute minimum just to get by; you'll never be able to get them to do extra. And if you're really in a jam and you need somebody to do some volunteering you can forget about it. Lastly, they never quite know what the priorities are so this type of supervisor is constantly facing the confusing situation of having people do the less-important work first.
  - Nobody wants to work for somebody who doesn't value them and is holding back information; the lack of transparency is devastating. Would you want to work for a person like this? Many are forced to do just that. Additionally when people are not given the big picture and they start having a sense that you're not being fully transparent with them it starts to make them very nervous about the potential of being rejected from the group.

They don't support their people with timely decisions and problem-solving.

- When people don't feel supported they don't really know what to do next. And they learn over time that their supervisor is not the person to ask when they need help. If productivity is so important, why aren't they making more decisions to keep things from getting stalled? That's the question the direct reports are asking themselves and it's a good one. There are certain roadblocks the direct reports don't have the authority to remove and they know their supervisor is not going remove it for them so why should they give a shit? They come into work and are constantly left dangling.

   °   No one works well in a situation like this. Supervisors who are not supporting their direct reports by making sure that problems are getting solved and roadblocks are getting removed trains the direct reports that solving problems is just not in the lexicon of this type of person—yet we find them in supervisory positions all the time. It's extremely stressful for people to not be supported by their supervisors in the areas of decision making and problem-solving.

   °   Special note: I'm sure you've heard a million times "If you bring me a problem bring me your solution too." There's actually a serious flaw in that approach. Just because the person finds a problem doesn't mean they are the best one to solve the problem. If they find a problem that they already know they can't solve and they know you're going to be asking them for a solution, well guess what? They're not going tell you about the problem and you'll never know there is a problem until it gets so large you have to find it yourself or somebody else tells you.

They don't give their people the training they need.

- When people are not getting the training that they need they feel incompetent, and when people feel incompetent they fear being humiliated. This is a fact. People that work for a supervisor like this know that they're taking a chance whenever they try to be extraordinary employees and the moment they mess up because they don't know what they're doing, they're going to be held responsible for something that is actually beyond their control to change. The entire planet is undertrained and supervisors who do not provide the training necessary for people to do their job are contributing to this problem. In situations where training isn't provided for safety-related issues, this type of behavior demonstrated by a supervisor is unconscionable. In order for people to be successful they need to be retrained on their performance expectations on a regular basis. Having very specific performance expectations like the ones I'm providing in this book and then just simply meeting every six months to dialogue about performance expectations is highly effective. If you're not regularly dialoguing concerning performance expectations *then your group members are undertrained.* People who receive *retraining* on performance expectations are psychically supported and emboldened to promote their own ability to achieve all their performance expectations. They are very empowered, become very sharp, and will become some of your highest performers.

   °   Nobody can feel good in this situation. Having expectations placed on you concerning outcomes that you cannot influence because you don't have enough training is a very difficult work situation to sustain yourself in. It sends a very clear message from the leader to the follower: *I do not care about you.*

They attempt to increase productivity by simply working people harder.

- That's right, just crack the whip harder, that's how you get more work done in a given amount of time. They increase direct supervision because they don't trust your decision making or they don't train you to make better decisions and they micromanage the hell out of you. In their mind that's the only way they know how to increase productivity. And nothing could be farther from the truth but they just don't get it. Working for somebody like this is a horrible experience. I know first-hand. They don't know how to give a directive, they're not clear on their expectations, they will often assign the directive to everybody all at the same time, and it's not unusual that the goals and objectives that they establish are not practical nor achievable. The phrase "work smarter" has never cross their mind. When it comes to issuing the deadline they can be unreasonable, causing short-term overtime that suddenly cuts into a person's personal time off. This is more than just being discourteous, it's preventable, and the lack of planning on the part of the supervisor creates a lot of resentment.
  - Nobody wants to work for a supervisor like this, and these are the types of supervisors people start referring to as *jerks*. Short notice, no planning, unclear objectives, and unachievable deadlines (unless you move heaven and earth to get there) create pure misery. What turns this sad story into a tragedy is that it's all preventable.

They don't want to hear your opinion about anything.

- They don't think the people that work for them have a brain in their head and as a result, these direct reports feel undervalued and disrespected at a human level not just an employee level. It's frustrating and disrespectful and meanwhile, given the opportunity and the training otherwise, everyone in the group could be solving problems and developing and innovating new ways of doing things that could increase productivity—and not only would this excite the group but it would make the supervisor look good to their supervisor too, right? But they just don't get it. Now there are a lot of reasons why that might be that are too long to go into here. Suffice it to say this supervisor will never Attract Power from the Bottom Up.
  - Nobody wants to go into work and constantly feel undervalued and that's exactly what's happening here. Everyone in a supervisory position should know by now you want every brain in the game and that you need innovation just to stay even. These types of supervisors are still out there. I can guarantee you.

They don't mentor their direct reports.

- Part of the job of any supervisor, at a minimum level, is mentoring their direct reports. And this is implemented in two ways. One is when the supervisor gives feedback to an individual who is suffering from less-than-standard performance. This is not corrective action, this is training. The second method that should be employed by the supervisor is to make sure they are appropriately mentoring their staff by encouraging them beyond a standard level of performance by raising their sights and assisting them to increase their level of performance to above standard or outstanding. The mentoring takes place by giving specific feedback that encourages the employee to do this. Certainly this behavior is self-serving for the supervisor because higher-functioning direct reports positively impact their output as a leader, but at the same time it also significantly empowers the direct report, so everybody's making out on this deal. When a person is performing in a less-than-standard rating of performance the supervisor *is required to give them feedback so they can improve their performance*. There is no shortage of supervisors who do not give feedback to employees who are suffering from less-than-standard performance. This disempowers the organization, it disempowers the supervisor, and it disempowers the employee in question. *Everybody loses.*

° Nobody's going to give this supervisor power. There is no doubt that when people receive feedback from their supervisor concerning their less-than-standard performance they're not very happy about it, especially if they think the supervisor is incorrect. Everyone knows, however, that the supervisor has an obligation to help individuals correct less-than-standard performance and every time the supervisor either improves the performance of someone who is suffering from less-than-standard performance or mentors a direct report who is missing an opportunity to accelerate and empower themselves with higher levels of performance we have found the supervisor who has succeeded in their mentoring role. The supervisor not appropriately mentoring their direct reports makes for a horrible workplace. Lastly, when individuals are suffering from less-than-standard performance and it remains uncorrected that usually means other people are doing more work they shouldn't have to. Whether you're laying bricks or collecting facts for a report, it's always true. This supervisor is just relying on other people to pull up the slack from those that are not doing what they need to do to contribute to the work, and the other direct reports that are having to pull up the slack know it, and it builds resentment. The number of supervisors that feel uncomfortable giving feedback to a person who is suffering from less-than-standard performance and therefore don't do it *are like stars in the sky*. And the number of people who feel some resentment for having to work with people who are performing at a less-than-standard level of performance can be found *everywhere*.

They don't help people recover after making an error.

• They just see people making the same mistake twice as something that is typical. They see different people making the same mistake as typical. *And they see typical as unavoidable.* When you combine the two it means the way they see the world is that most mistakes are unavoidable, it's just the way it is. So, they don't do anything to prevent the mistake in the future. Instead they punish and penalize the person making the mistake or error in their attempt *to punish their way to success. Supervisors attempting to punish their way to success are not rare and they are essentially following the current penal philosophies of the greater society.* I'm not saying there isn't a place for punishment, I'm just saying it's grossly overused as an instrument that has already proven itself to not be effective. What this supervisor doesn't realize is that if you have somebody on your team making the same mistake twice it's completely avoidable. What this supervisor doesn't realize is that if you have two different people making the same mistake it's probably a flaw in the training program and that as well is avoidable. Analyzing mistakes or errors, gaining an understanding of how they occurred and figuring out the preventative measures that could be taken instead, and then taking those preventative measures and incorporating them as teachable moments in future training programs result in the chances of the same mistakes being made dropping significantly and the resulting performance of the entire group improves, one person at a time but from a systematic approach to increasing the effectiveness of the training program. This approach is the reason the United States has the best fighter pilots in the world. However, these supervisors who continue to approach success by engaging various forms of punishment aren't very good at learning new ways of doing things. You can hit them with these words like a 2 x 4 in the forehead and they still won't believe you because they're just so used to using an ineffective and misdirected approach—in their simple world, punishing people and firing people when they make a mistake seems to be the most reasonable approach. Don't get me wrong, some people do need to be fired, but it's going to be for reasons that are far more significant than somebody simply making a series of mistakes.

- ° No one wants to work for a supervisor who is quick to punish mistakes or errors that in hindsight one recognizes could've been prevented. But prevented by whom? And prevented how? Pray tell a better training program, perhaps? When people work in an environment like this they become extremely risk averse and their work patterns become robotic, eliminating any possibility of risk by doing the least amount of work possible (because doing something extraordinary is risky). The other issue with this supervisor is that they have promoted a situation that has literally scared people away from any type of innovation, therefore squelching any possibility of the work group becoming better tomorrow than it was today. This type of supervisory approach survives from a draconian perspective founded within the tenets of the early industrialization age dating back hundreds of years and that didn't start to get corrected until the 1940s.

They don't recognize excellent or exceptional performance.

- This supervisor suffers from various maladies including one or more of the following: One, they simply don't see the significance of recognizing excellent or exceptional performance. Two, they think excellent or exceptional performance should be the standard. Three, they don't like saying nice things about other people because they may or may not suffer from an inferiority complex. Four, they think saying good things about someone inappropriately inflates the person's ego. Five, they think saying good things about a person's performance is like treating them like a child. Six, it's not unusual to find that supervisors that have never been recognized for their exceptional performance likewise do not want to recognize the exceptional performance of their direct reports. There's more but you get the picture. The fact is every direct report that is recognized for exceptional or excellent performance *will repeat the same performance.* Aside from the fact that for some supervisors it actually feels pretty damn good to give recognition to their exceptional direct reports, one of the most important reasons for any supervisor to recognize exceptional or excellent performance is because it means that *exceptional performance will be repeated.* Vaulting the entire group performance towards higher levels of mission success one exceptional performance event at a time.

o   No one wants to work for somebody who thinks everybody should get the same grade and that same grade is a "C." Did someone go beyond the call of duty? Has someone become the very best at a routine duty? Did someone do an exceptional job responding to an emergency? Did someone do an exceptional job responding to a customer complaint? Did someone take on additional duties or volunteer for something? Did someone solve a complex problem? Did someone help during a stressful situation? Did someone come up with a great idea for improvement? Did someone come up with a great idea for increasing productivity? Did someone perform CPR and save a fellow employee's life? Sure they did, and don't supervisors want to see that exceptional performance repeated? Of course they do. Just from a sense of fairness, shouldn't supervisors feel that these people deserve something more than a "C"? Of course! But not the supervisor we're describing here. They think people should just perform exceptionally as a regular course of their work and that with any recognition they're being treated like fourth graders, getting a participation prize that they can take home and put on the refrigerator. People typically reserve a stronger term than "jerk" when describing this individual.

These issues can be hard to remember so Figure #21 is provided as a quick guide to help you focus on what's important. .

Fig. #21: *If They Can't Attract Collaborative Power from the Bottom Up*

Why do leaders **fail** to attract power from their followers?

1. They don't emulate behavior they want from others.

2. They don't protect the culture & their people.

3. They treat their direct reports like mushrooms (...they keep them in the dark).

4. They don't support their people with timely decisions & problem-solving.

5. They don't give their people the training they need.

6. They attempt to increase productivity just by working people harder.

7. They don't want to hear your opinion about anything.

8. They don't mentor their direct reports.

9. They don't help people recover after making an error.

10. They don't recognize excellent or exceptional performance.

If you protect & support people, they begin to **trust** your leadership

When you can convince the people that follow you that they made a **good decision** by having you as their leader, it **expands** your power base.

Yes, you are the leader and you hold most of the cards, but when you support your people *in the ways they truly need,* you help them to be more effective humans & employees.

When your direct reports are expert problem solvers, super-high producers, & people who get the job done because they received expert training, **they empower you.** Direct reports like these enhance your performance and empower you to be The Exceptional Leader.

THEY CAN'T CULTIVATE COLLABORATIVE POWER FROM THE WORKPLACE LANDSCAPE

You will see as a reoccurring theme in this book and the books that follow that there is a long list of behaviors that if they are not being used in the group need to *start* being used if you want a more collaborative group. Likewise there is a long list of behaviors that humans participate in that need to *stop* being used if you want a more collaborative group.

This is the sophisticated human dos and don'ts list. By applying the two rules above you'll be moving everyone towards a Q2 status, which we talked about earlier.

You will see later in this book the collaborative group behaviors that need to be applied to the group AFTER you've invited enough power from the top and attracted enough power from the bottom. Once those early phases are completed then you're empowered to start Cultivating Collaborative Power by slowly implementing collaborative group behaviors. What I'm about to explain below is what happens when leaders are disempowered in corrosive workplace cultures.

Before reading any further please be assured that in Chapter 7: Cultivating Collaborative Power I give you the solution to all these problems.

No House Rules?

Every group needs a set of house rules in order to publicly announce a list of behaviors that the group can no longer tolerate. Without specifically calling out these negative behaviors your work environment will look like the nightly news.

You will notice that in the landscape environment of the powerless leadership team these negative behaviors are not called out. Most groups will list some of these items, but any item that hasn't been addressed from the list below needs to be added to the house rules. Whenever any of these behaviors is not held in check, group collaboration, and the mission achievement that is depending on that collaboration, is compromised.

Not every behavior listed in the House Rules section below is as important as every other behavior mentioned. Some items are fundamental good management practices while other items on the house rules list need to stop because they generate intense fear within the work environment, compromising your high performers and essentially encouraging them to go work someplace else.

Anytime the fear-generating items on the house rules list are not enforced in a group, your best talent is bleeding out. As the high performers leave group performance drops and mission success will be compromised over time. With each passing month there will be yet another nail in the coffin.

House Rules

Here is a list of the most basic behaviors that need to be called out as no longer being tolerated:

- Harassment
- Public shaming
- Abusive language directed at others
- Acts of intimidation
- Bullying
- Mobbing
- Angry public outbursts
- Unsafe behavior
- Stealing group or group members' property (including time meant to be spent on group activities)
- Excessive tardiness or absenteeism, or unexcused absences
- Falsifying or altering group records, including payroll information
- Insubordination by refusal to perform assigned work or by passively refusing to do assigned work
- Disorderly conduct, including but not limited to fighting and assault, refusing to share knowledge, habitually whining or complaining, being uncooperative or unreliable
- Habitually demonstrating a lack of humility

In some groups a significant number of these are missing from the house rules and it disempowers leaders within that group. One of the ways to Cultivate Collaborative Power is to make sure that the negative behaviors that compromise mission success are part of the house rules and *are trained out of the group*. It doesn't have to be heavy-handed training; most people most of the time will agree that the behaviors that are being called out in the house rules are behaviors that should not be pursued by anybody in the workplace, so the training can simply focus on raising awareness of the rules.

The reason for a house rules list is to give group members the opportunity to avoid these behaviors. However, because many of these behaviors can be so destructive, leadership needs to be ready to pursue and retrain anybody who is demonstrating these behaviors. If leadership finds that an individual continues demonstrating destructive behavior regardless of multiple attempts at retraining, it can be necessary to then remove the destructive behavior by removing the individual who is not favorably responding to multiple training attempts. Leaders not removing destructive behavior from the group environment when they should will always compromise efforts that support mission success.

These issues can be hard to remember so Figure #22 is provided as a quick guide to help you focus on what's important. .

Fig. #22: If They Can't Cultivate Collaborative Power from the Workplace Landscape

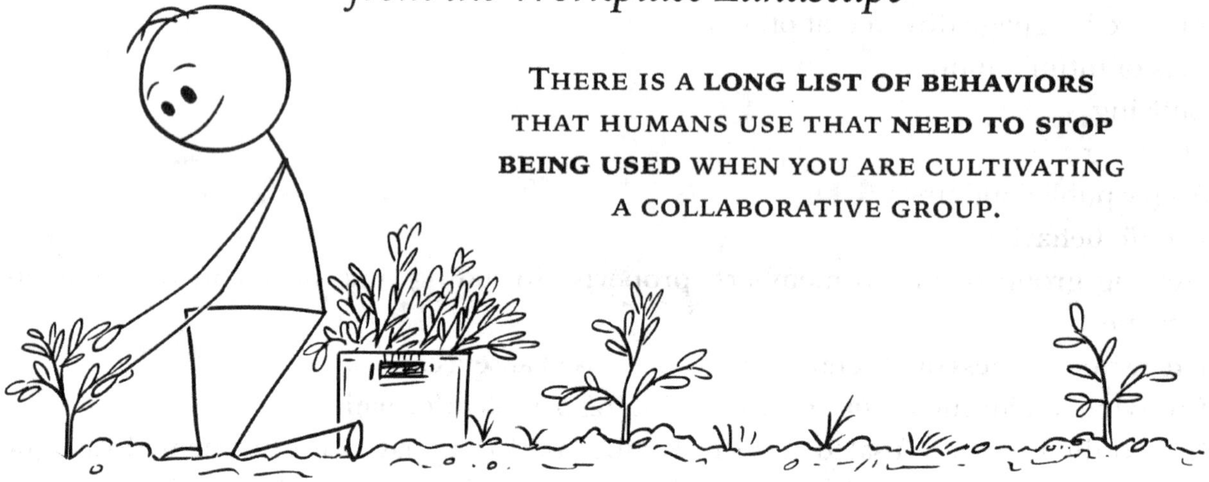

THERE IS A **LONG LIST OF BEHAVIORS** THAT HUMANS USE THAT **NEED TO STOP BEING USED** WHEN YOU ARE CULTIVATING A COLLABORATIVE GROUP.

This is the collaboration **DON'Ts** list.

First things first. Have your group use *a set of house rules* & publicly announce a list of behaviors that the group **can no longer tolerate.** These behaviors are like weeds in your workplace landscape. You need to remove them *before your group can effectively cultivate Collaborative Power.*

Harrassment

Angry public outbursts

Public shaming

Excessive tardiness or absenteeism

Bullying

Abusive language directed at others

Unsafe behavior

Mobbing

Acts of intimidation

Falsifying or altering group records

Stealing group or group members' property or time

Disorderly conduct

Refusal to perform assigned work

Habitually demonstrating a lack of humility

These are the basic behaviors that can <u>no longer</u> be tolerated.

Next I will go over what's missing in groups, using the Big 8 categories, that also denies leaders the ability to Cultivate Collaborative Power within the group.

Mission

The group is silo driven, meaning each department sees themselves as an independent entity. The problem with this is that as the departments are required to interact and are continuously placing demands on each other in order to have the group work as a collaborative holistic system, requests from other departments are systematically treated as the second-most-important task and the work-load generated internally within the department is always placed as the top priority.

With this narrow perspective the group runs the risk of routinely having the second-most-important tasks completed ahead of the first-most-important tasks. Groups that are silo driven chronically have their priorities mixed up, reducing the chance of generating higher group performance and threatening their ability to reach mission success.

Instead, the group needs to look at itself as a collaborative enterprise from a holistic perspective that helps people prioritize the demands from other departments and see them not as separate departments but just one group with just one mission statement. Oftentimes the demands between departments can be rated or routinized so that information and demands for action that flow between departments can be appropriately prioritized for the good of the entire group *in advance*, making sure that department A is satisfying the high-priority tasks of department B.

Culture

Group members making inappropriate comments or demonstrating inappropriate behaviors in public forums not only destroys collegiality, it generates fear in the brains of the people within the group. That fear shifts where decision making happens in the brain as explained earlier. With the prefrontal cortex in charge you have logical, rational, and ethical thinking which then promotes logical, rational, and ethical behaviors. When fear is created there is an unstoppable process of moving decision making to the amygdala. And at that point all the human brains in the group can do is fight, flight, or freeze. So therefore any type of unchecked harassment or bullying behavior is completely eviscerating the collaborative power of the group. Without consistently training and enforcing the group relationships towards empathy, dignity, and respect, the chances of Cultivating Collaborative Power *are nonexistent.*

Effective Interpersonal Relationships

At this point you already know how the number of relationships grows exponentially as you add additional group members. This is why defining what it means to have effective interpersonal relationships is an absolute imperative to a high-performing group that wants to Cultivate Collaborative Power. *Seeing your fellow group member as a contributing collaborative person and treating them that way on a regular basis is now a condition of employment.* If there are group members that are unable to keep their own biases in check whether that be in terms of political, religious, or ethnic differences, just to name a few for example, the work environment will be polluted with ineffective interpersonal relationships. If those biases are bleeding out into the work environment then Cultivating Collaborative Power will be impossible. From now on group members need to separate out what's good for the group and deal with adversity in a way that is supported by their training. Lastly, group members not mitigating their anger by first meeting with their supervisor instead of letting it spill out into the relationships within the group, regardless of the reason, makes Cultivating Collaborative Power *impossible*.

High-Quality Communication

Any group that isn't talking about talking or writing about writing or communicating about communication is creating a disaster that's mostly hidden from view. This disaster hobbles every group trying to Cultivate Collaborative Power. Let me explain. You cannot prove that there are lost opportunities because of low-quality communication because you can't prove that something didn't happen when it could've happened, but this malady is happening all the time if you're not addressing the issue in advance. When people are discouraged from communicating important information up to and through the chain of command about how a condition could have been improved, and that information flow is now also stymied from the top down in ways that discouraged a dialogue that could have otherwise improved the conditions of the group, the group's ability to Cultivate Collaborative Power is horribly stymied, *but you can't prove it*. And because of the uniqueness of this particular type of issue typically being hidden from view, the group members and their supervisors are unaware of its debilitating nature. With the loss of high-quality communication the group's ability to Cultivate Collaborative Power is significantly reduced.

Technical Competency

Group members not fully demonstrating their expertise at all times or operating outside their area of expertise creates massive inefficiencies and can even be dangerous depending on the nature of the work. If the technical expertise that's been trained into a person isn't used, it's as if it never existed. A person expressing knowledge when they haven't been trained in order to support that knowledge, or promoting themselves as an expert where no expertise exists, is not an unusual behavior in groups. While one can successfully argue that this is an individual that needs to be held in check, this situation can actually be considered a lack of training. If a group is not training their group members to expert levels of technical competency, Cultivating Collaborative Power is significantly compromised.

Productivity

If group members are not trained in the importance of productivity nor how increases in productivity promote mission success, then they have no idea how to work smart instead of simply working harder to increase productivity. If directives are not issued in a critical fashion as I describe in this book then work is being performed inefficiently, guaranteed. Group members not accepting delegated tasks with positive motivation starts to reduce the lubrication necessary to advance an agenda that supports Cultivating Collaborative Power. Without igniting innovation in the people that are doing the work and making sure they get recognition for their incredible ideas to reduce time-wasting procedures and to "think anew, out of the box," the opportunity will be lost to promote better operating methods that will cause explosive levels of opportunities for higher performance. When people are discouraged from innovation and are not listened to when they make suggestions about how to improve, those increases to productivity that would lead to explosive levels of performance go down the drain and your ability to Cultivate Collaborative Power disappears.

Problem-Solving

If group members are not trained to recognize problems and are not trained to communicate problems, if they're not trained to verify information as fact or fiction, if group members don't take an open-minded approach and allow new facts to change their minds, and if group members are not trained in the use of a systematic problem-solving process, the group will be buried in problems that remain unsolved and then with each passing day or week or month the next set of problems will remain unsolved and simply be added to the growing list of unsolved problems. Now with most groups 100 percent of the problems are not going unsolved. Yet even if 10 percent or sometimes even 1 percent of the most important problems are going unresolved, efforts to build a group that's able to leverage solutions and Cultivate Collaborative Power are buried in the morass of unsolved problems.

Continuous Improvement

Flawless Execution

Group members need to be trained to accept performance feedback with civil behavior in order to modify future behaviors based on the feedback. Likewise, supervisors need to be trained in how to give performance feedback in a civil manner that promotes the success of their direct reports. Many supervisors and many performance evaluation systems fail horribly at this most important task. When group members are given feedback to promote their success and they know that is the reason for the feedback, then it becomes *a success system*. But as just noted a lot of groups don't have the leadership and evaluation system creds necessary to do this well. As such, the ability to Cultivate Collaborative Power by building higher performance, one individual at a time, is miserably lost.

Innovation

Every system in nature, including human systems, is always advancing and innovating and filling new evolutionary niches by creating new mutations from existing organisms. That's the way nature works and that's the way the human systems of nature work. In other words, when somebody comes up with a new procedure by improving an old procedure, they are essentially creating a mutation within the workflow *that works better now* (however you define the word "better") *than how it worked before*. Innovation is not only necessary to move the group forward to higher levels of performance, innovation is also necessary to prevent the group from falling behind. If all the systems surrounding you are advancing and your group is not advancing with them, then by definition *standing still actually means you're falling behind*. The people that are "doing the work" will always be the greatest source of innovation that has a practical application to advancing mission success. ***Without encouraging them, without listening to them, and without implementing what they tell you,*** Cultivating Collaborative Power through innovation is so significantly retarded that even with a trickle flow of improvements that might be giving you the feeling as if you're moving forward, ***you're actually falling behind.*** Yes, this is very tricky stuff.

In order to have a highly functioning ecosystem that represents human innovation, people need to know and need to be trained in the appropriate risks to be taken in order to create a mutation that leads to an improvement. A scenario where we agree that the new concept represents something that we call an improvement over today's condition, so that tomorrow's condition looks different, looks better, ***requires risk taking.*** When placed in these terms it looks like innovation is an unachievable ballet but I'm here to tell you, it's all achievable. This is how innovation occurs within human systems, but if not done with the appropriate skill necessary it just simply doesn't work. This is a level of sophistication that many supervisors on staff may not have, which means Cultivating Collaborative Power as it relates to innovation ***is lost.***

THE BIG 8 CATEGORIES AND WHY THEY FEEL SO GOOD

Collaborative group behaviors fall into the same Big 8 performance categories of behavior:

1. **Mission**
2. **Culture**
3. **Effective Interpersonal Relationships**
4. **High-Quality Communication**
5. **Technical Competency**
6. **Productivity**
7. **Problem-Solving**
8. **Continuous Improvement**

When done right, which is what you will be doing, it feels good (yes, feels good) for all involved. Your supervisor, your direct reports, and your entire group start to live a life that's more effective and more sane in the methods that are used to pursue achievements. In many groups the quest for mission success comes at the expense of the individual. That's unfortunate because what we have learned is that treating people well is a complementary function to mission success. I know that for some of you that's an obvious point but for millions of groups across this planet right now it's simply not the case.

This is what is being said in people's heads once they get the correct and necessary training to support the Big 8 categories.

- It feels good to be involved and I'm happy to return that value in higher levels than I received (Mission).

- It feels good to not be afraid. It feels good to respond logically, rationally, and ethically instead of having to constantly be looking over your shoulder (Culture).
- It feels good to experience mutual healthy outcomes between group members (Effective Interpersonal Relationships).
- It feels good being well informed and being able to avoid misdirected stress because of misunderstandings (High-Quality Communication).
- It feels good to be an expert at what I do (Technical Competency).
- It feels good to know how to be a productive contributing group member in a group that appreciates my contribution (Productivity).
- It feels good to be an empowered expert problem solver (Problem-Solving).
- It feels good to be mentored and supported (Continuous Improvement – Flawless Execution).
- It feels good to be an innovator, to be creative, to charting new paths forward and to be appreciated for it. (Continuous Improvement – Innovation).

1 – MISSION

It feels good to be involved and I'm happy to return that value in higher levels than I received.

A clearly defined, practical, and well-used mission is the key to group success.

A group without a well-used mission may be hardworking and well intended but they won't be effective. They will go through the motions and may appear very busy, but their activity will be wasted activity.

Give group members a specific description for direction that will benefit the group then encourage *them* to influence outcomes. The mission is the "why" and everybody needs a "why" in order to give meaning to "what" they are doing.

Train on the definition of mission success. It's all the same rules in for-profit or non-profit group: include external customer needs and empower group members to create outcomes by training to the mission-defined objective then delegating management tasks (not leadership tasks) down into the group. Moving important management tasks down creates the conditions of inclusion, control, and openness.

We have for far too long looked to those who labor in our groups as just that, labor. In doing so, we continue to miss the greatest opportunity for group survival. The people who labor in our groups have brains that know how to improve group performance in ways the leaders will never know. They provide unique insights, great ideas, and mission-centered decisions that can be the determining factors in group success. Leadership needs to build an environment that treats everyone as a contributor to the mission. Training group members in mission-related skills will avail them of the opportunity to achieve great things.

Because achieving great things satiates the individuals in the group, giving them the opportunity to do so based on a purpose (a mission) pushes the group to success.

When a group is unaware of the importance of a mission or a set of values that direct group members towards unifying behavior, incompetence is prevalent. Yet this incompetence is not caused by a lack of desire or aptitude on the part of the individual. The cause is instead that they lack direction from a coherent unifying leadership message called a mission.

Without a mission, each member of your group will naturally use their own definition for success— and who can blame them? No one wants to suffer failure, and if leadership won't teach them how to succeed with a coherent mission and a clear sense of values then they are left to do the best they can to resolve the situation on their own. It's a dilemma they don't have the tools nor the authority to solve.

So, leadership blames the individual, perhaps even reprimanding their failure, and walks away, never understanding the hidden underlying systemic cancer of missing mission and value statements. Nobody is able to see the mission-less group environment as being the secret culprit of poor decision making. True, it's not the only reason poor decisions are made. But those decisions that are made poorly because of the absence of a mission statement are hidden from common understanding.

Does that make sense to you?

Have a clearly defined and practical mission statement. Make sure it's well used by providing training for how it can best be used on a day-to-day basis. Make sure it's well used by providing recognition every time you observe someone using it. Make sure it's well used by making sure it's used for prioritizing work.

Make sure group members, leaders and non-leaders alike, are using the related Collaborative Group Behaviors by integrating them into the performance expectation for every group member.

2 - CULTURE

> *It feels good to not be afraid. It feels good to respond logically, rationally, and ethically instead of having to constantly be looking over your shoulder.*

The primary reason for Collaborative Group Behaviors is to protect the group environment from obvious and not-so-obvious destructive behaviors.

Destructive behavior creates fear and fear then becomes the controlling factor in adversely impacting the many necessary prerequisites for human collaboration.

Collaborative Group Behaviors require training on the appropriate behaviors to use and the inappropriate behaviors to avoid so the individual can succeed in a group environment that is free of fear. Once fear is reduced the brain's decision making switches from the fight-or-flight amygdala to the prefrontal cortex with rational, logical, and ethical behaviors.

Protect the group environment from rogue destructive behavior. Train on the appropriate behaviors we need and the behaviors to avoid. Without protection against destructive cultural interactions the group environment will predominate in fear. Fear will create a fight-or-flight thinking process in group members, making collaboration impossible. Protection creates the conditions of inclusion, control, and openness.

Train to change concerning *who* needs to demonstrate *what* behavior in the group culture so *when* things change you still have safety in numbers. Culture plays a key role and is guarded without compromise as it comes up against any activity that adversely impacts dignity and respect of the individual. Without these safeguards in place, subterfuge starts to undermine any well-intentioned effort that leadership puts forth. It's more than "playing nice." Without drawing a line in the sand and having the courage to act against destructive behavior, passive leadership is generating hidden fears.

There are three essential human needs for eliminating fear within a culture (thank you, Will Schutz, and your book ***The Human Element***: *Productivity, Self-Esteem and the Bottom Line*):

1. Each person wants Inclusion to feel significant. When they don't feel significant their fear is being ignored.
2. Each person wants Control to feel competent. When they don't feel competent their fear is being humiliated.
3. Each person wants Openness to feel likable. When they don't feel likable their fear is being rejected.

An environment where these three needs are addressed is an environment where people are included, they are given control, and they are supported in their desire to be in an open and transparent work environment. Living in constant fear of being humiliated, rejected, or ignored—does that sound like a high-performing group? Of course not, because high-performing cultures have a culture that prioritizes sharing control by sharing responsibilities. Because high-performing cultures increase inclusion through recognition of good performance and because they encourage openness through transparency.

Without standards for maintaining a respectful environment, a culture that cannot be protected against destructive negative behaviors is formed. In this condition, we simply accept a fate of permanent failure masked as "things aren't too bad" when in fact we instead have proven alternatives that could result in success.

The destiny for each of us and our groups is not written, it is chosen. Start choosing a culture that will enhance everyone's future. When this choice is made and these behaviors are integrated into performance expectations over time, eventually what you are left with are people that want to collaborate.

Imagine that.

Reduce fear. Protect the culture from rogue distractive behavior immediately and privately.

Promote the culture by teaching people how to design professional relationships using everything you're reading here.

Make sure group members, leaders and non-leaders alike, are using the related Collaborative Group Behaviors by integrating them into the performance expectation for every group member.

3 - EFFECTIVE INTERPERSONAL RELATIONSHIPS

It feels good to experience mutual healthy outcomes between group members.

In order for a group to reach its potential for mission success, it needs to develop collaboration between the humans present in the group.

This is where the misunderstanding starts. Most people think that we are focusing on training the humans in the group to promote collaboration. But that is only partially true. ***It's more about creating collaborative relationships.***

Teach the keys to one-on-one relationship and insist they are used. It's training on how to create and maintain one-on-one collaboration through effective interpersonal relationships. Having differences is healthy; how the difference develops a healthy outcome, or not, becomes the issue.

A process to develop healthy outcomes is stressed and creates the conditions of inclusion, control, and openness.

As noted, while we are teaching collaboration to people, the express purpose is to ensure that their *relationships* are collaborative, not necessarily the individuals. Let me explain.

As I explained earlier, while the number of people in a group might rise in a linear fashion the number of relationships is rising logarithmically. With 10 people in a group there are 45 relationships. With a 100-person group it's 4,950 relationships. Yes, we added 90 more people and in doing so we added 4,905 relationships! If we add another 9,900 people to the group, the number of possible relationships skyrockets to nearly 50 million! We need each one of those relationships to be collaborative, but while we can't train 50 million relationships, we can train 10,000 people.

The success of the group effort is directly supported by the accumulation of effective one-on-one relationship-building efforts by each person. This is why each relationship is important and it's why building a capacity for professional relationship creation is important!

In our view, the ability of group members to hold themselves to professional relationship-building behaviors and to avoid behaviors that are damaging to relationship needs to become a job requirement. This is why many of the Collaborative Group Behaviors go beyond just holding people accountable for treating each other well. But now, more importantly, holding them accountable for holding themselves accountable for developing professional relationships. See the difference?

Having each person actively contribute to solutions for resolving interpersonal conflicts is a fundamental behavior necessary for collaboration.

The primary reason groups don't place a high priority on Effective Interpersonal Relationships (even if they think they do) is because they underestimate the magnitude of the issue. They think they are dealing with a 100-person issue when actually it's a 4,950-relationship issue. So it's not 100 reasons to require effective interpersonal relationships, it's actually 4,950 reasons to require effective interpersonal relationships, even though there are only 100 people in the group. Right?

People can think and feel whatever they want, that's their human right to do so, **but they can't do or say whatever they want, at least not without consequences.** And if you're in a group that has not clearly defined what people are not allowed to do or say then they can proceed without consequences, and that is a self-inflicted wound by leadership. Every negative leadership behavior mentioned in this book should be a performance expectation of what not to do and part of the training routine for your leaders to address behaviors *of what not to do.*

Make sure group members, leaders and non-leaders alike, are using behaviors to build effective interpersonal relationships. Make sure they are avoiding behaviors that can damage effective interpersonal relationships.

Finally, make sure all group members are using the related Collaborative Group Behaviors by integrating them into the performance expectation for every group member.

4 - HIGH-QUALITY COMMUNICATION

> *It feels good being well informed and being able to avoid misdirected stress because of misunderstandings.*

Communicate about how to communicate and how to listen, and insist those skills are used. Training on how to talk and how to listen significantly reduces fear.

With high-quality communication, problems can be addressed instead of suppressed. Group members are well informed on group issues from bottom to top and top to bottom, and group members are able to feed documentation up concerning their own performance achievements. All these actions create the conditions of inclusion, control, and openness.

Communication as we know it: a string of words coupled with body language and other behaviors that gets a point across. That are then endlessly connected end to end to other words and behaviors, resulting in an almost limitless stream of communication.

Communication is our ability to transfer thoughts and feelings. Once sent and accurately received, our communication usually results in a conclusion that requires some type of action. As the need for action changes so does the communication. As the need for high-quality action rarely stops, nor should the need for excellent, dynamic communication. If action occurs but communication is not keeping pace, it creates problems for the group. When the pace of initiating new communication is unable to keep pace with the need for the group to respond to new environmental changes, the group's current actions become ineffective. If left unaddressed, this fault will threaten mission success, simply because with each unaddressed action the group grows ever more irrelevant to the exact things it's wanting to impact in a positive fashion.

Communication is dynamic, meaning that it is ever changing. And in a group it is as complicated as the independent movement of each water molecule in a giant raging river. If we start to see communication this way, we start to come closer to treating it with the respect that it deserves.

Because communication is dynamic it is always either getting better or it's getting worse; it doesn't have the ability to stay the same. If you don't know for sure that communication is getting better, then it's usually getting worse.

Pause after reading each statement:

- We make judgments as we listen and filter out anything we don't believe and we don't realize we are doing it.
- We each use different pictures in our mind for the same words that are being used in the conversation and we don't realize we are doing it.
- We assume that the words we are using in our conversation represent reality with 100 percent accuracy. They don't and we don't realize it.
- We have a tendency to fill in the gaps between pieces of information instead of asking questions and we don't realize we are doing it.

- We can have difficulty communicating our own self-interest and we don't realize we are suffering from this inadequate or inaccurate communication.
- When we hear communication that makes us feel uncomfortable we have already decided that it is wrong or inaccurate *and we don't realize we are doing it.*
- If we hear a verified fact in a conversation that opposes one of our belief systems, we start to sabotage the dialogue *and we don't realize we are doing it.*
- Fear prevents us from conveying important information *and we don't realize it.*
- Talking about anything "new" can feel dangerous so we don't talk about it *and we don't realize we are avoiding it.*

Do you see anything that all of these communication issues have in common?

That's right; *we typically don't realize we are doing it.*

If we don't know we are doing it, we can't take the initial steps of correcting the situation. If we can't correct the situation, it continues to do damage and we don't even realize it.

High-Quality Communication creates such an opportunity for improvement in a group setting. Make sure group members, leaders and non-leaders alike, are using the chain of command up and down. Make sure group members are using the communication SOPs provided in Appendices 3 and 4.

Also make sure group members, leaders and non-leaders alike, are using the related Collaborative Group Behaviors by integrating them into the performance expectations for every group member. These are listed in Chapter 7.

5 - TECHNICAL COMPETENCY

> *It feels good to be an expert at what I do.*

Find out where people are weak in their skills and train people how to be fully competent at what they do—and when you think you're done, train them some more.

Finding the weak spot in anyone's skill set is no longer feared because the response is now train, train, train.

It's okay to say "I don't know" because it identifies where we need to train, benefiting the individual and the group.

Constantly seek out and train to the individual's and group's weakest skill set. In this way the competency safety net is actively driven towards the weakest, riskiest deficiencies first, *then from there upwards* in the group, dramatically increasing the individual's and group's reliability.

Technical competency creates the conditions of inclusion, control, and openness.

Train on how each person needs to fulfill their specific role in their technical competency at all times and how they should not operate outside their area of expertise.

Being able to make a "skilled" contribution is what makes you, as an individual, fundamentally valuable to your group. Having a group of technically skilled contributors advances the success of the group and its mission. It's that straightforward, yet technical competency within the group is often blocked from its full potential by roadblocks that most groups don't know about. As we don't know the problem we fail in applying technical skills for reasons we are unaware of.

As the collective skill level rises in a group, the chances of mission success also rise. As the skill level drops so does the success. We as individuals are married to group success and this group success is directly proportional to the collective technical skill level of the group.

There are two basic skill sets, hard skills and soft skills, or what I will call collaborative skills. Both are essential to a successful group.

Hard skills are those that are required to be performed by an individual related to a particular specialty or expertise. This specialty then adds to the group's other specialty roles provided by others. Whether you are an accountant for a hardware chain, a piano player in an orchestra, a machinist at an airplane factory, or an English teacher at a school, if you don't know how to do your job well the entire group is damaged, not just you.

And it can't just be one or two or ten people who know what they are doing. Groups of diversified skill holders *are complementary*. You can have the finest menu with the freshest ingredients, a famous chef cooking wonderful food, and friendly and competent servers pleasing diners, but if the dishwasher does a lousy job and everyone is eating off poorly washed dishes all of the rest just doesn't matter. If everyone is not technically competent in their specific area of expertise it lowers the group's ability to meet the mission *and it creates risk*.

A word of warning: When technical incompetency shows itself as a problem it typically appears at the individual level, so the typical group can misunderstand the issue as being a problem associated with only that particular individual. While this might be true, further investigation often uncovers another unrecognized problem.

When an individual is given effective training from a highly effective training program, their chances of demonstrating low technical competency are lowered; however, be aware that when the group member in question also has the aptitude and the desire to learn their technical training, any issues with low technical competency might be sourced back to a flaw in the training program. *This can also be recognized if you find more than one person making the same mistake.*

When a group has a coherent, focused, and effective training program that applies to all technical skills embedded in the group, the entire group advances towards success.

Additionally, if you train group members to expert levels you can almost completely eliminate any direct supervision resources. And in this respect training is also an investment in lowering costs while not losing value.

Having each and every group member fully competent within their specialty is an essential bottom-line necessity: technical skill-set competency creates group success.

Make sure group members, leaders and non-leaders alike, are adequately trained. Always train each group member starting at their weakest skill set first. Train to expert level to lower cost of direct supervision and increase value at the same time.

Also make sure group members, leaders and non-leaders alike, are using the related Collaborative Group Behaviors by integrating them into the performance expectation for every group member.

6 – PRODUCTIVITY

It feels good to know how to be a productive contributing group member in a group that appreciates my contribution.

Educate group members about how wealth is generated when products and services can be created at less cost or time to the group and continue to ask *them* how it can be done better. When they talk, listen to what they say. If their idea can be supported, implement it now.

One, they talk, two, you listen, three, develop support, four, implement now.

Working smarter makes the difference, resulting in explosive group success. Train on the wisest way to get the job done under less-than-optimal conditions by creating an environment that collaborates to success.

Delegating tasks down in a program management fashion and giving over control to highly trained staff rockets productivity. *In using the other Collaborative Group Behaviors to create collaboration, the end result shows itself as higher productivity.*

Simply put, productivity is the amount of effort or work per unit of time or money. Sounds a bit "stuffy," yet understanding it well has been responsible for building empires. Likewise, not understanding it, not protecting it or improving it, has led to their downfall as well. Productivity is such a consequential factor that it becomes the topic most likely to determine the success or failure of your group.

Like all Collaborative Group Behaviors, productivity is uniquely important. Without improving productivity over time the group fails. In essence, improved productivity generates increased wealth. As the cost of producing a product or service is reduced through innovation, the savings can be shared in a myriad of ways such as higher wages, more cash for capital purchases, and better dividends to the shareholders to name just a few.

Before it can be improved upon it needs at the very least to be maintained or sustained. If productivity is to be first sustained and then improved upon to generate wealth, the value it provides for the group needs to be fully understood. Once grasped, this understanding needs to be fully acted upon by every member of the group.

When productivity is growing on a regular basis from improvement strategies based on collaborative tactics, the group is in a mode of constantly generating wealth.

It's not necessarily about working harder. The central themes are the particular contributing behaviors that move the group towards higher productivity, and simply working harder is not a concept that a group can use to improve productivity. Working at a reasonable pace according to the task and conditions at hand is a baseline, but it's not the most powerful method a group uses to grow wealth.

It's really about "working smarter" and the possibilities of doing so never seem to be exhausted. There is always a new idea around the corner that drives productivity ever higher. And this stream of ideas for improvement comes from the people in your group.

We can't tell the future. But with an innovation process that drives productivity up, the group can get closer to a better future using one good idea at a time. Step by step.

Motivation and innovation pushing productivity up creates wealth within the group. And that wealth creates opportunity for meeting the mission. Working smarter means knowing how to be more productive today, tomorrow, and the next day and the next.

But the fact is, there is no improvement in productivity unless the group members possess the desire to improve. Generating the desire and the passion to improve in your group is not a hard skill, it's a soft skill. Without it, it is just a matter of time before your customers, competition, or board of directors notice you circling the drain towards mission failure.

The key to success is to use some of that productivity increase and plowing it back into the group. Anytime resources start dwindling below minimum, things start to go very wrong.

The competition for dwindling resources and the ongoing snipping and gossiping on paid time that can go along with it replaces cooperation, further exacerbating the problem of falling productivity. As fear grips the environment, cooperation begins a slow persistent drop that spells the fate of collaboration and trust amongst group members. Because of this, productivity loss accelerates the group into a death spiral, taking everyone's job along with it.

The good news is, exploiting productivity improvement opportunities in your group results in just the opposite. The desire to improve caused by working in a highly collaborative group creates opportunity, creates relationship, creates economic spirit, and, metaphorically speaking, allows everyone to move to a richer neighborhood.

Productivity, implemented by a group well versed in its power, becomes an explosive positive movement. **Esprit de corps** builds camaraderie and respect between group members. When a group becomes a high performer it's always because it became a high producer.

Success in productivity cements effective relationships when an individual is positively recognized for demonstrating productive behavior. This level of recognition communicates to group members a desire and commitment that others will observe then strive to repeat.

As productivity increases the group moves ever closer to its maximum potential of mission success.

Make sure group members, leaders and non-leaders alike, are using the related Collaborative Group Behaviors by integrating them into the performance expectation for every group member.

7 – PROBLEM-SOLVING

It feels good to be an empowered expert problem solver.

Instruct the group on how to use and guide the critical-thinking process in group environments, avoiding cognitive biases as a daily practice. Problem-solving becomes a team sport, reducing individuals' needless anxiety while simultaneously building more diverse solutions that have staying power. Better solutions with less anxiety, no argument there.

We are in a group that also prevents problems by using simple techniques such as *catching things falling through the cracks*. We are now in a group of people that has each other's back. This creates the conditions of inclusion, control, and openness.

Using a simple team problem-solving approach feels good and will make a significant difference in group success.

By definition, team problem-solving inherently adjusts to changing conditions.

Group members now have permission and are encouraged to bring problems of any sort forward. In fact, it's essential that they do. From technical problems to professional issues to personal disagreements. When they come forward with problems for examination and resolution and the problem is resolved effectively, you will have removed one of the most significant issues that keep a group from succeeding.

Having good problem-solving skills is not the same as being smart or intelligent. Just because a person is smart and has risen to prominence based on that intelligence does not mean they have good problem-solving skills. Believe it.

Problems solved and issues resolved as fast as they show up is one of the most important actions that a successful group does well. And problems can't be solved if they are not first known. It's a team sport where it now matters less who solves the problem; the only thing that matters, in the final analysis, is that the problems are resolved and the damage they create is stopped. Problems and issues left unresolved will suck the life blood from your group. Problems and issues have a life of their own and as long as they go unanswered they roam around doing a lot of damage to the group.

When a group can solve problems and resolve issues as fast as they show up, the group has maximized chances for success and minimized the significant tangible damage that unanswered problems will do. The damage includes making people's lives miserable, gutting productivity, and providing a major cultural impediment to collaboration that makes continuous improvement much more difficult than it would be otherwise.

If the number of unresolved problems escalates beyond a group's ability to solve them, then suddenly you have a list of problems piling up, growing longer with each passing day, month, and year. The tangible result becomes an unmanageable chaos that smothers collaboration.

Any chance at healthy collaboration is now buried under the debris from bad feelings, a lack of confidence in the mission, lost customers, and everything in between. When unsolved problems hurt people and mission success *and* it could have been prevented, it's more than a sad story—it's a tragedy.

For every issue or problem there is a solution that will help to mitigate the damage. Groups typically lack solutions in several critical areas, which ensures that unsolved problems stay unsolved. To name just a few: We haven't made recognizing and talking about problems a top operating priority in our group environment. We don't use a team step-by-step problem-solving philosophy, and therefore all of our collective knowledge, wisdom, and resident staff genius is left untapped and unleveraged. We don't realize that we don't know what we don't know. We don't understand that flawed thinking patterns like cognitive biases and fallacies are leading us to deny valid answers to pressing problems. We don't understand what a "fact" is. We lack imagination in the sense that we don't use the creative powers that we possess.

Make sure your group isn't ignoring small problems. Make sure your group uses a team step-by-step problem-solving system.

Make sure group members, leaders and non-leaders alike, are using the related Collaborative Group Behaviors by integrating them into the performance expectation for every group member.

8 - CONTINUOUS IMPROVEMENT

Continuous Improvement constitutes two independent processes: Flawless Execution and Innovation.

Flawless Execution

It feels good to be mentored and supported.

It's not a place, it's a direction. The process of continuous improvement is, well, continuous, and as it relates to each person's performance there are two primary areas to focus on. The first area is making sure people are meeting minimum performance standards and that they are given specific feedback in case they're not so they have the opportunity to improve. The second area is ensuring that those that are meeting minimum performance standards are given the opportunity to excel to higher levels of performance through the mentoring process. Give constant feedback to improve individual group member performance and system performance.

Feedback is designed to _improve_ conditions. We don't reprimand our way to success; feedback is _training_. When feedback is announced as a training program and given to improve a condition in human performance or process performance, redesigning how we achieve improvement becomes more understandable.

Knowing how to improve feels good, while receiving performance feedback on how to improve provides a _knowing_ but it doesn't always feel good when we are hearing it. The words we need to hear to preserve our security by improving our performance are subsequently the same words we have difficulty listening to because of our egoic filter. Let's know that. Let's speak to it and just know it's difficult. And if we avoid the difficulty we won't improve. What do you want more, to avoid difficulty or to improve your performance?

That being said, giving performance feedback effectively includes removing any personal or emotional issues and just focusing on the behavior. There are no "bad people" here, just behaviors that can be improved upon and negative events to be avoided or corrected. *Getting feedback to improve performance in our personal relationships and group relationships happens to everybody at some time or another, so when it is happening to you, it's just your turn.* Take it in, use the feedback, and become the greatest benefactor. We were not born knowing how to automatically improve our performance without getting some feedback from our supervisors, so don't beat yourself up.

Leadership should focus on improvement and not linger long on describing the negative event as long as the group member demonstrates an understanding of what happened. Good leaders want everyone to improve and will do somersaults to make that happen. They want to be as gentle as possible while getting the individual to essentially buy in to the fact that they do, indeed, need to improve. Once that understanding is established, instantly move the conversation forward to focus on describing what improvement looks like. There's no reason to dwell in the uncomfortable zone once they've agreed they need to improve. That agreement shows that they're moving forward and as a leader you want to instantly move forward with them.

Group members who adjust their behavior after performance feedback get high kudos for doing just that. Evaluations give special recognition to problems solved after feedback was given. By giving significant credit for correcting a performance issue, performance soars. I've seen it.

It's not about reprimand, per se, it's about training and improvement, even though it may not feel good to be held accountable for less-than-standard performance.

This is all that is required 98 percent of the time to help a group member to improve back to Collaborative Group Behaviors. The other 2 percent of the feedback sessions work their way out one way or another.

There is one single difference between humans and all other animals (as far as we know): we can "think about thinking." This is the fertile soil upon which conceptual thought turns into an activity that is beneficial to the human. Much of our thinking is prioritized towards activities that are more important, or more beneficial, for our survival. Much of this thought is unconscious; we are thinking about how to survive more than we probably know. And when faced with any type of threatening situation, real or imagined, physical or psychological, our brain definitely shifts to the survival mode.

Because their survival hung in the balance, humans throughout prehistory were highly motivated to develop innovative responses to effectively counter the unprecedented nature of their circumstances.

The ever-changing prehistoric environment begged an ever-changing response to maintain the conditions necessary for survival. Maintaining our survival conditions by responding to a changing environment is our fundamental adaptive response. This is why innovation is critical to a successful group. Successfully adapting to a new or unprecedented environmental condition creates a constant demand for the process of innovation. People innovate constantly but are rarely aware that they are doing it as much as they actually are.

In high-performing groups, people are encouraged to initiate ideas for improvement, ideas that solve problems, ideas that save time or save money, ideas that increase sales, and ideas that help other ideas for improvement to succeed. High-performing groups encourage people to do some research ahead of time that will help determine whether to take an idea to the next step. They encourage members to participate in brainstorming sessions that are focused on a particular issue and other sessions that are open forums for the specific purpose of gathering the problems for group members to solve.

Continuous improvement is a combination of constant innovation and constant recovery.

The main thrust of continuous improvement is that negative performance events, either within a system/process or within people-centered performance, are followed by a mission-conscious debriefing. From that debriefing adjustments are identified to improve future performance.

By prioritizing recovery from mistakes and focusing on the recommended changes for improved behavior instead of attacking the person, performance improves at an accelerated pace and less-than-desirable behavior drops and doesn't reemerge.

It is acceptable in the context of negative performance events that the communication be appropriately clear. Yet focusing on feedback that is designed to promote the individual's success will always be the most effective. Hardworking and well-intended people want to be effective, and recovery training gets them there.

With a constant and consistent flow of small improvements over time, mission success becomes bulletproof. Sorry to say it's not *talent* that will drive the world out of its problems, but *skill*. And if skill is to be developed it needs an objective that defines success coupled with an effective training program that uses constant feedback in order to make constant small adjustments towards success.

We can't just reprimand our way to success but we can "recover" our way to success. Do not underestimate the power of recovery behavior.

Combining innovation and recovery behavior keeps processes and people forever improving.

Make sure group members, leaders and non-leaders alike, are using the related Collaborative Group Behaviors by integrating them into the performance expectation for every group member.

Innovation

It feels good to be an innovator.

About 80 percent of what we know now has been learned in the last 15 years. The solutions we create today will start to become obsolete 15 years from now. If we don't adapt to the rapid change by innovating we fall behind when standing still. Moving forward to meet minimum change is also standing still. Moving forward beyond minimums is truly moving forward.

When leadership starts soliciting and using great ideas from everybody in the group, they have a running list of the credible ideas that are coming up from the bottom.

As you saw in the productivity section: One, they talk, two, you listen, three, develop support, four, implement now.

Unforeseen events that could have been anticipated and prevented cause a constant stream of surprise events, keeping the group locked in a reactive mode. Being effective "reactors" can be an emotionally fulfilling exercise (ask any firefighter) and is necessary to protect the group, but all you are doing is stopping a process that is creating *damage*, and every minute spent there is less time spent on the process called *improvement*.

When prioritizing innovative behavior we create an environment where ideas for improvement are in constant demand and welcomed with continuous invitations from leadership. This process creates the conditions of inclusion, control, and openness as *by-products*. The group product is pure success. And yet this success is born through a comfort level with experimentation and failure. The process of innovation may challenge many of the rules you are used to using to "succeed."

If there is a better way to do something then the group should do it that way.

As management tasks are moved downward in the group (as discussed under Mission earlier), implementing ideas for improvement grows organically and radically. It doesn't really matter where a good idea comes from because now everybody is involved. Every brain is now in the game. So let me repeat: If there is a better way to do something then the group should do it that way. *No matter its source.*

It feels good to group members to be able to put forward ideas for improvement. If you're now in a group who doesn't listen to you, doesn't it sound good to imagine that you are now heard? Innovation should also include staff training in how to innovate in the face of new conditions and encouragement to constantly modify your approach to match newly found actual conditions.

High levels of skill and desire will motivate the group to focus on the *actual condition* and the result will be near automatic modification (innovation) to task execution when conditions change. This is the essence of continuous improvement.

Appendix 5 offers a process group members can use to test their own ideas for improvement before they submit them. And note, this is not just giving group members the tools to analyze an idea for improvement but also giving them the permission and courage to be bold and audacious.

Put it all out there! If you absolutely, positively know you have an idea that will improve the group towards its mission, we want you to be relentless in the pursuit of getting it implemented. Relentless, please.

Listen, groups that use Collaborative Group Behaviors not only have a satisfying experience, they become very, very busy places. Everybody is on the move, so when something new comes up we need a little push from time to time to get it on the calendar. If typical business and group activities create a passive resistance to implementing new ideas from time to time, *it's just a reality check*. And if ideas are not implemented over time it's a death sentence for a group that is falling behind. So there's the challenge, *now go meet it*.

It's okay to be a busy highly effective human trying to save your piece of the planet with a well-designed human system, and if we don't improve to meet changing conditions your group, and you, will become obsolete.

Be relentless in the pursuit to innovate, break the rules if that's what it takes.

Make sure group members, leaders and non-leaders alike, are using the related Collaborative Group Behaviors by integrating them into the performance expectation for every group member.

These issues can be hard to remember so Figure #23 is provided as a quick guide to help you focus on what's important.

Fig. #23: The Big 8 Categories & Why They Feel So Good

THE BIG 8

COLLABORATIVE GROUP BEHAVIORS FALL INTO THE SAME BIG 8 PERFORMANCE CATEGORIES OF BEHAVIOR.

1. **Mission**
2. **Culture**
3. **Effective Interpersonal Relationships**
4. **High-Quality Communication**
5. **Technical Competency**
6. **Productivity**
7. **Problem-Solving**
8. **Continuous Improvement**

When utilized right, applying these performance categories feels good (yes, **feels good**) for all group members involved. Your supervisor, your direct reports, and your entire group start to live a life that's **more effective & more sane** in the methods used to pursue achievement.

Once people get **correct training** to support the Big 8...

...THEIR INTERNAL VOICE SOUNDS SOMETHING LIKE THIS:

It feels good to be involved and I'm happy to return that value in higher levels than I received (**Mission**).

It feels good to not be afraid. It feels good to respond logically, rationally, & ethically instead of having to constantly look over my shoulder (**Culture**).

It feels good to experience mutual healthy outcomes between me & other group members (**Effective Interpersonal Relationships**).

It feels good to be an expert at what I do (**Technical Competency**).

It feels good to be a productive contributing group member in a group that appreciates my contributions (**Productivity**).

It feels good to be an empowered expert problem-solver (**Problem-Solving**).

It feels good to be mentored & supported (**Continuous Improvement – Flawless Execution**).

It feels good to be an innovator, to be creative, to chart new paths forward & to be appreciated for it. (**Continuous Improvement – Innovation**).

Chapter 4

Understanding *Exactly* What's Going Wrong and What's Going Right in Your Organization

Bob interlaces organizational psychology and behavior, judgement, and high-level cognitive decision-making, and distills it into well-thought, practical and proven processes yielding high-functioning teams, positive work environments and successful outcomes.

—JOHN MAHONEY

DOWNLOAD A FREE COPY OF THE LANDSCAPE SURVEY AT THELOSTARTOFCOLLABORATION.COM

I wanted to make sure this book could stand on its own so I made sure that this landscape survey was included in the book. However, you can go to **thelostartofcollaboration.com** and download a very user friendly copy for free.

Okay, here goes:

Before you do anything, you need to figure out what the hell is going on. You need to know what's going right so you can check that box and not waste time addressing issues that don't exist. And you need to know what's going wrong not just with the group but with the current leadership group.

This takes a little bit of effort, but the answers to these questions will give you a massive amount of helpful information and the power that comes along with having that information.

As a friendly reminder, there's a bunch of stuff your group and leaders are doing *that they need to stop doing* if you want a more collaborative group, and there's a bunch of stuff your group and your leaders are not doing *that they need to start doing* if they want a more collaborative group.

CAUTION: No organization is perfect.

I'm about to give you over 200 metric questions and statements that allow you to measure your organization or at least start the process of discovering the answers to these questions and statements.

There are zero organizations on this planet that come through this series of questions and statements with 100 percent correctness.

There is no perfection in nature, there is no perfection in the human, and there is no perfection in the human group. You might find 50 separate issues that need to be improved upon *even though you exist in a relatively well-performing group.*

I want to caution you now against treating all of these items with equal standing. In other words, if you end up with a very long list of issues to improve, *make sure you prioritize the list based on importance.* From there you can determine where you want to start, making sure you're dealing with the most important items first and knowing at the same time there could be lower priority items *that you'll never get to.* For instance, multiple examples of egregious destructive behavior in the culture that you've discovered should be placed at a much higher priority to resolve than minor improvements to the performance evaluation system.

To offer a few examples, when using this survey you will start to discover how effectively (or not) your department or your division prioritizes its work according to the mission. The survey will also help you discover the types of cultural destructive behaviors that are currently demonstrated within your work environment. The survey will give you questions to ask yourself that will help determine the effectiveness of interpersonal relationships and the capacity for problem-solving. It will also give you a list of questions that allow you to determine how well your group is using innovation as a continuous improvement strategy.

That being said, when you move on to the process of Inviting Power from the Top Down (Chapter 5), in order to build your master list you will **need** to add what you discover here to the list of problems confronting your boss.

- After you have gone through the process of learning about the problems that are confronting your boss (and perhaps even your boss's boss) compare that list to your survey list and **group the like problems together as your next steps to looking at solutions.** The reason for doing this is you might be able to find **single solutions that solve multiple problems.**

If you can do that then you're going to be a home-run hitter.

Additionally, using the process of Attracting Power from the Bottom Up (Chapter 6) will go a long way to satisfying other issues that you are about to discover using the survey.

Don't be blinded by the snowstorm of information; make sure you're focusing on the most important issues. The solutions to many of the issues you uncover in this survey are integrated throughout the rest of the Collaborative Power Grab step-by-step process. In other words, those issues can be solved by Inviting, Attracting, and Cultivating Collaborative Power. **That's intentional, obviously.**

READING THE LANDSCAPE

You will be using a series of questions, statements, and insights in three main categories to assess what going right and what's going wrong in your group.

THE BIG 8 QUESTIONS

You have probably noticed that I break down almost everything I can into the Big 8 performance categories, which is true with this survey as well. The questions in the first section examine some of the things that people and leaders are doing and are not doing within those same eight categories.

1. Mission
2. Culture
3. Effective Interpersonal Relationships

4. High-Quality Communication
5. Technical Competency
6. Productivity
7. Problem-Solving
8. Continuous Improvement

LEADERSHIP QUESTIONS

Next, in the leadership category, leadership assessment tools are broken down into key leadership functions.

1. Leading
2. Managing
3. Requirements
4. Direct Supervision
5. Accountability, Recovery, Recognition
6. Training – Job Control
7. Productivity
8. Problem-Solving
9. Continuous Improvement

HYGIENE QUESTIONS

The last category looks at what I call "hygiene." These are issues that directly relate to job satisfaction *as a minimum*. In other words, these are problems you need to absolutely, positively get out of the way.

If you try to build a collaborative group by solving the Big 8 issues and solving the leadership issues without **ALSO** solving these issues, it's not going to work.

According to Frederick Herzberg—along with many others who agree with him, including me—there are two groups of conditions that are experienced by the people that work in our groups that either motivate or demotivate their actions. The first group of potentially dissatisfying conditions are called *hygiene* issues and the second group of conditions that actually motivate us to higher performance are called *motivators*. Much of the Collaborative Power Grab addresses the motivators and just a small number of the demotivators. The questions in this category will help identify the rest of the demotivators *that need to be addressed in order that motivation will grow as fast as you want it to or as fast as you need it to.*

KEEP NOTES AND KEEP EVERYTHING TO YOURSELF
As you do this assessment, write everything down.

Keep a comprehensive log on your assessment results so you can go back to add new answers to questions as you find out more information and to track progress. You most likely will not be able to answer all the questions at the same time. You might come across some information just in the course of doing your work, while for other pieces it might be months before you can gain enough information to really know what's going on.

Having a comprehensive logbook of the questions and statements and your responses will help you identify exactly how things are going right and how things are going wrong so, importantly, you can be focused on the issues that are hurting your group the most.

Keep this information to yourself.

This is not a public-facing survey; rather, you are gathering information behind the scenes and by observation. If people know you're working to find out exactly what's wrong with the organization it's going to make them feel nervous, especially the leadership staff.

In order to gain collaborative power and improve your group you need to reduce resistance to your process of gaining power. And making people nervous, especially your fellow leaders, is going to create resistance.

Here is the exception:

If you have successfully turned this book into a training manual that you are now using in your workplace, then you'll use all of these questions in an open discussion to assess where the group is strong and where the group is weak in order to help the group move forward.

HOW TO RESPOND TO THE ITEMS IN THE SURVEY

In each category I am going to give you a series of questions, statements, and insights. Respond to each question or statement with one of the following, as appropriate; your answers will give you insight about what's going on:

- ***Agree/Yes:*** If you can agree with or confirm the statement then you know the group is doing the right thing. And for every statement that you are agreeing with you know you don't have to address that as an issue.
- ***Disagree/No:*** For every statement or question you disagree with or answer in the negative, you know for sure that is an area that is ripe for improvement.
- ***Don't know/Not sure:*** For every statement that you can neither agree nor disagree with because you don't know, *you know you need to go find out the answer.*
- ***Give a percentage when asked for OR use a "don't know" if need be:*** Be aware that in some cases a higher percentage can indicate a positive attribute and in others it's the opposite, that a higher or lower percentage indicates a weakness in the group. Either way you'll be able to tell the difference based on the question.

Do not underestimate the value of what you are about to uncover by completing this survey.

Some questions are asked in the first person and some questions are asked in the second person. In all of these cases what you're trying to do is give simulated answers as if you were those other people in the group based on your observations.

Let me give you some examples.

When I say, "My supervisor keeps us focused on the mission and values," and the statement is in quotation marks, I want you to answer as if you were those other people in the group looking towards their supervisor in answering that question about their supervisor.

When I say, "The people in your organization are always working on the most important task first," confirm or deny that statement from your own perspective based on your observations.

Again, write it down, keep a log to track progress on each issue, and keep it to yourself.

THE BIG 8 QUESTIONS AND INQUIRIES

1 – Mission / What the people in your organization, in your division or department, or on your crew are thinking, saying, and doing.
"I think our workplace has a strong sense of mission. Nothing is perfect but most everyone seems to know the right priorities when it comes to determining what work is the most important to do. If not, they know where to go to find the answer."

"My supervisor keeps us focused on the mission and values."

"The people in our workplace are willing to explore a better understanding of what is hurting the success of other employees and other departments instead of demonstrating verbal bashing of other employees or other departments."

The people in your organization are supportive of cross-training by participating in cross-training activities when they are made available.

The people in your organization are supportive of cross-training that might include work tasks in other departments.

The people in your organization are always working on the most important task first.

The people in your organization use new information to reprioritize their current work tasks.

People in your organization are encouraged and actually do communicate with their supervisor if they are not sure of their work priorities.

What percentage of group members keep their work properly prioritized?
5% 10% 30% 50% 70% 90%

What percentage of group members are high performers?
5% 10% 30% 50% 70% 90%

What percentage of group members are average performers?
5% 10% 30% 50% 70% 90%

What percentage of group members are hard workers?
5% 10% 30% 50% 70% 90%

What percentage of group members know what it means to "work smart"?
5% 10% 30% 50% 70% 90%

What percentage of group members are always trying to do the right thing?
5% 10% 30% 50% 70% 90%

What percentage of group members are open minded and willing to change the way they are doing things in order to build a more effective organization in the future?
5% 10% 30% 50% 70% 90%

2 – Culture / What the people in your organization, in your division or department, or on your crew are thinking, saying, and doing.

"I think the people that work here treat each other with dignity. There are instances here and there where people don't, like most places, but those situations are very rare. Overall, people are respectful of each other and usually don't talk behind each other's backs."

"What I like about my workplace is that the exceptional work I do gets the recognition I think it deserves. It feels good to work someplace where I am appreciated."

"I think my supervisor protects the culture by holding people accountable for destructive behavior."

The people in your organization avoid aggressive behavior, angry outbursts, or overreactive behavior.

The people in your organization avoid inappropriate conversations, behaviors, or humor related to sexual content.

The people in your organization avoid inappropriate conversations, behaviors, or humor related to ethnic or racial subject matter.

The people in your organization meet with their supervisor in order to search for solutions to their problems instead of "mouthing off" and complaining in meetings because they are upset.

The people in your organization avoid demonstrating harassment and/or bullying behavior.

The people in your organization demonstrate respect, dignity, and empathy.

The people in your organization communicate with their supervisor if they need help because they are being subjected to harassment or bullying behaviors from a fellow employee.

What percentage of group members emulate the behaviors they want from others?
5% 10% 30% 50% 70% 90%

What percentage of group members try to protect the culture from destructive behavior?
5% 10% 30% 50% 70% 90%

What percentage of group members are promoting a culture of success by volunteering to help the people they work with?
5% 10% 30% 50% 70% 90%

What percentage of group members are often demonstrating positive behavior?
5% 10% 30% 50% 70% 90%

What percentage of group members hold themselves responsible for poor outcomes when they should?
5% 10% 30% 50% 70% 90%

What percentage of group members seem to be intent on promoting positive change?
5% 10% 30% 50% 70% 90%

What percentage of group members seem to be stirring up trouble and creating unnecessary drama, creating problems instead of solving problems?
0% 2% 5% 7% 10% 20% 30% 40%

What percentage of group members are honest?
5% 10% 30% 50% 70% 90%

What percentage of group members demonstrate anger in the workplace?
0% 2% 5% 7% 10% 20% 30% 40%

What percentage of group members intimidate others in the workplace?
0% 2% 5% 7% 10% 20% 30% 40%

What percentage of group members are good at "making positive things happen"?
5% 10% 30% 50% 70% 90%

3 - Effective Interpersonal Relationships / What the people in your organization, in your division or department, or on your crew are thinking, saying, and doing.
"People mostly work well together and seem to develop professional relationships with their fellow workers. Relationship building between employees is not perfect but is typically positive."

The people in your organization demonstrate that getting along with their fellow employees is part of their job.

The people in your organization understand they should demonstrate trustworthy behavior in order to maximize collaboration and mission success.

The people in your organization keep interpersonal problems or personal differences separate from work performance.

The people in your organization tolerate personal differences with fellow workers where those differences do not relate directly to mission success such as ethnicity, country of origin, sexual orientation, politics, religion, or other personal philosophies.

The people in your organization understand they should pause and think of other ways to express themselves when feeling angry about an issue.

The people in your organization understand the workplace is a social situation and that angry private or public arguments create fear that causes collaboration to drop.

What percentage of group members are good at resolving personal differences they have with a fellow team member?
5% 10% 30% 50% 70% 90%

What percentage of group members get along well with their fellow workers?
5% 10% 30% 50% 70% 90%

What percentage of group members DO NOT get along well with their fellow workers?
2% 5% 10% 30% 50% 70% 90%

What percentage of group members understand getting along well with others is a job requirement?
5% 10% 30% 50% 70% 90%

4 – High-Quality Communication / What the people in your organization, in your division or department, or on your crew are thinking, saying, and doing.
"Overall our communication, while not perfect, is really pretty good. We typically are informed about what is happening and what to expect next based on timely communication."

"I think my supervisor mentors me and gives me great professional advice."

"The company usually keeps me informed on the important matters that are confronting us as a group."

The people in your organization understand that if they have doubts about a policy, directive, statement, or anything that is expected of them, they should talk with their supervisor.

The people in your organization understand they should ask questions instead of making assumptions if they are not sure what to do next.

People in your workplace understand that when having a problem or a question they should follow the chain of command instead of seeking help or direction from others who are not their immediate leader-supervisors.

What percentage of group members reliably follow the communication chain of command?
5% 10% 30% 50% 70% 90%

What percentage of group members do you consider to be high-quality communicators?
5% 10% 30% 50% 70% 90%

5 - Technical Competency / What the people in your organization, in your division or department, or on your crew are thinking, saying, and doing.
"Our training program is pretty effective. Outside training is reasonably available and the in-house training gives me the confidence to do my job well. Training is obviously a high priority at my workplace."

The people in your organization understand they should provide value by executing technical skills the moment they are needed by the organization.

The people in your organization understand they should not operate outside their area of expertise and that anyone operating outside of their area of expertise can potentially create problems.

The people in your organization understand they should perform their jobs in a safe manner and comply with all safety policies, procedures, and regulations.

The people in your organization understand to always report unsafe conditions so they can be corrected.

What percentage of group members need significant training?
5% 10% 30% 50% 70% 90%

What percentage of group members have less-than-average technical competency?
5% 10% 30% 50% 70% 90%

What percentage of group members actively pursue more training to build their technical competency?
5% 10% 30% 50% 70% 90%

What percentage of group members are experts in their technical skill set?
5% 10% 30% 50% 70% 90%

6 – Productivity / What the people in your organization, in your division or department, or on your crew are thinking, saying, and doing.
"We get a lot done and most everybody is pulling their weight when it comes to getting things done. We work smart and somebody is always coming up with ideas that allow us to be a bit more efficient today than we were yesterday."

"I think my supervisor is great at getting things done."

The people in your organization understand they should make effective independent decisions to keep work flowing.

The people in your organization understand they should increase productivity by using creative thinking and by submitting ideas for improvement related to increasing productivity.

The people in your organization understand they should increase productivity by accepting and demonstrating cross-training and growth opportunities.

The people in your organization understand they should complete all directives as assigned and by the deadline given.

The people in your organization understand they should always ask their supervisor if they have questions or need clarification with an assignment.

The people in your organization know to contact their supervisor when they run into a roadblock while attempting to complete a directive.

The people in your organization understand they should not demonstrate negative behavior when receiving delegated tasks from their supervisor.

The people in your organization understand that they will be recognized for their positive contribution with submitting ideas that can save time or money.

The people in your organization understand they are to contact their supervisor with every new idea that they think might work to improve the success of the organization.

The people in your organization understand innovation and continuous improvement in productivity is not considered "extra" but is a typical way of doing day-to-day business in a high-performing group.

What percentage of group members get their work completed on time?
5% 10% 30% 50% 70% 90%

What percentage of group members get their work completed the right way the first time?
5% 10% 30% 50% 70% 90%

What percentage of group members ask questions if they are not sure about what to do next?
5% 10% 30% 50% 70% 90%

7 - Problem-Solving / What the people in your organization, in your division or department, or on your crew are thinking, saying, and doing.

"There are always problems but we do two things well. First, we are mostly focused on the more important problems and second, we follow a great step-by-step problem-solving process that is pretty effective."

The people in your organization understand they should communicate any problems they find to their supervisor.

The people in your organization understand that the fact-finding process to uncover real and actual conditions is important and they should avoid using information that is unreliable.

The people in your organization understand they should not operate outside their area of expertise when problem-solving.

The people in your organization understand they should not use theories and beliefs in place of facts.

The people in your organization understand they need to let new facts change their current way of thinking if the group is to improve.

The people in your organization understand they should work collaboratively.

The people in your organization understand they should avoid being argumentative.

The people in your organization understand they should contribute to solutions by realizing that somebody else might have a better idea than their own.

The people in your organization understand they should use a step-by-step problem-solving process.

The people in your organization *use* a step-by-step problem-solving process.

What percentage of group members are good at decision making?
5% 10% 30% 50% 70% 90%

What percentage of group members are good at recognizing problems early on while they are small?
5% 10% 30% 50% 70% 90%

What percentage of group members use a step-by-step systematic problem-solving process?
5% 10% 30% 50% 70% 90%

8 - Continuous Improvement / What the people in your organization, in your division or department, or on your crew are thinking, saying, and doing.
"What I like about working here is that I'm always being asked if I have any good ideas and when I tell them the ideas I have, I can tell they are taking me seriously. We all know that not every 'good idea' is really a good idea and will be implemented, but again I can tell they are taking the ideas we submit seriously."

The people in your organization understand they should accept performance feedback with civil behavior.

The people in your organization understand that not accepting performance feedback with civil behavior will hurt their future evaluation scores.

The people in your organization understand they should use performance feedback to improve their future performance when requested to do so.

The people in your organization understand they should submit ideas that they think might improve the organization generally and to increase productivity specifically.

The people in your organization understand that everyone gets credit for thinking about and then submitting ideas for improvement whether they turn out to be workable ideas or not.

What percentage of group members actively submit new ideas for improving and promoting a more successful organization?
5% 10% 30% 50% 70% 90%

LEADERSHIP QUESTIONS

1 – Leading / Answer the following questions and statements as you think people in your organization, in your division or department, or on your crew would. From your perspective and based on your observations of what's happening in the group, how would they respond to these statements?
"Our leadership team has an abundance mentality." (People who have an abundance mentality foster other people's dreams, have confidence, coach and mentor others, are optimistic, and are generous.)

"I think my supervisor models the same behavior they want from others."

"I think my supervisor cares about the people they lead."

"I think my supervisor keeps their cool under stressful situations."

"I think my supervisor makes it safe for me to bring up bad news."

"I think my supervisor is a good listener."

"Leaders help their direct reports to succeed. You can tell every team member is important."

Do leaders include their direct reports in decision making?

Do leaders actively use their performance expectations to successfully guide their own performance?

Do leaders develop a mentoring relationship with their boss?

Do leaders improve their performance once performance deficiencies have been identified?

Do leaders give accurate responses when answering questions?

Do leaders take responsibility for the poor outcomes of their group and the programs they are responsible for?

Do leaders actively use the organization's mission and values as performance expectations?

Do leaders demonstrate active buy-in for maintaining a strong leadership team?

Do leaders actively seek to resolve conflicts with other leaders?

2 - MANAGING
Do leaders manage their time effectively by using a time management system that places important issues ahead of urgent but less-important issues?

Do leaders train their direct reports to expert levels?

Do leaders train their direct reports by designing each person's training plan to address their weakest skill set first?

Do leaders encourage and train their direct reports to accept delegated management tasks as opportunities arise?

3 - REQUIREMENTS
Do leaders comply with all internal reporting, all regulatory, and all safety requirements?

Do leaders demonstrate the behaviors they want from others, including collaboration and leadership?

4 - DIRECT SUPERVISION
Do leaders give the appropriate level of direct supervision, with newer staff getting more supervision?

Do leaders give the appropriate level of direct supervision, with staff having performance issues getting more supervision?

Do leaders give the appropriate level of direct supervision, with staff having high levels of experience getting no or less supervision?

5 - ACCOUNTABILITY, RECOVERY, RECOGNITION
I think my supervisor is quick to give credit where credit is due and freely recognizes my accomplishments.

My supervisor appropriately handles delicate matters in private.

Do leaders meet with their direct reports for periodic performance check-in meetings to discuss their performance?

Do leaders regularly recognize the positive performance demonstrated by their direct reports?

Do leaders hold their direct reports accountable for less-than-standard performance related to performance expectations, agency policies, and all current standard operating procedures?

Do leaders help direct reports recover when their performance has dropped below minimum performance standards?

Do leaders mentor their direct reports?

Do leaders interrupt destructive behavior?

Do leaders pass along information to *their* higher-ups about the positive performance they are observing from their direct reports?

6 - TRAINING – JOB CONTROL

My supervisor makes sure I get the training I need to do a good job.

Do leaders reduce risk by training their direct reports to improve their weakest skill sets?

Do leaders empower their direct reports with effective delegation that encourages decision making?

7 – PRODUCTIVITY

My supervisor's delegation skills are excellent.

I think my supervisor is decisive.

Do leaders make decisions at an effective pace so as to maximize productivity?

Do leaders set deadlines and establish appropriate labor assignments in order to maximize productivity when delegating tasks?

Do leaders assign delegated tasks to individuals by name?

Do leaders encourage direct reports to come up with more effective ways of completing their assignments?

8 – PROBLEM-SOLVING

I think my supervisor is an excellent problem solver and is available to help solve the problems I encounter.

Do leaders verify the facts from the available information?

Do leaders let new facts change their minds?

Do leaders avoid the most common reasons problems don't get solved?

Do leaders use and teach an effective systematic step-by-step problem-solving process?

9 - CONTINUOUS IMPROVEMENT
My supervisor regularly asks for new ideas for improvement.

I think my supervisor takes my ideas for improvement seriously.

Do leaders actively solicit ideas for improvement from their group?

Do leaders actively implement improvement ideas?

Do leaders continuously improve the overall productivity of their work unit?

HYGIENE QUESTIONS

In my job role I have some control over how much achievement I can gain. I do have some limited freedom and authority to make some decisions related to my work and that gives me a feeling of achievement.

I am able to demonstrate achievement in my work.

I am typically recognized for doing a job well done when I do a good job.

As I achieve more accomplishments I am usually rewarded with more authority.

I have a clear understanding of what is expected of me in order to advance in the company.

If I work effectively, being able to advance in the company is a realistic expectation based on the method the company uses to promote people.

We have company policies and procedures like everyone else but they make sense and they are relatively easy to comply with.

We have to deal with a lot of red tape.

I'm becoming an expert in what I do.

We are expected to work hard but overall day-to-day working conditions are pretty good.

I think my job is interesting and from time to time I get to learn and do new things I haven't done before.

I make good money.

I like the people I work with.

I think my current typical work demands allow me time with my family.

In my work group courtesy, dignity, and respect are typical traits demonstrated by most people from top to bottom.

In my company "culture" means we are in the "people business" first and by placing people first our company will grow profits with most everyone's support to make it happen.

We have a clear definition for success and a clear purpose, and we work together to shape our future.

We engage to develop each other professionally and reinvent continuously.

We value results and relationships.

When our company hires people they hire for character and for competency.

Our company places a premium on helping its employees to be physically, mentally, and emotionally healthy.

In this company we tell our managers the truth and in turn they are willing to listen and act on the truth.

In this company people keep their word and say no to unrealistic expectations to avoid over-promising and under-delivering.

This company typically shows they care about people that work for them.

Chapter 5

Inviting Collaborative Power from the Top Down: Looking at Your Work World from Your Boss's Perspective

The steps for inviting and attracting collaborative power are things everyone should be doing on a daily basis.

—*John Schwarz*

Developing a Mentoring Relationship with Your Boss
    Problem-Solving
    Relationship
    Agenda
    Combining Their Needs with the Known Problems Revealed in the Landscape Survey
    Keep Gathering Intel
Step by Step/Listen – Integrate – Act
    Phase 1
        Step 1: Know and Exceed Your Performance Expectations
        Step 2: Basic Rules That Apply to Most Situations
        Step 3: Determine Which Quadrant Your Current Boss Falls Into
    Phase 2
        Step 4: Develop a Mentoring Relationship with Your Boss
    Phase 3
        Step 5: Start Initiating Your Support Role Activities
Knowing Which Quadrants You're Dealing With (Your Q and Your Boss's Q)
    Matrix
    Modifications to Your Approach: Quadrant Thinking
    The Q5 Supervisor
    High Technical Low Collaboration: The Q1 Supervisor
    Low Technical High Collaboration: The Q4 Supervisor
    High Technical High Collaboration: The Q2 Supervisor
    Low Technical Low Collaboration: The Q3 Supervisor

DEVELOPING A MENTORING RELATIONSHIP WITH YOUR BOSS

Understanding your boss's agenda and understanding the agenda of your boss's boss is the key to knowing how to support them. If you can make a deep dive into understanding what the entire leadership hierarchy is needing in terms of the support that you can provide, all the better.

Inviting Collaborative Power from the Top Down means relationship building with your boss to understand the roadblocks facing them along with some of the problems that they are confronting so you can contribute solutions that can enhance higher levels of performance towards mission success.

PROBLEM-SOLVING

Of all the actions that we'll be talking about here, perhaps the single most supportive activity you can offer to your boss is to help solve and eliminate the problems that are confronting them.

As I have noted in my introduction, *the gateway* to inviting power from the top down *is being able to solve problems.* When you become an expert problem solver everybody around you is going to hand you power. My entire career, with its many jobs and experiences, has taught me that, without exception, becoming an expert problem solver is the most important thing you can do to make sure you're in the club.

This book includes two sections on problem-solving: **Appendix 1**: Recognizing Problems SOP and **Appendix 2**: Eight-Step Problem-Solving Process SOP. *A pivotal move on your part is to read, reread, understand and integrate this material until it becomes second nature.* Everyone thinks they are great problem solvers and the simple truth is: most people aren't. *However, by mastering the knowledge provided in Appendices 1 and 2 you will become a master problem solver.*

One of the ways you're going to help support your boss is by Attracting Power from the Bottom Up from your direct reports. We'll talk more about that later.

As you empower the leadership group above you they're going to respond by handing you a significant amount of power after they've had a chance to experience your support of them.

Once they figure out you're a highly competent direct report who knows how to help drive the group towards mission accomplishment, you're going to be considered an extremely valuable member of the team. And they will figure out as well that the smartest thing they can do is to empower you so you can keep supporting them in ways they previously never thought possible.

RELATIONSHIP

Inviting Collaborative Power through a relationship with your most immediate supervisor means you are taking an active role in developing that relationship. One of the best ways to develop a relationship is to play a supportive role. We will talk about the different types of relationships below, but the basic game plan is the same.

Find out what they need from you so can support them and do so in such a way that they notice that you're supporting them. You don't want the reality of you supporting them to get mistakenly buried in the frenetic pace of day-to-day work activities. Rightfully managing their perception of you so it accurately reflects what you're doing *is important*.

Ask them if there are problems they want you to start working on. Find out what's bothering them and *make it part of your work to help them achieve it*. Look how powerful that statement is.

The more you pursue this approach the more power they will hand over to you because it's the next best legitimate response for them to pursue and it works to their favor to do so. When you're never a threat and you're always a support mechanism who is intelligent , savvy, active, and responsive, *you are empowering them*.

Keep the dialogue going so they know exactly what you're doing. Find out how often they want you communicating with them and promote regular check-ins. Regular communication is essential to help you stay on top of their needs and allows you to keep being the *up-to-date thoughtful response machine* that you need to be. When things are not going well for you, you'll now also be able to rely on them to help you get unstuck at the roadblocks you are encountering down at your level of the organization.

AGENDA
Inviting Collaborative Power from the Top Down by understanding your boss's agenda and your boss's boss's agenda is developed during your conversations with your boss. You want to get a clear picture of what demands are being placed on your boss.

Over time, you also want to gain a thorough understanding of *what* they're needing to accomplish, *how* they're planning on meeting those needs, *who's* placing those demands on them and if they're obtainable, and *when* your boss is needing to accomplish the ongoing demands being placed on them. *From this point forward you want to incorporate your boss's agenda into everything you do.*

As time goes on you want to start understanding your boss's boss's agenda as well. When you do that you are now supporting the larger enterprise because you're incorporating a larger, more expansive agenda into your daily tasks.

The more you're supporting the larger agenda the more power people will hand over to you because it's the next best move for them to make. You are a team member who is *all in*. Not only can you demonstrate this approach consistently, you are going to make sure they understand you are an ally and not a threat.

COMBINING THEIR NEEDS WITH THE KNOWN PROBLEMS REVEALED IN THE LANDSCAPE SURVEY

Once you understand what is driving your boss's and your boss's boss's daily actions you're going to start to gather information that tells you where the organization is wanting to go and helps point you in that direction. As you gain that information, start comparing your boss's agenda with the results of your Landscape Survey and *prioritize your problem-solving by combining information from those two inputs*.

It's not unusual that the roadblocks you or your boss might be facing are rooted in one or more of those issues revealed in the Landscape Survey. It is also for this reason that Attracting Power from the Bottom Up and Cultivating Power from the larger workplace landscape are some of the solutions being provided to you in the other Collaborative Power Grab sections of this book; *they directly contribute to solving the problems you found in the Landscape Survey.*

In other words, whether it's Inviting Collaborative Power from the Top Down or Attracting Collaborative Power from the Bottom Up or Cultivating Collaborative Power from the larger workplace landscape, the information that is provided in all these step-by-step instructions is designed to solve the problems that are revealed in the Landscape Survey.

KEEP GATHERING INTEL

Are there directives from your boss's boss that you can read? Are there strategy statements? Are there value statements? Are there mission statements from the senior leaders or mission statements posted to the entire group that you can read? You'll find out a lot about your boss three levels up just by gathering information whenever you can and do so with the express purpose of focusing on how you can support them.

When you've developed a relationship with your boss by helping to support them with problem-solving, when you've started to address the strategy agenda of your boss's boss, when you find out how to address the needs of your boss three levels up, you are going to invite power. And it's power that was legitimately invited and you can now use to support the larger enterprise.

There is one golden rule here: You don't bypass your current supervisor. You need to keep the chain of command strong to keep confidence up. If your immediate supervisor thinks you're bypassing them as a power move, it's not good for any of you. Nothing will stop their mentoring faster than the thought that you're bypassing them to senior management. It's deadly to your power gathering strategy and it's inappropriate.

- *The only exception to this rule is if for some reason your immediate supervisor is directing you to perform activities that are clearly either illegal, unsafe, against company policies or is diametrically opposed to the directives issued by senior management.*

Inviting Power from the Top Down is not going to happen by itself. You have to go out and be *intelligent* in your approach to mission success, *savvy* in knowing the steps to empower those around you, *active* in implementing plans and solving problems, and *responsive* to the needs above you and below you.

The most important set of skills you need to gain in order to make the following step-by-step process successful is listening, integrating, and then acting on every step I'm about to give you.

I have a question for you: are you a good listener? If you're not then you're going to have to improve. Because that's what's really happening here in the step-by-step process. To improve your listening skills: 1) stop talking or interrupting the speaker 2) stop thinking about your response while you are listening and 3) take notes. When you're invited to speak, pause, check your notes, formulate a response and deliver your response. If you do not fully understand the messaging being delivered, after the speaker's presentation, ask questions until you have a complete understanding.

The most important task I bring to your attention is this:

From this day forward every single word that comes out of your supervisor's mouth needs to be *listened to* and then *integrated into your planning on your next steps* and *acted upon as you implement your plan.*

The advice in this last paragraph alone is worth the price of this book. When you can *listen, integrate, and act* on the words that leave your supervisor's mouth that represent the thoughts in their head, *you become a powerhouse for the people you work for* and over time they will return the favor by naturally and legitimately empowering you and making sure you are an integral part of the leadership team.

So it's Listen – Integrate – Act.

STEP BY STEP/LISTEN – INTEGRATE – ACT

— PHASE 1 —

STEP 1: KNOW AND EXCEED YOUR PERFORMANCE EXPECTATIONS

- Build a plan for how you are going to exceed all your performance expectations.
  - **Starting now:** Take your logbook and write down in two or three sentences *exactly* how you're going to exceed each and every performance expectation. This is your *recipe for success.* As new expectations might be placed on you, stop and create a plan that describes in two or three sentences how you're going to exceed that performance expectation. *Take an active and thoughtful approach to planning out how you're going to exceed your performance expectations.*
  - **Starting now:** Take note of any performance expectation you don't completely under-stand and use that as part of your conversation with your supervisor. Always: If you need

input on filling out your *recipe for success* go ask your mentor—yes, that's also your boss. See Step 2.

○ **Starting now:** Start acting on your plan. Start implementing your *recipe for success* and make adjustments to the plan *when you find opportunities to improve* your approach. You want to start to integrate a *continuous improvement strategy* into how you're going to exceed your performance expectations. Your question: what do I need to learn next in order to improve my performance? Once you answer that question: *implement*.

- Note: Building a recipe for success requires some work up front. However, the mere fact that you are methodically assessing each performance expectation and adding the actions you are going to pursue *is extremely powerful*. For any performance expectation that requires a more complex approach just break down your recipe for success into easily understood steps. Any complex concept or practice can typically be broken down into sequential steps and *I can honestly say every time I did this it was time well spent investing in my successful future.*

These issues can be hard to remember so Figure #24 is provided as a quick guide to help you focus on what's important. .

>INVITING< COLLABORATIVE POWER FROM THE TOP DOWN

PHASE 1: STEP 1: *Know & Exceed Your Performance Expectations*

HOW TO **EXCEED** ALL OF YOUR PERFORMANCE EXPECTATIONS (P.E.s)

Preparation:
- Purchase a spiral **notebook**
- Locate your **company P.E.s**

A–Starting Now: *Recipe for Success*

- *Copy down your P.E.s into **your logbook**.*
- *For each P.E., write down **two or three sentences** describing exactly how you're going to exceed each and every performance expectation.*

B–Starting Now: *Clarify Unclear P.E.s*

- *Note the P.E.s you **don't fully understand** as you go.*
- *Take "unclear" P.E.s **to your Boss**/mentor for discussion.*

C–Starting Now: *Take Action on the Plan*

- ***Take action** on the "Recipe" you created in Step A.*
- ***Make adjustments** to your Recipe for Success as you find opportunities to improve it.*

D–Starting Now: *Continuous Improvement*

- ***Ask daily:** What do I need to learn next in order to improve my performance?*
- *Once you answer that question: **implement.***

Recipe For Success

PE #4: Make sure all product received from the factory is packaged in 24 hours + shipped within 24 hrs of packaging.

MY NOTES

- Check SOPs in the packaging + shipping departments – update as necessary
- Meet w/ Jane in packagine on a regular basis to solve problems
- Meet w/ David in shipping on a regular basis to solve problems
- Do we need new equipment to meet these goals more efficiently?
- Do we need a training program to meet this goal? If so, build/implement program
- Check w/ factory on an "early warning statement" about notifying us what is about to be delivered to packaging

Fig. #1 & #24

STEP 2: BASIC RULES THAT APPLY TO MOST SITUATIONS

- One of the best ways to make your boss a success is to complement their weaknesses by supporting them with skills they don't have. This can be very tricky. If you are supporting your boss with a strength that you have in order to compensate for one of their weaknesses, it can appear to them as if you are trying to *one up them* or you are intending to outcompete them in this performance category. Examine the quadrant information below and, depending on your boss's quadrant, instead of overtly disagreeing with your boss in order to help complement their weaknesses you might just find ways to do it anyway without asking for permission. I know this advice could seem controversial and perhaps potentially antithetical to everything I'm saying here, but it's not. *Smart leaders intentionally surround themselves with people who are better than they are at certain skill sets.* Tread carefully here but just know that one of the ways you can make your boss a success is to support them where they are weak, just don't be overt about it.
  - ° **Starting now:** Examine the quadrant advice given below and follow it.
  - ° **Starting now:** If it looks like one of your boss's weaknesses is about to blindside them: *immediately meet with them privately and bring it to their attention.* If they insist on disagreeing with you let the issue go. If the issue becomes a reality then the second time you bring something up they will probably be listening a little more closely and will be less likely to disagree with you. However, if the issue does not become a reality they may still realize that you brought it to their attention because you care about their success. If for some reason they do not come to that same conclusion you are free to remind them that the way you see your job, in part, as their direct report is for you to protect them and in doing so protect mission success.
- Take extreme care in how or if you disagree with any of your supervisors, if ever: *it needs to be done in private.* Anytime you're in a situation where it appears that you're having to disagree with your supervisor in public, *just don't do it.*
  - ° **Starting now:** If you're going to be in a meeting with your boss and you know that your boss's boss will be there, *first have a pre-meeting meeting with your direct supervisor and ask them how they want things to go.* Then do as they say. *From this point forward treat your boss with dignity and respect whether that be in private or public meetings.* Note: there is a lot going on in the leadership stack above you that you may never know about. And this means you don't want to assume that you know the whole situation. If you do make this assumption it could lead to serious mistakes that could mortally wound your relationship with your boss. This is why it's always important to take your boss's behavior as an example of the dynamics in larger meetings that have higher level management around the table.
- Don't complain about your boss to your followers.
  - ° **Starting now:** When you receive information from your boss that you know your followers are going to have problems with, you need to soften the blow. Yes, certainly acknowledge any faults in the information, but at the same time acknowledge that the boss has their eye on a larger field than what we are participating in and it's our job to get the job done. *Do not under any circumstances participate in a whine session with your direct reports about your boss*

or their directives. The more you can draw parallels between yourself and your supervisor and the group's mission statement in the eyes of your followers, the more you become an extension of your leadership team and therefore an extension of their power as well. ***The only specific exceptions to this rule are found within the quadrant information below.***

- Something going wrong?
  - **Starting now:** Get to your supervisor ASAP and let them know what's going on. The sooner you do it the better off you are. Some supervisors may criticize you for not solving the problem when they think you should have, but the alternative of you knowing about a problem and not contacting them sooner is orders of magnitude worse for you and your supervisor. Note: as noted previously, train yourself on Appendices 1 and 2 and know the material like the back of your hand. When you become an expert problem solver the whole world will want you around.
- Take responsibility for poor outcomes.
  - **Starting now:** If you or your crew is responsible for a poor outcome, the sooner you bring that to the attention of your supervisor the better. It doesn't mean you won't get a dose of medicine that may leave a very bad taste in your mouth, but over time this falls under the category of perception management. By demonstrating that you hold yourself responsible, ***they learn that you are somebody they can trust.*** This is big. The moment your supervisor *is convinced that you are legitimately trustworthy, your power expands massively.*
- Don't bypass your boss.
- **Starting now:** Always follow the chain of command and do not bypass your boss on the way up. Nor should you let your boss bypass you on the way down to your direct reports. There is no other situation that is more ripe for misunderstanding and misdirected perceptions along with misdirected anger than the chain of command getting bypassed or the chain of command going unused. The messaging can get confusing and people won't really know what to do next or they will think they know based on poor-quality information. When bypassing has occurred and nothing goes wrong it gives people the impression that bypassing the chain of command is not only not wrong but it can be very effective and useful. However, whenever a breakdown in the chain of command causes problems it's usually a very messy situation with a lot of finger-pointing to go around. Essentially with a healthy chain of command in use it will make sure that the right decisions are being made at the right authority level with the right people being held responsible. Note: the only exception to this rule is if for some reason your immediate supervisor is directing you to perform activities that are clearly illegal, unsafe, against company polices or are diametrically opposed to the directives issued by senior management. If that happens you have to have a, probably uncomfortable, conversation with your direct supervisor before you go over their head. In any situation like this, which we can all agree is a difficult situation, you need to talk to your direct supervisor first before you do anything else. ***Welcome to leadership.*** The only exception to this rule is if you suspect the end result of your conversation could be violence. In that rare situation going directly to your boss's boss before a conversation with your supervisor, is entirely appropriate. Study, follow and enforce Appendices 3 and 4 and billeted chapter 7 high quality communication collaborative behaviors in order to promote a high quality communication system.

Figure #25 is provided as a quick guide to help you focus on what's important.

>**INVITING**< Collaborative Power from the Top Down

PHASE 1: STEP 2: *Basic Rules That Apply To Most Situations*

Fig. #2 & #25

MAKE YOUR BOSS **A SUCCESS** - COMPLEMENT THEIR WEAKNESSES BY SUPPORTING THEM WITH SKILLS THEY DON'T HAVE

Warning: When supporting your boss with a *strength of yours* to compensate for a *weakness of theirs*, it can appear to them *as if* you are trying to **one up** them.

Basics... {
- AVOID OVERTLY DISAGREEING WITH YOUR BOSS
- FIND WAYS TO SUPPORT THEM W/O ASKING PERMISSION

A–Starting Now:
Use the Four Quadrants

- *Examine / Place yourself in the Four Quadrants*

- *Examine / Place your boss in the Four Quadrants*

- *Without asking, and being careful not to one up them, take action on shoring up your boss's weaknesses*

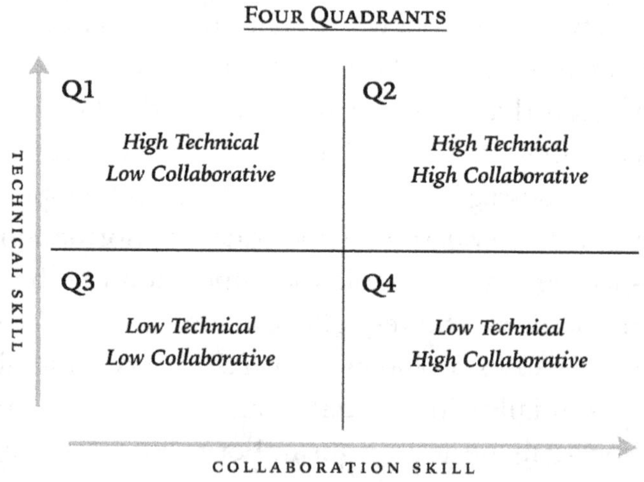

FOUR QUADRANTS

Q1 *High Technical Low Collaborative*	**Q2** *High Technical High Collaborative*
Q3 *Low Technical Low Collaborative*	**Q4** *Low Technical High Collaborative*

TECHNICAL SKILL

COLLABORATION SKILL

B–Starting Now:

*If it looks like one of your boss's weaknesses are about to blindside them, **immediately meet with them privately** & bring it to their attention.*

C–Starting Now:

*If a meeting is taking place with your boss and your boss's boss, **meet with your direct supervisor first** and ask them how they want the meeting to go.*

D–Starting Now:

*When you receive information from your boss that you know your followers are going to have problems with, **you need to soften the blow.***

E–Starting Now:

*Something going wrong? **Get to your supervisor ASAP and let them know what's going on.** The sooner you do it the better off you are.*

F–Starting Now:

Take responsibility for poor outcomes. If you or your crew is responsible for a poor outcome, the sooner you tell that to your supervisor the better.

G–Starting Now:

Always follow the chain of command and do not bypass your boss on the way up. UNLESS—you are asked to do something illegal or unsafe.

STEP 3: DETERMINE WHICH QUADRANT YOUR CURRENT BOSS FALLS INTO

- **Starting now:** Carefully and slowly examine the quadrant descriptions of the various bosses in the section below. This guide is just that: a guide. Everybody has fingerprints, but it's those same fingerprints that make us very different. The quadrant thinking of your boss is no different. There is no doubt that your boss is going to land predominantly in one of these quadrants, *just as you do.* By combining your understanding of your quadrant and your boss's, you can bring a very intelligent level of support to your boss. Step 3 is imperative before you make any future moves into Phase 2.

- **Starting now:** This guide is provided so not only do you understand what quadrant your boss is in but what quadrant you are in. If you haven't already figured out which quadrant you are in, do so now by referring to the Quadrant Thinking section in Chapter 3 and the quadrant information provided below. The advice that's given to you in this section when comparing your quadrant to your boss's quadrant *needs to be an essential component of your plan moving forward if you want to succeed._*

Note: there are many benefits to understanding Quadrant Thinking, however one of the primary purposes of understanding your and your boss's quadrant is to *protect mission success against your combined inherent weaknesses.* Your boss could be very strong in an area where you are weak, and that's *complementary strength.* You could be very strong in an area where your boss is weak, and that is also *complementary strength.* However, when discovering areas where you're both weak you can empower the both of you by *acquiring the resources and knowledge necessary to resolve your combined weakness.*

Figure #26 is provided as a quick guide to help you focus on what's important. .

>INVITING< COLLABORATIVE POWER FROM THE TOP DOWN

PHASE 1: STEP 3: *Detect What Quadrant Your Current Boss Falls Into*

Fig. #3 & #26

UNDERSTANDING YOU AND YOUR BOSS'S QUADRANT **PROTECTS MISSION SUCCESS** AGAINST YOUR COMBINED INHERENT WEAKNESSES.

FOUR QUADRANTS

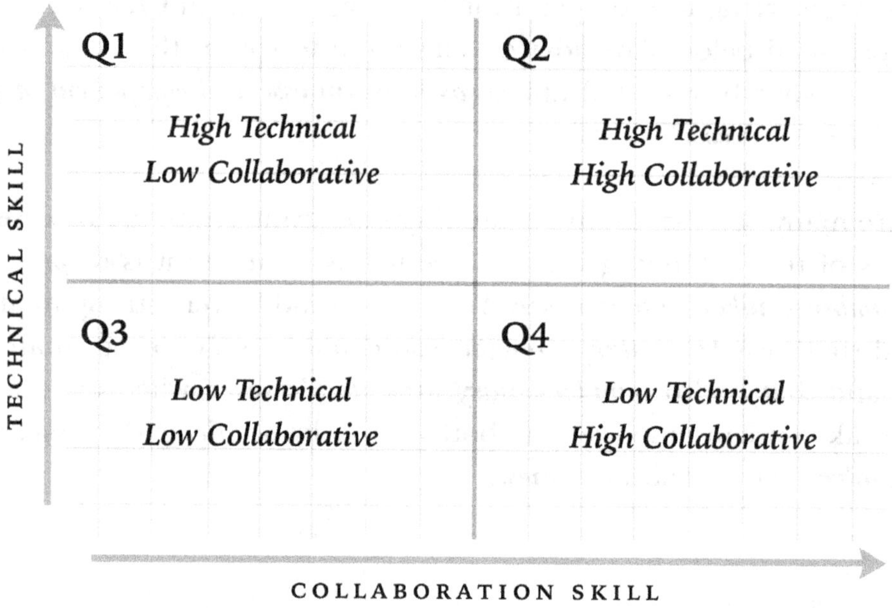

Q1
*High Technical
Low Collaborative*

Q2
*High Technical
High Collaborative*

Q3
*Low Technical
Low Collaborative*

Q4
*Low Technical
High Collaborative*

TECHNICAL SKILL

COLLABORATION SKILL

Start Now Actions — *More Info*

A–Starting Now: *Read the Quadrant Descriptions*
• *Go to chapter 5 and study the quadrant descriptions.*

B–Starting Now: *Place Your Boss In the Quadrants*
• *Using the material you've read, place your boss in the appropriate quadrant.*

C–Starting Now: *Place Yourself In the Quadrants*
• *Using the material you've read, place yourself in the appropriate quadrant.*

D–Starting Now: *Protect Mission Success From You & Your Boss's Combined Weaknesses.*
• *Find where you and your boss are weak.*

E–Starting Now: *Where You're Both Weak: Secure Outside Help.*
• *Protect your weaknesses as necessary and recruit outside help if needed.*

— PHASE 2 —

STEP 4: DEVELOP A MENTORING RELATIONSHIP WITH YOUR BOSS

- *Always-always-always have a notepad and pen in your hand when you meet with your supervisor. Take a lot of notes, refer to them often, and update them as necessary.*
- You are asking: What are their expectations of you?
  - **Starting now:** Ask them in exact terms what they want and need from you and then follow those instructions with a 110 percent execution response. Finding out what they want from you next is a continuous routine conversation from this point forward. Note: Any type of routine meeting with your supervisor needs to be placed on your calendar. I shouldn't have to say that but after *writing things down* this is the second largest area where I find people hurting their own success.
  - **Starting now:** *Request, accept, and integrate critical performance feedback.* Ask them to please give you direction when they think you're doing something wrong so you can correct your performance immediately. Just know that once they start doing this it might not feel very good, but it's the exact thing you need to know. Every time they give you critical feedback on your performance *and you make an adjustment they're going to be very impressed with you*, as well they should. Professionals making adjustments in their performance quickly and effectively is always an impressive power play. One of the reasons it's so impressive is because this is a very difficult thing for many people to do. *You, however, are going to become an expert at it.*
  - **Starting now:** When setting the goals for your performance objectives try to ensure that you have a clear and realistic approach to achieving those objectives. Ask your supervisor for any *practical advice* that they can offer so you have a better chance of achieving those objectives.
  - **Starting now:** Make sure every directive you receive has a clear objective, an achievable deadline, and the resources available to complete the directive as assigned. Talk things out with your supervisor until those three requirements are met with each assignment they give you. By approaching every directive this way it increases your chances of success, which increases your supervisor's chances for success. Lastly, if you find during implementation of your assignments that for whatever reason you're not going to be able to meet the deadline, *the earlier you inform your supervisor the better.* Prior to you presenting this information think through the options of what could be offered to help move the objective forward in spite of the new roadblock just encountered, *but don't take too long doing this.*
  - **Starting now:** Have and demonstrate a strong work ethic. Certainly having a strong worth ethic will benefit your entire life, however the key word there is *demonstrate.* It's not enough to be good at what you do; if your boss doesn't know it then their perception of you is incomplete. As I'm sure you've heard before: *perception is reality.* It's up to you to make sure

their perception of you matches the reality. *You are an authentic support to the leadership structure above you. There's nothing wrong with you making sure they know that.*

° **Starting now:** Have periodic meetings with your supervisor from this point forward. Keep your communication level with them extremely high. Again, any routine meeting with your supervisor needs to be placed on your calendar.

- However, ***don't get in the way of their already crowded calendar.***
- You want to keep them informed of ***all the information you're in possession of that can help them do their job.***

Figure #27 is provided as a quick guide to help you focus on what's important. .

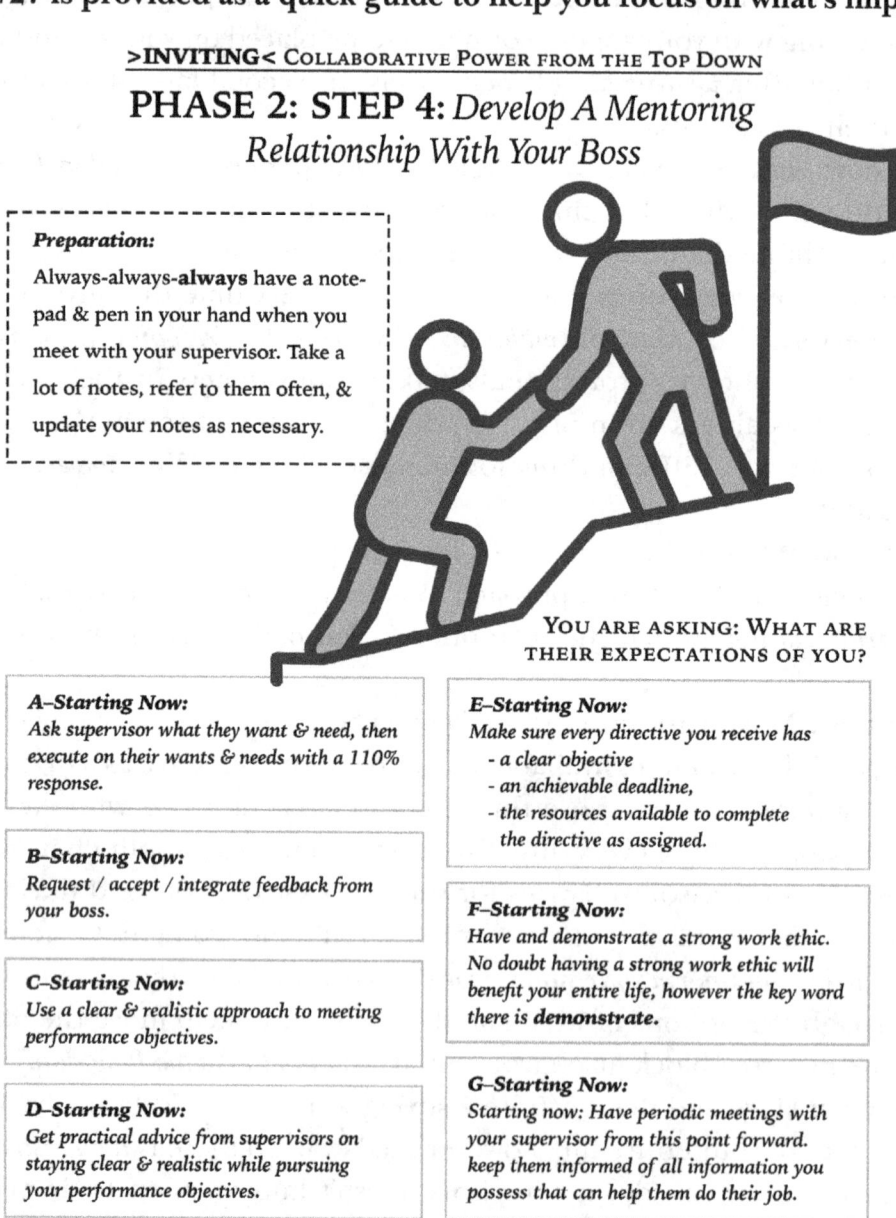

>INVITING< COLLABORATIVE POWER FROM THE TOP DOWN

PHASE 2: STEP 4: *Develop A Mentoring Relationship With Your Boss*

Preparation:
Always-always-**always** have a note-pad & pen in your hand when you meet with your supervisor. Take a lot of notes, refer to them often, & update your notes as necessary.

YOU ARE ASKING: WHAT ARE THEIR EXPECTATIONS OF YOU?

A–Starting Now:
Ask supervisor what they want & need, then execute on their wants & needs with a 110% response.

B–Starting Now:
Request / accept / integrate feedback from your boss.

C–Starting Now:
Use a clear & realistic approach to meeting performance objectives.

D–Starting Now:
Get practical advice from supervisors on staying clear & realistic while pursuing your performance objectives.

E–Starting Now:
Make sure every directive you receive has
- a clear objective
- an achievable deadline,
- the resources available to complete
 the directive as assigned.

F–Starting Now:
*Have and demonstrate a strong work ethic. No doubt having a strong work ethic will benefit your entire life, however the key word there is **demonstrate**.*

G–Starting Now:
Starting now: Have periodic meetings with your supervisor from this point forward. keep them informed of all information you possess that can help them do their job.

Fig. #8 & #27

— PHASE 3 —

STEP 5: START INITIATING YOUR SUPPORT ROLE ACTIVITIES

...by supporting your boss. Find out from them, *over time during the course of your conversations with them* or by asking them directly, if you think they would be comfortable discussing these issues with you at some point in the future *once you've had the chance to establish a good relationship*:

- What are their goals for the group?
  - ° **Starting now:** Make them your goals as well.
- What are their most important priorities?
  - ° **Starting now:** Those are your most important priorities as well.
- What are the problems they are facing?
  - ° **Starting now:** Those are the same problems you're going to start working on the solutions to in addition to your normally assigned work.

Note: The power of these three actions cannot be overstated. In fact if I was going to distill the idea of inviting collaborative power to just three actions it would be these. They are pivotal both to the success of your boss and to you.

At some point your boss is going to realize this as well, either by you practicing these start now actions or because they are reading the book too. Either way, when that starts to happen, this realization *has the tendency to morph your relationship into a partnership*.

In terms of inviting power down, *this type of relationship change is the epitome of success*.

Important Side Note:

- It would also be good to know what performance expectations are being placed on your supervisor by their higher-ups. However, this is a bit tricky as your boss probably won't feel comfortable discussing these items with you. Extreme caution needs to be exercised here. If they ever think that you're wanting to find out their performance expectations so you can determine whether you think they're meeting those expectations, it's a *game stopper* in building the mentoring relationship you need to build. If you can't safely find out what expectations are being placed on your boss by their boss, it's best to leave it; it is not necessary to find out.
  - ° **Starting now:** If you are able to find out over time then indeed use their performance expectations to guide your future decision making so can support your boss where they need you the most.

Figure #28 is provided as a quick guide to help you focus on what's important. .

>INVITING< COLLABORATIVE POWER FROM THE TOP DOWN

PHASE 3: STEP 5: *Start Initiating Your Support Role Activities By Supporting Your Boss*

THROUGH THE COURSE OF **CONVERSATIONS** WITH YOUR BOSS, OR BY ASKING THEM **DIRECTLY** (IF YOU THINK THEY'D BE COMFORTABLE WITH THAT), FIND OUT ABOUT THEIR PRIORITIES IN THE FOLLOWING **3 CATEGORIES.**

1. What are your boss's goals for the group?
Starting now, make their goals into your goals.

2. What are your boss's most important priorities?
Starting now, those are your most important priorities as well.

3. What are the problems your boss is facing?
Starting now, support your boss by taking owner--ship of those problems where it makes sense.

NOTE: THE POWER OF THESE THREE ACTIONS **CANNOT BE OVERSTATED.** IN FACT, IF I WAS GOING TO DISTILL THE IDEA OF INVITING COLLABORATIVE POWER TO JUST THREE ACTIONS, **IT WOULD BE THESE.** THEY ARE PIVOTAL, BOTH TO THE SUCCESS OF YOUR BOSS AND TO YOU.

Fig. #12 & #28

KNOWING WHICH QUADRANTS YOU'RE DEALING WITH (YOUR Q AND YOUR BOSS'S Q)

You'll need to make modifications to the Step 2 instructions above based on the type of supervisor that you're working for, so we're going to go back to the quadrant method of measuring people's technical and collaborative capacities as a way of understanding how they're going to supervise.

It is essential that you modify the Step 2 instructions above based on the quadrant in which your supervisor currently resides.

MATRIX

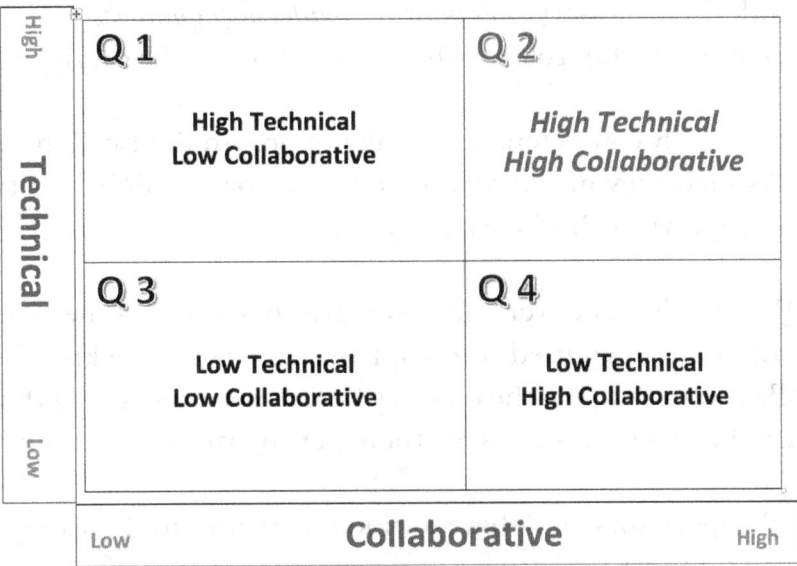

MODIFICATIONS TO YOUR APPROACH: QUADRANT THINKING

If you haven't already read the section Operating Rules of the Human Brain and Quadrant 2 Behaviors in Chapter 3, please go read that section before going any farther.

THE Q5 SUPERVISOR

I want to avoid any Pollyannaish viewpoints about people in power and mention that there's another type of or Supervisor that I will call the Q5 "boss." That's correct—they're not on the quadrant matrix because **they actually operate with a very different set of rules.** They could very well be a Q1, Q4, or a type of Q2, but the different rules that they're following are the rules of the self-serving leader. The transactional leader, the corrupt leader, the liar leader. While they're spouting a well-managed message that is supporting the people and supporting the group mission they are actually just feathering their own nest in ways that are uncompromisingly corrupt. Further discussion about corrupt leaders is beyond the scope of this book, but suffice it to say that if you run into a Q5 boss you have two choices.

First, you can choose to not see the signs of how they manipulate the situation to their own benefit and go through life blindly thinking they really do care about you and the mission. Second, you can figure out what they're doing and decide whether it hurts you enough to leave if you do have an option to leave. Q5 bosses are rarely overt in their deception and can possess the skills to appear as a Q2. They can be extraordinarily covert in their activities in order to hide the agenda that is the real driver behind their true but unknown-to-all goals.

HIGH TECHNICAL LOW COLLABORATION: THE Q1 SUPERVISOR
The Q1 supervisor is the most common type of supervisor you will encounter on the planet.

The reason for this is that leaders are often hired because of their demonstration of high technical competency while in the position *they had prior to the one they have now*. Obviously those technical skills have little to do with the necessary *collaborative leadership qualities* that the Q1 leader does not possess (but needs in their leadership role) as they now arrive to take on their new leadership duties.

Q1s are typically very technically competent and weak not only in their collaborative skills but in their collaborative *thinking*. As such they may have a tendency to bark orders and to freely micromanage because they know a lot about what they're asking you to do.

It's not unusual that Q1 supervisors are very outcome driven and can sometimes skip over the collaborative options that could have been used to complete tasks more quickly. They are not necessarily empathetic towards collaborative approaches, simply because it's something that was not part of their training and wasn't part of the requirements for them getting the job that they now hold.

This is not to say that Q1 supervisors don't have a wide spectrum with how they emotionally deal with people. Some of the nicest and very effective supervisors I'm ever met were Q1s and some were the worst. Not worse because they were bad people but as supervisors they were just so unskilled in the use of collaboration and any knowledge of how it's essential to mission success when involving an enterprise that relies on humans. Their ignorance is hard on the group and can lead to insufficient fear reduction if there is a people problem that *goes unaddressed because it is not recognized by the Q1 leader*.

If you want to impress a Q1 supervisor you need to stay on task and you need to meet the objective by deadline exactly as outlined in the directive. Q1s like to be agreed with because they're not sure how to handle disagreement. With a lot of Q1s when you disagree with them they're hearing you say that they are wrong.

Now, how you use your collaborative skills with your work crew to get things done as quickly as possible and stay as focused on objectives as possible *gets to be your call*. Just know that when you're speaking in terms of the raw, more advanced aspects of collaboration the Q1 supervisor can misunderstand fear reduction as coddling.

While the Q1 supervisor is definitely the sharpest knife in the drawer when it comes to the technical aspects of getting their particular job done (or your particular job, for that matter), don't rely on them for advice on superior psychological approaches to uncomfortable situations.

Oftentimes they're very good at getting things done that are immediately in front of them. However, if it is sometimes necessary to accept short-term loss to accomplish long-term strategies, don't be surprised if this is something that they are not good at. Q1s are typically repelled by short-term losses even if enduring such pain *now* could pay off handsomely *later*. They see all short-term losses as failures.

As always, there are exceptions. I'm speaking to tendencies here and Q1 supervisors can be very mechanical ***because they know that's what has paid off for them in the past***, which causes them to undervalue more advanced collaborative techniques that include a different way of planning or a different way of achieving longer-term projects.

People who are not strong collaborators have a tendency to undervalue human collaboration and will be unaware of the lost opportunity that investments in collaboration can provide the group in the long run. Because they are unaware of the lost opportunity, ***they don't change***.

It's for this reason that it's not unusual for the Q1 supervisor to have a few black marks on their performance evaluations related to longer-term projects that were relying on collaboration. To them, strategy, collaboration, advanced logistics, and planning related to ***human capital*** can all, or separately, be considered gobbledygook.

The Q1 supervisor will have a tendency to psychologically project their own qualities, good or bad, upon other people. While to one extent or another everybody psychologically projects, I find that the Q1 has a tendency to make assumptions about other people more than a Q4 or a Q2. It's just the reality of this type of supervisor. But when it comes to your relationship with your direct reports, even if you have a Q1 supervisor you can and should be a Q2 supervisor to your direct reports.

How the perspective of the Q1 leader can hurt the group can show up in many ways. For instance you might hear them saying: "If the training program was good enough for me and it got me where I am today, why do you think you need to spend precious time and money improving the very same training program for the people that are working for you?"

When a Q1 supervisor cogently extends that type of logic thread (and others like it) to deciding how to ***allocate resources (time and money) to the organization*** based on a set of values that don't excite improvement in collaboration, the group may look great from a short-term task execution perspective yet actually be falling behind from a collaborative long-term investment perspective.

The Q1 supervisor wants results, and sometimes those results are acquired at the expense of the investment necessary for developing collaboration. The same collaboration that can provide extremely high levels of performance *tomorrow but not at the moment while you're having to make the investment.*

Steady resolve coupled with a strong sense of how best to leverage the future to the benefit of mission success is required to justify the short-term burdens that may be needed to see long-term benefits that directly impact human collaboration. This is where Q1 leaders can be weak.

If you are having to make the argument to your Q1 supervisor that you want to deny short-term resources for long-term benefits, you have to make sure you have a good case before making the pitch.

Again you might hear them saying: "Shouldn't you be getting the directive I just gave you completed instead? What's wrong with you?"

With a Q1 supervisor you're going to have to convince them that collaboration has value, but you can't do it face-to-face. Instead you have to do it by demonstrating the high performance that collaboration makes possible by following the steps above.

Summary of the Q1 Supervisor

- High technical low collaboration
- Outcome/results driven
- Can have a tendency to micromanage
- Avoids short-term losses necessary to make long-term gains
- Typically does not relate to efforts like fear reduction
- Doesn't necessarily realize the importance of empowerment
- Can be highly demanding
- Can be highly productive
- Does not do well if working for a Q4 supervisor

Comparing Your Quadrant to Your Q1 Boss

If you are a Q1 you are going to get along pretty well with your boss. However, you're not going to be able to support them where they are weak, which is in the collaboration part of their job. What you're wanting to achieve here is for your boss to be a success and, as noted previously, one of the best ways to make your boss a success is to complement their weaknesses by supporting them with skills they don't have. *If you remain a Q1, you will certainly look pretty good to your boss but you're not going to be able to help them in their weakest skill set.*

If you are a Q4 your Q1 boss is going to drive you crazy. It's going to be essential that you follow my exact instructions as noted in the steps and phases. In addition to that you are going to have to buck up on the technical aspects of your job—if not, you're going to be picked apart detail by detail and you'll end up being extremely micromanaged. The only way to avoid that is to demonstrate that you have the technical prowess necessary to do the job. In other words, you need to become a Q2.

- *As a Q4 you have a prime opportunity to help support your boss in their collaborative weaknesses. Take the time to think about how you can do that as you simultaneously work on increasing your technical competencies.*

If you are a Q2 then you're set to not only meet your boss's technical requirements but also complement their weaknesses with your collaborative skills. *Go for it.*

If you are a Q3 things are not going to go well unless you become a Q1 as quickly as possible. While becoming a Q2 should be everyone's goal, *your immediate goal needs to be bucking up on your technical skills so you can meet the expectations of your Q1 boss*. If your technical skills do not improve in a way that your boss notices, you're going to be picked apart detail by detail, you'll end up being extremely micromanaged, and most likely you'll get the worst assignments requiring the least amount of thinking and hurting your job satisfaction. That being said, the Q1 boss won't want an unimproved Q3 on the team for long, so if you want to stick around you need to improve your technical competence right away.

Figure #29 is provided as a quick guide to help you focus on what's important. .

Fig. #29: Knowing the Quadrants:
The Q1 Supervisor

Q1

Knowing Which Quadrants You're Dealing With
(Your Q and Your Boss's Q)

- **High** technical, **low** collaboration

- **Outcome/results** driven

- Can have a tendency to **micromanage**

- *Avoids* short-term losses necessary to make **long-term gains**

- Typically *does not* relate to efforts like **fear reduction**

- Doesn't necessarily realize the importance of **empowerment**

- Can be *highly demanding*

- Can be *highly productive*

- Does **not do well** if working for a Q4 supervisor

LOW TECHNICAL HIGH COLLABORATION: THE Q4 SUPERVISOR

Of all the supervisor types, the Q4s compete with the Q2s as being equally prevalent in the general population but a distant second to the large number of Q1 supervisors out there.

It's always a positive sign when your supervisor is wanting to make sure that collaboration is taking place at the appropriate levels, at the appropriate times, and in the appropriate meetings to make sure everyone is part of the process. For a Q4 *how it was done is just as important as what was done*. But that's where the positive signs start to stop with a Q4.

Whenever tasks go unaccomplished and become a problem, the leopard can sometimes suddenly change spots. They're going to want to know what went wrong and they're not going to be very patient with you just concentrating on the fact that *how it was done was just as important as what was done*. Even though that's what you were told at the front end of the directive.

People typically appropriately prioritize based on the impression that they're getting from their supervisor. In this case, because some of the Q4's directives are technically flawed and as a result things don't work out as intended with the directive they handed out, the Q4 stops caring how things were done and just wants to know why it wasn't technically correct in its implementation.

The other dynamic you need to be aware of is if you are working for a Q4 supervisor and they have a Q1 supervisor, it's a horrible mix that will most likely trickle downhill and negatively impact your work life.

In fact it's worth mentioning now that anytime you have a Q4 working for a Q1 supervisor, or anytime you have a Q1 working for a Q4 supervisor—especially when it involves two leaders *directly above you*—you're looking at a shit storm that's probably going to land on your desk in the form of mixed messages, hard feelings, and directives that were not completed according to *somebody's* expectations.

Your response: you need to stay out of that fight as much as you possibly can.

If your direct supervisor is the Q1 and they're working for the Q4 *then you need to incorporate some collaborative aspects to whatever directive is coming your way in order to support your supervisor.*

Alternatively, if your direct supervisor is the Q4 and they're working for the Q1 *then you need to incorporate the technical aspects into whatever directive is coming your way in order to support your supervisor.*

Even though the Q4 supervisor can be very good at making sure people feel included, by the very nature of this quadrant they lack technical skills that are important to managing and leading the group. If somebody is feeling bad about a particular decision that feeling might become more important than meeting objectives, and without meeting objectives there is no mission success. For some Q4 supervisors it can be difficult for them to deal with uncomfortable situations.

This is what Q1 and Q4 have in common—they sometimes have a difficult time dealing with uncomfortable situations—*but for different reasons.* The Q1 is uncomfortable dealing with uncomfortable situations because they simply don't know what to do. However, the Q4 is uncomfortable dealing with the situation because *they have a tendency to treat everybody's feelings as equally important.*

Fear reduction includes clamping down on destructive behavior and because the Q4 supervisor *is essentially treating everybody's feelings with equal importance* they may be unsure of what to do next so they are susceptible to do nothing when they should certainly be doing something. And of course doing nothing in this situation is the worst thing you can do.

Other Q4 supervisors, however, can be very active at fear reduction, which can make the workplace a great place to work in spite of their technical deficiencies, as long as the Q4 supervisor has surrounded themselves with, and easily yields to, a technically sound and supportive staff. There are multiple links in that chain: First, the Q4 has a good number of technically competent staff; two, this staff is also supportive; and three, the Q4 will also cooperatively yield to their direct reports' recommendations concerning technical matters. *Note: If any of the three links in that chain just described fail, the Q4 supervisor's performance will be negatively impacted.*

With Q4 supervisors wearing their feelings on their sleeve, it's not unusual that they give everybody on the crew the same performance evaluation score: outstanding! Feels good, right? It feels good giving people those ratings and it feels good receiving those ratings, regardless of the actual performance that's being demonstrated by each individual on the crew. Everybody knows it's bullshit, but who's going to rock that boat? But evaluating an entire crew with the same performance rating results in plenty of negative feelings on the part of your high performers. Therein lies another Q4 self-made dilemma where they want to promote good feelings (and avoid uncomfortable conversations with their low performers) but that backfires with those they rely on the most: *their high performers.*

When you have a Q4 supervisor you can backfill their lack of technical competency with your skill set, making a great team. The Q4 supervisor needs mission accomplishment and you can help them get there by making sure your group is staying on task and making sure that the objectives the Q4 supervisor is giving you *are very clear to you at the moment of delegation.*

With the Q4 supervisor you also want to be making sure that the process that you're going to use to achieve the objective is integrated into the directive. Remember, to them how things are done is just as important as what gets done. The Q4 supervisor wants to make sure that you are taking into consideration a highly collaborative approach with all your fellow leaders as you move forward in completing your assignments. This is a very rational and important way to approach your work, as any Q2 would agree.

The Q4 supervisor is very process heavy, sometimes so much so it has a negative impact on meeting the objective by the deadline established. The best thing you can do is to bolster their confidence by making sure they know that you're including all the right people around the table as you're moving forward making decisions and meeting objectives prior to deadline. This is something you should be doing anyway as a Q2, but for the process-heavy Q4 supervisor you might need to be even more explicit about it.

Lastly, with a Q4 supervisor you have to be careful not to show them up technically. It can be easy to do even accidentally, so caution is required here.

Summary of the Q4 Supervisor

- High collaboration low technical
- Process driven
- Can have a tendency to under-supervise when giving directives
- May or may not relate to efforts like fear reduction
- Can have tendency to avoid uncomfortable situations
- Has the tendency to prioritize good news over bad news
- Has a tendency to inappropriately prioritize all feelings as *equally important.*
- Does not do well when working for a Q1 supervisor

Comparing Your Quadrant to Your Q4 Boss

If you are a Q4 you are going to get along pretty well with your boss. However, you're not going to be able to support them where they are weak, which is in the technical part of their job. What you're wanting to achieve here is for your boss to be a success and, as noted previously, one of the best ways to make your boss a success is to complement their weaknesses by supporting them with skills they don't have. *If you remain a Q4 ,you will certainly look pretty good to your boss but you're not going to be able to help them in their weakest skill set.*

If you are a Q1 your Q4 boss is going to drive you crazy. *It's going to be essential that you follow my exact instructions as noted in the steps and phases.* In addition to that you are going to have to buck up on the collaborative aspects of your needed skill sets (as described in this book); if not you will potentially be seen as uncaring, pushy, and someone who just wants to do things their way and not consider other, perhaps better, opportunities at getting task assignments completed with a higher level of collaborative performance. Besides following the advice above the other way to avoid problems is to simply become a Q2.

- *As a Q1, you have a prime opportunity to help support your boss in their technical weaknesses. Take the time to think about how you can do that as you follow the step-by-step instructions provided in this book that can increase your collaboration skills.*

If you are a Q2 then you're set to not only meet your boss's collaborative requirements but also complement their weaknesses with your technical skills. *Go for it.*

If you are a Q3 things are not going to go well unless you become a Q4 as quickly as possible. While becoming a Q2 should be everyone's goal, *your immediate goal needs to be bucking up on your collaboration skills so you can meet the expectations of your Q4 boss.* If your collaborative skills do not improve in a way that your boss notices, you're going to be viewed as somebody who should not be in charge of people because you lack the people skills necessary to be a leader. As a result you will most likely be passed over for future leadership positions, and they won't be wrong in this assessment. That being said, Q4 bosses sometimes have a problem firing anyone, so Q3s just might retain their positions.

Figure #30 is provided as a quick guide to help you focus on what's important. .

Fig. #30: Knowing the Quadrants:
The Q4 Supervisor

Q4

Knowing Which Quadrants You're Dealing With
(Your Q and Your Boss's Q)

- **High** collaboration, **low** technical

- **Process** driven

- Can have a *tendency* to **under-supervise** when giving directives

- *May* or *may not* relate to efforts like **fear reduction**

- Can have tendency to *avoid* uncomfortable situations

- Has the tendency to **prioritize good news over bad news**

- Has a tendency to **inappropriately prioritize** *all* feelings as equally important.

- **Does not do well when working for a Q1 supervisor**

HIGH TECHNICAL HIGH COLLABORATION: THE Q2 SUPERVISOR

Of all the supervisor types, the Q2s compete with the Q4s as being equally prevalent in the general population but a distant second to the large number of Q1 supervisors out there.

They get it. By definition, Q2s have excelled in the technical area of their life and the collaborative area of their life and they're really smart about what they do next. They're genuine and straightforward, but this doesn't mean they can't be demanding.

Their type of demanding, though, is slightly different than the Q1 simply because they understand the training it takes to turn you into an expert. They're always looking towards the horizon, making sure that the general direction they're moving syncs with goals that may not be achieved for a couple of years. They are typically very realistic when handing out directives, but just make sure you're checking all the boxes when they hand down and delegate tasks to you. Like I said they can be demanding and sometimes they're so busy they leave stuff out. And everything they leave out can hurt you.

At the same time, because of their Q2 rating they might expect you to fill in the gaps, so sometimes part of the conversation with your Q2 supervisor will be about filling the gaps in the directive as it's being issued.

As noted, Q2 supervisors have a tendency to move very fast and that's where they will trip themselves up from time to time. They will have a tendency to check in with you and while they do have a tendency to coach you along the way you need to make sure that you're not skipping steps.

The compass point for the Q2 supervisor is typically pointing towards the question **What is important?** Concentrating on the next most important thing they need to do is one of the things that makes them super effective. However, this means they typically **leave a long trail of urgent but unimportant items** that you might have to clean up after. As a Q2 follower to a Q2 supervisor, you're more than happy to do that.

These are the types of supervisors who might also want you to show up with a solution to every problem that you bring them…that's the Q1 in them speaking. There is an inherent risk in this type of an approach and I address this in other parts of the book. Suffice it to say if that's the demand they place on you, don't take the bait **if it means operating outside your area of expertise.**

- **The great thing about Q2 supervisors is they are going to respond well to your support. It's one of the reasons they are a Q2 leader.**

As noted with a Q1 supervisor, you're going to have to convince them that collaboration has value but you can't always do it in a face-to-face conversation; instead you have to do it by demonstrating high performance. With a Q4 supervisor you have to be careful not to show them up technically because it can be easy to do. But **with the Q2 supervisor you don't have either one of these problems.**

What you really want in life is to be involved in a leadership team that is stacked heavy with Q2 leaders. If you can find a group like that which is ready-made, don't go anywhere.

If you are in a group with a bunch of Q1s and a bunch of Q4s, that's exactly why you're following the directions in this book. The endgame is to empower everybody towards Q2 by inviting power from above you and attracting power from below you.

Summary of the Q2 Supervisor

- High collaboration high technical
- Process and outcome driven
- Good at giving directives
- May or may not relate to efforts like fear reduction
- Tendency to not avoid uncomfortable situations
- Prioritizes important tasks well but can leave many less-important but urgent tasks undone
- Does not like to work for a Q1 or Q4 supervisor but will help them improve if its' practical
- Always on the lookout for a Q2 boss and will leave for another group to have one

Comparing Your Quadrant to Your Q2 Boss

If you are a Q1 your Q2 boss is going to place expectations on you concerning your lack of collaborative skills. ***It's going to be essential that you follow my exact instructions as noted in the steps and phases.*** You are going to have to buck up on the collaborative skill sets (as noted in this book); if not you will potentially be seen as uncaring, pushy, and someone who just wants to do things their way and not consider other, perhaps better, opportunities for getting task assignments completed with a higher level of performance. Besides following the advice above the other way to avoid problems is to simply become a Q2.

If you are a Q4 your Q2 boss is going to place expectations on you concerning your lack of technical skills. ***It's going to be essential that you follow my exact instructions as noted in the steps and phases.*** You are going to have to buck up on the technical skill sets required by your job; if not you're going to be micromanaged by necessity. Q2 bosses don't like doing stuff like that, but they will in the short term if they have to in order to get the job done. They're going to be watching closely to see if you're responding favorably to your technical training and if you're not they'll be sitting down with you to talk about why that is. The other way to avoid problems besides following the advice above is to become a Q2.

If you are a Q2 you are going to excel working for your Q2 boss. To them you will simply be a breath of fresh air and somebody they can trust to get the job done collaboratively and technically. If there's anybody that will hand power down to you once you've proven yourself as a Q2 it will be the Q2 boss. Follow the advice above in the steps and phases ***and prepare yourself for one of the most rewarding relationships you may ever have in your career.***

If you are a Q3 things are not going to go well unless you become at least a Q1 or a Q4 as quickly as possible. While becoming a Q2 should be everyone's goal, your immediate goal needs to be bucking up on *any skills so you can start to provide value as part of any of the other three quadrants.* The good news about a Q3 working for a Q2 boss is that if the Q3 *makes improvements in their performance* the Q2 boss (typically more than a Q1 or Q4 boss) will see that improvement and will acknowledge it. In this sense, at least early in the game, the Q2 boss will give credit for the initial efforts of the Q3 attempting to improve. However, know that this is a honeymoon period. In the longer term the Q2 boss is going to want to see actual results from the Q3 effort to improve that brings value to the group. If that doesn't happen, the Q3's days in the group are numbered.

Figure #31 is provided as a quick guide to help you focus on what's important. .

Fig. #31: Knowing the Quadrants:
The Q2 Supervisor

Q2

Knowing Which Quadrants You're Dealing With
(Your Q and Your Boss's Q)

- **High** collaboration, **high** technical
- **Process & outcome** driven
- Good at giving **directives**
- *May* or *may not* relate to efforts like **fear reduction**
- Tendency to *not avoid* uncomfortable situations
- Prioritizes **important tasks well** but can leave many less-important but urgent tasks undone
- *Does not* like to work for **a Q1 or Q4 supervisor** but will help them improve if it's practical
- *Always* on the lookout for a Q2 boss and *will leave for another group* to have one

LOW TECHNICAL LOW COLLABORATION: THE Q3 SUPERVISOR

You might be asking, wait a minute, how could that be? Someone becomes a supervisor when they have low technical skills and low collaboration skills? Well, let me tell you, there are two primary reasons as to why this happens, or at least two reasons I know about.

The first reason is there are leaders that want the leaders below them to just simply be their eyes and ears, reporting back what they see and hear and carrying out directives without thinking and without questions.

They just want the Q3 supervisors that work for them to carry out directives blindly, exactly as instructed, and basically just say yes to their boss every time they are told to do something. That is something the Q3 followers to a Q3 supervisor can do quite well.

Now if you're a Q1 or Q2 or Q4 this is just going to drive you crazy and you're not going to last very long. But for some Q3s they can spend their entire career like this. How do I know? Because I've seen it. Here's the way a Q3 sees it: I don't have any stress because I'm not saddled with any responsibility. I don't have to mull over multiple options to make a decision; instead all I have to do is what they tell me to do, so **life is good**. I can pay the rent and I don't have to think or stress in order to make a living.

The second reason a Q3 becomes a supervisor is that they happen to be related to the boss. Now this might drive the boss a little crazy from time to time, but there may be alternative reasons for them doing this, hidden deep someplace in a personal commitment that you may never know about (but given enough time, if you last that long, you probably will find out).

If you're a Q1 you're going to recognize your boss's lack of technical skills and have no respect for them whatsoever. If you're a Q4, their lack of tact and diplomacy and their inability to give a shit about another person's feelings will drive you nuts. I'm not saying Q3s lack empathy, but they just don't care as a general rule. There's nothing in their skill set that tells them **caring** is something that is to their advantage. In fact, **not caring** is one of the ways they keep their job.

If you are a Q2 you are either going to leave or end up getting their job and both options are always on the table when a Q2 is working for a Q3. That being said, it has to happen fast because Q2s run the other direction from Q3 supervisors as fast as they humanly can, so long as the Q2 can find another way to get a paycheck.

Because of this Q3 supervisors, if they last long enough—and they can for one of those two reasons I explained—have a tendency to collect a whole bunch of Q3 followers on their crew. Any Q3s that happened to stumble by are the ones that end up staying, so the population of Q3s rises while all the Q1s, Q4s, and Q2s **head for the door**.

Summary of the Q3 Supervisor

- Low collaboration low technical
- Typically demonstrates behavior that results in corrective actions by superiors
- Obedient if they've been held accountable for past instances of not being obedient
- Can be good at passing on instructions but not necessarily understanding what they're saying at an in-depth level
- Avoids taking responsibility
- Extremely risk averse
- This is your typical "yes man" when found in leadership positions.
- Is constantly checking in with higher-ups to establish priorities between competing tasks to avoid corrective of actions
- They have difficulty working for any supervisor including Q1s and Q fours, *they really don't do well* when working for a Q2 supervisor

Comparing Your Quadrant to Your Q3 Boss

If you are a Q1, Q2, or Q4 your Q3 boss is going to drive you crazy *but the reasons are different for each of you*. Based on your knowledge so far you should be able to extrapolate in which ways that will occur depending on which quadrant you are in.

Their expectation of you doesn't really change depending on what quadrant you're in because it doesn't really matter. They're not asking you for ways to improve the group, so don't clutter their busy schedule with suggestions they are not asking for. Blindly performing the tasks you are assigned and not asking questions is something you'll never be able to get used to, though, unless you yourself are also a Q3.

Interestingly enough, however, if you are also a Q3 that can't follow orders as directed, things are not going to go well unless you change quickly to providing some level of value that directly relates to following the orders they're giving you. The best way for a Q3 to survive under a Q3 is to switch over to a Q1 as quickly as possible with as much technical training as possible. Switching over to a Q4 from a Q3 while working for a Q3 supervisor has zero advantages. All in all, the Q3 boss won't want an unimproved Q3 on the team for long so the Q3s will have to meet the minimum qualifications of just blindly following orders without screwing things up.

Figure #32 is provided as a quick guide to help you focus on what's important.

Fig. #32: Knowing the Quadrants: The Q3 Supervisor

Q3

Knowing Which Quadrants You're Dealing With
(Your Q and Your Boss's Q)

- **Low** collaboration, **low** technical

- *Typically* demonstrates behavior that results in **corrective actions** by superiors

- **Obedient** if they've been *held accountable* for past instances of not being obedient

- Can be good at **passing on instructions** but *not necessarily understanding* what they're saying at an in-depth level

- **Avoids taking responsibility**

- Extremely *risk averse*

- This is **your typical "yes man"** when found in leadership positions.

- Is **constantly checking in with higher-ups to establish priorities** between competing tasks to avoid corrective of actions

- **They have difficulty working for any supervisor including Q1s and Q4s. They really don't do well when working for a Q2 supervisor**

Chapter 6

Attracting Collaborative Power from the Bottom Up: Looking at Your Work World from Your Followers' Perspective

His book captures all these attributes which can now provide any leader the instructions necessary for their successful collaborative power grab, if they merely follow the instructions provided.

—TODD BECCHER

Positive Long-Term Impact on the Culture

"Starting Now" Actions

10 Steps for Attracting Collaborative Power

Each Step Will Follow the Same Format

Phase 1

    Step 1: Emulate the Behaviors You Want from Others

    Step 2: Support Timely Decision Making and Problem-Solving

    Step 3: Build to Expert Levels of Technical and Collaborative Competency

    Step 4: Continually Make Observations of Examples of Good Performance

Phase 2

    Step 5: Keep the Group Focused on the Mission, Values, Directives, and Their Performance Expectations at All Times

    Step 6: Teach and Promote All Productivity Behaviors

    Step 7: Encourage the Group to Innovate New Ideas for Mission Success

Phase 3

    Step 8: Help Your People Recover from Low Performance or Errors with Training Sessions Focused on Improving Performance

    Step 9: Protect and Promote the Culture

    Step 10: After Full Implementation, Implement, Implement, Implement All the above at Every Chance

---

POSITIVE LONG-TERM IMPACT ON THE CULTURE

Everything you are about to do will have a *positive long-term impact on the culture*. I want to emphasize what this means:

- *Positive:* Meaning the results stimulate job satisfaction, first to support mission success, and second it does so in an almost guaranteed fashion *if applied consistently over time without letting up.*
- *Long term:* Meaning months and years, not days and weeks. Also meaning that once the culture initially matures from these application steps it will remain in its advanced state as long as these expectations are used as a method of measuring the performance of the individuals in the group.
- *Impact on Culture:* Over time the cascade of empowerment moves downward throughout the extended followers beyond your immediate direct reports. As it does these group members hand back to you high levels of performance.

"STARTING NOW" ACTIONS

The step-by-step Starting Now instructions I'm about to give you will enhance the group to higher mission success, supporting performance by *specifically*:

- Encouraging and supporting the movement of all Q1, Q3, and Q4 followers to advance towards a Q2 status. It will also cause the explosive growth of the Q2 followers already in your group. Over time the population density of Q2 employees increases through training and turnover. Expect that Q1, Q3, and Q4 followers will need much more *guidance* at the initial stages. They will also be the ones to most resist this new level of empowerment.
- Reducing fear in the workplace that maximizes the use of the prefrontal cortex and minimizes the need to access the amygdala. This advances logical, rational, and ethical thinking that precedes logical, rational, and ethical behaviors. This reduces the amount of inappropriate conflict (which we call *fighting*), reduces avoidance behaviors (we call *flighting*), and reduces passive non-conformance to the new cultural rules now being applied (we call that *freezing*).
- Understanding that in any unhealthy environment, prior to establishing the empowered work environment, *the healthy actor existing within that unhealthy environment may first appear as an antagonist*. At the beginning of the process it's important to understand whenever you *encounter anger* that not all *angry encounters* are for the same reason. If you have Q2 employees who have had to work under a Q1, Q3, or Q4 supervisor *for an extended period of time, expect to encounter some initial frustration from them* that you're going to have to deal with. Also know that Q2 employees that have been working under a Q3 or Q4 for an extended period of time typically have become *independent contractors of sorts* who are used to calling their own shots because of the vacuum of leadership that existed above them. It might take some time and there could be resistance while they get accustomed to actually being led again by a competent supervisor.

- Providing training that meets six direct specific objectives:
  1. *Always* start with each individual's weakest skill set.
  2. *Always advance the trainee to an expert level* for whatever task they are being trained on.
  3. *Always* provide regular periodic refresher training that directly supports a person's performance expectations.
  4. *Always* modify the training program based on the error experience of the staff.
  5. *Always* train your Q1 and Q3 followers with more collaboration training and guidance.
  6. *Always* train your Q4 and Q3 followers with more technical training.

Teaching that maximum group performance is achieved by *error recovery* and learning from mistakes versus using punishment as a form of motivating the behavior change of group members.

Certainly, disciplinary action has its necessary place, but only as described here:

You want to go heavy on the "carrot" when building an enhanced culture and only use the "stick" as needed to stop destructive behaviors, versus heavy use of both the stick and carrot. Encourage the use of motivating Q2 behaviors and reduce demotivators while saving the heavier behavior correction efforts for the *chronically underperforming who are not responding well to multiple training attempts and those who compromise the culture through uncorrectable anger issues and bully-type behaviors.*

Teaching and significantly supporting systematic problem-solving techniques and requiring their use as a performance expectation, while also using your authority power to actively remove the roadblocks getting in the way of and frustrating your direct reports.

Commingling continuous improvement with reducing complexity, improving working conditions, and addressing safety issues *all* results in increased productivity.

Recognizing exceptional behavior that you want to see repeated.

10 STEPS FOR ATTRACTING COLLABORATIVE POWER

It might seem like a lot to do to use these 10 steps for Attracting Collaborative Power, but these actions will become second nature over time.

Not every step will be needed every day. However, each step needs to be used *at the appropriate time*. Therefore *timing is very important* to using many of these steps.

Don't underestimate your power to empower those below you; wield it at every opportunity. If you're used to not feeling empowered as a supervisor everything has just changed as long as you recognize the fact that you have always had more power than you have been led to believe.

You are now Captain Kirk on your own starship *Enterprise* or Kathryn Janeway on your own starship *Voyager* and ***it's time for you to use your power to empower.***

Mentor, coach, promote, stop destructive behavior, and hold accountable all those that follow you.

Simply stated: ***Reduce complexity, reduce fear, teach them how to solve problems, help them to recover when they err, listen to them about new ways of doing things, and make sure they get the recognition they have earned.***

Be lavish in your praise when it is deserved and focus on the same excellent performance behaviors you want repeated.

Hold all the leaders that follow you to these very same 10 steps for Attracting Collaborative Power.

EACH STEP WILL FOLLOW THE SAME FORMAT

Here's a quick description of each section of the step-by-step process.

- **Introduction** describes why this important step needs to be taken.
- **Quadrant Thinking** will explain which quadrants will be resistant or more accepting or will thrive with this new information.
- **Important Takeaway** will explain a major focus point that you should be aware of with using the step.
- **Starting Now** will explain the exact **THREE** actions you want to start taking *now. Follow the description exactly when you pursue each action.*
- **Looking at It from Your Follower's Perspective** will explain how your followers are feeling about what you're doing, using the dialogue of what their inner voice is telling them *after they get used to this new approach to being supervised.* Take note, this is after they get used to this new approach *but not at the beginning.* You might disagree with my assessments; all I can tell you is they are based on my experience.

— PHASE 1 —

STEP 1: EMULATE THE BEHAVIORS YOU WANT FROM OTHERS

Introduction
It's a reminder for all of us, most notably during stressful situations. Demonstrating behaviors you don't want others demonstrating will make you rightfully appear as inconsistent, unreliable, and unpredictable. Don't underestimate the power this has on the people who follow you. By ***reducing inconsistent and unpredictable behaviors*** and instead increasing the consistent and predictable use of a

positive work ethic, dignity, and respect, the supervisor is significantly reducing fear in the work environment because the decision areas of the brain are also those that are responsible for our emotions. *As collective fear goes down, group performance goes up.*

The next point that I'm going to make I can't emphasize enough, and it may be the first time you have heard this: As a leader, when you consistently demonstrate predictable behaviors your direct reports *learn how to develop a relationship around YOUR needs.* If you are unpredictable, the people that work for you become nervous and fearful not knowing how their supervisor will react in any given situation. That is the worst approach any leader can employ. A supervisor will not get what they need from their direct reports in the way they are wanting because they have sent confusing signals, and all the while this ignorant supervisor will complain about their direct reports underperforming.

The direct reports don't know what their supervisor wants, so they understandably avoid their supervisor as much as they can. This supervisor is oblivious to these avoidance behaviors, but another telltale sign that this is happening is when direct reports try to keep their meetings with their supervisor as short as possible with one eye on the door.

Quadrant Thinking
This will appeal to all quadrants.

Important Takeaway
When you *predictably demonstrate a positive work ethic, dignity, and respect,* people will follow your lead; they will emulate your behavior and help reduce fear and increase group performance *in ways you can't measure and without you knowing it.* It will take a while for people to design relationships around your predictable behaviors so this is a medium- to long-term investment. If you don't push yourself to demonstrate dignity and respect every day you will undercut the high ground you need to stand on. *Do as I say not as I do* has hidden devastating consequences for your leadership power position. This is one reason why it's Step 1.

Starting Now
Here are the three actions you need to start taking immediately:

1. **Starting now:** Consistently demonstrate a positive work ethic *by reliably and consistently demonstrating all the following Steps 2 through 10 in Attracting Collaborative Power.*
2. **Starting now:** Consistently demonstrate your dedication to integrity and professionalism *by treating all your followers with the dignity and respect that every one of us deserves.*
3. **Starting now:** Build predictability in your relationships *by explaining your decision-making philosophy.* As noted, by building in predictability your direct reports will start to *design their decision making based on your philosophies*!

Looking at It from Your Follower's Perspective
(After implementing for several months)

- I feel safe because my boss is predictable and consistent.
- Because I know how they think I have a good idea of how they are going to react even to new situations.
- It feels good to know how they think because it helps me create the outcomes they are wanting from me.

Figure #33 is provided as a quick guide to help you focus on what's important.

>**ATTRACTING**< COLLABORATIVE POWER FROM THE BOTTOM UP

PHASE 1: STEP 1: _Emulate the Behaviors_
You Want From Others

Don't underestimate the power this has on the people who follow you. _**By reducing inconsistent and unpredictable behaviors**_ and instead increasing the consistent and predictable use of a positive work ethic, dignity, and respect, the supervisor significantly reduces fear in the work environment.

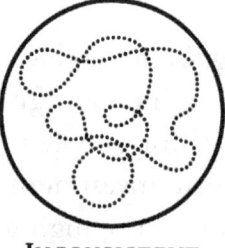

INCONSISTENT BEHAVIOR	CONSISTENT BEHAVIOR
• _Unpredictable / no pattern_	• _Predictable_
• _No set example to follow_	• _Reliable example to follow_
• _Generates fear_	• _Generates safety_
• _Destroys productivity_	• _Maximizes productivity_

As **COLLECTIVE FEAR** GOES DOWN, GROUP **PERFORMANCE** GOES UP

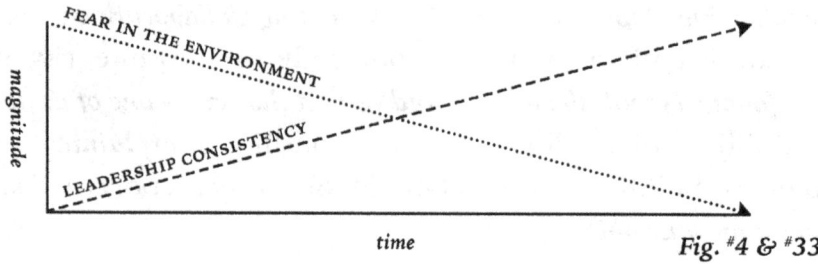

Fig. #4 & #33

188

STEP 2: SUPPORT TIMELY DECISION MAKING AND PROBLEM-SOLVING

Introduction

"Be there" for your direct reports with *timely solid decision making* and by removing roadblocks to progress and adjusting resources as necessary to help them get that day's job done. Every time *field personnel are waiting an inordinate amount of time on a management decision*, by definition the group is already falling behind on meeting its deadline.

Each day: *Ask them if there is anything getting in their way of doing a good job today*. If you can't solve it right away write it down and get to work on it. Contrary to popular belief, you shouldn't force them to suggest solutions to problems they find *that they may not have the training or experience to solve*. This approach can actually reduce communication over time.

Instead, teach them *a step-by-step problem-solving process*. Teach them *how to recognize problems and how to use the step-by-step problem-solving process*.

- *I have supplied both of these in this book (see Appendices 1 and 2); use them as your teaching materials.*

Promote that highly effective people ask for help when they need it and so should they. This doesn't mean that you have two people doing a one-person job. What this does mean is that we solve problems, remove roadblocks, and adjust resources *as a team in order to get the job done*.

We all succeed or we all fail *together, never separately*. Including people in other departments.

Problem-solving requires a particularly high cognitive function, and if people are not trained on a successful problem-solving methodology individual and group problem-solving will not occur consistently.

There are many reasons problems don't get solved. I'm providing you with a list of those reasons in Appendix 1 so you can train your group on how to recognize problems as a precursor to solving them. One of the things that gets in the way of good problem-solving is our own cognitive biases.

- Most complex problem-solving occurs in the prefrontal cortex, so once again if fear reduction is not part of your program and people's decisions are being made from the amygdala then you're not going to get the problem-solving capacity in your group that you need. In one way or another every one of the steps that you're following promotes fear reduction. If you want good problem-solving you need to have effective fear reduction behaviors.

People can be trained away from their biases. To help you out Appendix 1 also includes a list of the more common cognitive biases that we are confronted with, which you can use to train your people about biases.

Recognizing problems and following a step-by-step problem-solving process is a life skill that everyone in the group can take to the other areas of their lives beyond the work environment.

Quadrant Thinking

Quick decision making will appeal to **Q1s, Q2s,** and **Q4s.** Quick decision making on your part *makes their life easier.* And if they've worked for a past supervisor who was not making quick decisions you will become a breath of fresh air.

Some **Q1s** and most **Q3s** will resist problem-solving training and might resist appeals to *allow new facts to change their minds.*

All the quadrants suffer to some extent from the "I already know how to solve problems" syndrome. As well, because many of the quadrant performers rely on traditional thought patterns and rely heavily on an accumulated library of knowledge, they may not do well with the *allowing new facts to change their minds* approach. But with training they will.

Important Takeaway

It's not unusual that people see their own problem-solving skills as being a lot better than they actually are. This is a well-known fact for those that are in the problem-solving industry. The stories of very intelligent people making horrible decisions during problem-solving efforts are limitless. You might get some resistance as this process will be accused of being *too cumbersome, too time consuming, and essentially unnecessary (after all, I already know how to solve problems).*

- Remember that when fear or perceived threat is present and people are dropping out of the prefrontal cortex and into their amygdala, problem-solving will become hampered. When use of the amygdala is combined with people's cognitive biases then problem-solving capacity is significantly and negatively impacted.

Stick with teaching the problem-solving protocols, require a step-by-step process to be used by everyone who works for you, and over time the resistance will fall away. If you have to read out loud the problems with problem-solving noted earlier in various sections of this book, please do so (don't leave out the space shuttle disaster scenarios).

Starting Now

Here are the three actions you need to start taking immediately:

1. **Starting now:** Hold training sessions on how to recognize problems and train your group to *always communicate to you about any problems* they know about, including roadblocks they encounter during their workday. Each day: remind them to tell you about *anything getting in them way of doing a good job today.*

2. **Starting now:** Train your direct reports on the first step of the problem-solving process, which is you want them to communicate problems to you *immediately.*

    Note: when a problem occurs, the statement I hear from leaders most often is: *"If they had just told me about the problem earlier a lot of damage could have been avoided!"*

3. **Starting now:** Hold training sessions on *how to use the step-by-step problem-solving process and require its use.* Use Appendix 2 for training your direct reports on the step-by-step problem-solving process. Make sure to also go over the list of cognitive biases supplied in Appendix 1. It's a real eye-opener if people are learning about cognitive biases for the first time.

4. **Starting now:** Promote that every group member have an open-minded approach that (a) encourages people to *allow new facts to change their minds* and (b) ensures that finding the right answer is more important than *being right.* It's *not about being right,* it's about *learning right* so we can *do right,* therefore they need to leave their ego at the door.

Looking at It from Your Follower's Perspective

(After implementing for at least three months if you are aggressive at helping them remove roadblocks and improving working conditions in Step 6.)

- I feel empowered.
- I feel like I have a capability that's been missing.
- I feel in control.
- I feel trained.
- I don't fear humiliation.

Figure #34 is provided as a quick guide to help you focus on what's important. .

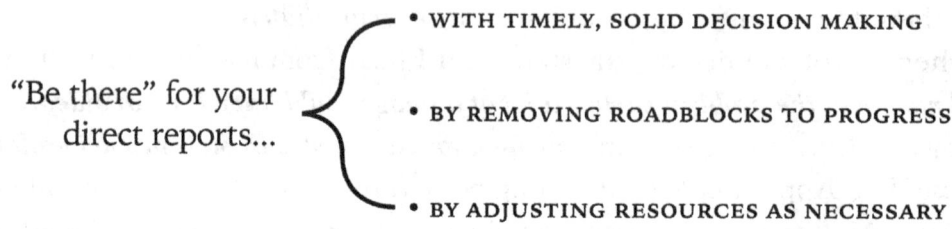

>ATTRACTING< Collaborative Power from the Bottom Up

PHASE 1: STEP 2: *Support Timely Decision Making & Problem Solving*

"Be there" for your direct reports...

- WITH TIMELY, SOLID DECISION MAKING
- BY REMOVING ROADBLOCKS TO PROGRESS
- BY ADJUSTING RESOURCES AS NECESSARY

When field personnel are waiting an inordinate amount of time on a management decision, *the group is falling behind on meeting its deadline.*

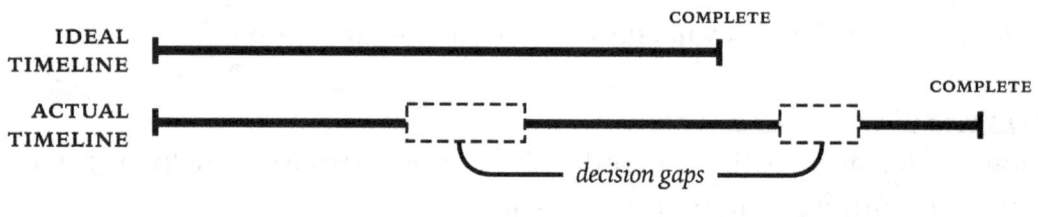

IDEAL TIMELINE — COMPLETE

ACTUAL TIMELINE — COMPLETE

decision gaps

Everyday...

A ✓ ...ASK THEM IF THERE IS ANYTHING GETTING IN THEIR WAY OF DOING A GOOD JOB TODAY.

B ✓ IF YOU CAN'T SOLVE IT RIGHT AWAY, WRITE IT DOWN AND TAKE ACTION.

Mon	Tue	Wed	Thu	Fri
A ✓ B ✓	A ✓ B ✓	A ✓ B ✓	A ✓ B ✓	A ✓ B ✓

Starting Now, train your group on...

> how to recognize problems

> telling you any time a roadblock appears

> communicating problems to you immediately

> using the step-by-step problem solving process

> taking an open-minded approach that:
  • allows new facts to change their mind
  • prioritizes the right answer over being right
  • prioritizes leaving their ego at the door

Fig. #5 & #34

STEP 3: BUILD TO EXPERT LEVELS OF TECHNICAL AND COLLABORATIVE COMPETENCY

Introduction

Building to expert levels of technical and collaborative competency is perhaps one of the most important steps you can make as a leader, though it might be most impactful in ways you might not completely understand.

The entire planet is essentially *undertrained*. Don't let your group fall victim to this same error. People who are undertrained will either create risk or they will fear being humiliated. Either possibility is unacceptable and tragically unnecessary. Most of the error and destruction you observe in the world around you *is not caused by a diabolical plot* but instead is caused by incompetence. While diabolical plots certainly exist and they get the most press, it's actually incompetence that holds back humanity from advancing.

The risk this incompetence is causing results from the activities of the *underinformed and the undertrained*. We have become used to being undertrained, and normalized mediocre performance allows us to accept incompetence without knowing it.

Having people in your group who are chronically undertrained creates a significant amount of risk to mission success. So get used to training people to expert levels of competence, both technically and collaboratively, and then turn around and rely on them now as the experts that you have just created.

Always provide training for each individual's weakest skill set first. And then the next weakest skill set, working your way up from the weakest to the strongest skill set. *This will eliminate the maximum amount of risk for the minimum amount of resource necessary for the training.*

Always provide training that advances the trainee to an expert level for whatever task they are being trained on. *Once you've created the expert your direct supervision requirements drop significantly. The quality of independent decision making skyrockets.*

- This one idea of training everybody to expert levels, implemented consistently, will allow management time dedicated to direct supervision *to drop significantly.* I cannot stress this enough: if you want to reduce (and in some cases eliminate completely) the demands placed on you by the burden of direct supervision then *build all the skill sets below you to expert levels.* Once they've been trained as experts you then encourage them on making more independent decisions which will free you up to do the other important jobs you're responsible for.
- When training standards drop, direct supervision goes up. *But almost everybody is not measuring this.* Trust me: as training standards increase enough for people to reach expert levels the *direct supervision burdens on you will drop significantly and can oftentimes be eliminated completely.*

Always provide regular periodic refresher training that directly supports a person's performance expectations. On a quarterly basis make sure that each person that works for you directly or indirectly is receiving refresher training on exactly how they can meet their performance expectations. It seems obvious but the vast majority of groups fail in this area, simply relying on the years-old training that each person received during the onboarding process when they were first hired. It sounds boring and repetitive but when you combine it with the other training requirements in this section it significantly improves group performance in ways you can't always measure.

Always modify the training program based on the error experience of the staff. *Every time somebody makes an error modify the training program so future activities do not replicate the same error.* Train your people that error is good as long as we learn from it, and learning from it means you modify the training program so the same errors are not repeated.

How many training programs do you know about where somebody is in charge of modifying the training program specifically based on the error experience of the current staff?

Quadrant Thinking

Always train your **Q1 and Q3** followers *with more collaboration training and guidance.*
Always train your **Q4 and Q3** followers *with more technical training.*

If a person is strong technically but not strong collaboratively they are a Q1 and they need more collaboration training to bring them towards Q2. Make sure they get the collaboration training that this book describes.

If a person is strong collaboratively but not strong technically they are a Q4 and they need more technical training to bring them towards Q2. Make sure they get the technical training their job requires and at a level that allows them to become an expert.

In some cases Q4s are *misplaced technically within the group when first hired* or they advance within the organization to a job that demonstrates their incompetency from a technical standpoint. When that happens, the Q4 not gaining enough technical expertise (even with repeated attempts at training) sometimes calls into question whether they'll be able to keep their job. If they're very collaboratively competent and they're not technically competent in their current job, *look for another role within the organization that they would be technically competent at.*

- Having an accumulation of Q4s in the organization means you have another pool of potential Q2s from which to draw. Moving your Q4s to jobs that are more technically amenable to their skill set *works to the group's advantage* because this is another way you can quickly turn the Q4 into Q2. Make sense?

<u>*Important Takeaway*</u>
Assign someone in your group to collect errors and mistakes and turn those into teachable moments by modifying the training program. In every situation in which an error was made, *modify the training program so future activities do not replicate the same error.* Train your people that error is good as long as we learn from it, and learning from it means you modify the training program so the same errors are not repeated by others in the future.

<u>*Starting Now*</u>
Here are the three actions you need to start taking immediately:

1. **Starting now:** Provide training for each individual's weakest skill set first. And then the next weakest skill set, working your way up from the weakest to the strongest skill set. Ask them what they think they need training on and make sure they know why you're asking. *This should be a routine training process within the entire group.*

2. **Starting now:** Provide training that advances the trainee to an expert level for whatever task they are being trained on. *Once they are an expert ,start relying on them as an expert.* Start encouraging them to make independent decisions so you can relieve yourself of the burden of direct supervision. Note: training your people to be experts might seem like overkill, especially in a world that has normalized mediocre performance. However, I'm of the opinion that most of the planet is under-trained. And if you look deeply into the problems of many organizations the biggest issue is almost always *incompetency*. When people are trained to expert levels, both the tangible and intangible advantages are significant towards achieving mission success. Tangibles are results such as less direct supervision, better decision making, and fewer problems. Intangibles include increased job satisfaction from increased job control, higher self-esteem, and significant fear reduction.

3. **Starting now:** Provide *quarterly refresher training on the performance expectations* everyone is expected to meet. This would include making sure that Q1 and Q3 individuals receive more collaboration training and that Q4 and Q3 individuals receive more technical training. This also includes moving Q4s to jobs that better fit their skills if it looks like training is not resolving their technical incompetencies. *The moment the Q4 is moved to a job where they are very technically competent they instantly become a Q2.*

<u>*Looking at It from Your Follower's Perspective*</u>
(After implementing for several training cycles beyond the training they were used to experiencing in the past)

- I feel well trained.
- I feel like I have the capability to do what I need to do and feel very competent.
- I don't fear humiliation.
- I feel empowered.
- I feel like I'm ready for anything.

Figure #35 is provided as a quick guide to help you focus on what's important.

>ATTRACTING< COLLABORATIVE POWER FROM THE BOTTOM UP

PHASE 1: STEP 3: *Build to Expert Levels*
of Technical & Collaborative Competency

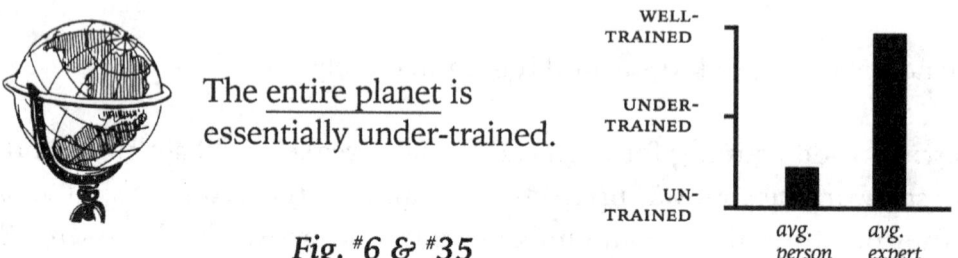

The <u>entire planet</u> is essentially under-trained.

Fig. #6 & #35

WELL-TRAINED
UNDER-TRAINED
UN-TRAINED

avg. person   *avg. expert*

MOST ERROR & DESTRUCTION IN THE WORLD...   *...is a result of...*   ...INCOMPETENCE RATHER THAN MALICIOUSNESS.

Warning: Having chronically undertrained people in your group poses significant risk to mission success.

TRAINING BEST PRACTICES

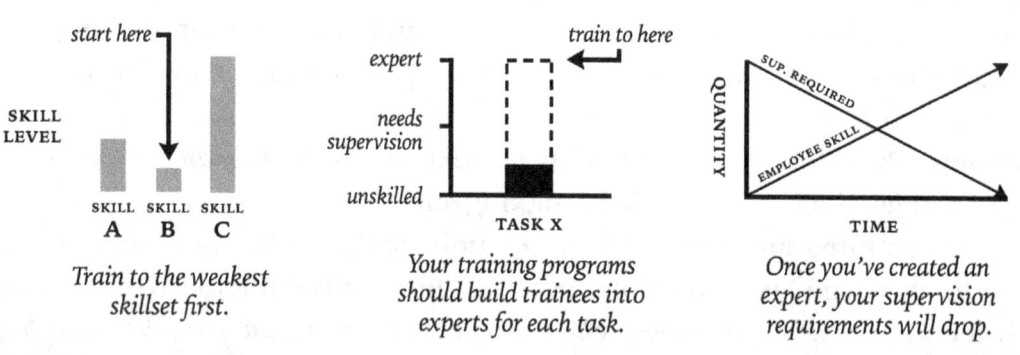

start here
SKILL LEVEL
SKILL A   SKILL B   SKILL C

Train to the weakest skillset first.

expert
needs supervision
unskilled
train to here
TASK X

Your training programs should build trainees into experts for each task.

QUANTITY
SUP. REQUIRED
EMPLOYEE SKILL
TIME

Once you've created an expert, your supervision requirements will drop.

Train Q1s & Q3s in **collaboration**. Train Q3s & Q4s in **technical skills**.

Starting Now:

A—Provide training for each individual's weakest skillset first.

B—Provide training advances the trainee to an expert level in the task they are being trained.

C—Provide everyone with quarterly refresher training on their performance expectations.

STEP 4: **CONTINUALLY MAKE OBSERVATIONS OF EXAMPLES OF GOOD PERFORMANCE**

Introduction

Make observations of examples of good performance, including those that are not your direct reports by sending a note to their supervisor. If we don't define success by recognizing actions that represent excellence and positive examples of performance, we fail as leaders. Behaviors that are recognized with positive feedback are always repeated. And that is exactly what you want: *repeated examples of good performance* and then even more *repeated examples of good performance* as more and more examples of good performance continue to be observed. Go heavy, start early, and don't let up. Use the following list as your guide.

Did someone:

- go beyond the call of duty?
- become the best at a routine duty?
- do an exceptional job responding to an emergency?
- do an exceptional job responding to a customer complaint?
- take on additional responsibilities?
- volunteer?
- solve a problem?
- help during a stressful situation?
- come up with a great idea for improvement?
- come up with a great idea for increasing productivity?

I know I'm repeating myself here, but it's worth repeating. Every single positive behavior that is recognized as a desired performance behavior **will be repeated by that individual and others in the group that witnessed or learn of the recognition.**

Recognition should be (a) verbal at the time of discovery and (b) coupled with extended official written recognition.

As long as it is sincere and based on the list above (or similar actions) you are going to find people can be extremely excited about being recognized for doing great work. And while they might be bashful externally, internally it has a very positive impact—as it should.

Remind them: they're not getting anything free; they've **earned this recognition.**

The sad and true fact of the matter is that for many adults in our world, **being rightfully recognized for exceptional performance is rare.**

Quadrant Thinking
Every quadrant will respond very favorably to this feedback.

Four Important Takeaways

1. If you think that giving positive recognition is a form of coddling you couldn't be more wrong. The fact is people should be rightfully recognized for the accomplishments that they've produced because they made a positive difference in the group's attempt at mission success. ***When your direct reports see themselves as being part of something larger than themselves, authentic and sincere recognition leaks into the group psyche and has very positive impacts on both the sender and the receiver.***

2. If you have difficulty finding something good to say about somebody on your crew then it's your job as the leader to motivate them to higher levels of performance. Ask them to do a special project or special assignment. It can be something simple like reorganizing the stockroom or cleaning out a part of the workshop or writing a simple report or gathering some information for you. There are a lot of different ways people can and ***will shine*** and you as the leader need to find a way to make that happen. It's only in very rare cases in my decades of experience that I couldn't find something good about somebody and usually that was because of an organic problem. Here's the bottom line: if you can't find anything good to say about somebody who works for you ***the problem might be you.***

3. When these recognition reports start happening on a regular basis for an entire department or entire organization it really has a significant impact on the entire culture. Once these reports become a way of communicating positive information about people working in the group up to the higher echelons of leadership it creates an extremely positive contagion response. A virus whose infection results in high performance and yes, very good feelings.

4. It's perfectly legitimate to be recognizing a person for exceptional performance in one area while at the same time counseling and helping them recover from an error or event of less-than-standard performance in another area of their responsibilities. We are people, we are mixed bags, right? Remember the fighter pilots? They are continuously working on areas where they can improve their performance and at the same time they're getting recognized for exceptional performance under difficult circumstances.

Starting Now
Here are the three actions you need to start taking immediately:

1. **Starting now:** If somebody qualifies for recognition go up and tell them that you're aware of what they did and personally thank them.
2. **Starting now:** The next thing you're going to do is write a short one-on-one email to your supervisor noting the individual and the exceptional performance. Then copy that email and

send it to the person who you are recognizing. This is a very powerful way of recognizing some-body, when they know that you're passing this information on to your boss. Do not underesti-mate how empowering this is.

3. **Starting now:** As you train more people to become Q2s their performance will start to increase and you need to be ready and willing to recognize them *as quickly as possible.* Your goal is to send one of these emails *about once every two months for each person on your crew.* And you want to make sure that all of these events are collected and placed in their semi-annual or annual evaluation so people understand that what they do in the field *directly impacts their performance evaluation scores.*

Looking at It from Your Follower's Perspective

(After two or three emails for each person, so say approximately nine months)

- I feel in control.
- I feel significant.
- I do not fear rejection.
- I do not fear being ignored.
- I do not fear being humiliated.
- I am at the top of my game.
- I know exactly what to do next to keep my standing in the group.
- I feel powerful.

Figure #36 is provided as a quick guide to help you focus on what's important.

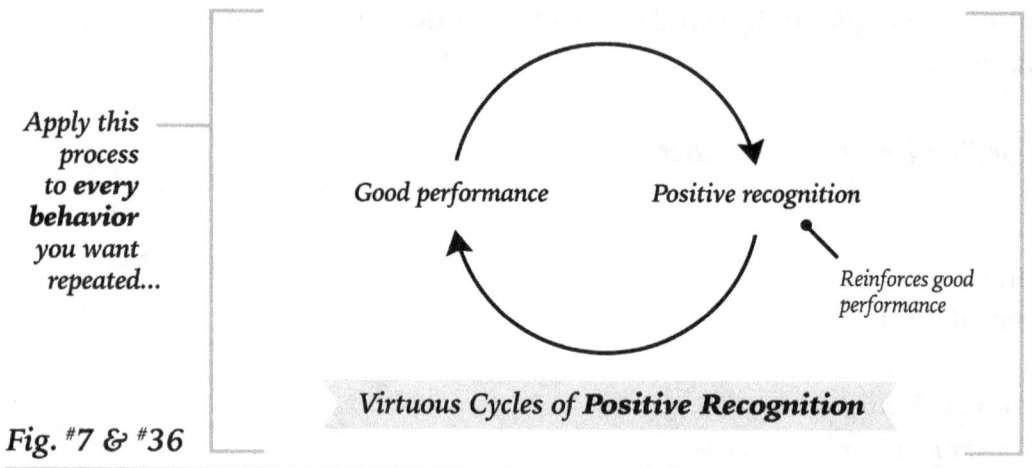

>ATTRACTING< COLLABORATIVE POWER FROM THE BOTTOM UP

PHASE 1: STEP 4: *Continually Make Observations of Examples of Good Performance*

*Apply this process to **every** behavior you want repeated...*

Good performance → Positive recognition

Reinforces good performance

*Virtuous Cycles of **Positive Recognition***

Fig. #7 & #36

Behaviors that are recognized with positive feedback are *always* repeated.

DID SOMEONE...

- ☐ *...go beyond the call of duty?*
- ☐ *...become the best at a routine duty?*
- ☐ *...respond exceptionally to an emergency?*
- ☐ *...respond exceptionally to a customer complaint?*
- ☐ *...take on additional responsibilities?*
- ☐ *...volunteer?*
- ☐ *...solve a problem?*
- ☐ *...help during a stressful situation?*
- ☐ *...come up with a great idea for an improvement?*
- ☐ *...come up with a great idea for increasing productivity?*

...THEN LET THEM KNOW WITH POSITIVE RECOGNITION.

Starting Now:

A—If somebody qualifies for recognition, go up and tell them you're aware of what they did and personally thank them.

B—Next you're going to write a short one-on-one email to your supervisor noting the individual and the exceptional performance.

C—Then copy that email and send it to the person you are recognizing. This is a very powerful way of recognizing somebody.

D—As you train more people to become Q2s, their performace rises and you need to be ready to recognize them as quickly as possible.

— PHASE 2 —

STEP 5: KEEP THE GROUP FOCUSED ON THE MISSION, VALUES, DIRECTIVES, AND THEIR PERFORMANCE EXPECTATIONS AT ALL TIMES

Introduction

Mission statements, company value statements, strategy statements or reports, directives, and the performance expectations listed on everyone's performance evaluations are all fuel for taking the steps necessary for creating a dialogue ranging from where the group is going and what the group hopes to achieve all the way down to highly detailed meetings talking about performance expectations.

Keeping the group focused on mission, values, directives, and performance expectations at all times is an opportunity for increasing facetime with short and frequent one-on-one meetings with your direct reports. Promote transparency and get them talking.

Periodically meet with each person in your charge and give them copies of the mission statements, value statements, or other reports from the senior leaders that give direction to the entire group.

Also periodically meet with them as a group and provide copies of the performance expectations and review them, taking questions as necessary.

Initially, start out with one-on-one meetings to lay the groundwork. Once your one-on-one meetings have developed a basic understanding, you can switch over to group meetings.

Actively promote these ideas and information and encourage conversation and transparency. No one is required to memorize the mission and values; just keep them part of the conversation.

While it might take some time, this type of training will result in a common mission perspective on the part of your direct reports, as well as common values and common performance expectations. This commonality ***builds very strong relationships if consistently applied over time.***

Promote ***our*** common purpose and ***our*** mission.

Quadrant Thinking

This will appeal to most **Q2s** and **Q4s**. May appeal to some **Q1s**, though some may be resistant. Most **Q3s** will be ambivalent.

Important Takeaway

You might think you don't have enough time for these meetings. And one of the reasons might be that you're so busy in your *management* job. What's being proposed here is an essential, absolute no-substitutes-allowed action requirement to support your *leadership* job. You're not going to be able to exert leadership from the backseat. Once you become the symbol of moving your group forward and taking the time to make sure that your followers are convinced you are out front, then and only then do you actually become a leader. Anybody can be a leader by title, but there's no such thing as a leader without followers. And to take it one more step: there's certainly no such thing as a **successful** leader without **dedicated** followers. Get out front and stay out front from this point forward.

Starting Now

Here are the three actions you need to start taking immediately:

1. **Starting now:** Meet periodically (say, once a quarter) with your entire follower group with handouts of the mission, values, and other senior leadership materials and directives. Go over the materials and specifically promote that ***every group member brings value to support the overall mission and in this sense everyone should be considered important regardless of rank or standing.*** Open up the conversation and get people talking. During meetings promote that ***"If it's important to you then it's important to me"*** ethos and specifically speak to the need for breaking down barriers between departments. We all succeed or we all fail together, including the people in other departments. As noted earlier, initially start out with one-on-one meetings to lay the groundwork. Once your one-on-one meetings have developed a basic understanding you can switch over to group meetings. You might be asking yourself whether you have the time to do this. Once you've started the group meetings, we're only talking about an hour every three months.

2. **Starting now:** Meet often with your immediate direct reports. Give them sufficient facetime so they are able to talk about the directives they have received from you and ***focus on giving them the right priority for the day and reprioritizing their work as necessary.*** Encourage them to contact you anytime concerning any challenges they might be having. ***Of all the meetings you hold as a leader, these should be considered the most important.***

3. **Starting now:** Meet occasionally with your larger follower group, separate from the mission and values meetings, and give training presentations on their performance expectations and answer any questions they might have. I'll talk about this in the building experts step as well.

Looking at It from Your Follower's Perspective

(After implementing for at least 3 to 6 months' worth of meetings. This step is also highly dependent on all the other steps being implemented at the same time.)

- I feel like I am part of something larger than myself and I feel good about being part of the conversation.
- I feel like there is a high level of transparency and I feel safer as a result of this transparency.
- I know exactly what is expected of me and because I know what is expected of me I feel more in control.

Figure #37 is provided as a quick guide to help you focus on what's important.

>**ATTRACTING**< COLLABORATIVE POWER FROM THE BOTTOM UP

PHASE 2: STEP 5: *Focus Your Group on The Mission, Values, Directives, & Performance Expectations*

CREATE A GROUP DIALOGUE USING THE FOLLOWING TOOLS:

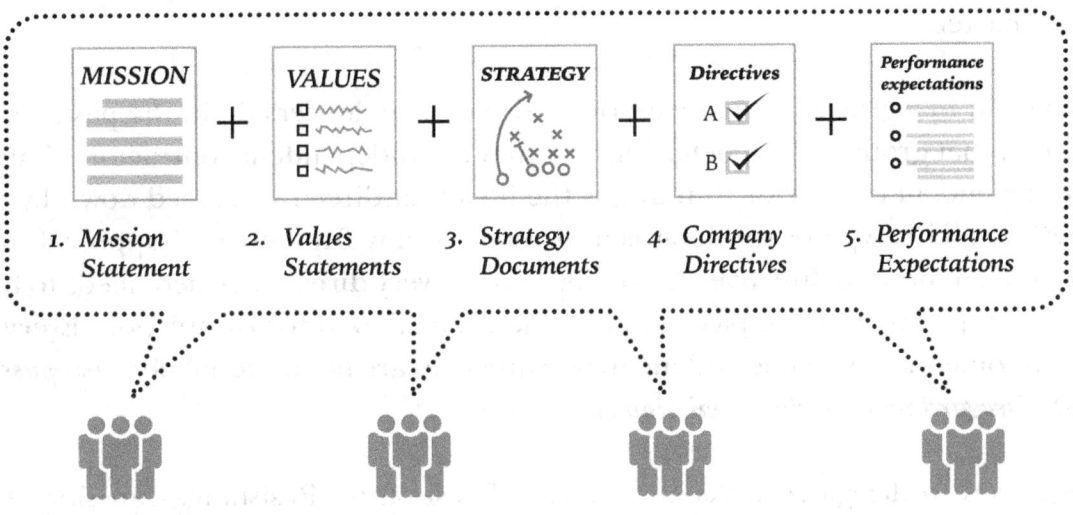

1. Mission Statement + 2. Values Statements + 3. Strategy Documents + 4. Company Directives + 5. Performance Expectations

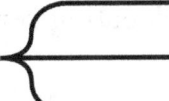

This dialogue will range from...

- WHERE THE GROUP IS HEADING...
- & WHAT THE GROUP HOPES TO ACHIEVE...
- TO HIGHLY DETAILED MEETINGS DISCUSSING PERFORMANCE EXPECTATIONS.

Keep the group focused on mission, values, directives, and performance expectations *at all times.*

Starting Now: *Fig. #9 & #37*

A—Meet periodically with your entire follower group with handouts of the mission, values, and other materials.

- Go over the materials
- Promote the message that every individual brings value
- Promote that: "if it's important to you, it's important to me."
- Lay the groundwork with 1-on-1 meetings.
- When your 1-on-1s have built understanding, meet as a group.

B—Meet often with your immediate direct reports.

- Give them sufficient facetime so they are able to talk about the directives you've given them and help them prioritize those directives.
- Consider these your most important meetings.

C—Meet occasionally with your larger follower group and give training presentations on their performance expectations. Also provide Q & As.

STEP 6: TEACH AND PROMOTE ALL PRODUCTIVITY BEHAVIORS

Introduction

The better we become at our jobs the less direct supervision we require, which gives supervisors more time to do other things they need to do. Teaching direct reports how to make good independent mission-centered decisions increases productivity by reducing the need for direct supervision while simultaneously supporting mission success. It's not really working harder; it's really just working smarter. As in Step 5, when you give expert training that's what you're doing—you're teaching everybody to work smarter.

If you find yourself in a group that has experienced very weak leadership in the past, it's not unusual for the people in that group to start behaving as if they are independent contractors. And what comes along with independent-contractor thinking is the idea that directives passed down by direct supervisors are *optional*. This type of thinking is a disaster for any fundamental approach to increasing productivity, so from now on directives are not optional. Every directive issued needs to be completed according to its objective and completed within the time allowed for completion. Everyone receives directives from someone, so no one is alone here. Directives are not optional because *passive inactivity or intentional disregard will scuttle the mission-success ship.*

Negative responses to delegated tasks are a form of resistance. Resistance can slow the work and in turn lower productivity levels, which is a sign the group is moving away from mission success. Leadership guides the group to mission success by delegating certain tasks, so it's important for followers to accept assigned tasks in a positive fashion.

- *Reporting time-wasting procedures and suggesting improvements are key to increasing productivity.*

Any task that takes longer than it should or having three people doing a two-person job is a loss of opportunity to improve productivity. Efforts need to be made in eliminating or improving time-wasting procedures. *No one knows better the way to save time than the people actually doing the work.* Leaders should be asking their followers about this, and when people start talking leaders need to listen and start implementing the ideas that are being proposed. Some of this bleeds over to Step 7.

One of the very best ways for a leader to get higher productivity from the people that work for them is to describe the exact outcome they are expecting from their direct reports. It's called *leading through expectations*. People love it because they feel secure in knowing exactly what their supervisor wants.

It's not a good feeling for direct reports when they don't know what their boss expects from them. If that's what's happening then this is a failure in leadership *not followership*.

Quadrant Thinking

Q2s typically have a very well-balanced approach to excepting, implementing, and delegating tasks. They are also ready to contribute to new ways of thinking. (All of which are reasons they have this rating to begin with.)

Q4s will do well when working on tasks with others, less so independently.

Q1s often *thrive* when given the permission and the request to modify procedures to reduce effort, time, and cost. For some Q1s this turns into a passion; if you end up with somebody like this they could single-handedly save your group thousands of hours of effort. (I know because I've seen it more than once.)

Important Takeaway

If you're supervising a group that's not used to completing directives it's going to take some time for them to acclimate to this new approach where you expect them to follow through (more on this below). If the people in your group are not used to getting a deadline when they're delegated the task, they're not going to like it at first. You might ask: "How am I going to Attract Collaborative Power by making people do things that they don't like doing?"

In my observation if you combine this with all the other steps you are taking you're actually going to give each person and your team a feeling of accomplishment. ***Eventually, meeting the deadline becomes equivalent to mission success because it authentically does become the same.*** This takes time and patience so you have to stick with it.

Improving productivity has within its roots all the other steps we've talked about previously and the subsequent steps we'll talk about after this:

- *Emulating work ethic behaviors* you want from others (Step 1)
- *Supporting quick decision making and problem-solving* so personnel are not having to wait (Step 2)
- *Training to expert levels* on everything they're required to know and do (Step 3)
- Making sure people are *recognized for their incredible efforts* (Step 4)
- Properly *prioritizing work based on the mission* and values (Step 5)
- Encouraging *submitting new time-saving ideas for improvement* (Step 7)
- *Reducing error* and low performance *with recovery* (Step 8)
- *Protecting and promoting* the culture (Step 9)

ALL these steps favorably impact upward movement in productivity levels.

- The other important takeaway to mention here is the importance of ***reducing complexity***. Many workplaces gain more complexity as they age. You'll find much of this complexity the brainchild of past good ideas. ***The more you can reduce complexity the more you will be able to improve working conditions and productivity.*** Go after complexity and try to reduce it as aggressively as possible. And once again one of the ways you do that is to get every brain in the game and let them know by simplifying (not dumbing down) their work approaches, working conditions improve and productivity goes up. This coincides with another gem you will read in Step 7, which is ***improving working conditions.***

Starting Now

Here are the four actions you need to start taking immediately:

2. **Starting now:** ***Identify a time period within which each and every task needs to be completed.*** If the people who work for you are not used to this it gets a little tricky when you first introduce this concept. But it's an essential move, because if you don't have specified time limits for all tasks, ***there's no way to predict or track productivity.*** And if you can't predict and track productivity, I don't care what your mission statement says, it can't be achieved. ***If you are not tracking productivity you have normalized mediocre performance.*** Be willing to take the time and explain this to everybody that works for you. Reason this is tricky is because if the members of your group have not been given deadlines and timelines in the past then they are essentially used to being ***independent contractors*** so with that change there might be resistance at first , however everyone will get used to it at some point.

1.
    ° One of the best ways to approach this is to simply negotiate what seems to be a reasonable time frame in which to complete the task ***by collaborating with your direct reports.*** It's a simple request: we need to make sure we are completing work in a reasonable amount of time, how much time would you recommend that this task require? ***Then use the time frame that they recommend.*** Note: Using the time THEY recommend is the key to removing resistance because they're able to control the destiny of how long things take. If you think some of the time frames are too long you can always come back and modify them later but start by using their recommended time frames.

    ° If they don't know what the timeframe should be just keep negotiating and ***help them come to the right answer that works for them.*** Over time people will get better and better at this and in my experience the time frame they give you is oftentimes very reasonable. It's very, very rare that anybody tries to ***game the system by padding the time required*** when you approach this process in the way that I'm recommending here.

    ° Be sure to let them know that if for some reason something comes up that was unexpected, they should simply communicate with you ***before the deadline*** and let you know that it might take more time than was originally anticipated. This gives you the option to add more resources or to solve the problem that they are encountering in order to still meet the deadline.

- ° When giving directives always include these eight important components:
  1. **A clear and achievable objective**
  2. **A time-frame/deadline**
  3. **The number of people assigned to the job**
  4. **The name of the responsible party for completing the directive**
  5. **The reason the assignment needs to be completed**
  6. **The request for any ideas that can get the assignment completed with in less time or for less money**
  7. **The request that they contact you before the deadline in case it appears the deadline cannot be met**
  8. **Encourage questions and discussion and give advice as requested**

2. **Starting now:** Teach your direct reports that it's about working smarter by constantly reviewing how work is being completed. ASK them to tell you about procedures currently in use *that can be changed or eliminated to reduce the effort, time, or cost of completing tasks.*

3. **Starting now:** Reduce complexity at every opportunity. *Complexity is the archenemy of higher productivity.* Having everyone on your team constantly looking for ways to reduce complexity is highly effective. If you find somebody who's especially good at it *then make them the person in charge of reducing complexity.*

4. **Starting now:** While always making yourself available for advice, solving problems, or using your authority for removing roadblocks, also encourage your new experts to make more independent decision making. *As your experts improve the quality of their decision making give them more responsibilities over time.* Give them positive feedback each and every time they make good independent decisions (See Step 9).

Looking at It from Your Follower's Perspective
(After they've gained expert status and/or after implementing their improvement ideas as part of Step 7)

- I feel empowered.
- I feel confident at working smart.
- I'm getting feedback that tells me that I know what I'm doing.
- I feel appreciated for coming up with ideas for increasing productivity

Figure #38 is provided as a quick guide to help you focus on what's important.

>ATTRACTING< COLLABORATIVE POWER FROM THE BOTTOM UP

PHASE 2: STEP 6: *Teach & Promote*
All Productivity Behaviors

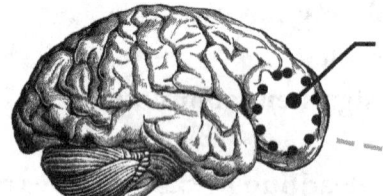

TRAINING DIRECT REPORTS TO MAKE **INDEPENDENT MISSION-CENTERED** DECISIONS...

...**REDUCES** THE NEED FOR DIRECT SUPERVISION ACROSS THE BOARD...

Fig. #10 & #38

...WHICH IN TURN LEADS TO **INCREASED PRODUCTIVITY.**

This approach supports **mission success.** *It's working smarter,* **not** *harder.*

Starting Now:

A—Identify a time period for completing each task.

- If you don't have specified time limits for all tasks, there's **no way** to predict or track productivity.

- If you can't predict and track productivity, *it can't be acheived.*

- *Collaborate with your direct reports:*

  "We need to make sure we are comp--leting work in a reasonable amount of time, how much time would you recommend that this task require?"

  Then use their timeframe.

- If they don't know what the time--frame should be, *keep negotiating* and help them come up with an answer that works for them.

- Let them know that if something comes up that was unexpected, they should communicate with you before the deadline.

B—When giving directives, always include these 8 components.

  1. A clear & achievable objective.
  2. A timeframe/ deadline.

B—(cont'd)

  3. The number of people assigned to the job.

  4. The name of the person responsible for completing the directive.

  5. The reason the assignment needs to be completed

  6. A request for any ideas that can get the assignment completed with--in less time or for less money

  7. A request that they contact you if they think the deadline can't be met.

  8. Encourage discussion and give advice as requested.

C—Teach your direct reports to work smarter **by constantly improving** how work is being completed.

D—Reduce complexity at every opportunity.

E—While **always** making yourself available for advice, solving problems, or using your authority to remove roadblocks, also **encourage your new experts** to make more **independent decisions.**

STEP 7: ENCOURAGE THE GROUP TO INNOVATE NEW IDEAS FOR MISSION SUCCESS

Introduction

You want every brain in the game. While the supervisor might know what needs to be done and when it needs to be done, they don't actually do the work—and encouraging people that actually do the work is the key to innovation.

- Because it's all about changing *how* you are doing something. *It's the people who are actually doing the work that will come up with the best ideas.*

When they start talking, you start listening. After listening, implement the ones that will lower effort, save time, and save money with the lowest risk.

At all times you should have a running list of ideas that they have collected and are working to implement. Implementing 10, 30, or even 50 large, medium, and small time- and money-saving ideas over a one-year period can create epic outcomes. Don't underestimate the POWER of continuous improvement!

Train your people on how to define what a good idea is or what an improvement is and allow their creativity to drive innovation. I have included this training in Appendix 5 of this book.

Once people catch on to this game, it is tantamount to a treasure hunt. Creating new ideas becomes an intoxicating practice. Eventually continuous improvement becomes organic and starts to bypass the original authorization processes because everybody knows what a good idea is and how to implement it.

Training your group in the use of Appendix 5: Submitting Ideas for Improvement SOP is your longer-term goal. Depending on the level of current skill, some people will learn this standard operating procedure very quickly but others will need a little more handholding during the training process.

- The reason Appendix 5 is so important for your long-term goal is that once this training is integrated into your group, *innovation and continuous improvement become organic functions within each group activity,* requiring little to no attention on your part.

Quadrant Thinking

All quadrants can thrive when it comes to creativity.

Your **Q1s** will focus on the technical changes that can be made and you want to help them by emphasizing their skills in the ideas related to increasing productivity.

Your **Q4s** will focus on the collaborative changes that can be made that help things run more smoothly and more efficiently, which also increases productivity.

Your future and current **Q2s** will obviously focus on both technical and collaborative changes.

If you have **Q3s** that are responding well to training, they'll come up with ideas as well!

Important Takeaway
You should always have a logbook with the list of good ideas that are being submitted by your people that you are working to implement. Study closely the standard operating procedure for submitting improvement ideas in Appendix 5 of this book. If anyone has ideas that lower effort, lower cost, or lower time demand and they are low risk for implementation, *you need to be implementing those as fast as you can. I can't state the importance of this enough.*

One of the primary reasons you exist as a leader is to motivate your group to continuously improve. One of the best ways to do that is to get every brain in the game and have people start submitting ideas like a conveyor belt. If you're not getting a regular flow of good ideas then the group is not continuously improving. And if your group is not continuously improving your group is falling behind.

- As part of combining Steps 6 and 7, pay special attention to ideas that improve working conditions. Implementing ideas that improve working conditions elevates a positive perspective on the part of your followers and can have significant positive impacts on productivity. This is another hidden gem along with reducing complexity.
- *And if there are safety problems, improving working conditions to make the workplace a safer place to be holds moral implications as well as being critical to better productivity.*

Starting Now
Here are the three actions you need to start taking immediately:

1. **Starting now:** At your various meetings start promoting this process. Let people know that if they have an idea that they think can improve productivity, you want to hear about it. *Along with improvements to productivity be sure to mention that the improvement of working conditions will not only make our lives better but it will make our lives smarter.*
   - *Improving working conditions also means that safety issues should be communicated and addressed, with unsafe conditions being mitigated effectively, so everybody goes home to their families at the end of their workday.*

   Ideas that improve productivity and improve working conditions at the same time get special focus. Encourage people to submit ideas and come to you and talk about what they're thinking. When they start talking you start writing down their ideas start working on implementation for high-benefit, low-cost, low-risk ideas (see Appendix 5).
2. **Starting now:** Provide training on the standard operating procedure that helps people understand and define what a good idea actually is (see Appendix 5). *This should be a routine training process within the entire group.*

3. **Starting now:** Keep your logbook handy. You should have a running list of all the ideas you have implemented, all the ideas that have been submitted, and all the ideas that you are actively working on implementing now.

Looking at It from Your Follower's Perspective
(After implementing their improvement ideas as a routine activity and by improving working conditions, in particular unsafe working conditions)

- I feel confident and competent in knowing how to improve my group.
- It's fun coming up with ideas for improving the group.
- I feel a lot better about our working conditions now.
- I feel like they care about me now that the safety issues are being addressed.
- I feel appreciated for using my creativity.
- I don't fear humiliation.
- I feel empowered.

Figure #39 is provided as a quick guide to help you focus on what's important.

PHASE 2: STEP 7: *Encourage the Group to Innovate New Ideas for Mission Success*

INNOVATING MEANS CHANGING **HOW** YOU ARE DOING SOMETHING.

The people **actually doing the work** will come up with the best ideas for innovation.

Fig. #11 & #39

 When they start talking, you *start listening.* After listening, implement the ones that will *lower effort, save time,* and *save money* with the lowest risk.

 **At all times** you should have a running list of ideas that your people have collected and are working to implement.

Implementing 10, 30, or even 50 large, medium, and small time & money-saving ideas over a one year period creates epic outcomes. Don't underestimate the *POWER* of continuous improvement!

Starting Now:

A—At your various meetings start promoting this process. Let people know that if they have an idea that they think can improve productivity, **you want to hear about it.**

B—Provide training on the standard operating procedure that helps people **understand** and **define** what a good idea actually is (see Appendix 5). This should be a routine training process within the entire group.

C—Keep your logbook handy. You should have a **running list** of all the ideas you have *implemented,* all the ideas that have been *submitted,* and all the ideas that you are *actively working on* implementing now.

— PHASE 3 —

STEP 8: HELP YOUR PEOPLE RECOVER FROM LOW PERFORMANCE OR ERRORS WITH TRAINING SESSIONS FOCUSED ON IMPROVING PERFORMANCE

Introduction

Help improve their performance by helping them *recover after making an error or recover from any instances of less-than-standard performance.*

The United States has some of the best fighter pilots in the world. There are a couple reasons for that, but one is they sit down with their pilots after every sortie and review any mistakes or errors to correct or improvements in performance to implement. Group commanders learned early on that after spending millions of dollars on training a single pilot they simply couldn't wash them out because they had erred. After all, to err is to be human. Certainly, erring when flying a $40 million machine at supersonic speed with a lot of lives on the line can take exceptional courage to own up to, but when you create a psychologically safe space people will step up. This psychologically safe environment has been responsible for everything from redesigning cockpit instrument placement to modifications in the training program for the newer pilots coming up, as well as same-day changes to the tactical plans for the sorties leaving in the next hour.

The fact is when you can help people improve their performance and recover from an error the chances of them repeating the mistake is much lower than if you were to reassign a new person to the job who hasn't committed the same error. Think about that for a moment.

Teach a person how to recover from error or low performance by giving them a helping hand and the effort can be returned to the group as extraordinary levels of high performance. Look for similar errors being made in seemingly unconnected events and trace them back to their common source with the intent of eliminating *systemic error generation by turning them into teachable moments for future training.* When you change the training program as a preventative measure against future instances of the same error by converting it into a teachable moment, group performance again climbs systematically.

When people do err: keep the feedback session private and safe; deliver the feedback unemotionally, without anger; focus on improvement; and be specific so the individual receives usable information for improvement. And as noted earlier, take this information and modify the training program to prevent the error from being repeated by others in the future.

We cannot punish our way to success and there are smart ways to deal with people that don't want to protect and promote a culture. It's done privately, and it's done continuously until you know that either the issue is remedied or can't be fixed by retraining after multiple attempts (which means the problem needs to be addressed by other means).

A note of caution: The world has a tendency to remove the people who create *people problems* too quickly. Before determining that these people are untrainable because they're not responding to the training you're giving them, you want to make sure that your workplace culture is not the source of the people problems. In other words, if your workplace culture is not reducing fear, that is going to impact the human brains in your group and promote what look like individual deficiencies in performance when actually a systemic issue is promoting their lack of cooperation. Then what is actually happening is individuals are being held responsible for systemic issues. If you are determining too early that somebody is untrainable when it's actually a systemic issue, you could be removing somebody that could have otherwise been saved and turned into a high performer. Additionally, any leader that's making this mistake will continue to repeat this mistake over and over again until they realize there may be a systemic source that is negatively impacting the performance of their direct reports.

Lastly, never, ever publicly embarrass your followers. Publicly shaming them concerning performance issues is not only ineffective, it's inhumane.

Quadrant Thinking
The **Q1s'** needed performance improvements will typically be found in the area of additional collaboration training in order to improve performance or correct errors.

The **Q4s'** needed performance improvements will typically be found in the area of additional technical training in order to improve performance or correct errors.

The **Q3s'** needed performance improvements will typically be found in the areas of both additional technical training and collaboration training in order to improve performance or correct errors.

All of these quadrants just mentioned are potentially your future **Q2s**.

The need for **Q2s** to recover from errors is not unusual. While their performance improvements aren't necessarily just focused on technical or collaboration training, many times your feedback to them will be helping them recover from an error and not less-than-standard performance issues.

This type of error making is often caused by them *performing at a very high level.*

High-performing **Q2s** do not always take failure well. In these situations you're going to have to counsel them and encourage them to keep striving by helping them recover from any mistakes they have made. You won't have to push the point too hard; they typically integrate corrective measures quickly.

Important Takeaway
For some supervisors giving feedback to help people recover from errors or from less-than-standard performance *is a difficult conversation for them to have with their direct reports and therefore they sometimes*

avoid the conversation entirely. In any situation that demands action from the leader and inaction, by definition, damages the group, *this can't be you.* If you're going to be a Q2 supervisor and empower yourself by empowering your supervisor and empowering your direct reports, you need to get comfortable with what are potentially uncomfortable conversations, or you just will not be as successful as you should be.

Starting Now

Here are the five actions you need to start taking immediately:

1. **Starting now:** If someone has made an error or is suffering from substandard performance in any of their performance expectations, pause and plan ahead exactly what you want to say to the individual before you meet. You should be making notes to yourself that you will use in your meeting with them and *your advice to them for making improvements should be very, very specific.*

2. **Starting now:** Meet with them one-on-one and make sure the *first* thing you tell them is that you're meeting with them *to help them improve their performance.* The *second* thing you want to tell them is that you understand they might be feeling uncomfortable, and that you understand why that might be. *Keep the meeting psychologically safe* and reduce fear by reassuring them over and over again, as many times as necessary, that the reason for the meeting is to improve their performance. *Be specific*—the more specific you are the better chance they have at recovering. *Schedule a follow-up meeting* so you can give feedback on their improvement. *This second meeting is very important—don't skip it.* Always keep the meeting as a private one-on-one meeting and the contents of the meeting should always be confidential.

3. **Starting now:** If it's the *second time correcting the same problem*, place some additional pressure by mentioning this fact. If a person persists in substandard performance after repeated retraining sessions, consult your supervisor for next steps.

4. **Starting now:** Bullying behavior, acts of intimidation, or other hostile behaviors need immediate action on the part of the leader. Regardless of how busy you might be destructive behavior needs to be dealt with at the moment it's discovered. Also, the solution needs to have staying power which means if continue training does not bring about the desired outcome your immediate supervisor needs to be involved. More detail is provided below in Step 9.

5. **Starting now:** Do not over-supervise or micromanage your veterans. It's inefficient and ineffective, not to mention demoralizing and demeaning. That being said, do not under-supervise your newcomers. They can become anxious when they're not quite sure what to do. Your steady guidance is critical to their future success. Note: I have seen many situations where supervisors do not adjust their level of direct supervision according to the experience of their individual team members. This becomes just another way of normalizing mediocre performance. When you successfully train people to expert levels, the best thing you can do is get out of their way.

Looking at It from Your Follower's Perspective

(Approximately 6 to 12 months after implementation; coincides with Step 9: Protecting and Promoting the Culture.)

Before and during the first meeting:

- I don't feel good when I make an error.
- I feel embarrassed and I feel incompetent when meeting with my supervisor about these things, so I fear being humiliated.
- They tell me the reason we're meeting today is to help me improve my performance but it doesn't feel that way.
- I feel like they might be picking on me, I'm not completely sure I agree with them.

After the second meeting if performance issues have improved:

- I feel liked, I feel supported, I feel like they care about me.
- I'm getting the training I need in a situation where I was originally feeling very bad.
- I'm feeling more competent.
- I'm feeling more significant.
- I'm fearing less humiliation even though I made an error or was suffering from less-than-standard performance.

Figure #40 is provided as a quick guide to help you focus on what's important.

>ATTRACTING< Collaborative Power from the Bottom Up

PHASE 3: STEP 8: *Help Your People Recover from Errors with Training Focused on Improving Performance*

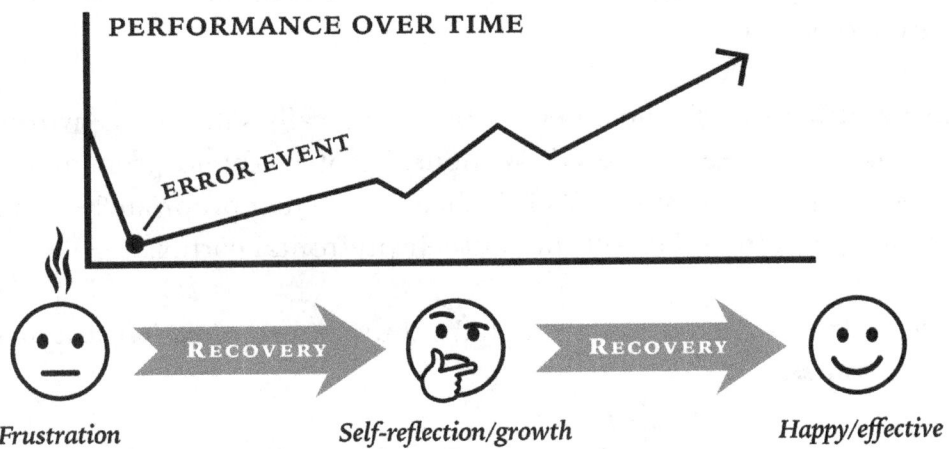

Help them improve their performance by helping them recover after making an error or *any instance* of less-than-standard performance.

When you *help people improve their performance* and *recover from an error* the chances of them repeating the mistake is much lower than if you were to reassign a new person to the job who *hasn't* committed the same error. Think about that.

Starting Now:

A—If someone made an error, pause & plan exactly what you will tell them be--fore you meet. *How you suggest they improve should be **very specific.***

B—Meet with them one-on-one. The first thing you say: this meeting is to help you improve. If they feel uncomfortable, reassure them of the meeting's purpose.

"THIS IS TO HELP YOU IMPROVE."

Fig. #13 & #40

C—If it's the second time correcting the same problem, place some additional pressure by mentioning this fact.

D—Bullying behavior, acts of intmidation, or other hostile behaviors need im--mediate action on the part of the leader.

E—Do not over-supervise or micromanage your veterans. It's ineffcient and in--effective, not to mention demoralizing and demeaning.

That being said, do not under-supervise your newcomers.

STEP 9: PROTECT AND PROMOTE THE CULTURE

Introduction

How people treat each other is important to mission success and is critical to *building a workplace where people want to be*. Support your people by simultaneously being a *good listener* and *privately holding people accountable for inappropriate behavior*. As a leader, if you ignore destructive behavior *you have become the problem*. Remind your group when they are feeling frustrated to come to you so they have a chance to talk it out and search for solutions.

High performance and high performers need a psychologically safe work environment for all the human brain reasons we've already covered. Without a protected and promoted culture your best performers will leave for greener pastures. Weird, chaotic, and inappropriate behaviors in the culture definitely generate fear, pushing everybody out of their prefrontal cortex.

This is not a *nice to have*; a protected and promoted culture is a *required intrinsic foundation to a high-performing human enterprise*.

Civility promotes dignity and respect and creates a psychologically safe environment where high performers feel good about coming forward and making things happen. Bullying behavior, public anger events, inappropriate comments in the public forum, and behind the scenes intimidation are things that you will need to address immediately.

Keep the group in their prefrontal cortex by evoking logical, rational, and ethical thinking which turns into logical, rational, and ethical behaviors. This is done by *protecting* the culture by having people *stop behaviors that they shouldn't be using* and *promoting* the culture by having people *start to do things they're not doing now*.

These two approaches of simultaneously *protecting and promoting* essentially become coequal branches of the future culture expectations you will place on your group. Aside from the obvious moral imperative of requiring respectful behavior, development of collaborative relationships between team members is essential for a group seeking high performance.

Quadrant Thinking

This will appeal to **Q2s** and **Q4s**. It may appeal to some **Q1s**, but some **Q1s** and **Q3s** may be very resistant.

Important Takeaway

In groups where leadership has not been protecting and promoting the culture people have become used to doing and saying whatever they want. As you start to impose new rules for the culture expect some resistance from these *independent contractors*. That resistance can occur in the form of the more hidden conversations behind the scenes between staff all the way to and including more public messages during meeting settings. In this takeaway I don't want to overblow this point; the overwhelming (oftentimes silent) majority is wanting a safe and sane culture. In the protected culture they will continue to get to think and feel however they want *but now people will no longer be allowed to do or say whatever they want.* No more anarchy, no more chaos. What people do and say about each other or to each other *now matters.*

Starting Now
Here are the four actions you need to start taking immediately:

1. **Starting now:** *Don't allow inappropriate comments and behaviors in public forums.* This includes, but is not limited to, angry outbursts, inappropriate humor, any type of harassment, and bullying behavior. Have a private meeting with these folks and let them know it's not okay to pursue this type of behavior. If it seemed to them that this behavior was acceptable in the past, let them know you are trying to build a better workplace and that you need their help to do that. If the behavior persists, escalate your response by bringing this to your supervisor's attention and seek their guidance on next steps.
2. **Starting now:** Protecting the culture from destructive behaviors is critical because it protects your high performers. As I mentioned in Step 8, no matter how busy you might be, destructive behavior needs to be dealt with at the moment it's discovered. If you are unable to create the outcome you need from repeated retraining, you need to involve your immediate supervisor. Uncorrectable destructive behavior needs to be removed from the group culture one way or the other.
3. **Starting now:** *Promote that getting along with your fellow employees is now part of their job.* Stress to your direct reports that from now on their ability to develop professional collaborative relationships is as important as their technical competency.
4. **Starting now:** Teach all your followers that when they feel angry that they are not to attack. Instead they are to step back, reassess, and *go talk with their supervisor about finding solutions.*

Looking at It from Your Follower's Perspective
(Approximately 6 to 12 months after implementation; coincides with Step 8: Help Your People Recover from Low Performance or Errors with Training Sessions Focused on Improving Performance. And obviously these are not the thoughts of somebody who's been a bully and is needing their behavior corrected.)

- I feel like my environment is more predictable.
- I feel safer from people that feel the need to treat other people poorly.
- I feel protected.
- I feel more in control and more bold, and I feel supported.

Figure #41 is provided as a quick guide to help you focus on what's important.

>ATTRACTING< COLLABORATIVE POWER FROM THE BOTTOM UP

PHASE 3: STEP 9: *Protect and Promote the culture*

USE YOUR LEADERSHIP POWERS TO PROTECT YOUR PEOPLE.

High performance & high performers **need a psychologically safe work environment** for all the human brain reasons we've already covered.

A protected and promoted culture is *not a nice to have.* This is **a required intrinsic foundation** to a high-performing human enterprise.

Weird, chaotic, and inappropriate behaviors in the culture definitely **generate fear**, pushing everybody out of their prefrontal cortex.

Without a protected and promoted culture your best performers **will leave** for greener pastures.

Keep people **in their prefrontal cortex** by evoking *logical, rational, & ethical thinking* which turns into *logical, rational, & ethical behavior.*

Protecting the culture is done through having people **stop** behaviors that they shouldn't be using and *promoting the culture* by having people **start** to do things they're not doing now.

Starting Now: Fig. #14 & #41

A—*Don't allow inappropriate comments & behaviors in public forums.* This includes, but is not limited to, angry outbursts, inappropriate humor, any type of harassment, & bullying behavior.

B—No matter how busy you might be, *destructive behavior needs to be dealt with at the moment it's discovered.*

C—Promote that getting along with your fellow employees is *now part of their job.*

D—Teach all your followers that *when angry that they are not to attack.* Have them step back, assess, & discuss solutions with their supervisor.

STEP 10: AFTER FULL IMPLEMENTATION, IMPLEMENT, IMPLEMENT, IMPLEMENT ALL THE ABOVE AT EVERY CHANCE

Introduction
Need I say more? Implementing all the steps simultaneously and continuously occurs after you've completed all the phasing as outlined in the implementation section.

Quadrant Thinking
Keep quadrant thinking in the forefront of your mind as you implement Attracting Collaborative Power.

Important Takeaway
Implementing anything new is always going to have a little messiness to it. This is not a physics problem per se. This is changing a group to increase its performance. This means it's dynamic in its application and people are dynamic in their response, but much of it is very predictable. The key here is to keep at it. There will be a little chaos here and there but if you stay with it people will start to acclimate to the new ways of doing things and then after acclimation will actually start to see the value and enjoy your approach. That's when the big payoff occurs. That's when you start getting the power back.

Starting Now
Here is the one action you need to start taking immediately:

1. **Starting now:** Implement the steps in *Chapters 2 and 3 in order to fully integrate Attracting Power from the Bottom Up.*

Figure #42 is provided as a quick guide to help you focus on what's important.

>ATTRACTING< COLLABORATIVE POWER FROM THE BOTTOM UP

PHASE 3: STEP 10: *After Implementing Steps 1-9, Implement, Implement, Implement*

Fig. #15 & #42

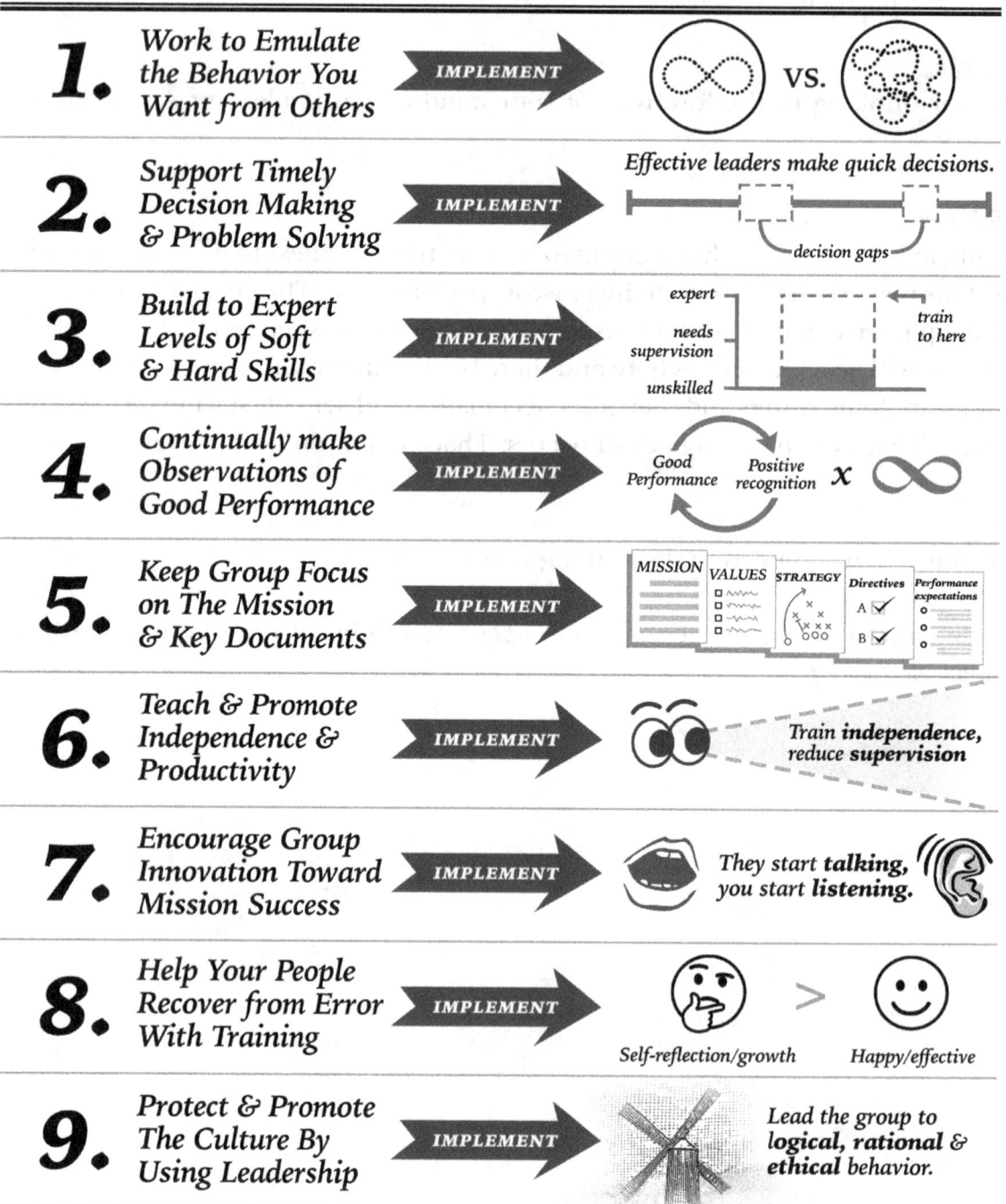

1. *Work to Emulate the Behavior You Want from Others* — IMPLEMENT — ∞ VS.

2. *Support Timely Decision Making & Problem Solving* — IMPLEMENT — Effective leaders make quick decisions. — decision gaps

3. *Build to Expert Levels of Soft & Hard Skills* — IMPLEMENT — expert / needs supervision / unskilled — train to here

4. *Continually make Observations of Good Performance* — IMPLEMENT — Good Performance / Positive recognition x ∞

5. *Keep Group Focus on The Mission & Key Documents* — IMPLEMENT — MISSION / VALUES / STRATEGY / Directives / Performance expectations

6. *Teach & Promote Independence & Productivity* — IMPLEMENT — Train **independence,** reduce **supervision**

7. *Encourage Group Innovation Toward Mission Success* — IMPLEMENT — They start **talking,** you start **listening.**

8. *Help Your People Recover from Error With Training* — IMPLEMENT — Self-reflection/growth > Happy/effective

9. *Protect & Promote The Culture By Using Leadership* — IMPLEMENT — Lead the group to **logical, rational & ethical** behavior.

Chapter 7

Cultivating Collaborative Power: Implementing Collaborative Group Behaviors

Bob has encapsulated decades of collaboration and leadership
experience into a single recipe for success.

—E. J. SHALABY

Problem-Solving
Continuous Improvement
Training for Each Collaborative Group Behavior
  Mission
  Culture
  Effective Interpersonal Relationships
  High-Quality Communication
  Technical Competency
  Productivity
  Problem-Solving
  Continuous Improvement

IT'S OPTIONAL

I want to start out by saying that implementing the content in this chapter—Phase 4: Cultivating Collaborative Power—*is optional*.

If you're a first-line supervisor or middle manager or even a department head and you have implemented and are following the Starting Now actions of Inviting Power from the Top Down and Attracting Power from the Bottom Up described in the previous two chapters, that may well be all you will need to do.

You're Inviting Collaborative Power and Attracting Collaborative Power so you can have a positive impact on supporting your supervisor and their success and supporting your direct reports and their success. Then, *as the people in your immediate sphere of influence become successful, so do you.*

Cultivating Collaborative Power is a completely different animal. How much power you have in your organization will dictate how successful you can be at implementing this process.

And truth be known, as you read about the Collaborative Group Behaviors used to Cultivate Collaborative Power you'll notice that many of them are embedded within the Attracting Collaborative Power section.

To recap, Inviting Power from the Top Down allows you to gain power by first empowering everybody above you; power is then returned to you as the second step in the process. The same thing happens with Attracting Power from the Bottom Up: you empower them as a first step and they return power as a second step.

With Cultivating Collaborative Power, you are reversing the order. It's a power play on your part as a first step to manage behaviors, which will then ultimately empower them as a second step.

Empowering anybody as a first step which then results in power coming back to you as a second step is super effective and very low risk. However, having your power play be the first step so you can then create a result or outcome that empowers them as a second step is a different proposition, and while it can be very effective it's not low risk.

Let me repeat this earlier statement: Cultivating Collaborative Power is a completely different animal. *How much power you have in your organization will dictate how successful you can be at implementing these Collaborative Group Behaviors.*

All this said, this is exactly why you need to pay attention to the following 11 rules of implementation before deciding whether to implement Cultivating Collaborative Power.

RULE #1: IT'S OPTIONAL
If you have successfully implemented Inviting Collaborative Power from the Top Down and Attracting Collaborative Power from the Bottom Up, Cultivating Collaborative Power *is optional*.

The primary reason I offer Phase 4: Cultivating Collaborative Power as an option is in case the CEO or general manager wants to convert the entire organization over to the same high-performing group of Q2s that you have created in your smaller group within the larger organization.

RULE #2: IT'S BEST TO INVITE AND ATTRACT FIRST
The best way for a CEO or GM to implement Cultivating Collaborative Power is to first have the entire leadership team in the organization trained on how to Invite and Attract Collaborative Power.

CULTIVATING COLLABORATIVE POWER

You can influence the workplace environment with the Collaborative Group Behaviors that you're going to be exposed to in this section. These behaviors assert human collaboration as a priority, and **practically any leader** can inspire and promote the desired mission-centered outcomes *simply based on the proper caretaking of the human psyches under their charge* by fostering collaboration. In this section you'll find sophisticated human *dos and don'ts lists:* a list of behaviors that people are not using that should now be used in order to promote collaboration within the group, and a list of behaviors that people are demonstrating now that need to stop if you want to build collaboration within the group.

Remember that in deteriorated conditions our thinking is affected by the amygdala, which results in our decision-making capacity having only a short-term toolbox of fight, flight, or freeze. When we remove threats and fear and add collaboration training and recognition for the best skills demonstrated by group members, decision making advances to the prefrontal cortex, whose toolbox uses logical, rational, and ethical thoughts as the precursors to logical, rational, and ethical actions.

RULE #3: UNDERSTAND THE HUMAN BRAIN TOOLBOX OPTIONS
We know which human brain toolbox results in the best group performance and we also know we do not get the toolbox we need unless we favorably influence the work environment as it's experienced by the group members.

There is a long list of human behaviors that naturally excite the human brain to create an environment of collaboration. But as we have learned there is also a long list of human behaviors that naturally generate threat, fear, and hidden fears that demotivate the human brain and destroy collaboration. The dos and don'ts lists presented in this section will help us focus on the right toolbox.

- The fear toolbox or amygdala toolbox creates destructive behaviors, which we can address with the don't list. The **don't list** is a list of behaviors **people are using now that we want them to stop using** in order to create a more collaborative high-performing work group. This list usually includes behaviors that are destructive and that reduce group members' capacity for developing professional collaborative relationships because members' ability to trust other people is significantly reduced by these same behaviors.
- The reduced-fear toolbox or prefrontal cortex toolbox promotes logical, rational, and ethical behaviors as seen on the do list. The **do list** is a list of behaviors **that people are not using right now that they need to start using** if we want a more collaborative high-performing work group. The do list typically includes behaviors that promote trust within the relationship and when logical, rational, and ethical behaviors become typical in the work environment, the outcomes realized are mission success, improved performance, and better job satisfaction all at the same time.

RULE #4: FOCUS ON THE DOS AND DON'TS
Some people will resist accepting the *don't list* of behaviors that negatively impact the work environment and some people will resist accepting the *do list* of behaviors that favorably impact the work environment.

Quite frankly, Cultivating Collaborative Power can be met with some resistance by some people if the group is not used to learning about and using the actions and behaviors that encourage human collaboration. As you look at the list of Collaborative Group Behaviors, please know that some of the don't list behaviors are behaviors people have been using and will want to continue using. When a group has been experiencing a weak leadership environment for quite some time, as noted previously, the individuals within the group are operating as if they are independent contractors, and they don't like being told what to do.

Building a highly collaborative group requires that group members develop professional relationships with **all** fellow group members. If this has not been a requirement before and group members have been able to decide on their own who they are willing to develop positive workplace relationships with and who they aren't, some might not like the new requirement to have this type of relationship with *all* fellow group members.

I'm giving you a lot of dos and don'ts, but you can also make your own!

Look at your group right now and ask yourself: what are people doing that you want them to stop doing?

Again, look at your group right now and ask yourself: what are people not doing that you want them to start doing?

Write them down, train everybody on their use, incorporate them as performance expectations, hold people accountable to using the new performance expectations when they err, give people recognition when they use them, and retrain everybody about every three to six months.

It's worth mentioning house rules again because these are the types of behaviors that destroy relationships and create large amounts of fear in the workplace forcing poor decision making from the Amygdala.

HOUSE RULES

Here is a list of the most basic behaviors that need to be called out as no longer being tolerated:

- Harassment
- Public shaming
- Abusive language directed at others
- Acts of intimidation
- Bullying
- Mobbing
- Angry public outbursts
- Unsafe behavior
- Stealing group or group members' property (including time meant to be spent on group activities)
- Excessive tardiness or absenteeism, or unexcused absences
- Falsifying or altering group records, including payroll information
- Insubordination by refusal to perform assigned work or by passively refusing to do assigned work
- Disorderly conduct, including but not limited to fighting and assault, refusing to share knowledge, habitually whining or complaining, being uncooperative or unreliable
- Habitually demonstrating a lack of humility

In some groups a significant number of these are missing from the house rules and it disempowers leaders within that group. One of the ways to Cultivate Collaborative Power is to make sure that the negative behaviors that compromise mission success are part of the house rules and *are trained out of the group*. It doesn't have to be heavy-handed training; most people most of the time will agree that the behaviors that are being called out in the house rules are behaviors that should not be pursued by anybody in the workplace, so the training can simply focus on raising awareness of the rules.

The reason for a house rules list is to give group members the opportunity to avoid these behaviors. However, because many of these behaviors can be so destructive, leadership needs to be ready to pursue and retrain anybody who is demonstrating these behaviors. If leadership finds that an individual continues demonstrating destructive behavior regardless of multiple attempts at retraining, it can be necessary to then remove the destructive behavior by removing the individual who is not favorably responding to th multiple training attempts. Leaders not removing destructive behavior from the group environment when they should will always compromise efforts that support mission success .

RULE #5: MOVE TO Q2 THINKING

If the group is predominantly Q1 in its thinking patterns and the group members have essentially been left on their own to decide if they will collaborate or not collaborate with other members of the group, using Collaborative Group Behaviors can be met with resistance. Attempting to excite high performance that prioritizes mission success by moving the group to Q2 thinking patterns takes time, persistence, and consistent training and retraining.

It is for this reason that the order of implementation is important and that Cultivating Collaborative Power is always the last step in the process. Once you have *successfully Invited and Attracted Collaborative Power* over an extended period of time and have seen the benefits, Cultivating Collaborative Power will not come as a shock to the group and will be invited by most of the people in the group.

The phenomenon of people not wanting to change how they act in the workplace is not a big deep dark secret by any means. As you already know I'm encouraging this book to be used as your training manual so either way the cat is out of the bag so to speak. I think the sooner people start talking about the list of Collaborative Group Behaviors I'm providing here *the better*.

The primary reason I want you to wait on promoting Cultivating Collaborative Power is that it's best to wait until you have fully vetted out the first three phases. This fourth phase can be the most challenging and its success (or failure) is highly dependent on how much power you have in the organization.

When you start implementing the Cultivating Collaborative Power process it's not going to be a surprise to anybody at this point because they will already realize that building Q2 thinking is all about valuing and encouraging the human collaborative process *by empowering everyone in the group*.

RULE #6: BE PREPARED FOR RESISTANCE

Meeting resistance consumes your collaborative power—the same collaborative power you need to help the group switch to the Q2 behaviors that are needed for high performance. If you don't have enough power in the organization, you don't need to institute Cultivating Collaborative Power.

The most effective way to reduce resistance in advance of Cultivating Collaborative Power is to make sure that you have completed and effectively implemented Inviting and Attracting Collaborative Power.

We've already talked about some of the sources of resistance—in particular, if people have been used to using one set of behaviors and now they're asked to use a different set of behaviors, we know people don't always like doing that.

Another source of resistance is that if you use the Collaborative Group Behaviors as performance expectations, Collaborative Group Behaviors become more than just nice reading, they become requirements for employment. It's one thing to talk about using Collaborative Group Behaviors as a way of improving performance and job satisfaction, but the moment you make it a condition of employment it's basically communicating to all the group members that by not participating in the use of Collaborative Group Behaviors *you could lose your job.*

Whenever someone does not want to participate in Collaborative Group Behaviors and you've simultaneously made the use of these behaviors a condition of employment, you will typically have reached a point where you will experience maximum resistance from that individual.

PEOPLE WITH THE MOST POWER

RULE #7: NEXT MOVES ARE POWER DEPENDENT

The farther down the leadership stack you reside, success with Cultivating Collaborative Power becomes MORE dependent on a strong foundation of Inviting and Attracting Collaborative Power for as long as it takes in order to set the stage for Cultivating Collaborative Power. Conversely, the farther up the leadership stack you reside and the more position power you possess, success with Cultivating Collaborative Power becomes LESS dependent on a strong foundation of Inviting and Attracting Collaborative Power.

For instance:

- The CEO, general manager, and leaders higher in the leadership stack—meaning those with the most power organization-wide—can easily implement these Collaborative Group Behaviors as performance expectations that would be required to be used by all the group members.
- Division chiefs that have a lot of power within their division also have a lot of flexibility in implementing these Collaborative Group Behaviors. The extent to which they could actually be used as performance expectations depends on the organization. *If they are not used as performance*

expectations, implementation and success rates go down. However, they could be used as guidelines to at least influence the behaviors to the degree the division chief is able.

- As we travel down the pecking order in the leadership stack you encounter leaders with slightly less power. Middle managers with several crews under their purview and each crew having its own leader can again at least influence the leaders and crews underneath them with these Collaborative Group Behaviors as guidelines. It's entirely possible that the middle manager could appeal to the senior staff above them to institute them as performance expectations.
- A first-line supervisor with a single crew might find it much more difficult, and perhaps impossible, to implement Collaborative Group Behaviors as performance expectations.

The important reminder I want to pass on to you is this: if you have been Inviting and Attracting Collaborative Power and it is successfully impacting your sphere of influence in the organization, you don't really need the Cultivating Collaborative Power behaviors for your piece of the company.

For a CEO or general manager who wants the whole group to shift towards Q2 thinking, they will also want to Invite and Attract Collaborative Power first. *But then as a necessary second step* they will want to use these Collaborative Group Behaviors as performance expectations in order to *move the entire group in the same direction towards Q2 thinking*, instead of a piecemeal approach with different smaller groups within the larger organization Inviting and Attracting Collaborative Power while other smaller groups *within the same organization are not Inviting and Attracting Collaborative Power.*

RULE #8: COLLABORATIVE POWER GRABS HAVE A POSITIVE IMPACT AT ANY LEVEL
Inviting and Attracting Collaborative Power is going to have a huge positive impact on the people around you and that will be enough to create a huge positive impact on the people that work with you, which is why Cultivating Collaborative Power is optional. If you don't have enough power to convert the Collaborative Group Behaviors into performance expectations, leave that task to those that are higher in the leadership hierarchy.

It might take some time; remember it's not days and weeks, it's months and years. But over time you will be able to make the following statements by simply Inviting and Attracting Collaborative Power for your immediate sphere of influence. I give you this list to convince you that if you don't have enough power in the group to Cultivate Collaborative Power you are still making an incredible positive impact.

Once you've completed and continue to implement your Starting Now action items, you'll be able to say the following.

People know:

- you are there to help them recover when they make a mistake.
- you are there to guide them and help them recover from errors and train them in their weakest skill set.

- that when they demonstrate extraordinary performance they are going to be rightfully recognized.
- they can come to you to help them prioritize their work.
- they have an open invitation to communicate with you.
- you are there to support them ***when they need you the most.***
- that when they give you a new idea that they've come up with that they think can improve the work environment, save money or time, or make life safer at your organization, you're serious about implementing improvements.

You have been able to:

- get people to use the mission, strategy documents, values, company policies, and directives to help guide them on how best to prioritize their work.
- solve some of the mission-related problems you identified in your survey.
- influence people and get them to use more of the collaborative behaviors that you are modeling.
- effectively deal with the bullies that are under your control.
- influence how people communicate with each other.
- increase the amount of training your people receive.
- train your people on how best to recognize and solve problems.
- issue directives that are more effective at getting the job done.

Your boss:

- knows that when they come up with an idea for improvement that you're going to implement it full steam ahead 100 percent.
- supports you because they have been supported by you.

Lastly:

- Your fellow leaders know that you're there to support them too.

COLLABORATIVE GROUP BEHAVIORS

RULE #9: CONVERT TO PERFORMANCE EXPECTATIONS
When you are able to instill the following list of Collaborative Group Behaviors into the group as performance expectations, the entire group will shift towards Q2 thinking over time. Getting people to use these Q2 behaviors may encounter initial resistance and will require training and persistent and consistent application over time.

RULE #10: CREATE LESS RESISTANCE WITH UNIVERSAL TRAINING APPROACH
If the entire leadership staff has been using this book as a training manual, teaching all leaders how to Invite Power from the Top Down and How to Attract Power from the Bottom Up over a reasonable period of time, instituting Collaborative Group Behaviors as performance expectations will be met with minimal resistance.

RULE #11: CHERRY PICK IF YOU NEED TO!
Read all of the Collaborative Group Behaviors below in great depth. There is nothing that says you can't cherry pick some of the behaviors you like the most or use the ones that you think could solve a problem and then add them to your Starting Now list of action items for Attracting Collaborative Power.

PERFORMANCE EXPECTATIONS FOR LEADERS AND NON-LEADERS ALIKE

Collaborative Group Behaviors are categorized according to the Big 8:

1. Mission
2. Culture
3. Effective Interpersonal Relationships
4. High-Quality Communication
5. Technical Competency
6. Productivity
7. Problem-Solving
8. Continuous Improvement

MISSION
1.1 Assume every group member brings value to support the overall mission. Adopt an "If it's important to you then it's important to me" ethos.
1.2 Keep work prioritized according to the mission and value statements. Prioritize all tasks and if necessary reprioritize all tasks as new tasks arrive.

CULTURE
2.1 Avoid inappropriate comments and behaviors in public forums. This includes, but is not limited to, angry outbursts and inappropriate humor.
2.2 Any type of harassment and/or bullying behavior is unacceptable. Demonstrate empathy, dignity, and respect.

EFFECTIVE INTERPERSONAL RELATIONSHIPS
3.1 Getting along with your fellow employees is now part of your job. Your ability to develop professional relationships is now as important as your technical competency.

3.2 Must have the ability to deal with adversity and an ability to keep interpersonal relationship problems or personal differences separate from work performance.

3.3 When you feel angry, don't attack. Stand down with savoir faire and reassess the situation.

HIGH-QUALITY COMMUNICATION

4.1 When in doubt, pass it up.

4.2 Follow the Communication Chain of Command SOP.

4.3 Keep information flowing in order to support high performance by following the Communication Email SOP.

TECHNICAL COMPETENCY

5.1 Fully demonstrate your technical expertise at all times.

5.2 Operating outside your area of technical expertise is unacceptable.

5.3 Avoid injury by using safety practices and safety equipment related to the job.

PRODUCTIVITY

6.1 Understand and demonstrate the importance of productivity in achieving mission success.

6.2 Directives are not optional. Every directive issued needs to be completed according to its objective and completed within the time allowed for completion.

6.3 Accept delegated tasks with positive motivation.

6.4 Report time-wasting procedures and suggest improvements (this is also a Continuous Improvement expectation; see 8.3).

PROBLEM-SOLVING

7.1 Always communicate to your direct supervisor about any problems you know about.

7.2 Always get the facts, verify information, or assist in verifying information; recheck facts if something isn't making sense.

7.3 Demonstrate an open-mind approach and allow new facts to change your mind.

7.4 Leave your ego at the door.

7.5 Use the Eight-Step Problem-Solving Process SOP and the Recognizing Problems SOP.

CONTINUOUS IMPROVEMENT

8.1 Accept performance feedback with civil behavior. Demonstrate taking responsibility for your behavior.

8.2 Demonstrate integration of performance feedback by modifying future behavior using recovery behaviors.

8.3 Promote a continuous improvement strategy by using the Submitting Ideas for Improvement SOP.

TRAINING FOR EACH COLLABORATIVE GROUP BEHAVIOR

In this section, for each Collaborative Group Behavior I will give:

- A background description of the behavior,
- performance requirements—the specific actions that if performed will cause a person's evaluation scores to go up, and
- the recommended recovery behaviors that supervisors can use to help people in case they have not met minimum performance standards in this area. Note that these recovery behaviors are also provided so that every group member is made aware that this is what their supervisor will be saying if performance drops below standard.

Prior to incorporating these behaviors into performance expectations, a thorough training program should be offered to present this information to the individuals involved. This means a supervisor in a room with a small number of people reading this information out loud and going step-by-step through each particular Collaborative Group Behavior or performance expectation (which are now one and the same). For each individual Collaborative Group Behavior, after presenting the behavior take questions and encourage conversation.

At the risk of repeating some of what you read in the 11 rules for implementation, I will just add this: resistance to change has its basis in loss. When a person experiences change in a group setting, it's not unusual for their greatest fear to be that it will lower their social standing in the group. Resistance to change almost always emanates from this fear, regardless of any other reasons presented by the individual themselves. I will go into more depth on this subject in another book because it deserves its own book.

That being said, let me remind you of *four critical factors* that will help reduce resistance to these Collaborative Group Behaviors.

One, **IF** your entire leadership staff has been exposed to the contents of this book and most all of them are Inviting Power from the Top Down and Attracting Power from the Bottom Up, **THEN** instituting these Collaborative Group Behaviors as *performance expectations* becomes an easy next step to get the entire organization moving in the same direction from a performance standpoint.

Two, the farther up you are in the leadership hierarchy the easier it will be to make sure implementation of these Collaborative Group Behaviors as performance expectations will take place. Basically, the higher up you are in the hierarchy the more power you have, and if that power is used appropriately implementation is essentially guaranteed as long as the entire leader-manager staff is following up after these performance expectations are implemented.

Three, *combining* the previous two points becomes the most powerful way to move forward with implementing the steps to Cultivate Collaborative Power. That is, if most of your leadership is already Inviting and Attracting, and you are higher up in the leadership hierarchy, your chances of success with Cultivate are much better.

Four, regardless of the resistance encountered:

- *Perform the training in a full-disclosure format as recommended here.*
- *Don't apologize.*
- *Implement.*
- *Don't look back.*

Eventually the resistance will fall away and these performance expectations will become second nature.

1 - MISSION

1.1 Assume every group member brings value to support the overall mission. Adopt an "If it's important to you then it's important to me" ethos.

Background
No more silos. No more "us versus them" behaviors. No more bashing other departments. Remember we all have the same mission and values.

Performance Expectations

- Support other departments when they need help for the challenges facing them.
- Explore a better understanding of what is hurting their success instead of verbal bashing.
- Be supportive and create value by promoting cross-training and by participating in cross-training activities such as cross-configuring work tasks across silos.
- Anyone not sure of how to meet this or other performance expectations should consult their supervisor.

Recovery Behavior

- Stop determining the value of a request based on what department that request is coming from.
- Everyone should be following the chain of command, which means another department asking for your services should be going through your supervisor and you should be ready to help another department when directed by your supervisor.

- Anyone not promoting cross-training or bashing other departments is not doing their job.
- If a person is not meeting this performance expectation, they need to modify their future behavior using the recovery behavior as described here to at least meet minimum performance standards.
- Not using recovery behaviors will cause evaluation scores to go down.
- Anyone not sure of how to meet this or other performance expectations should consult their supervisor.

1.2 Keep work prioritized according to the mission and value statements. Prioritize all tasks and if necessary reprioritize all tasks as new tasks arrive.

Background

The only way for the mission to be successful is through the collective behaviors of the group members to support that mission by making sure they are always working on the most important task first.

Performance Expectations

- When you are working on a task make sure it's a first- or top-priority task. Be careful to not be working on the second-most-important task first.
- When new information arrives that might cause you to have to reprioritize your current work, make a determination as to which task is more important and if necessary switch tasks to the new work so you are always doing the most important task first and the second-most-important task second.
- Anyone not sure of how to meet this or other performance expectations should consult their supervisor.

Recovery Behavior

- The appropriate priority between two (or more) competing demands can present a dilemma at times; don't live with this dilemma, consult your supervisor for assistance.
- Anytime you are not sure how to prioritize your work according to the mission, values, or your performance expectations, consult your supervisor.
- If a person is not meeting this performance expectation, they need to modify their future behavior using the recovery behavior as described here to at least meet minimum performance standards.
- Not using recovery behaviors will cause evaluation scores to go down.
- Anyone not sure of how to meet this or other performance expectations should consult their supervisor.

2 - CULTURE

2.1 Avoid inappropriate comments and behaviors in public forums. This includes, but is not limited to, angry outbursts and inappropriate humor.

Background

No more doing or saying whatever we want and wherever we want. A collaborative culture can't be promoted if it's not first protected. With mission success hanging in the balance this is an area that can't be compromised. See House Rules.

Performance Expectations

- Aggressive behavior, angry outbursts, overreactive behavior, or inappropriate humor targeting fellow employees or related to political or sexual content is not allowed in public forums.
- A public forum is any place there are more than two people present, including but not limited to control rooms, locker rooms, company trucks, and work areas.
- Mouthing off and complaining in meetings because you're upset needs to be turned into a search for solutions by working with your supervisor instead of having a public venting session.
- Anyone not sure of how to meet this or other performance expectations should consult their supervisor.

Recovery Behavior

- Forcing a lunchroom full of people to listen to someone's passionate political views or jokes that they should be saving for their friends at the bar after work is not okay. These types of behaviors are not acceptable and never have been, really, even if they were passively not addressed in the past.
- Anyone having problems with anger needs to find an effective way of not demonstrating that behavior in the work environment. If a person has anger issues they themselves can't solve, they should consider getting some professional assistance.
- If a person is not meeting this performance expectation, they need to modify their future behavior using the recovery behavior as described here to at least meet minimum performance standards.
- Not using recovery behaviors will cause evaluation scores to go down.
- Anyone not sure of how to meet this or other performance expectations should consult their supervisor.

2.2 Any type of harassment and/or bullying behavior is unacceptable. Demonstrate empathy, dignity, and respect.

Background

As with inappropriate comments in public forums, no more doing or saying whatever we want, wherever we want. Destructive human behavior hijacks mission success and develops fear, and the human brain can't collaborate when it's in that type of an environment.

Performance Expectations

- Any type of harassment and/or bullying behavior is not allowed. This includes any prohibited behaviors listed in company policies.
- Instead of destructive behaviors, the following behaviors should be used instead: Demonstrate respect, dignity, and empathetic behaviors by expressing admiration for those who are able to demonstrate collaborative behavior in the group.
- Anyone being subjected to harassment or bullying behaviors from a fellow employee should consult their supervisor immediately.
- Anyone not sure of how to meet this or other performance expectations should consult their supervisor.

Recovery Behavior

- Each person has beliefs, perspectives, and opinions, just like you. They have hopes, anxieties, and vulnerabilities, just like you. They have friends, family, and perhaps children who love them, just like you. They want to feel respected, appreciated, and competent, just like you. And they wish for peace, joy, and happiness, just like you.
- Anyone not able to stop demonstrating destructive behavior in the group should seek professional help through the employee assistance program; if they are not successful at modifying future behavior they will need to be processed through the disciplinary process.
- If a person is not meeting this performance expectation, they need to modify their future behavior using the recovery behavior as described here to at least meet minimum performance standards.
- Not using recovery behaviors will cause evaluation scores to go down.
- Anyone not sure of how to meet this or other performance expectations should consult their supervisor.

3 - EFFECTIVE INTERPERSONAL RELATIONSHIPS

3.1 Getting along with your fellow employees is now part of your job. Your ability to develop professional relationships is now as important as your technical competency.

Background

Mission success is entirely dependent on the collective collaborative behaviors demonstrated by group members. We are no longer in a group where people are "at each other's backs"; instead the future holds that we are in a group where we now "have each other's backs."

Performance Expectations

- Getting along with our fellow employees is now part of our job.
- We are now required to develop professional relationships.
- We are now required to demonstrate trustworthy behavior that will maximize collaboration and mission success.
- Anyone not sure of how to meet this or other performance expectations should consult their supervisor.

Recovery Behavior

- If this type of performance expectation is new, it might take some getting used to.
- Acquiring this skill and demonstrating the ability to get along with fellow group members to support the goals of a collaborative group is so necessary that it is now part of our job.
- The ultimate responsibility of being able to develop collaborative professional relationships with fellow employees rests upon each and every individual in the group.
- If a person is not meeting this performance expectation, they need to modify their future behavior using the recovery behavior as described here to at least meet minimum performance standards.
- Not using recovery behaviors will cause evaluation scores to go down.
- Anyone not sure of how to meet this or other performance expectations should consult their supervisor.

3.2 Must have the ability to deal with adversity and an ability to keep interpersonal relationship problems or personal differences separate from work performance.

Background

While working with fellow group members, each person should focus on the tasks at hand not on the personal differences they might have with their fellow team members. The days of interrupting production because of arguments that are not focused on seeking solutions are over.

Performance Expectations

- The ability to keep interpersonal problems or personal differences separate from work performance is now a job requirement.
- Differences that don't relate directly to mission success, such as our ethnicity, country of origin, sexual orientation, politics, religion, and philosophy, have no place in the workplace.
- Anyone not sure of how to meet this or other performance expectations should consult their supervisor.

Recovery Behavior

- The ability to keep interpersonal problems or personal differences separate from work performance may not have been asked of group members before, so this might take some getting used to.
- Leaders will no longer be making assignments to separate group members that don't get along with each other.
- If a person is not meeting this performance expectation, they need to modify their future behavior using the recovery behavior as described here to at least meet minimum performance standards.
- Not using recovery behaviors will cause evaluation scores to go down.
- Anyone not sure of how to meet this or other performance expectations should consult their supervisor.

3.3 When you feel angry, don't attack. Stand down with savoir faire and reassess the situation.

Background

We can think and feel whatever we want but we can't do or say whatever we want. "Savoir faire" is defined as the ability to act or speak appropriately in social situations.

Performance Expectations

- When upset at work, PAUSE and think of other ways to express yourself to get your point across. Anger typically wants instant expression or gratification. PAUSING allows reflection. Some conflicts may not be without emotion but presenting your perspective with blinding rage doesn't allow the receiver to understand your position much less develop empathy.
- The workplace is a social situation and angry private or public arguments result in fear building that causes collaboration to drop, which then threatens mission success. Bottom line: no more attack behavior.
- Anyone not sure of how to meet this or other performance expectations should consult their supervisor.

Recovery Behavior

- The next time you feel pissed off your first move needs to be: do nothing.
- If it makes you feel better to write a blistering response, go ahead—BUT DON'T SEND IT. NEVER SEND IT.
- This is not about playing nice so much as it is starting the process of dropping blind emotional reactions and instead getting your brain-reaction-thinking away from the amygdala (the

source of fight-or-flight behaviors) back into the prefrontal cortex (the source of logical, ethical, and rational behaviors).

- If any of these first steps don't solve the problem the next step is a very simple piece of advice we are now required to use: we now take issues that are driving conflict to our supervisor for advice or additional action.
- If a person is not meeting this performance expectation, they need to modify their future behavior using the recovery behavior as described here to at least meet minimum performance standards.
- Not using recovery behaviors will cause evaluation scores to go down.
- Anyone not sure of how to meet this or other performance expectations should consult their supervisor.

4 - HIGH-QUALITY COMMUNICATION

4.1 When in doubt, pass it up.

Background

"When in doubt, pass it up" brings forth real-time quality information that becomes a customized self-identified training program. When complexity rises and when operating standards become more advanced, more questions are always in store for the people experiencing that advanced culture. If the group is going to succeed everyone needs to respond to doubt or missing information with a request for information, not incorrect assumptions.

Performance Expectations

- If anyone is in doubt regarding a policy, directive, statement, and/or anything that's expected of us then they need to pass it up to their supervisor to receive clarification.
- Knowing to ask questions if someone is not sure what to do or think next, instead of making assumptions, is now a performance requirement.
- Anyone not sure of how to meet this or other performance expectations should consult their supervisor.

Recovery Behavior

- Anytime the "right information" is not used at the "right time" the fault will lie with the person who wasn't using high-quality information.
- The mission is asking that everyone use "when in doubt, pass it up." Ask questions, remove doubt, and save the group time.
- If a person is not meeting this performance expectation, they need to modify their future behavior using the recovery behavior as described here to at least meet minimum performance standards.

- Not using recovery behaviors will cause evaluation scores to go down.
- Anyone not sure of how to meet this or other performance expectations should consult their supervisor.

4.2 Follow the Communication Chain of Command SOP.

Background

Everyone is now required to follow the Communication Chain of Command SOP (described in Appendix 3).

When the chain of command is skipped, it does damage.

If the boss is skipping the chain of command on the way down, the people receiving those directives will start to perform work that may not be consistent with the priorities of that shift, crew, department, or division. Sometimes the middle managers and first-line supervisors don't realize that's happening until they find work that wasn't completed and discover that the boss came into the room and told everybody to do something different than what the organization really needed them to do for mission success. This also completely guts the power base of your middle managers and first-line supervisors.

When the chain of command is skipped on the way up by having people bypass their supervisors to go to the next supervisor up, the wholesale removal of a leader from the needed level of involvement *will always contribute to mission failure if not corrected*. This failure will be accelerated if this is happening in multiple places within the organization. Anytime a strata of the leadership team is unilaterally removed by the people they supervise and it's not enforced by upper management, the decay encountered over time will typically be mostly **hidden** until one day when upper management realizes that the organization is now filled with well-intended, hardworking individuals in an otherwise ineffective organization.

Performance Expectations

- Everyone is now required to follow the Communication Chain of Command SOP.
- Anyone not sure of how to meet this or other performance expectations should consult their supervisor.

Recovery Behavior

- Anyone who bypasses the chain of command is essentially damaging the group.
- Not following the chain of command is disruptive and results in resources expended that would have otherwise been used in helping the group and its people succeed.

- If a person is not meeting this performance expectation, they need to modify their future behavior using the recovery behavior as described here to at least meet minimum performance standards.
- Not using recovery behaviors will cause evaluation scores to go down.
- Anyone not sure of how to meet this or other performance expectations should consult their supervisor.

4.3 Keep information flowing in order to support high performance by following the Communication Email SOP.

Background

Everyone is now required to follow the Communication Email SOP (described in Appendix 4). Almost every group is a combination of different types of experts. An organization of varied experts is like a long chain with each link being a different type of expert, all necessary and all having to work together, just like the links in a chain, to pull the mission and values forward. The key to collaboratively have each link in the chain communicate effectively is having rules for the group's information highway.

Performance Expectations

- Everyone is now required to follow the Communication Email SOP.
- Anyone not sure of how to meet this or other performance expectations should consult their supervisor.

Recovery Behavior

- Not following these guidelines of how to respond appropriately or not sending responses when they should have been sent according the SOP is problematic behavior.
- Study the Expectations and if you slip up take responsibility for your actions and get back on track.
- Anyone continuing to make the same errors over and over again will essentially bypass the effectiveness of the recovery behavior retraining process.
- If a person is not meeting this performance expectation, they need to modify their future behavior using the recovery behavior as described here to at least meet minimum performance standards.
- Not using recovery behaviors will cause evaluation scores to go down.
- Anyone not sure of how to meet this or other performance expectations should consult their supervisor.

5 - TECHNICAL COMPETENCY

5.1 Fully demonstrate your technical expertise at all times.

Background

In order for a group to excel each member needs to use their technical skill each and every time it's called upon. Every time a skill is not demonstrated at the exact moment it's needed means the past skill training didn't pay off and mission success suffers.

Performance Expectations

- It is now a job requirement that when a skill set is called upon each and every group member needs to provide value by executing the technical skills the moment they're needed by the group.
- Anyone not sure of how to meet this or other performance expectations should consult their supervisor.

Recovery Behavior

- Fully demonstrating technical skills to bring value to mission success applies to everyone in the group from top to bottom. We don't add value if we don't use our knowledge and skills.
- Anyone not stepping up their performance by allowing the group to capitalize on their existing skill set is demonstrating less-than-standard performance.
- If a person is not meeting this performance expectation, they need to modify their future behavior using the recovery behavior as described here to at least meet minimum performance standards.
- Not using recovery behaviors will cause evaluation scores to go down.
- Anyone not sure of how to meet this or other performance expectations should consult their supervisor.

5.2 Operating outside your area of technical expertise is unacceptable.

Background

The act of operating outside our area of expertise can be a common behavior in a group. Group members need to practice not operating outside their technical expertise.

Performance Expectations

- Not operating outside your area of expertise is now a job requirement. Anyone operating outside of their area of expertise damages the problem-solving process and can potentially create unsafe conditions.

- Anyone not sure of how to meet this or other performance expectations should consult their supervisor.

Recovery Behavior

- When someone doesn't know information but instead gives a "best guess" it can result in problems, injury, or even death. Don't be one of these people.
- If it is beyond your expertise, then let the experts do it. If you want to gain that expertise, then go get the training required to do so.
- If a person is not meeting this performance expectation, they need to modify their future behavior using the recovery behavior as described here to at least meet minimum performance standards.
- Not using recovery behaviors will cause evaluation scores to go down.
- Anyone not sure of how to meet this or other performance expectations should consult their supervisor.

5.3 Avoid injury by using safety practices and safety equipment related to the job.

Background

Injury hurts the individual and the group. Emotional fallout for the victim, their family, and the group can be catastrophic when we a group member suffers a severe injury. Not "acting safe" can result in trauma, cultural discord, lower productivity, mission failure, and "emotional liability" for everyone involved in an incident.

Performance Expectations

- Everyone needs to perform their jobs in a safe manner and comply with all safety policies, procedures, and regulations.
- Always report unsafe conditions so they can be corrected.
- Anyone not sure of how to meet this or other performance expectations should consult their supervisor.

Recovery Behavior

- Anyone having a history of placing themselves or others in unsafe conditions by demonstrating unsafe practices needs to improve their performance.
- The group is counting on everyone to recover from any unsafe behavior by meeting all safety Expectations .
- If a person is not meeting this performance expectation, they need to modify their future behavior using the recovery behavior as described here to at least meet minimum performance standards.

- Not using recovery behaviors will cause evaluation scores to go down.
- Anyone not sure of how to meet this or other performance expectations should consult their supervisor.

6 - PRODUCTIVITY

6.1 Understand and demonstrate the importance of productivity in achieving mission success.

Background

The better we become at our jobs the less direct supervision we require, which gives supervisors more time to do other things they need to do. Demonstrating the importance of productivity by making good independent mission-centered decisions increases productivity by reducing the need for direct supervision to support mission success. It's not really working harder, just working smarter.

Performance Expectations

- Make good independent mission-centered decisions.
- Increase productivity using creative thinking by submitting ideas for improvement related to increasing productivity.
- Increase productivity by accepting and demonstrating cross-training and growth opportunities.
- Anyone not sure of how to meet this or other performance expectations should consult their supervisor.

Recovery Behavior

- If you want to be in a group that values productivity this means that you will have to be open to new ways of doing things.
- Don't avoid work tasks or cross-training opportunities.
- Accept tasks with positive behavior.
- Comply with all productivity Expectations from your supervisor.
- Demonstrate open-minded behavior as the group moves to "work-smart" initiatives that will increase productivity and mission success.
- Increases in "work-smart" productivity will always, ultimately, be dependent upon those in the group who are doing the work.
- If a person is not meeting this performance expectation, they need to modify their future behavior using the recovery behavior as described here to at least meet minimum performance standards.
- Not using recovery behaviors will cause evaluation scores to go down.
- Anyone not sure of how to meet this or other performance expectations should consult their supervisor.

6.2 Directives are not optional. Every directive issued needs to be completed according to its objective and completed within the time allowed for completion.

Background

Everyone receives directives from someone, so no one is alone here. Directives are not optional because passive inactivity or intentional insubordination promotes anarchy.

Performance Expectations

- Complete all directives as assigned.
- Always ask your supervisor if you have questions or need clarification with an assignment.
- Once all the questions or issues are cleared up, it is essential that each member follow through and meet the deadline for the delegated tasks coming from their supervisor.
- Anyone not sure of how to meet this or other performance expectations should consult their supervisor.

Recovery Behavior

- The supervisor needs to make sure that the more significant or complicated assignments include:
  1. A clear and achievable objective
  2. A time limit/deadline
  3. If necessary, the number of people assigned to the job
  4. Name of the responsible party for completing the directive
  5. The reason the assignment needs to be completed
  6. Request for any ideas that can get the assignment completed with less time or less money
  7. Request that they contact the supervisor before the deadline in case it appears the deadline cannot be met
  8. Encourage questions and discussion and give advice as requested

  The group will fail if directives are not followed.
- Whether it be passive inactivity or intentional insubordination, pushback by the leadership-management staff in dealing with these situations will be significant because following directives is an intrinsic requirement for the success of any human enterprise.
- It's not unusual for managers to discipline a person who is not doing their job.
- In some cases, termination can result when insubordination creates great damage or harm to another group member or becomes a repeated problem that can't be corrected.
- If you're not used to being led by a professional leader, or you don't like being told what to do, or you treat directives as optional, then you will have problems.

- If a person is not meeting this performance expectation, they need to modify their future behavior using the recovery behavior as described here to at least meet minimum performance standards.
- Not using recovery behaviors will cause evaluation scores to go down.
- Anyone not sure of how to meet this or other performance expectations should consult their supervisor.

6.3 Accept delegated tasks with positive motivation.

Background

Negativity is resistance. It can slow the work and in turn lower productivity levels, which is a sign the group is moving away from mission success. Leadership delegation guides the group to mission success so supporting leadership's role to assign tasks is important.

Performance Expectations

- Accepting delegated tasks with positive motivation and avoiding resistance is now a job requirement.
- When delegated tasks arrive it's your job to accept them without resistance and without demonstrating negative behavior.
- Anyone not sure of how to meet this or other performance expectations should consult their supervisor.

Recovery Behavior

- Whining and eye rolling will not cut it here.
- If a directive is unclear, you definitely want to have a dialogue with your supervisor to clear up any confusion. That type of dialogue is invited. If you have problems with clarity or safety with an assignment definitely ask questions and get it cleared up. This is not negative behavior.
- Questioning why you have to do the assignment is negative behavior.
- If a person is not meeting this performance expectation, they need to modify their future behavior using the recovery behavior as described here to at least meet minimum performance standards.
- Not using recovery behaviors will cause evaluation scores to go down.
- Anyone not sure of how to meet this or other performance expectations should consult their supervisor.

6.4 Report time-wasting procedures and suggest improvements (this is also a Continuous Improvement expectation; see 8.3).

Background

Any task that takes longer than it should is a loss of opportunity to improve productivity. Efforts need to be made in eliminating or improving time-wasting procedures. No one knows better the ways to save time than the people doing the work. The new personnel evaluation system will be working over-time to give special recognition for your efforts at finding and eliminating or modifying time-wasting procedures.

Performance Expectations

- Everyone needs to demonstrate passion for and be relentless in submitting ideas that can save time or money or both.
- Contact your supervisor with every idea that you think might work.
- Innovation and continuous improvement is no longer considered "extra."
- Anyone not sure of how to meet this or other performance expectations should consult their supervisor.

Recovery Behavior

- "Because we have always done it that way" is the worst reason to continue to do anything.
- Everyone in the organization needs to be a productivity inventor.
- We want to watch ourselves and how we work.
- It does take initiative to stop people from doing things the way they have been used to doing them for years and years, which is why we need everyone on board seeking out and eliminating time-wasting, outdated procedures or methods.
- If this is something you have never done in the past, we need you to start now.
- Submitting ideas for improvement will drive your personnel evaluation ratings up.
- If a person is not meeting this performance expectation, they need to modify their future behavior using the recovery behavior as described here to at least meet minimum performance standards.
- Not using recovery behaviors will cause evaluation scores to go down.
- Anyone not sure of how to meet this or other performance expectations should consult their supervisor.

7 – PROBLEM-SOLVING

7.1 Always communicate to your direct supervisor about any problems you know about.

Background

One of the most common reasons for problems not being solved is because the "right" person doesn't know about the problem in the first place. A very common misunderstanding in groups is that everyone assumes everyone else that needs to know about the exact nature of a problem already knows, when in fact they don't know.

Performance Expectations

- Always communicate any problems you find to your supervisor. Never assume that others know about a problem.
- Gather information and, if you can do so quickly, determine the facts. Then communicate those facts to your supervisor.
- Quickly obtain the answers to the following questions: who's involved, what's happening, where it's happening, when it's happening, and how it's negatively impacting the group.
- Anyone not sure of how to meet this or other performance expectations should consult their supervisor.

Recovery Behavior

- The process of problem-solving can stumble badly when the number of problems is very high.
- Solving problems needs to be a very active process. This is because the problems not solved today are added to the problems that weren't solved yesterday, both of which will now be added to the problems not solved tomorrow.
- Problem-solving requires training and the first thing we learn is: if we find a problem we need to tell our supervisor.
- If we find a problem and we don't tell our supervisor, then we have two problems: the original problem and now the second problem, a lack of communication. Anyone having questions should consult their supervisor.
- If a person is not meeting this performance expectation, they need to modify their future behavior using the recovery behavior as described here to at least meet minimum performance standards.
- Not using recovery behaviors will cause evaluation scores to go down.
- Anyone not sure of how to meet this or other performance expectations should consult their supervisor.

7.2 Always get the facts, verify information, or assist in verifying information; recheck facts if something isn't making sense.

Background

Many people don't verify information as fact, which then results in beliefs or feelings being accepted as facts. To the extent the group is right or wrong about the facts, the group will get closer to or farther from a solution to the problem. A fact is a true statement or condition that actually exists.

Performance Expectations

- Fact find information with the intent to find reality and not ignore or deny what you hear simply because it causes you to have to change your mind or causes discomfort or confronts a long-held belief.
- Do not operate outside your expertise when problem-solving. While anyone can opine, they are not experts if they are operating outside their area of expertise.
- Theories and beliefs are not facts.
- Anyone not sure of how to meet this or other performance expectations should consult their supervisor.

Recovery Behavior

- If you are relying on unverified information and it results in a problem, you will be held responsible for making poor assumptions. Remember, when in doubt, pass it up.
- If your solution to the problem doesn't seem to be working, go back and look at your information, piece by piece. Review and, if necessary, retest all the information and assumptions.
- When the problem persists after you have applied what you think is the solution, it is often because the true cause was not adequately identified through the fact-finding process.
- If your investigation reveals the possibility or probability of inaccurate information, check it out again!
- Take the time to reconfirm and revalidate the facts, as if you were doing it for the first time with fresh eyes. Once you find the error, have the guts to admit it and move forward.
- If a person is not meeting this performance expectation, they need to modify their future behavior using the recovery behavior as described here to at least meet minimum performance standards.
- Not using recovery behaviors will cause evaluation scores to go down.
- Anyone not sure of how to meet this or other performance expectations should consult their supervisor.

7.3 Demonstrate an open-mind approach and allow new facts to change your mind.

Background

If we don't allow new facts to change our minds, our changing environment causes us to grow more obsolete each day until our approach becomes irrelevant. The safest thing any of us can do when in a changing environment is to change with that environment. The common term used for changing one's approach in response to one's changing environment is "adaptation." Being able to adapt allows you to blend your personal mission with the group mission and if you don't let new facts change your mind you will not be able to adapt.

Performance Expectations

- When presented with new facts you are now required to change your mind.
- Anyone not sure of how to meet this or other performance expectations should consult their supervisor.

Recovery Behavior

- Not adapting and not allowing new facts to change your mind will not only make you more irrelevant over time, it can harm you and the group. As irrelevancy grows the value you can provide to the group is diminished.
- New facts that make us feel uncomfortable typically cause us to believe more strongly in what we already think we know—the original incorrect information—even if we are exposed to new facts that counter our original belief.
- Being open minded takes courage.
- If you don't allow new facts to change your mind your performance will become more irrelevant with each new fact you don't accept.
- Any human enterprise that doesn't remain relevant in a changing world suffers mission failure.
- If a person is not meeting this performance expectation, they need to modify their future behavior using the recovery behavior as described here to at least meet minimum performance standards.
- Not using recovery behaviors will cause evaluation scores to go down.
- Anyone not sure of how to meet this or other performance expectations should consult their supervisor.

7.4 Leave your ego at the door.

Background

Group environments are filled with challenges, all of which require collaboration among group members. And sometimes the problems are so numerous and the complexity of the problems so significant that the felt need to be right starts to overwhelm some of the brains in the group. This behavior is significantly encouraged by the knowledge that when a group member doesn't know something they fear appearing as someone who isn't giving value to the group.

Performance Expectations

- Working collaboratively is now a job requirement.
- Avoid being argumentative.
- Contribute to solutions by realizing that somebody else might have a better idea than yours.
- Contribute to solutions by admitting someone else might have the correct answer instead of you when the situation presents itself.

- Anyone not sure of how to meet this or other performance expectations should consult their supervisor.

Recovery Behavior

- It's no longer about being right. It's now just knowing the right thing to do next.
- If you are someone who always needs to be right even though it's well known that it's humanly impossible to be so, you will be part of problem instead of being part of the solution.
- We all have a tendency to remember the problems we have solved successfully in the past but not the ones we didn't do so well at solving. This results in a distorted perspective that reinforces a belief that we are better problem solvers than we actually are (this has been scientifically proven).
- If your ego is in the way of buying into the collective approach to getting problems solved or new ideas implemented it's not going to go well. Don't get this one wrong.
- We need you to speak up and be heard, but in the final analysis if someone else has a better idea or your idea isn't worth trying we need you to see yourself as still providing value as a contributing member to an effective human enterprise.
- We are all important to the group even if we don't have the right answer every time.
- If a person is not meeting this performance expectation, they need to modify their future behavior using the recovery behavior as described here to at least meet minimum performance standards.
- Not using recovery behaviors will cause evaluation scores to go down.
- Anyone not sure of how to meet this or other performance expectations should consult their supervisor.

7.5 Use the Eight-Step Problem-Solving Process SOP and the Recognizing Problems SOP.

Background

There are a few reasons why problems don't get solved and one of the most important is that people do not use a systematic step-by-step process. Instead it can be a jumbled approach, grabbing only the most available information instead of digging for the most relevant information, starting to create solutions before the facts are gathered, and not having the right people/skill sets involved that are necessary for that particular problem. Lastly, which problem gets solved can sometimes be prioritized on the ease of coming up with a solution instead of going after the most important problem to solve, easy to solve or not. These issues will now be addressed by using the Eight-Step Problem-Solving Process SOP (described in Appendix 2) and the Recognizing Problems SOP (described in Appendix 1).

Performance Expectations

- Using a step-by-step problem-solving process is now a job requirement.

- Making sure you tell your supervisor about any problems you are confronting is very important communication and is also now a job requirement.
- Anyone not sure of how to meet this or other performance expectations should consult their supervisor.

Recovery Behavior

- If you are not using a step-by-step problem-solving process, you are not helping and could be hurting the overall problem-solving process.
- Problems not solved today are added to the pile we already have and not using a step-by-step process hurts the group's chances for mission success.
- If you are not communicating to your supervisor about the problems you are encountering, it's a big mistake. Start now! You need to know that just because you find a problem doesn't mean it's just left to you to solve. So asking for help is NOT a sign of weakness.
- If a person is not meeting this performance expectation, they need to modify their future behavior using the recovery behavior as described here to at least meet minimum performance standards.
- Not using recovery behaviors will cause evaluation scores to go down.
- Anyone not sure of how to meet this or other performance expectations should consult their supervisor.

8 - CONTINUOUS IMPROVEMENT

8.1 Accept performance feedback with civil behavior. Demonstrate taking responsibility for your behavior.

Background

It's okay to disagree with the information you are given in your performance feedback sessions or evaluations. Asking to discuss the details is perfectly legitimate. It's not okay, however, to blame others for your behavior or to demonstrate angry outbursts, name calling, or other negative behaviors during your performance evaluation feedback sessions. If you become upset when receiving your evaluation, it's okay to ask for a break and meet later, but the follow-up meeting will have to take place soon thereafter. *Just know the evaluation isn't going to change just because you don't like what it says.* The very best thing you can do is accept the feedback and modify your future performance from that point onward.

Performance Expectations

- Accepting performance feedback with civil behavior is now a job requirement.
- Not accepting performance feedback with civil behavior will hurt your future evaluation scores.

- Anyone not sure of how to meet this or other performance expectations should consult their supervisor.

Recovery Behavior

- For those who can't control their behavior, the focus will always be on recovery behavior until the time it becomes apparent that the less-than-standard behavior can't be corrected.
- Have the frame of mind that the evaluation is NOT a "guilty verdict" and that it is NOT saying you're a bad person.
- The feedback is designed to help you recover from less-than-standard performance and to promote your success and therefore the group's success.
- The more you succeed the more the group succeeds, so the group has a vested interest in your success, not your failure.
- Not accepting performance feedback and as a result not improving your future performance will only further hurt your future evaluation scores.
- If you don't improve then you are not providing value to the group.
- Not meeting the minimum standards of this performance expectation will result in lower evaluation scores.
- If a person is not meeting this performance expectation, they need to modify their future behavior using the recovery behavior as described here to at least meet minimum performance standards.
- Not using recovery behaviors will cause evaluation scores to go down.
- Anyone not sure of how to meet this or other performance expectations should consult their supervisor.

8.2 Demonstrate integration of performance feedback by modifying future behavior using recovery behaviors.

Background
Feedback typically falls into three basic categories:

1. We have done something we aren't supposed to and we are told it can't happen again.
2. Our performance doesn't include a desired behavior and we are being asked to start using it.
3. We demonstrated a more extreme behavior that is considered unacceptable and we are told to stop using that behavior immediately.

All three performance feedback categories are designed to promote success of the individual and the group. If a group member's performance evaluation rating drops to less-than-standard performance and they recover by using recovery behaviors, then their evaluation ratings go up. This includes a special recognition on their next review for using the recovery behaviors. Everyone gets recognition for using recovery behaviors.

Performance Expectations

- It is now a job requirement to use performance feedback to improve your future performance when requested to do so.
- Anyone not sure of how to meet this or other performance expectations should consult their supervisor.

Recovery Behavior

- If you're not familiar with or are resistant to modifying your behavior based on performance feedback you might not be used to being in a collaborative group or may not be wanting to comply for a lot of different reasons.
- Perhaps you are unable to control your behavior.
- If you are unable to modify your future performance (so you can demonstrate improvement) because you can't control your behavior, then there is very little leadership can do to help.
- It's always ultimately up to you (as it is up to any of us as individuals) to find ways to integrate performance feedback to improve your future performance when required to do so.
- If you can't correct your behavior and you continue to demonstrate behaviors that you are continually being asked to correct, it's going to be a big problem.
- The group becomes successful one successful group member at a time. Your success is intrinsically tied to the success of the group. The group has every motivation to promote each person's success and no motivation to see a group member fail.
- If a person is not meeting this performance expectation, they need to modify their future behavior using the recovery behavior as described here to at least meet minimum performance standards.
- Not using recovery behaviors will cause evaluation scores to go down.
- Anyone not sure of how to meet this or other performance expectations should consult their supervisor.

8.3 Promote a continuous improvement strategy by using the Submitting Ideas for Improvement SOP.

Background

The group moves forward by always improving, by changing according to a changing environment, and by always looking for new ways to support mission success. We need to assume that everyone's perspective can add to the list of ideas that can improve group performance. Based on observations of human systems we know this to be true: every group member has unique perspectives and therefore unique ideas that can contribute to continuous improvement. We want and need every brain in the game!

Use the Submitting Ideas for Improvement SOP (described in Appendix 5) to determine if you have a good idea and submit your idea to your supervisor.

The key here is to keep submitting ideas whether they turn out to be workable or not. The group needs to be continuously improving and the main way that is going to happen is by using the ideas submitted by the people who are doing the work. If you submit an idea and on further consideration it's not workable, do not get discouraged. If people stop submitting ideas for improvement continuous improvement will falter and mission failure becomes more likely as time goes on.

Performance Expectations

- If you have an idea that you think might improve the group we need you to submit it. Use the Submitting Ideas for Improvement SOP (see Appendix 5).
- Everyone gets credit for thinking about and then submitting ideas for improvement whether they turn out to be workable or not. The key here: keep submitting!
- Anyone not sure of how to meet this or other performance expectations should consult their supervisor.

Recovery Behavior

- The group needs you to be naturally curious. We say "needs" instead of just "wants" because constant improvement is what every high-performing group does and it's the people actually doing the work that come up with the best ideas.
- Don't get discouraged. If you're not familiar with this process the following information is very important for you to know. About 10 to 30 percent of ideas make it through the process and become successful. Some ideas for improvement won't be worth trying while others will be tried but won't work out as originally intended. This 30 percent success rate is just the way the new idea process seems to roll in most human enterprises. Herein lies the problem. When people submit ideas for improvement and it's determined that it won't work or it's not worth trying, people get discouraged and stop submitting ideas. We do not want anyone to get discouraged!
- It doesn't matter who it is; everyone submits ideas that might not work, even the boss. Here is a key insight: If everyone is submitting ideas for improvement and a 30 percent success rate is high enough for the group to see high levels of mission success then the group is growing at a very high "continuous improvement" rate. And it's happening because the group has every brain in the game!
- What we also know about human systems is that a 30 percent success rate is enough to make a group wildly successful at using a continuous improvement strategy. Don't get discouraged; keep submitting ideas you think might save time or money or both.

Appendices

Appendix 1

Recognizing Problems SOP

INTRODUCTION

The first step to solving a problem is recognizing you have one. Not recognizing or simply minimizing the problem is the critical failure in almost all problem-solving, so this SOP is focused on this first step. The full Eight-Step Problem-Solving Process SOP is outlined in Appendix 2. Talking and training about preventing, recognizing, and solving problems in general and in terms of any specific problems the group is experiencing at the moment *should be part of a larger routine, ongoing conversation amongst all the group's members.* Some large percentage of every leader-manager's time should be spent on this.

Assume the following four pieces of information are true as you engage in increasing your problem-solving performance:

1. Problem-solving requires very high cognitive function.
2. Problem-solving is an acquired skill and actually has very little to do with the given intelligence of the individual.
3. Some of the simplest problems have gone inadequately solved by very intelligent people.
4. Most people are not adequately trained to recognize or solve problems.

WHY HUMANS DON'T SOLVE PROBLEMS

There are SEVEN main reasons we aren't able to successfully solve problems:

1. We don't recognize the problem as being a problem and we don't prioritize problem-solving.
2. We don't have an open-mind approach; we don't allow new facts to change our minds.
3. We are unable to avoid cognitive biases, fallacies, and blocks.
4. We don't get the facts.
5. We don't follow a step-by-step problem-solving process.
6. We don't take the time to properly identify the problem.
7. Any combination of the above.

If we don't avoid these behaviors we never get to the next steps *of actually identifying and solving the problem.*

HOW TO AVOID THESE BEHAVIORS

This section presents ways to address each of the issues above so we can improve our problem-solving.

1. DEMONSTRATE A KEEN EYE FOR RECOGNIZING PROBLEMS AND MAKE SOLVING PROBLEMS A PRIORITY

Mission success is unlikely when we don't recognize problems as problems, we don't think they're important to solve, we don't see another person's problems as important, or we don't see small problems as being important even though many big problems start out small. Problems accumulate over time because of the lack of desire and/or aptitude to solve them, which starts to bury group morale. A constant fire-fighting environment with a steady flow of small emergencies becomes the new normal. Problems arrive at a constant and sometimes relentless rate. If they are not resolved as fast as they arrive, today's problems are added to the list of yesterday's problems, which will then have added to them the unsolved problems discovered tomorrow.

Solution: **Actively look for and don't ignore problems of any sort.**

2. DEMONSTRATE AN OPEN-MIND APPROACH, NEGATE YOUR OWN IGNORANCE, AND ALLOW NEW FACTS TO CHANGE YOUR MIND

When we don't know what we don't know and are not willing to admit it, ignorance prevails. I know this gets a bit circular but if you want to minimize surprises that can hurt you, you need to be more aggressive in this approach. Issues that can hurt you and issues that suddenly seem to pop up out of nowhere have something in common: chances are somebody in the group could have seen it coming had they been a bit more curious or a little less dismissive. Catching problems early on allows for more options to solve them, typically at less cost and before they have caused a lot of damage.

ALWAYS be asking yourself: What else do we need to know about what we don't know? Having this level of sensitivity will lead to some false alarms but it will pay off big time the moment you find a big problem early on and avert disaster.

This is why people who are naturally curious are usually pretty wise. People with open minds are on a quest for the truth. They employ the high standards necessary to ferret out fact from belief.

If you don't allow new facts to change your mind, you will steadily grow more obsolete each day and as your ability to adapt consistently drops, at some point in the future you, your methods, and your approach will become irrelevant.

Solution: **Allow new facts to CHANGE YOUR MIND.**

3. DEMONSTRATE BEHAVIOR THAT AVOIDS COGNITIVE BIASES, DON'T SUCCUMB TO FALLACY ARGUMENTS OF FALSE REASONING, AND BE AWARE OF BLOCKS

Cognitive biases, fallacies, and blocks are different but equally devastating issues because they all prevent problem-solving. Being aware of our own and others' biases, fallacies, and blocks helps us and our group avoid being a victim of these traits that enhance the likelihood that we will be blindsided.

In my experience very few ever take the time to learn the following subject matter, but if you choose to and do an honest evaluation I suspect you'll be surprised to see yourself here. Additionally, it gives you a skill set that allows you to see what's going on around you with X-ray glasses on. Whether it's in business meetings or watching the news you can start to see exactly how people get caught in all of these biases, fallacies, and emotional blocks.

It's part of being human to succumb to these blindsiding weaknesses, but with a little more awareness, a little more training, and a little more scrutiny we can help prevent the damage they do to us and our groups.

>>> **We are unaware that we have them or that they are controlling our thoughts!** <<<

Cognitive Biases formed early in our evolution. They allowed us to make quick decisions with a minimum of information.

Fallacies are a type of error in reasoning. Fallacies are arguments or explanations that may sound reasonable at first glance but actually lead us away from coherent reasoning.

Blocks can come from cultural, environmental, or emotional sources. The term *blocks* is used to refer to anything that actively inhibits our participation or otherwise influences us to *not act*.

Cognitive Biases

There are over 100 examples of cognitive biases. Look them up on Google and start studying!!

Here are some examples:

- **Anchoring** is where we grab on to a particular idea and do not stop believing in it regardless of the overwhelming evidence to the contrary.
- **Confirmation Bias** is where we actively seek out information that supports our position and avoid or ignore information that discredits or works against our position (**this is perhaps the most common bias I see on the planet, competing only with Anchoring**).
- **Irrational Escalation (Super Defensiveness)** happens because after we heavily invest in a particular idea with our time, energy, money, emotion, pride, or any combination of those, we

don't stop supporting the idea even though it's been proven wrong because of the sizable investment we have made in it being correct.

- **Semmelweis Reflex** is the automatic rejection of a new piece of information without any thought or investigation.
- **Bias Blind Spot** is a cognitive bias that doesn't allow people to see their own biases.

Recovery Behavior: *Learn about biases so you can AVOID THE BEHAVIOR.*

Figure #43 is provided as a quick guide to help you focus on what's important.

Fig. #43: Cognitive Biases

Note: There are *over 100 examples* of cognitive biases. Look them up on Google and start studying!

HERE ARE SOME FAMOUS EXAMPLES:

Anchoring is where we grab on to a particular idea & do not stop believing in it regardless of the overwhelming evidence to the contrary.

Confirmation Bias is where we actively seek out information that supports our position and avoid or ignore information that discredits or works against our position (this is perhaps the most common bias I see on the planet, competing only with Anchoring).

Semmelweis Reflex is the automatic rejection of a new piece of information without any thought or investigation.

Irrational Escalation happens because after we heavily invest in aparticular idea with our time, energy, money, emotion, pride, or any combination of those, we don't stop supporting the idea even though it's been proven wrong because of the sizable investment we have made in it being correct.

Bias Blind Spot is a cognitive bias that doesn't allow people to see their own biases.

Fallacies

There are numerous examples of tricky fallacies, which again you can learn more about online.

- **Accidental Fallacy:** We often arrive at a generalization but don't or can't list all the exceptions.
- **Ad Hominem Fallacy:** You commit this fallacy if you make an irrelevant attack on someone making an argument and suggest that this attack undermines the person's argument.
- **Appeal to Consequence Fallacy:** We use this kind of fallacy when we argue that a piece of information is false because it being true implies something we'd rather not believe.
- **Appeal to Emotions Fallacy:** We commit is fallacy when we accept someone's appeal to us merely because the appeal arouses our feelings of anger, fear, grief, love, outrage, pity, pride, sexuality, sympathy, relief, and so forth.
- **False Cause Fallacy:** This fallacy, also called *non causa pro causa*, occurs when we improperly conclude that one thing is the cause of another.
- **Tokenism:** If you interpret a merely token gesture as an adequate substitute for the real thing, you've been taken in by tokenism.
- **Traditional Wisdom Fallacy** is if you say or imply that a practice must be okay today simply because it has been the apparently wise practice in the past. ("But we've always done it that way; what's the problem?")
- **Tu Quoque Fallacy** is committed if, when we point out that the arguer doesn't practice what he preaches, we therefore suppose that there must be an error in the preaching.
- **Two Wrongs Make a Right Fallacy:** When you defend your wrong action as being right because someone else has acted wrongly previously, you commit the fallacy called "two wrongs make a right."
- **Vested Interest Fallacy** occurs when you argue that someone's claim or recommended action is incorrect because the person making it is motivated by his interest in gaining something by it.
- **Willed Ignorance Fallacy:** occurs when someone says (or is thinking): "I've got my mind made up, so don't try to convince me otherwise with new facts."
- **Wishful Thinking Fallacy** is committed when a reasoner suggests that a claim is true or false merely because he strongly hopes it is.

Recovery Behavior: *Learn about fallacies so you can AVOID THE BEHAVIOR.*

Figure #44 is provided as a quick guide to help you focus on what's important.

Fig. #44: Logical Fallacies

THERE ARE **NUMEROUS** TRICKY **FALLACIES**. LOOK AT THESE EXAMPLES, THEN SEARCH GOOGLE TO DISCOVER MORE.

➤ **Accidental Fallacy:** We often arrive at a generalization but don't—or can't—list all the exceptions.

➤ **Ad Hominem Fallacy:** When you make an irrelevant personal attack to suggest this attack undermines the person's argument.

➤ **Appeal to Consequence Fallacy:** Suggesting a piece of information is false because we'd rather not believe it is true.

➤ **Appeal to Emotions Fallacy:** When we accept or reject an argument because it appeals to our feelings of anger, fear, grief, outrage, & so forth.

➤ **Tokenism:** This fallacy occurs when we incorrectly identify one thing as the cause of another.

➤ **Traditional Wisdom Fallacy:** "But we've always done it that way; what's the problem?"

➤ **Tu Quoque Fallacy:** When we point out that the arguer doesn't practice what he preaches, we suppose that makes the argument false. A point can be valid even if the source makes it sound hypocritical.

➤ **Two Wrongs Make a Right Fallacy:** When you defend your wrong action as being right because someone else has acted wrongly.

➤ **Vested Interest Fallacy:** When you argue that a claim or recommended action is incorrect because the person making it stands to gain from the argument—it's suspicious, but not fallacious.

➤ **Willed Ignorance Fallacy:** when someone says (or is thinking), "I've got my mind made up, so don't try to change my mind with new facts."

➤ **Wishful Thinking Fallacy:** Wishful Thinking Fallacy is committed when a reasoner suggests a claim is true or false merely because he strongly hopes it is.

Blocks

Blocks are specific conditions, attitudes, or perceptions that work against problem-solving.

- **Perpetual Blocks:** This is when I think my approach is always a "better" process for taking action. People with perpetual blocks are the ones that always **need to be right** and if you don't follow their advice you're making a mistake. Chances are, reading that sentence made somebody's face pop into your mind.

- **Emotional Blocks:** This is when we fear looking bad, making mistakes, or appearing ignorant so we avoid important information. So much of how we think the world interprets us is based on the value that we provide, and there's nothing wrong with that way of thinking—to a certain extent, it's absolutely true. However, when we start to feel emotionally fearful or threatened with the possibility of humiliation our ability to think clearly is significantly and negatively impacted.

- **Intellectual Blocks** are thinking patterns that cause a person to assume they know something they don't, which prevents them from investigating the facts that are available but undiscovered, and therefore they come to an incorrect conclusion based on limited information. Making assumptions without investigation is a horrific and devastating roadblock to solving problems. If there is any block that stands out as perhaps the one that's cost the most money or the most loss of life, this could be it. Somebody assumed they knew better simply because they were in charge, somebody assumed they had all the information when they didn't, somebody assumed that other people would think like them when making the same decisions, or somebody assumed that past risks not turning into disasters meant future disasters wouldn't happen from taking the same risks (see the discussion of the *Challenger* and *Columbia* disasters in Chapter 3).

- **Expressive Blocks** refer to *how* you say what you say, which becomes just as important as *what* you are saying. ("It's hard for me to concentrate on the factual information you are presenting because I'm upset about you treating me like a jackass.")

Recovery Behavior: *All blocks can be avoided by following a step-by-step approach to problem-solving.*

Figure #45 is provided as a quick guide to help you focus on what's important.

<u>*Solution:*</u> **Avoid allowing these biases, fallacies, and blocks to control your thinking.**

Fig. #45: Internal Blocks

Blocks are specific conditions, attitudes, or perceptions that work against problem-solving.

Perpetual Blocks: This is when I think my approach is always a "better" process for taking action. People with perpetual blocks are the ones that **always need to be right** & if you don't follow their advice you're making a big mistake.

Intellectual Blocks are thinking patterns that cause a person to **assume they know something they don't**, which prevents them from investigating the facts that are available but undiscovered, & therefore they reach an incorrect conclusion. Making assumptions without investigation is a horrific & devastating roadblock to solving problems.

Emotional Blocks: This is when we fear looking bad, making mistakes, or appearing ignorant **so we avoid important information.** So much of how we think the world interprets us is based on the value that we provide, & to a certain extent, it's true. BUT—when we feel threatened by the **possibility of humiliation** our ability to think clearly is negatively impacted.

Expressive Blocks refer to how you say what you say, which becomes **just as important as what you are saying.** ("It's hard for me to concentrate on the factual information you are presenting because I'm upset about you treating me like a jackass.")

4. ALWAYS GET THE FACTS, VERIFY INFORMATION, AND RECHECK FACTS IF SOMETHING ISN'T MAKING SENSE

When we don't verify information as facts, we allow information from untested judgments to be accepted without critique. This results in beliefs or feelings being accepted as facts. We are influenced by how bad we want to believe the information to be true, but beliefs and opinions are not facts.

It's not a fact unless the information has been:

- *questioned*
- *tested*
- *or verified*
- *using high standards of investigation*
- *as part of a reasonable pursuit for finding an objective reality.*

Anything less is not a fact.

To the extent the team is right or wrong about the facts, the group will get closer to or farther away from a solution to the problem. Take care with cognitive biases, fallacies, and blocks when verifying facts. *Relying on a supposed fact "verified" by someone operating outside his or her area of expertise is deadly to the problem-solving process.* If the person doesn't know and gives you the impression or purports to "know" that he does know, then it's *no better than a guess and you don't know it's a guess until you try to use the information and find out it doesn't work.*

A fact is a true statement or condition that actually exists. Believing **strongly** in something doesn't make up for it not being proven to be a true, verifiable fact.

- Beliefs are based upon the unique needs of the believer.
- They ignore the importance of validation.
- A belief may turn out to be factual and a fact may have started out as a belief.

But it's not a fact unless it can be proven through a verification process.

Beliefs can make us feel good, chase away whatever we may fear, help us "make sense of our world perspective," or any combination or all three. If your solution doesn't seem to be working, go back and look at your information!

<u>Solution:</u> **Don't use unverifiable information as facts.**

5. RESIST TEMPTATION TO MAKE SNAP JUDGMENTS; CAREFULLY AND METHODICALLY ESTABLISH FACTS AND CREATE OPTIONS FOR SOLUTIONS USING PROBLEM-SOLVING EXPERTISE

- We **ALL** tend to be overconfident in our problem-solving capabilities.
- We have a tendency to remember the problems we successfully solved and not remember the ones we didn't or couldn't solve.
- We typically pick the solution that first comes to mind.
- We limit the number of choices or options for solutions because we lack imagination or expertise.
- We do not methodically use a step-by-step process to solve problems.
- We now know that even if you are smart you're not necessarily a good problem solver.
- Problem-solving is a different kind of intelligence.
- Problem-solving is an acquired skill.
- Problem-solving skill only exists when we are using critical thinking and a step-by-step method to solve the problem.

Solution: **Avoid "shooting from the hip."**

Figure #46 is provided as a quick guide to help you focus on what's important.

Fig. #46: Resist Temptation to Make Snap Judgments

Resist Temptation to Make Snap Judgments; Carefully & Methodically Establish Facts & Create Options for Solutions Using Problem-Solving Expertise

---

We tend to be **overconfident** in our problem-solving ability...

We have a tendency to remember the problems we **successfully** solved & **not** remember the ones we **didn't** or **couldn't** solve...

We typically pick the solution that **first** comes to mind...

We **limit** the number of **choices** or options for solutions because we lack imagination or expertise...

We do not **methodically** use a step-by-step process to solve problems.

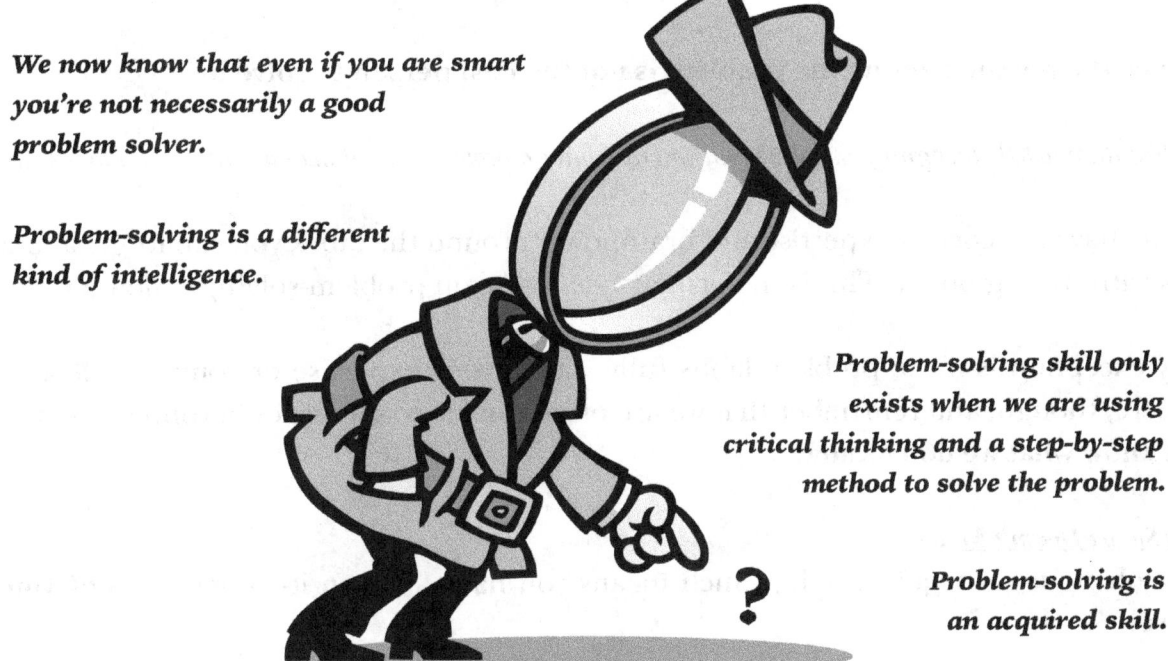

We now know that even if you are smart you're not necessarily a good problem solver.

Problem-solving is a different kind of intelligence.

Problem-solving skill only exists when we are using critical thinking and a step-by-step method to solve the problem.

Problem-solving is an acquired skill.

6. TAKE THE TIME TO IDENTIFY THE EXACT CAUSE OF THE PROBLEM

When we don't clearly define the problem we cannot find the true cause. Taking time to identify the cause of the problem is Step 4 of the problem-solving process (see Appendix 2). I mention it here because not taking this step is a reoccurring nemesis to problem solvers everywhere. Finding a problem's TRUE cause is the **gateway to the solution**.

There are numerous roadblocks that get in the way of our finding the causes of problems. Here are three very practical issues we all need to be aware of so we don't fall victim to their impediment.

6A. We Run Out of Time

If the solution isn't delivered in the amount of time necessary in order to be effective, it's as if the solution didn't exist. Time pressure is a reality: act on it before it acts on you.

When does this problem need to be resolved? If the answer is now, no matter what you thought you were going to be doing today you're now doing this instead.

6B. We Go It Alone

We have a bad tape playing in our heads that says we need to solve problems on our own or we are not good problem solvers.

Because "your" unsolved problem can negatively impact the group, the group has an inherent right to make sure the problem gets solved, so as a group member in good standing you are obligated to share the information about this problem with your supervisor.

Oftentimes the person finding the problem is not the best person to solve it.

It's your obligation to tell other group members that you (we) have a problem: you don't have an option to not say anything.

If you don't have the correct expertise and brainpower around the table, you can forget about finding solutions with staying power. This is the primary reason team problem-solving is now a requirement.

The only exception is if the problem lands fully within your expertise or your knowledge base. Be careful here, though, and remember that we are often unable to see issues beyond our expertise and **we don't know what we don't know.**

6C. Being Smart Doesn't Matter

Problem-solving is an acquired skill, which means you have to learn it—**regardless of your intelligence level.**

(Remember two words: "space shuttles.")

7. ANY COMBINATION OF THE ABOVE

Problem-solving is a very dynamic process. However the problem, your enemy, *is very dynamic as well.*

If your problem-solving process is not as dynamic as the problem development, you're going to lose this battle.

In most cases, when a problem is being created, *your inability to solve it is usually a combination of the six issues above.* The best way you can start to improve your organization's problem-solving capacity, regardless of the group's current performance level, is to train everybody in your group with this standard operating procedure.

In a group that is suffering from the often hidden Normalize Mediocre Performance, training everybody on why problems don't get solved along with a solid problem-solving process *is nothing short of revolutionary.*

Figure #47 is provided as a quick guide to help you focus on what's important.

Fig. #47: The SEVEN Problem-Solving Concepts

1.

Demonstrate a Keen Eye for Recognizing Problems & Make Solving Problems a Priority.

Solution: **Actively look for, & don't ignore problems of any sort.**

2.

Demonstrate an Open-Minded Approach, Negate Your Own Ignorance, and Allow New Facts to Change Your Mind.

Solution: **Allow new facts to change your mind.**

3.

Exemplify Behaviors That Avoid Cognitive Bias, Don't Succumb to Fallacy Arguments of False Reasoning, & Be Aware of Blocks.

Solution: **Avoid bias, fallacies, & blocks when possible.**

4.

Always Get the Facts, Verify Information, & Recheck Facts if Something Isn't Making Sense.

Solution: **Don't use unverifiable information as facts.**

5.

Resist Temptation to Make Snap Judgments; Carefully & Methodically Establish Facts & Create Options for Solutions Using Problem-Solving Expertise.

Solution: **Avoid "shooting from the hip."**

6.

*Take Time to **Identify** the Exact Cause of the Problem*

6A. *We Run Out of Time*
6B. *We Go It Alone*
6C. *Being Smart Doesn't Matter*

7.

Any Combination of the above.

There are **SEVEN** concepts that help us successfully solve problems.

...

Eight-Step Problem-Solving Process SOP

INTRODUCTION

For small problems that are easily solved, your supervisor always has the option to modify this approach by combining steps, but without skipping any of them.

Smaller problems can be solved immediately by the person finding the problem, *BUT only if they are trained to do so. Any solution requiring specialized training should not be attempted by those not specifically trained to do so* (e.g., fire extinguisher training, use of personal protective equipment, scaffolding mishaps, car repair, etc.)

Beware: because you don't know what you don't know, you might choose to solve a problem you shouldn't be solving.

Beware: eliminating steps completely will start to throw you back into the seven most common reasons problems don't get solved.

WHY HUMANS DON'T SOLVE PROBLEMS

There are SEVEN behaviors that stop us from successfully solving problems:

1. We don't recognize the problem as being a problem and we don't prioritize problem-solving.
2. We don't have an open-mind approach; we don't allow new facts to change our minds.
3. We are unable to avoid our cognitive biases, fallacies, and blocks.
4. We don't get the facts.
5. We don't follow a step-by-step problem-solving process.
6. We don't take the time to properly identify the problem.
7. Any combination of the above.

The Eight-Step Problem-Solving Process described in this appendix will help you avoid all of the items on this list.

Getting your boss involved (and whoever they want to include) and understanding how fast you have to get this process completed as opposed to your other important duties will (a) get the right people around the table and (b) allow the team to prioritize this problem-solving task in light of other important duties that still need to get done.

The quality of your problem-solving effort will increase significantly if you follow a disciplined three-step process that recognizes three separate, distinct activities: getting information and determining the facts first, focusing on cause second, and then, and only then, proceed to the third step, developing solutions.

That same three-step process can also contribute to developing more than one solution, perhaps with one of the solutions being less risky, less costly, or less time consuming than another. These can be very valuable options from which to select in order to get a problem solved with low stress while not needing to throw money at the problem and to do so quickly so the group can get on with other important work.

Lastly and importantly—though this is a step that is often skipped—is the plan for applying the selected solution *and the follow-up actions necessary to confirm the problem was indeed solved.* Not embedding follow-up within the problem-solving process can result in big fat problems. Even for the very best of us.

The 1991 Oakland firestorm started out as a small grass fire *everyone thought had been successfully put out on the day prior to the event.*

It suddenly "*restarted*" the next day, and *over a mere 72-hour period* 25 people were killed, 150 others injured, and 2,843 single-family dwellings and 437 apartment units were destroyed, totaling $2.6 billion in 2020 dollars. Aside from those who sadly burned to death, suffered from smoke inhalation, or were injured, an average of 45 homes and $35 million were lost *every hour* over that three-day period until the firestorm was finally stopped. It was heartbreaking for everyone involved, including the firefighters *who thought the fire was already out the previous day.*

Can you imagine how they felt?

Let's make sure we follow up.

EIGHT-STEP PROBLEM-SOLVING PROCESS

Step 1: **Contact Your Supervisor (Never Skip)**
Step 2: **Do a Damage and Time Survey**
Step 3: **Explore Information and Determine the Facts**
Step 4: **Decide on the Cause of the Problem (Not the Solution)**

Step 5: Look at the Various Possible Solutions for Solving the Problem After Determining If It's an Open- or Close-Ended Problem

Step 6: Select the Best Possible Solutions to Be Implemented

Step 7: Create an Implementation Plan and Implement

Step 8: Evaluate How Well the Selected Solution Solved the Problem, If Not Repeat Step 5 or Step 6

Figure #48 is provided as a quick guide to help you focus on what's important.

Fig. #48: The 8-Step Problem-Solving Process

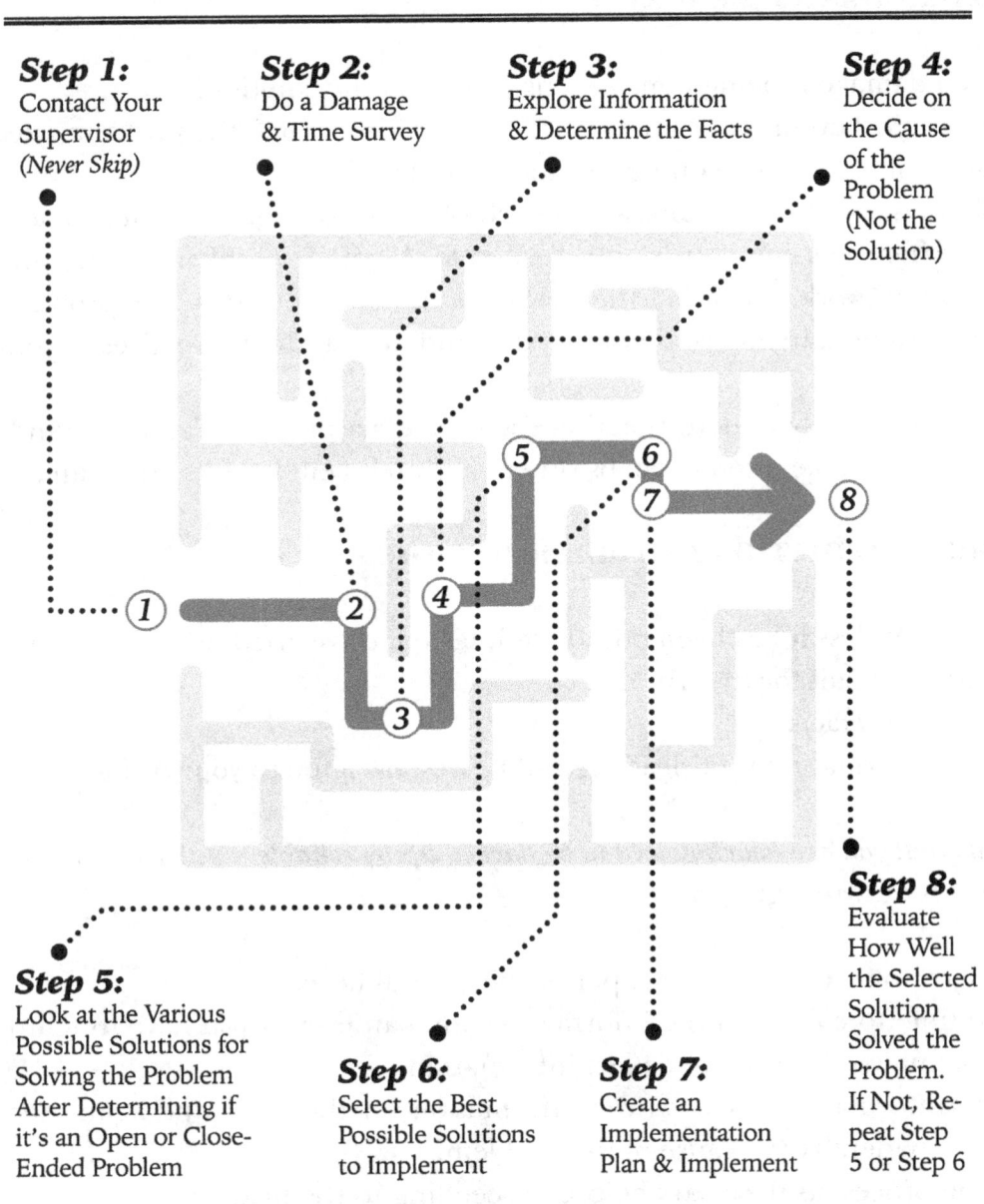

Step 1:
Contact Your Supervisor
(Never Skip)

Step 2:
Do a Damage & Time Survey

Step 3:
Explore Information & Determine the Facts

Step 4:
Decide on the Cause of the Problem (Not the Solution)

Step 5:
Look at the Various Possible Solutions for Solving the Problem After Determining if it's an Open or Close-Ended Problem

Step 6:
Select the Best Possible Solutions to Implement

Step 7:
Create an Implementation Plan & Implement

Step 8:
Evaluate How Well the Selected Solution Solved the Problem. If Not, Re-peat Step 5 or Step 6

STEP 1: CONTACT YOUR SUPERVISOR AND BUILD A TEAM

- The person that finds a problem is not always the best one to solve it!
- It could be a team of two (i.e., just you and your supervisor).
- Or the supervisor may choose to take the problem over from there, allowing you to get back to work.
- Or it might be a larger group if the supervisor feels that the problem-solving team requires further expertise.
- **NEVER SKIP THIS STEP when you find a problem.**

STEP 2: DO A DAMAGE AND TIME SURVEY

- How much damage is being done as long as there is no solution?
- Is there a critical event that creates a time limit within which the problem needs to be solved?
- Is this problem creating second-generation problems?
- If so, ask the same two questions about each of the second-generation problems.
- Compare where this new issue stands related to the other problems facing your group.
- Reprioritize all work, including the new information about this new problem using the mission, vision, value statements, best practices, and outstanding directives as your guide.

WARNING: Inappropriately underestimating the damage a problem can cause and not solving the problem in time is a mistake often made by otherwise intelligent leaders and managers.

STEP 3: EXPLORE INFORMATION AND DETERMINE THE FACTS

- It's not a fact unless it has been questioned, tested, or verified using high standards as part of a reasonable pursuit for the truth.
- Opinions are *not* facts.
- Unverified information is misleading and represents a foe to your problem-solving efforts.

Do the statements that you are hearing need to be backed up by reliable data? Expert testimony is acceptable if the expert is duly recognized.

- Non-experts love acting like an expert so be careful here.
- Take the time to collect all the information you can even if you have to temporarily stop the process of analysis in order to collect information.
- Bring the information back, vet the information for the facts, and again decide if you need more facts to identify the cause of the problem.
- Repeat the process as necessary before proceeding to the next step.

STEP 4: **DECIDE ON THE CAUSE OF THE PROBLEM (NOT THE SOLUTION)**
KEEP asking yourself "Why is that happening?"

- As you dig down into the information, symptoms, and observations that may be baffling you, KEEP asking yourself "Why is that happening?" and let your investigation take you where the answers to that question leads.
- If it takes the investigation to another set of information, symptoms, and observations that are baffling, still KEEP asking yourself "Why is that happening?" and, again, let your investigation take you where that question leads.
- KEEP asking yourself "Why is that happening?" and let your investigation take you where that question leads until you reach a point where the information, symptoms, and observations *start to reveal the root causes of the problem.*

List the symptoms you are experiencing from the problem; this is known as a problem statement.

Use the following to describe what is happening:

- What is happening?
- How is it showing itself?
- Where is it happening?
- When is it happening?
- Why is that happening?
- **Use "Why is it happening?" over and over again as noted.**

STEP 5: **LOOK AT THE VARIOUS POSSIBLE SOLUTIONS FOR SOLVING THE PROBLEM AFTER DETERMINING IF IT'S AN OPEN- OR CLOSE-ENDED PROBLEM**
Identify whether the problem is an open- or close-ended problem:

- **Close-ended** problem: A narrow field of possible solutions (*e.g., finding out why the dumpster behind the welding shop caught fire would probably be a **close-ended** problem*).
- **Open-ended** problem: Problem appears to entail a myriad of possible solutions (*e.g., finding out how we can recruit more students to our school next year is an **open-ended** problem*).

The ultimate solution to an open-ended problem will usually result from implementing multiple possible solutions either simultaneously or in sequence

STEP 6: **SELECT THE BEST POSSIBLE SOLUTIONS TO BE IMPLEMENTED**

- If the cause of the problem becomes very obvious during the investigation, apply a solution and it's case closed.

- Once the list of possible causes is determined, rank them in order of likelihood of being the authentic cause of the problem.
- For the most likely cause, list the best possible solutions that could be applied to resolve the issue.
- All things being the same, you have a tie, seek the simplest possible solution if there is more than one solution on the "try list."
- The team should work up towards the more complicated possible solutions only as necessary.
- To *keep the process moving forward*, the highest-ranking leader on the team will settle stalemates on what is the list of best possible solutions to be applied, and in what order.
- Leaders are supposed to make unilateral decisions, if necessary, when they think they have enough facts to implement a possible solution.
- Keeping the process moving forward is the leader's job, so help them do it by contributing in a way that doesn't bog down the process.

STEP 7: CREATE AN IMPLEMENTATION PLAN AND IMPLEMENT

If desired, more than one solution can be tried at the same time, but only *if you don't care about knowing which one worked. Take care here.*

In some cases when experiencing emergency situations, a group can implement all the best possible solutions at the same time just to stop the damage and then go back later to find out what happened (**exactly** what happened) so the group can keep it from happening again.

When resolving **open-ended** problems, implementing a list of possible solutions simultaneously can add effectiveness to solving the problem. Simultaneous implementation can add synergy between possible solutions, accentuating a more positive outcome than if they had been implemented in sequence.

Create an Organizational Chart

Determine when the implementation needs to be completed by adding a time and/or a date. Determine your organizational chart:

- **Who** is responsible for implementing the solution?
- **Who** is going to monitor and lead the implementation process?
- **Who** will be responsible for evaluating whether the selected "solution" was effective at solving the problem and will be responsible for either making small adjustments or starting the process over again in case the solution selected falls short of solving some or all of the problem (Step 8)?

The evaluation role will typically fall to the team leader, but the team leader can delegate the task of determining whether the problem is solved to another team member.

Finally: **Implement the selected solution(s) and see if they work at solving the problem.**

STEP 8: **EVALUATE HOW WELL THE SELECTED SOLUTION SOLVED THE PROBLEM**
The person who was placed in charge of monitoring and leading the implementation process will report back to the leader and members of the problem-solving team.

If the problem is solved, as a last action, this individual will now be responsible for:

- Memorializing the problem/solution with all the necessary information and publishing it to the group to support group learning.
- Changing any procedures as a result of what was learned to avoid the issue re-emerging.
- Identifying possible policy changes that need to be made and passing those on to the policy makers.

If the problem remains unsolved: double check you have adequately identified the cause in *Step 4*, then go back to the list of possible solutions in *Step 5 or 6* and try the next most likely possible solution or solutions.

Repeat – Repeat – Repeat the problem-solving process until the problem is solved.

Three Special Notes A / B / C :

A - WHEN THE FACT-FINDING DISCOVERS SOMEONE IS AT FAULT:

- IF the insinuating information does *not* make a material difference to the process of establishing the cause, then discretion should be used and the information can be removed from the problem-solving process.
- IF the insinuating information DOES make a *material difference* in determining the cause it needs to be included in order to establish a cause for the problem and should be de-personalized. (E.g., Paul Stevens is now identified as "Individual 1," Jane Robinson is now identified as "Individual 2," etc.)
- Include all the material facts when problem-solving and use discretion when dealing with personnel performance issues. *Information that may impact a person's performance evaluation should remain appropriately confidential and be handled by that person's supervisor.*

B - THE THREE TYPES OF ISSUES THAT CAN CREATE CHALLENGES FOR PROBLEM-SOLVING:

1 - The Two-Problem Combo – One Set of Symptoms, Two Embedded Problems

- You know you have this dual issue, in which there are two unknown problems, *when the current symptoms list eludes even your best troubleshooting experts and efforts.*
- When encountering these situations, start by separating the symptoms' list into two lists. Use various methods of separating out the single list into separate lists, so you can start to identify the two problems independently.
- Try as many combinations of the two-list approach as you need to until you see the two separate possible causes start to appear that will help highlight the two separate problems.
- *This can be a tedious process, but an effective one if you stay with it.*
- Using this process, I once found I had three problems not two!

2 - The Intermittent Problem

It comes and goes; it's not always there, but even if it goes away, it has shown up more than once and it will probably be back:

1. Acknowledge you have an *intermittent* problem.
2. Gather the symptoms you were able to identify before the problem went away, even if they are very limited.
3. From those symptoms, decide what *additional information should be collected at the moment the problem reemerges.* In other words leaning on what little evidence you have, be ready to collect information the moment it shows up again. This might include training your group or using technology to gather data. *This is a key step to solving intermittent problems.*
4. Gather the information when the problem shows up again based on the actions established in step 3.
5. Troubleshoot the cause of the problem with the new information.
6. Repeat 1-5 as often as needed.

3 - The Conflict with Original Design and Theory

Finding a solution can be tough when there is no solution because *the system or equipment is operating outside of its original design intent.*

Make sure to double check that the problem is not based on a simple misunderstanding. Asking more from a system than it was designed to deliver will often show up as a problem because the unexpected outcome is not meeting your desired expectations.

If you find this to be the case, it's time to re-design the system so it addresses your needs.

C - IF YOU ARE STUCK ON STEP FOUR:

Step four is a notorious place for getting stuck.

Getting back on the trail:

- As new information comes in, talk about what is being revealed and ask, "Why is that happening?"
- As new information comes in, ask yourself what other new questions it might be creating.
- As possible causes are listed, start further investigations *until you get to the root cause of the problem.*
- Keep examining the facts as they are determined and look for information gaps.
- Keep listing the possible causes, as they are determined.
- Use logic to keep the list of possible causes "clean" – careful here and remove information that clearly shows itself as being either unrelated *or as a separate problem.*
- As new information comes in, start group discussions about what the cause of the problem might be.
- Use brainstorming sessions if necessary to discover possible causes.
- Keep the conversation going.
- Add more experts / more different disciplines around the problem-solving table if you need to.
- If the conversation is not collaborative, make the moves necessary to get the problem-solving team back on track.
- With any group problems-solving process, everyone on the team needs to stay calm; remind your team: "we need to stay in our higher brain function"
- Help other people's ideas to be examined by helping them present their information.
- When having discussions, use intuition and "hunches" to promote the investigation. Their intuition creates a feeling or emotion that helps give them insight…. That being said **these gut reactions need to be backed up by factual information gathering**….
- Allow "suitable" feelings and emotions – Some people "feel" their way through problem-solving. It's not unusual for problem-solving to require more than one skill set.
- Always, keep the conversation focused on *observable symptoms* without making a conclusion that falls outside of your area of expertise.
- Always ask: what additional information needs to be collected?
- And: why are we seeing what we are observing?

The interplay between technical skills can be a source of friction in relationships. *At this point, everyone must suspend judgment and just listen when others are talking…*

- The conversation needs to circle back to facts, *not opinions,* at all times.
- Eventually the causes and your solutions will pop like stars in the night sky.
- Just remember everybody speaks: Your team's guiding principal needs to be as follows: words not spoken *are potential solutions not spoken.*

KEEP asking yourself "Why is that happening?"

Communication Chain of Command SOP

INTRODUCTION

The most important aspect about following the chain of command is that it results in high-quality information given by the appropriate authority who is held responsible for making a decision on the issue at hand.

Whenever somebody is taking responsibility for that over which they have no authority, or they're taking authority over that for which they're not held responsible, the information delivered is low quality. Low-quality information can be highly destructive to the performance necessary for mission success.

Many of us have heard the term "chain of command" but don't know what it means and don't realize the impact it has on the effectiveness of a group.

The chain of command essentially asks that everyone follow the same lines you find on your official organizational chart for your group when communicating important information and when making decisions.

When different levels or different positions of the organization are skipped when important communication is being conveyed, input from the people in those positions is not available and can lead to some horrible decision making. Additionally, when levels or positions are skipped in the communication loop people can be held responsible for outcomes they're not even aware of.

It works in both directions: a senior staff member skipping levels and positions on the way down in communicating with lower-level personnel, or lower-level personnel skipping supervisors on their way up. Either way, not following the chain of command does nothing but add chaos and anarchy to a process that needs to otherwise have a coherent and rational approach to information and decision making if the group desires mission success.

When the chain of command is not used in a group, it undermines the group's ability to *move* information and make decisions, to make sure the *right person knows the right information,* and to *solve problems while they are still small.*

The chain of command process does not, and should not, prevent someone from reaching someone at the highest levels of the organization. Instead, it should resolve the issue or answer the question effectively and quickly as low in the organization as possible, which works to the benefit of the individual and the group.

Every leader in this group has an open-door policy and that door is only open if you have exhausted the line of leaders that precedes them. This SOP will ensure access to the very highest leader in the group and it will do so by insisting that a series of required rational and beneficial steps be taken prior to that access. Those required steps are described in this SOP.

Everyone has a right to the chain of command as well as a duty to the chain of command.

The Right to the Chain of Command

Groups that are effective at dealing with problems, issues, and questions are demonstrating the characteristics of a high-performing group. In a high-performing group leadership wants everyone to have the right to the chain of command to support the process of expediting accurate information, resolving issues, and promoting transparency.

The Duty to the Chain of Command

In addition to their right to the chain of command, everyone also has *duty* to the chain of command. In other words, (1) no one gets to skip the chain of command, and (2) just as important, the group requires you to report issues **instead of leaving them unresolved**! These are two very important points about the *duty* of the chain of command. It's important that everyone report problems (and not avoid reporting them) and to do so to their immediate supervisor.

THE PROCESS

STEP 1

If you have an issue or question, you need to go to your immediate supervisor. If your supervisor needs some time to resolve the issue, answer your question, or go find the answer, you need to give them a reasonable time frame in which to get back to you with an answer.

Typically if the supervisor is being asked a question that is new to them they will consult their supervisor before getting back to you. This might take a little additional time but it'll give you a more high-quality answer.

STEP 2

Once your supervisor provides an answer, this is usually the end of the process. If you have questions and want to dialogue concerning the answer you received, that conversation is invited.

Ultimately, if the solution is not to your liking, you can tell your supervisor that you're going to take the issue the next step up in the chain of command. Note: With some issues it's not unusual that your supervisor will discuss your question with their supervisor prior to getting back to you.

Note to supervisors: If an individual is wanting to go up the chain, place a courtesy call to your supervisor. Outline the issue and the answer you gave.

STEP 3

Next, call your supervisor's supervisor and schedule an appointment. Tell them (a) that you have already spoken to your supervisor and (b) the answer you received. If the supervisor can resolve the issue, then you're done. Note that the answer may be similar to the previous supervisor's answer, because this is the person your supervisor likely got the original answer from in Step 2.

Note to supervisors: As a supervisor, or anyone in the chain of command, there are important obligations to supporting a well-run chain of command:

- If you get an email or a visitor seeking information or alerting you to a problem, you are obligated to respond *in a timely manner* with some information even if you don't have all the immediate needed information or a solution.
- This required response should include (a) the next steps that will be taken and (b) the approximate time at which a follow-up communiqué can be expected.
- The key here is that an active dialogue continues until (1) the information is provided, (2) the problem is solved, or (3) it's determined the person should go up the next step in the chain of command.

STEP 4

If your issue still isn't resolved, then you have the right to go up the chain of command to the point where you get to the very highest person in the group who is available for access. Whether you finally receive an answer to your liking is a separate issue, but at least you had access to the chain of the command.

The only exception to this rule is if you know of unethical or illegal activity, or you feel you are suffering some harassment, by your immediate supervisor. These cases are the only situations in which it is okay to jump a link in the chain of command and go to the next senior leader up. In these cases, intentionally bypassing your immediate supervisor in the chain of command is perfectly acceptable and greatly encouraged.

In any other case, anyone who bypasses the chain of command is essentially damaging the group.

It's a very simple process to comply with: Just go ask your immediate supervisor FIRST, regardless of the question or issue. Not following the chain of command is disruptive and results in resources expended that would have otherwise been used in helping the group mission and its people succeed.

If you continually attempt to bypass the chain of command after being told not to, eventually the issue will escalate and show up as a downgraded performance evaluation. If you have any questions, consult your supervisor.

Appendix 4

Communication Email SOP

INTRODUCTION

Most every group is comprised of different types of experts. Some lead and manage, some operate machinery, some market, some maintain, some do accounting, some drive trucks or fly airplanes, some drill holes while others build strategic plans. In terms of their expertise they actually have very little in common with the other experts in the group, yet what they do have in common is the mission and values of the organization they belong to. So, in a sense, the organization is like a long chain with each link being a different type of expert, all necessary and all having to work together, just like the links in a chain.

In order support mission success and promote the values of the organization this chain of experts is completely and wholly dependent on the group's information highway.

Just as our roadways need to effectively move people, goods, and services, it is also true for the group's *information highway*. From a communication perspective, it is essential to keep the flow of high-quality information moving as quickly as it needs to in order to support mission success, but this flow can encounter significant obstacles. There are a number of well-known challenges that can get in the way of information flow and create massive "information" traffic jams and significantly contribute to mission failure. Some of those challenges are listed below.

One, we are very busy, which therefore forces us to prioritize our responses. Ergo we have a tendency to prioritize the information in our own silo as being more important, which increases our likelihood that we will respond to those in our silo and makes us less likely to respond to those outside of our silo.

Two, because expertise typically generates esoteric terms not familiar to other experts in the group, words or language not understood can be underrated in their importance and even *ignored*.

Three, some group members use the group's information highway as a catharsis, sending inappropriate or accusatory "shotgun" emails to a long list of receivers as a way of getting attention paid to their "**problem**."

Most of the following guidelines will assume communication is via email, but it applies to most forms of communication. I first list the eight communications Requirements then provide the specifics for each one.

THE EIGHT COMMUNICATIONS REQUIREMENTS

1. **Every employee is required to check and respond to emails every workday.**
2. **All communications sent require a response.**
3. **Communication should always follow the chain of command.**
4. **Stop sending shotgun emails.**
5. **Take request for information (RFI) emails seriously.**
6. **Don't take the bait on tension emails.**
7. **Misdirected RFIs should be forwarded.**
8. **Change the subject header when the topic of the email thread changes.**

1. Every employee is required to check and respond to emails every workday.

Email communication is a vital information highway within the group. *Each and every employee is required to check their email every workday.*

What to do: Whenever you are going to be away from your email, set up an automated response that either notifies the sender that you will get back to them later or offers them somebody else to reference if they need an answer right away—typically the best automated response gives both pieces of information. You can also articulate different sources for different responses: "For project A please contact Sue, and for project B contact Jack." Whether it is your boss or your direct reports trying to reach you, the worst response to any email is crickets.

2. All communications sent require a response.

Every single communication a group member receives from another group member that is asking a question or requesting your effort *requires a response.*

What to do: *Responses are not optional. Study the following six items in this list that provide the most likely responses that you can use.* If you get a communication that you are not sure how to respond to, *go see your supervisor.*

3. Communication should always follow the chain of command.

This will simultaneously lower the number of requests for information and increase the quality of each request.

What to do: If it's a request for information that is not following the chain of command, send a copy of the email to your supervisor with your own notation pointing out the irregularity. The more group members are made to follow the chain of command *now*, the more likely they will follow the chain of command *in the future*. The exception to this rule is applied when the people involved are members of a multidisciplinary or cross-silo work team. And obviously, true emergencies are also the exception. *The key here is stopping the chaotic "no-rules-for-email" communication process that is a hallmark of low-performing groups.*

4. **Stop sending shotgun emails whenever it can be avoided.**
Unless it is part of your job description to do so, don't send shotgun emails. "Shotgun" emails are those sent to a high number of recipients—far more people than what is necessary to address the issue at hand. They're also a way for some group members to essentially throw tantrums.

Even with the best of intentions shotgun emails can cause major information traffic jams and cause productivity to drop as a significant number of people in the group are consuming unnecessary information instead of doing something more important. If you're in a group that sends a lot of shotgun emails, this eye-rolling amount of information basically teaches people to ignore their emails.

What to do: *Before you send an email,* stop and think about who should get it based on the specific goal you are needing to achieve. If you're not sure, go ask your supervisor. *This will lower the amount of traffic on the information highway and <u>increase the ability for the more important information to get to its destination for a response</u>.* If you receive a shotgun email and you think it was inappropriate that you were on that send list, send a copy to your supervisor with your own notation pointing out the irregularity.

5. **Take request for information (RFI) emails seriously.**
RFI emails can be critical to mission success and are often the very necessary links in the group chain moving the group ever closer to mission success. As such, RFI emails should be treated with the importance they deserve. If you can't supply what they need right away or you can't delegate the task, *respond with a message that proposes a future time when you can supply the information.* If you can't meet their deadline for the information then get off email and get on the phone with them to determine how mission critical the information request is.

What to do: If you and the sender can't work out the priority question, *it should not be considered a failure to pass it up to your supervisor. Some RFIs can require a considerable amount of time and effort.* We all have our work prioritized by our supervisors, so when things get busy and work demands climb high enough that an RFI threatens completing the tasks your supervisor is asking of you, the next logical step is to bring the supervisor(s) in on the decision-making process concerning this new request. If there is an impasse, both the sender and receiver should pass it up to their respective supervisors to adjudicate the question of mission-related priority. Again, the primary reason passing it up to the supervisors is not a performance failure is because it is our supervisor who is in charge of prioritizing our work, *not other group members in lateral positions or silos other than our own.* The task that stands before the two supervisors is to specifically determine if the information that is being proposed laterally or from another silo needs to be completed as a first priority in order to meet the larger group's mission. Remember that the task proposed by another silo within your organization could very well be a task that's more important than the task you are completing now within your own silo. It's the job of these two supervisors to keep that larger picture in mind, which is why they should be brought into this process.

6. Don't take the bait on tension emails.

Any email communication that is introducing or evoking tension or anger—for the sender or receiver—needs to have a change of "venue," meaning the conversation should be shifted over to oral communication. Even though emails jumping back and forth appear as a dialogue, it's actually a form of *serial monologue* that can be very ineffective because the correspondence is missing key (and essential) pieces of information like *voice inflection and body language.*

What to do: This is hard to do sometimes, but it's necessary. Once things heat up, *get off email and pick up the phone.*

7. Misdirected RFIs should be forwarded.

If you receive an RFI that actually requires a decision to be made by someone else in the group, *and you have no control over how or when that decision will be made,* don't just respond with the "not my job" default explanation.

What to do: Let the sender know *and forward that request to the appropriate decision maker.*

8. Change the subject header when the topic of the email thread changes.

Email thread histories can be a very effective way of documenting logic threads and can help to provide information at a later date to backfill reports, show how decisions were made, or show how strategies were developed. In these email conversations, just as with live verbal conversations, the thread can branch off to different subjects.

What to do: When the subject being discussed in an email thread changes, <u>*also change the subject header of the email.*</u> If you ever need to go back to your email repository looking for key pieces of information, it can save you a lot of time.

>>> *When the information highway is flowing with high-quality information and is not impeded by traffic jams of low-quality information that will harm productivity, it promotes a higher likelihood of mission success.*<<<

Again:

1. **Every employee is required to check and respond to emails every workday.**
2. **All communications sent require a response.**

3. **Communication should always follow the chain of command.**
4. **Stop sending shotgun emails.**
5. **Take request for information (RFI) emails seriously.**
6. **Don't take the bait on tension emails.**
7. **Misdirected RFIs should be forwarded.**
8. **Change the subject header when the topic of the email thread changes.**

Anyone not responding to communication—which is now a required activity—or using the group's information highway in a way that is inappropriate as just noted is moving towards a downgraded performance evaluation.

Not following these guidelines of how to respond appropriately, or not sending responses at all when you should, is problematic behavior. ***Study the guidelines and if you slip up, take responsibility for your actions and get back on track.*** Continuing to make the same errors over and over again will essentially bypass the effectiveness of the recovery behavior retraining process and cause performance scores to drop. If you have questions, consult your supervisor.

Figure #49 is provided as a quick guide to help you focus on what's important. . .

Fig. #49: The 8 Email Communications Requirements

1. *Every employee is <u>required</u> to check & respond to emails every workday.*

2. *<u>All communications</u> received require a response.*

3. *Communication should <u>always</u> follow the chain of command.*

4. *<u>Stop</u> sending shotgun emails.*

5. *Take <u>Request For Information</u> (RFI) emails seriously.*

6. *<u>Don't take the bait</u> on tension emails.*

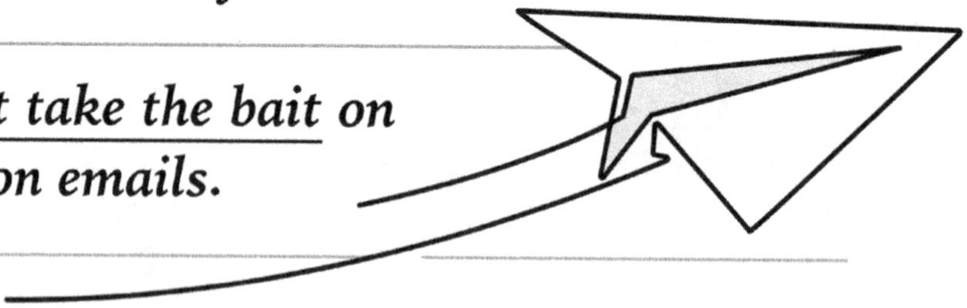

7. *Misdirected RFIs should be <u>forwarded</u>.*

8. *<u>Change the subject header</u> when the topic of the email thread changes.*

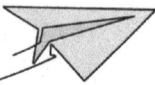

Appendix 5

Submitting Ideas for Improvement SOP

INTRODUCTION

The group moves forward by always improving, by always changing according to a changing environment, by always looking for new ways to support mission success. The group needs to assume that everyone's perspective can add to the list of ideas that can improve group performance. Based on the observations of human systems we know this to be true: every group member has a unique perspective and therefore potentially unique ideas that can contribute to continuous improvement.

Leadership wants every brain in the game!

If you have an idea that you think might improve the group, use this SOP.

Over time, every organization with complex systems will be able to point to hundreds of examples of ideas that led to SOP improvements, some saving 10, 20, 30, 100, or 300 hours a year, some saving $1,000, $10,000, or $20,000 a year, *all adding up to very significant, permanent year-in and year-out savings IN TIME AND MONEY !*

Here are some typical examples:

- A staff inquiry results in a study that demonstrates the grease-concentrating system is not necessary, saving 400 labor hours per year.
- A staff member unilaterally constructs a hose/nozzle system that directs floatables to a trough, saving 300 labor hours annually.
- A staff idea to "pre-flush" primary tanks that need to be cleaned to prepare for maintenance cuts turnaround time for tank cleaning in half while saving 200 hours of labor per year.
- A staff idea cuts the time required to place a clarifier into service, turning a two-person job into a one-person job and saving 100 hours of labor per year while simultaneously increasing process stability.

The group needs you to be naturally curious. If you're not familiar with a continuous improvement process, the following information is very important for you to know.

About 10 to 30 percent of continuous improvement ideas make it through the process and become successful. Some ideas for improvement won't be worth trying while others will be tried but won't work out as originally intended. This 30 percent success rate just seems to be the way the new idea process rolls in most human enterprises.

Herein lies the problem: *When people submit ideas for improvement and it looks like the idea won't work or it's an idea not worth trying, people get discouraged and stop submitting ideas. We do not want anyone to get discouraged!*

Everyone submits ideas that might not work, even the boss. Here is a key insight: **IF** everyone is submitting ideas for improvement and a 30 percent success rate is high enough for the group to see high levels of mission success, **THEN** the group is growing at a very high "continuous improvement" rate. What we also know about human systems is that a 30 percent success rate is enough to make a group wildly successful at using a continuous improvement strategy. Don't get discouraged. Keep submitting ideas you think might save time or money or both.

Batting a lifetime average of 30 percent ("batting 300") will get you into the National Baseball Hall of Fame. No difference here—when you have THE ENTIRE TEAM hitting 30 percent, the group's continuous improvement strategy is up and running.

GETTING STARTED

The ideas that help the most are ideas that:

  A. Save effort, time, and/or money or increase productivity for the same or less cost,
  B. Don't cost too much time or money to try out, and
  C. Are low risk.

So if you have an idea, ask yourself these corresponding questions:

  1. How much effort, money, and/or time will it save?
  2. How much will it cost to implement?
  3. What is the return on investment (ROI—or how long will it take for the savings to compensate for or pay back the implementation costs)? Not every idea for improvement will require an ROI, depending on the type of improvement it will provide the group.
  4. What are the risks with implementing this idea?

If you have some answers to those questions but not all of them, go ask your supervisor for help and start following the four-step process outlined below. If you are confident that you have accurate data that answers these key questions, this process allows you to continue with the next steps prior to meeting with your supervisor. However, because *we don't know what we don't know*, an early visit to the supervisor might be very advantageous to show them what you have so far.

STEP BY STEP

The following process is one way to see an uptick in the conversion rate that leads a *new idea* to become an *improvement idea that works*. These are the four steps to understanding if a ***new idea*** is a ***good idea***.

Step 1: Focus Areas – These are the questions that should be answered so the group knows what improvement to expect from the idea once it is implemented.

Step 2: Benefit vs. Cost Matrix – This step weighs what was found out in Step 1 with the cost of implementation.

Step 3: Benefit vs. Risk Matrix – This step weighs what was found out in Step 1 with the risk of implementation.

Step 4: Ranking Matrix – This step uses the information in Steps 1, 2, and 3 to rank the value of the idea and to determine its order of implementation as compared to other ideas being submitted.

STEP 1: FOCUS AREAS
An idea for improvement is a change in the group environment that advances the group towards its mission-centered potential. Therefore, ideas for improvement need to present a benefit to the group. The benefit should fall under at least one of the four following focus areas.

To prepare to pitch your new idea to your supervisor, make sure you have at least attempted to answer these four important questions:

1. How much effort, money, and/or time will it save?
2. How much will it cost to implement?
3. What is the return on investment (ROI—or how long will it take for the savings to compensate for or pay back the implementation costs)? Not every idea for improvement will require an ROI, depending on the type of improvement it will provide the group.
4. What are the risks with implementing this idea?

If you think you are on to a good idea but are having a hard time answering one or more of these questions, go see your supervisor. Part of their job is to support the continuous improvement process by supporting ideas that might have merit and just need a little help to go from a promising idea to an idea that's worth trying.

Once you have these questions answered and you weigh the information using the matrixes in Steps 2–4, you can determine if your idea is worth taking forward. And again, if you are not sure then get your supervisor involved to help out.

STEP 2: BENEFIT VS. COST MATRIX

Typically the best idea is a **Q1** idea using the chart below: High Benefit/Low Cost.

That being said, a "good" idea can also be a **Q2** idea: Low Benefit/Low Cost. These ideas can be a gold mine when added up over time. For example, a Low Benefit/Low Cost idea that saves only an hour a day in a 24-hour operation by simply removing or changing a time-wasting procedure saves 365 hours a year!

Some "good" ideas can also be a **Q3** idea: High Benefit/High Cost. These ideas, however, will find a more challenging road to implementation because the higher cost will need a higher justification based on risk. If the idea doesn't work out there is a higher initial investment that has been lost. In other words, the funds and time initially invested will not be recovered, making this a higher-risk idea.

Place your prospective good idea in the Benefit vs. Cost Matrix below.

Benefit vs. Cost Matrix

		-Benefit-	
		High	**Low**
-Cost-	**Low**	Q1: Benefits are high and costs are low.	Q2: Benefits are low and costs are low.
	High	Q3: Benefits are high, but so are the costs.	Q4: Benefits are low and the costs are high.

What type of a good idea do you have? **Q1? Q2? Q3? Q4?**

Return On Investment

The Benefit vs. Cost Matrix will help you figure out how much time or money it will cost to implement your idea. This is called the "return on investment" or ROI. Ideas that lead to cost savings that will recover the initial cost of implementation more quickly are typically more favorable for the group. The more quickly the initial cost is paid for, the sooner the benefit to the group is realized. That being said, ideas that create significant long-term savings that take months or even years to recover the initial investment for implementation can be very worthwhile. This question is examined on a case-by-case basis. In order for the Benefit-Cost rating to be a **Q1** or **Q2** the ROI should be determined to be acceptable.

STEP 3: BENEFIT VS. RISK MATRIX

Typically the best idea is a **Q1** idea on the chart below: High Benefit/Low Risk. That being said, a "good" idea can also be a **Q2** idea: Low Benefit/Low Risk. Even though the benefit might be low, the risk is also low and as such not much harm can come from simply "trying it out to see what happens."

Place your prospective good idea in the Benefit vs. Risk Matrix.

Benefit vs. Risk Matrix

		-Benefit-	
		High	**Low**
-Risk-	**Low**	Q1: Benefits are high and risks are low.	Q2: Benefits are low and risks are low.
	High	Q3: Benefits are high, but so are the risks.	Q4: Benefits are low and the risks are high.

What type of a good idea do you have? **Q1**? **Q2**? **Q3**? **Q4**?

If you have a **Q1** or **Q2** from the *Benefit vs. Cost Matrix* and that same idea is a **Q1** or **Q2** from the *Benefit vs. Risk Matrix*, the idea should be implemented ASAP!

Again, keep your supervisor in the loop and ask for their assistance when you need it.

1. Check the benefits in terms of effort, money, or time saved and/or productivity increased.
2. Check the benefits in terms of the cost of implementation.
3. Check the benefit of how long it takes the proposed idea to deliver an ROI if it indeed does. Not every idea for improvement will require an ROI, depending on the type of improvement it will provide the group.
4. Check the benefits in terms of the risk of implementation.

STEP 4: RANKING MATRIX

You now have your Benefit ratings (high or low), Cost ratings (high or low), and Risk ratings (high or low). Take those ratings and apply them to the following Ranking Matrix.

When applying the quadrant ratings from the Cost and Risk Matrixes to the Ranking Matrix, you'll get a *tier rating*. Each tier rating tells you when the idea should be implemented and, if you have multiple ideas at the same time, it can tell you how to prioritize their implementation.

For instance, if you have five different ideas going into implementation and they are a combination of Tier 1 and Tier 2 ideas, the Tier 1s go first if you can't implement them all at the same time.

If you have a Tier 2 idea going into implementation and you suddenly discover a Tier 1 idea, slow the Tier 2 idea's implementation if you have to and let the Tier 1 idea go ahead of it.

Ranking Matrix

Tier	Cost Matrix	Risk Matrix	Action Ranking
1	Q1	Q1	First choice: implement now
2	Q2	Q1	After Tier 1 or same time as Tier 1 if time allows
2	Q1	Q2	After Tier 1 or same time as Tier 1 if time allows
3	Q2	Q2	After Tiers 1 and 2 or same time as Tier 2 if time allows
4	Q2	Q3	Nonstarter, unless you can lower risk
4	Q3	Q2	Nonstarter, unless you can lower cost
5	Q3	Q3	Any idea involving a Q3 in either category is a nonstarter, unless you can significantly lower risk and/or cost

Cases involving Q4 ratings are ideas that are not under consideration. Ideas that are low benefit and are simultaneously high cost or high risk are by definition *not a good idea for providing improvement.*

Once you have your tier ratings, your supervisor will start implementing the top-tier ideas in the order recommended in the Ranking Matrix. The higher an idea's *tier rating*, the faster you want to implement it to start receiving the benefits.

Implementing a constant flow of Tier 1 and Tier 2 ideas will change your group forever.

The moment you have time for Tier 3 ideas get them implemented also.

While Q1s are your best "go to" ideas, do not underestimate the cumulative effect of a constant flow of low-benefit ideas that don't cost much to implement and have very low risk—**they all add up**!

Management Tasks versus Leadership Responsibilities

INTRODUCTION

The distinction between Management tasks and Leadership responsibilities is an important one.

Not delegating management tasks will swamp your calendar and work against your ability to have enough time to exercise your leadership responsibilities. Meanwhile, not exercising your leadership responsibilities when they are called for is abdication.

- *In a group with normalized mediocre performance, it's not unusual to find a high population of overworked managers who are also abdicating their leadership responsibilities.*

MANAGEMENT *TASKS*

With management tasks, after the training has occurred and the delegation of that task to a direct report is completed, your time dedication to that task essentially nearly ends. Other than using standard supervisory practices that support your direct report in the form of answering questions and assisting with problem-solving when requested, the delegated task and its new owner are saving you time and opening up your calendar for performing more leadership responsibilities.

You might own the needed outcome of the delegated task but you no longer own the time demand that comes along with it. Once the new owner of the task becomes highly experienced and proficient, you can walk away from thinking or acting on the task and only concern yourself with 1–2 percent of its original time demand. That's your goal.

LEADERSHIP *RESPONSIBILITIES*

With leadership responsibilities, you teach them to everyone on your leadership team and the entire leadership team, *including you and most notably you*, are all exercising these responsibilities at the same time.

In this case you are not delegating an activity that you walk away from. Instead, this is an activity where you and your fellow direct-report-leaders *are co-active*. *These are responsibilities you don't walk away from, ever.*

All of you, together, are now spending a maximum amount of time on delegating more management tasks so you can create more time to exercise more leadership responsibilities.

Important to know: while actually delegating management tasks is a management activity, *knowing that you want to delegate management tasks to create more time for implementing leadership responsibility is a leadership responsibility.*

WHERE THINGS GO REALLY WRONG

Many leader-managers feel extremely productive by working overtime on a huge number of management tasks they are not delegating. As a result, they end up not having time to exercise their leadership responsibilities, and they don't even realize this is what they're doing.

When a leader-manager is not exercising their leadership responsibilities *when they should be*, it's called abdication!

In fact, it gets worse.

Many overworked managers *delegate the leadership responsibilities to their direct reports* while they themselves don't exercise or demonstrate their own leadership responsibilities. *So, not only are they abdicating their own leadership responsibilities, they're forcing overworked direct reports to backfill the vacuum that they as the abdicating leader have created.*

Below I provide a list of management tasks and leadership responsibilities. Based on what I just explained, *read those leadership responsibilities with abdication in mind* and think about what your group is like if leadership is not pursuing these critical leadership responsibilities.

That's exactly what overworked managers do: they don't delegate tasks, don't have time for their leadership responsibilities, and therefore *abdicate those responsibilities.*

Figure #50 is provided as a quick guide to help you focus on what's important.

Fig. #50: Where Things Go Really Wrong

X   X   X   X   X   X

*Many leader-managers **feel** extremely productive by working overtime on a **huge number** of management tasks they are not delegating.*

*As a result, they end up **not having time** to exercise their **leadership responsibilities,** & they don't even realize this is what they're doing.*

When a leader-manager is **not** exercising their leadership responsibilities when they should be, it's called **abdication!**

When leaders fail in this way, the ***entire chain of effective action*** is negatively impacted.

Many overworked managers **delegate the leadership responsibilities to their direct reports** while they themselves don't exercise or demonstrate their own leadership responsibilities. *So, not only are they abdicating their own leadership responsibilities, they're forcing overworked direct reports to backfill the leadership vacuum that they as the abdicating senior leader have created.*

That's **exactly** what overworked managers do: they *don't* delegate tasks, *don't* have time for their leadership responsibilities, and therefore abdicate those responsibilities.

WHAT GOOD MANAGERS DO

- Good managers are able to analyze process, technical situations, and data.
- They are good problem solvers for technical issues and troubleshooting process problems.
- They build work plans, budgets, and cashflow projections.
- They develop procedures and schedules.
- They become a source of sound decision-making fundamentals as it relates to the "process of doing," such as machining, marketing, accounting, packaging, installing, building, operating, etc.
- They know where to find information they will need. If they don't know where to find it, they *always know* where to start looking.
- They know how to communicate complex concepts in usable terms as the expert they are.
- They insist on high technical standards to promote quality and productivity.
- *Lastly, they train everybody that works for them on how to do all these things well and once they've completed that training they start delegating these tasks to the people that they've trained.*

Figure #51 is provided as a quick guide to help you focus on what's important.

Fig. #51: What Good Managers Do

"A SOURCE OF SOUND DECISION-MAKING FUNDAMENTALS"

 Good managers are able to **analyze** process, technical situations, and data.

 They are good **problem solvers** for technical issues & **troubleshooting** process problems.

 They **build** work plans, budgets, and cashflow projections.

 They **develop procedures and schedules.**

 They become **sources of sound decision-making** fundamentals as it relates to the "process of doing," such as machining, marketing, accounting, packaging, installing, building, operating, etc.

 They know how to **communicate complex concepts in usable terms** as the expert they are.

 They insist on **high technical standards** to promote quality and productivity.

 Lastly, **they train everybody that works for them on how to do all these things well** and once they've completed that training they start delegating these tasks to the people that they've trained.

WHAT GOOD LEADERS DO

- Leaders create a culture that protects success. Great leaders are no-nonsense defenders of the culture that encourages and yes, **sometimes demands**, that everyone be the best that they can be.
- They protect the culture from destructive behavior. The mission is the only agenda now, and uncooperative and destructive behaviors need to change or leave.
- They're always looking for ways to increase inclusion, control, and openness for their followers. They're getting people involved, helping them grow, and being honest with them. They will always advance the mission **through their** followers not **over their** followers whenever possible.
- They know that recovery from mistakes is more important than blame. Great leaders are always counseling followers and helping them recover from poor performance. They know they can't punish their way to success.
- They know that high levels of training are critical in helping a group achieve great things, and that high levels of training give people the opportunity to grow and have more job satisfaction.
- They know that honest, ego-defying integrity is more important than how things look. Great leaders focus on how things are, not always how they look.
- They focus on importance, not popularity.
- They understand that while knowing how to delegate some of their management tasks is what a good manager does, **knowing that they need to delegate those management tasks in order to have more time to lead is the sign of great leadership**.
- Great leaders have the intestinal fortitude to hold people accountable to their responsibilities even when it's not popular. Courage, not comfort, is their clarion call.
- They have the intestinal fortitude to clamp down on toxic behavior. They know that toxic behavior paralyzes hardworking collaborators in their group. As long as the bullies are in charge, they are not.
- Great leaders are always helping those who demonstrate destructive behavior to either change or leave and showing them respect while they do.
- Great leaders always focus on behavior instead of personality: what behavior is wrong, not who is wrong, unless who is wrong is the problem.
- They make exceptions to the rule as warranted. Not easy to do. They explain themselves and don't expect approval. Move on.
- Great leaders enjoy strategy building with the intent of advancing effectiveness towards mission success. Let me repeat that. Great leaders enjoy strategy building with the intent of advancing effectiveness towards mission success. **As a leader, that's why you're breathing.**
- They present and re-present very clear expectations and achievable goals as a top priority.
- Great leaders typically have a natural curiosity. They love innovation. They love great ideas to improve the group towards mission success, regardless of who that idea comes from.
- Great leaders develop a healthy relationship with calculated risks. They understand that failure is an inherent function in a long-term successful enterprise. They also know the risks of not innovating and of not implementing the ideas necessary to move the group forward.

- *They know that while the rest of the world innovates, if they don't, the group is not standing still but actually falling behind.*
- Great leaders are willing to be fired instead of compromising their moral principles. They know that keeping a get-out-of-town fund on the side with six months' worth of cash to keep them and their family above water is highly recommended. *And the higher one climbs the leadership ladder, the more it's recommended.*
- They don't mind being different. In fact, you might notice they typically enjoy it.

Figure #52 is provided as a quick guide to help you focus on what's important.

Fig. #52: *What Good Leaders Do*

BUILDING WITH THE INTENT OF **ADVANCING EFFECTIVENESS** TOWARDS MISSION SUCCESS.

 Leaders create a culture that **protects** success. Great leaders are no-nonsense *defenders of the culture.*

 Leaders protect the culture from *destructive behavior.* Those who are uncooperative or destructive are lead to **change** or **leave.**

 Leaders are looking for ways to increase **inclusion, control, & openness** for their followers. They will always advance the mission *through* their followers, not *over* their followers when possible.

 They know that **recovery** from mistakes is more important than blame. Great leaders know *they can't punish their way to success.*

 Leaders know that *high levels of training are critical* in helping a group achieve great things, & great training gives people the opportunity for **growth** & **job satisfaction.**

 Great leaders know that honest, **ego-defying integrity** is more important than how things look.

 Leaders focus on **importance, not popularity.**

 Great leaders understand *that they need to delegate management tasks in order to have more time to lead, & that doing so is the sign of great leadership.*

 Great leaders have **intestinal fortitude** & hold people accountable to their responsibilities *even when it's not popular.* **Courage > comfort.**

 Leaders have the intestinal fortitude to clamp down on **toxic behavior.** *As long as the bullies are in charge, they are not.*

 Great leaders always focus on **behavior** instead of personality: *hat behavior is wrong, not who is wrong,* unless who is wrong is the problem.

 They **make exceptions to the rule as warranted.** Not easy to do. They explain themselves & don't expect approval. Move on.

 Great leaders enjoy **strategy building** with the intent of advancing effectiveness towards mission success. *As a leader, that's why you exist.*

 They present and re-present very **clear expectations** & **achievable goals** as a top priority.

 Great leaders develop a healthy relationship with **calculated risks.** They understand that failure is an inherent function in a long-term successful enterprise.

 They don't mind **being different.** In fact, you might notice they typically enjoy it.

HOW TO MAKE A DIFFERENCE

Whether you're a first-line supervisor, a middle manager, a GM, or a CEO, all of the advice is the same, *and you've got to get this one right.*

If you use this information exactly as described, it could be the single most powerful thing you do as a leader-manager.

Do the management job just as described above.

Do the leadership job just as described above.

The point is this: don't mix them up.

Don't hold on to management tasks. Instead, train and delegate.

Never abdicate leadership responsibilities. Instead, train and demonstrate.

If you are a senior leader-manager in your group, you can turn this appendix into a training program then convert what's been taught into performance expectations.

Imagine that!

Influencers / References / Bibliography

Allen, Steve: *Dumbth, And 81 ways to Make Americans Smarter*

Babiak, Paul / Hare, Robert / *Snakes in Suits, when psychopaths go to work*

Bowles, Samuel / Gintis, Herbert, *A Cooperative Species - Human Reciprocity and its Evolution*

Campbell, Joseph, *The Hero with a Thousand Faces*

Covey, Stephen: *Seven Habits of Highly Effective People*

Dana, Daniel: *Conflict Resolution: Mediation Tools for Everyday Work Life*

Darwin, Charles: *Origin of Species*

Frankl, Victor, *Man's Search for Meaning*

Fehr, Ernst/ Fischbacher, Urs/ Gächter, Simon; Strong Reciprocity, Human Cooperation and the Enforcement of Social Norms, HUMAN NATURE 13(2002) pages 1-25

Goleman, Daniel, *Social Intelligence*

Goulston, Mark, *Just Listen*

Carnegie, Dale, *How to Win Friends and Influence People Copy #26673323*

Hare, Robert, WITHOUT CONSCIENCE, *The Disturbing World Of The Psychopaths Among Us*

Hare, Robert, *Aftermath-surviving psychopathy.org*

Herzberg, Fredrick, *One More Time: How Do You Motivate Employees?* Harvard Business Review, 1968

International Labor Organisation, *bureau/magazine/26/violence*

Kotter, John / Heskett, James: *Corporate Culture and Performance*

Krugman, Paul: *The Age of Diminished Expectations: US Economic Policy in the 1980s*, MIT Press, Cambridge, p. 9.

LeDoux, Joseph, *The Emotional Brain*

Murphy, James D.: *Flawless Execution*

National Aeronautics and Space Administration - **Columbia** Accident Investigation Board - *final report on August 26, 2003*

National Safety Council *2005; United Nations worker safety study*

Patterson/Grenny/Maxfield/McMillan/Switzler: *Influencer, The Power to Change Anything*

Paul, Richard, *Keynote address at* the *27th Annual International Conference on Critical Thinking in 2007*

Peter, Dr. Laurence / Hull, Raymond, *The Peter Principle*

Pfeiffer, Jeffrey, *Leadership BS, fixing work places and careers one truth at a time*

Sapolsky, Robert, BEHAVE, *the biology of humans at our best and our worst*

Schutz, Will, *The Human Element, productivity self-esteem and the bottom line*

Society for Human Resource Management, *Research/Articles/Articles/Pages/Dealing with violence*

Space Shuttle (Challenger) Accident and Rogers Commission Report – *final report February 18, June 10 and 17th 1986*

Tamm, James W. / Luyet, Ronald J.: *Radical Collaboration, five essential skills to overcome defensiveness and build successful relationships*

U.S. Constitution: *Bill of Rights*

Walker, Kathy et al; *"Communication Basics"* LEADS curriculum, Unit 2 Module 2-1 (Kansas State University 2002)

Williams, Kipling , *Scientific American Mind, Jan/Feb 2011,* The Pain of Exclusion, pages: 30-37

World Health Organization, *mental health/prevention*

Index

Printed in the USA
CPSIA information can be obtained
at www.ICGtesting.com
LVHW020852110823
754885LV00020B/1865